NETWORKING WITH MIKROTIK

Other Works

MikroTik Security Guide, Second Edition

Ubiquiti EdgeRouter Hardening Guide

Networking with MikroTik®
MTCNA Study Guide
First Edition

Tyler Hart

Copyright © 2017 by Manito Networks, LLC. All rights reserved.

No part of this publication may be reproduced or utilized in any form or by any means, electronic or mechanical, including photocopying, recording, or by any information storage and retrieval system, except as permitted by the United States Copyright Act, without permission in writing from the publisher.

Author: Tyler Hart

ISBN: 9781973206354

The author(s) and publisher(s) make no warranties or representations with respect to the wholeness, completeness, or accuracy of the contents of this work. The author(s) and publisher(s) disclaim all warranties including any warranties of fitness for a particular purpose. Every network and information system is different, and you should consult with a professional before implementing the solutions or suggestions in this publication.

Vendor and product names are displayed in caps or initial caps, and every effort made to respect trademarks where Manito Networks, LLC is aware a trademark is claimed. Usage of trademarked product or vendor names does not constitute an endorsement of or by the trademark owner. Manito Networks, LLC is not affiliated with any vendor or product mentioned in this publication. For more information on copyrights and trademarks in this document see the online resources at https://www.manitonetworks.com.

"MikroTik" is a registered trademark of Mikrotikls, AKA MikroTik LLC.

"CCNA" and "Cisco" are registered trademarks of Cisco Technology, Inc.

"Apple" and "iOS" are registered trademarks of Apple Inc.

"Android" and "Google" are registered trademarks of Google, Inc.

"Microsoft", "Windows", and "Windows Server" are registered trademarks of Microsoft Corporation.

"FileZilla" is a registered trademarks of Tim Kosse.

"Ubiquiti", "EdgeOS", "EdgeSwitch", "EdgeMax", and "EdgeRouter" are registered trademarks of Ubiquiti Networks, Inc.

All other trademarks are the property of their respective owners.

Any IP addresses and DNS names used in this guide are strictly for demonstration purposes. Some public services currently available as of this writing are referenced, and you should research the viability of those service before deciding on their use in your own networks.

For more information on Manito Networks, LLC books, online publications, and articles visit our website at the following URL:

`https://www.manitonetworks.com`

Acknowledgments

Thanks to my wife Kristi for all the support during long days and evenings writing articles, books, curriculum, and emails.

Thanks as well to my parents for encouraging me to take risks and do it myself.

About the Author

Tyler Hart is a network and security professional who started working in the field in 2002. He holds a Business degree in IT Management, as well as the CISSP® certification and others from Microsoft®, CompTIA®, Cisco®, (ISC)2®, Tenable Network Security®, and more. For over 15 years he has worked and consulted with large and small organizations including hospitals and clinics, Internet Service Providers (ISPs) and Wireless ISPs (WISPs), U.S. Defense organizations, and state and county governments.

In 2015 he started ManitoNetworks.com, the leading English-language MikroTik blog. His MikroTik Router Security and VLAN guides became the standard online, referred to and recommended by MikroTik users and staff alike. In the following years the website expanded to include Ubiquiti, network security, and penetration testing articles. Tyler is also a professional trainer and teaches courses on service provider networks, cyber security, and compliance.

Contents

1 MikroTik   **1**
- 1.1 The MikroTik Company . . . 1
- 1.2 MikroTik Distribution . . . 1
- 1.3 RouterOS Software . . . 2
- 1.4 MikroTik Resources . . . 2
  - 1.4.1 MikroTik Newsletter . . . 2
  - 1.4.2 RouterOS Changelog . . . 2
  - 1.4.3 MikroTik Wiki . . . 3
  - 1.4.4 MikroTik Forum . . . 3
  - 1.4.5 MikroTik User Meetings . . . 3
  - 1.4.6 Distributor and Consultant Support . . . 3
  - 1.4.7 Reddit . . . 4
- 1.5 MikroTik Support . . . 4
  - 1.5.1 Emailing Support . . . 4
  - 1.5.2 Autosupout.rif File . . . 5
  - 1.5.3 Support Best Practices . . . 5
- 1.6 RouterBOARD . . . 6
  - 1.6.1 RouterBOARD Features . . . 8
  - 1.6.2 Cloud Core Router . . . 10
  - 1.6.3 Cloud Router Switch . . . 12
- 1.7 Cloud Hosted Router . . . 14
- 1.8 RouterOS Licenses . . . 16
  - 1.8.1 Level 0 Trial . . . 17
  - 1.8.2 Level 1 Demo . . . 17
  - 1.8.3 Level 2 . . . 17
  - 1.8.4 Level 3 . . . 18
  - 1.8.5 Levels 4 and 5 . . . 18
  - 1.8.6 Level 6 . . . 18
  - 1.8.7 CHR License . . . 18
- 1.9 Review Questions . . . 20
- 1.10 Review Answers . . . 22

2 RouterOS Software   **23**
- 2.1 RouterOS Installations . . . 23

		2.1.1	Pre-Installed RouterOS	23
		2.1.2	RouterOS Virtual Hard Disks	24
	2.2	RouterOS Packages		24
		2.2.1	Installed Packages	27
		2.2.2	Package Format	28
		2.2.3	Downloading Packages	28
	2.3	RouterOS Releases		28
		2.3.1	Current	28
		2.3.2	Bugfix Only	29
		2.3.3	Legacy	29
		2.3.4	Release Candidate	29
	2.4	Updating RouterOS		29
		2.4.1	Check for Updates	30
		2.4.2	Upgrading Software	31
		2.4.3	Downgrading Software	32
		2.4.4	Disabling RouterOS Packages	33
	2.5	RouterBOOT Firmware		34
	2.6	Review Questions		35
	2.7	Review Answers		37
3	**Defaults**			**39**
	3.1	Credentials		39
	3.2	Interfaces		40
	3.3	Local Area Network Addresses		40
	3.4	Dynamic Addresses		40
		3.4.1	WAN DHCP Client	41
		3.4.2	LAN DHCP Server	41
	3.5	Firewall		42
		3.5.1	Forward Traffic	42
		3.5.2	Input Traffic	42
		3.5.3	Output Traffic	42
		3.5.4	NAT	42
	3.6	IP Services		43
	3.7	Review Questions		44
	3.8	Review Answers		46
4	**Accessing the Router**			**47**
	4.1	Access Methods		47
	4.2	Serial Port		48
	4.3	LCD Touchscreen		48
	4.4	Telnet		49
	4.5	Secure Shell		49
	4.6	Winbox		50
	4.7	Winbox Device Access		53
	4.8	MAC Winbox		54

	4.9	Webfig	54
	4.10	API	55
	4.11	FTP	56
	4.12	Review Questions	57
	4.13	Review Answers	59

5 Configuring RouterOS   61
  5.1 Command Structure 61
      5.1.1 Moving Up and Down Commands 62
  5.2 Shortcuts and Help 63
      5.2.1 Console Colors 63
      5.2.2 Tab Key 64
      5.2.3 Question Mark Key 66
      5.2.4 HotLock 67
      5.2.5 Clearing the Screen 67
  5.3 Command History 67
      5.3.1 Viewing Command History 67
      5.3.2 Rolling Back Commands 68
      5.3.3 Clearing Command History 68
  5.4 Quick Set 69
  5.5 Safe Mode 70
  5.6 System Hostname 71
  5.7 Login Banner 71
  5.8 Time Zone and Clock 72
  5.9 Network Time Services 73
  5.10 Configuration Management 74
      5.10.1 Device Backup 74
      5.10.2 Device Restore 75
      5.10.3 Configuration Export 75
      5.10.4 Hide Sensitive 77
      5.10.5 Configuration Restore 77
  5.11 Using USB Storage 78
  5.12 Device Reset 79
  5.13 Review Questions 80
  5.14 Review Answers 82

6 Managing Users   83
  6.1 Default Admin User 83
  6.2 User Best Practices 84
      6.2.1 Least-Privilege 84
      6.2.2 Nonrepudiation 84
      6.2.3 Accountability 85
      6.2.4 Passwords and Comments 85
      6.2.5 Rename Admin Account 86
  6.3 User Operations 87

		6.3.1	Creating Users	87

        6.3.1   Creating Users 87
        6.3.2   Disabling and Enabling Users 87
        6.3.3   Removing Users 88
   6.4   Groups 89
        6.4.1   Read Group 90
        6.4.2   Write Group 90
        6.4.3   Custom Groups 90
   6.5   Active Users 91
   6.6   Further Reading 91
   6.7   Review Questions 92
   6.8   Review Answers 94

7 Interfaces   **95**

   7.1   Interface Types 95
   7.2   Interface Listing Commands 96
   7.3   Interface Statistics 97
   7.4   Ethernet Interfaces 97
   7.5   Power Over Ethernet 99
        7.5.1   POE Modes 99
        7.5.2   POE Priority 100
        7.5.3   Power-Cycle POE 100
   7.6   SFP Modules 101
   7.7   Wireless 103
   7.8   Bridge Interfaces 104
        7.8.1   Creating Bridges 105
        7.8.2   Fast Forward 105
        7.8.3   Adding Ports 105
        7.8.4   Removing Bridge Ports 106
        7.8.5   Removing Bridges 106
   7.9   Interface MTU 107
   7.10   State 108
   7.11   Duplex 108
   7.12   Flow Control 109
   7.13   Spanning Tree Protocol 109
        7.13.1   Configuring STP 110
   7.14   Cable Test 111
   7.15   Physical Security 111
   7.16   Review Questions 112
   7.17   Review Answers 114

8 Addresses   **115**

   8.1   Static Addresses 115
   8.2   Dynamic Addresses with DHCP 116
        8.2.1   DORA Exchange 116
        8.2.2   DHCP Server 117

		8.2.3	Client IP Pool 117
		8.2.4	DHCP Networks 118
		8.2.5	Leases 118
		8.2.6	DHCP Options 121
		8.2.7	Managing Static Addresses with DHCP 122
		8.2.8	DHCP Client 123

- 8.3 Point-to-Point Addresses 124
  - 8.3.1 Legacy /30 Addressing 124
  - 8.3.2 Modern /32 Addressing 125
  - 8.3.3 West Router Configuration 125
  - 8.3.4 North Router Configuration 126
  - 8.3.5 East Router Configuration 126
- 8.4 MAC Addresses 126
  - 8.4.1 ARP Table 127
  - 8.4.2 ARP for Inventory 127
  - 8.4.3 Finding MACs by OUI 128
  - 8.4.4 ARP Modes 128
  - 8.4.5 Disabled 128
  - 8.4.6 Proxy ARP 129
  - 8.4.7 Reply Only 130
- 8.5 Wake on LAN 130
- 8.6 DNS and Name Records 130
  - 8.6.1 RouterOS DNS Server 131
- 8.7 Review Questions 134
- 8.8 Review Answers 136

9 Routing 137
- 9.1 Routes 137
- 9.2 Administrative Distance 138
- 9.3 Static Routes 139
- 9.4 Dynamic Routes 140
- 9.5 Default Routes 141
- 9.6 Blackhole Routes 143
- 9.7 Prohibit Routes 144
- 9.8 Route States 144
  - 9.8.1 Active 144
  - 9.8.2 Connected 145
  - 9.8.3 Disabled 145
  - 9.8.4 Unreachable 146
- 9.9 Check Gateway 146
- 9.10 Source Routing 146
- 9.11 Review Questions 147
- 9.12 Review Answers 149

10 VPNs and Tunnels 151

10.1	PPP	151
	10.1.1 PPP Profiles	151
	10.1.2 IP Pools for PPP	153
	10.1.3 PPP Encryption	153
	10.1.4 PPP Secrets	153
	10.1.5 RADIUS Users	153
	10.1.6 Monitoring PPP Users	154
10.2	PPTP	154
	10.2.1 PPTP Server	154
	10.2.2 PPTP Users	154
	10.2.3 PPTP Client	155
10.3	PPPoE	155
	10.3.1 PPPoE Server	155
	10.3.2 PPPoE Client	156
10.4	SSTP	157
	10.4.1 SSTP Server	157
	10.4.2 Securing SSTP Access	157
	10.4.3 Creating an SSTP User	158
	10.4.4 SSTP Client	158
10.5	Review Questions	159
10.6	Review Answers	161

11 Queues — 163

11.1	Scheduling Algorithms	163
	11.1.1 FIFO	164
	11.1.2 RED	164
	11.1.3 SFQ	164
	11.1.4 PCQ	164
	11.1.5 None	165
11.2	Priority Levels	165
11.3	Simple Queues	165
11.4	Bursting	166
11.5	Interface Queues	167
11.6	Queue Trees	167
11.7	Review Questions	169
11.8	Review Answers	171

12 Firewalls — 173

12.1	Best Practices	173
12.2	Firewall Components	174
12.3	Firewall Chains	175
	12.3.1 Input Chain	175
	12.3.2 Forward Chain	176
	12.3.3 Output Chain	177
	12.3.4 Custom Chains	178

- 12.4 Firewall Rules 178
  - 12.4.1 Rule Evaluation 179
  - 12.4.2 Rule Sorting 179
- 12.5 Default Firewall Rules 179
  - 12.5.1 Default Input Rules 180
  - 12.5.2 Default Forward Rules 181
  - 12.5.3 Default Output Rules 182
- 12.6 Connection Tracking 182
  - 12.6.1 Connection States 182
- 12.7 Firewall Actions 184
  - 12.7.1 Accept 184
  - 12.7.2 Add to Address List 184
  - 12.7.3 Drop 185
  - 12.7.4 FastTrack Connection 185
  - 12.7.5 Jump 186
  - 12.7.6 Log 186
  - 12.7.7 Passthrough 187
  - 12.7.8 Reject 188
  - 12.7.9 Return 189
  - 12.7.10 Tarpit 189
- 12.8 Address Lists 189
- 12.9 Comments 190
- 12.10 Review Questions 191
- 12.11 Review Answers 193

13 NAT 195
- 13.1 NAT Overview 195
  - 13.1.1 Source NAT 196
  - 13.1.2 Destination NAT 197
- 13.2 RFC-1918 Addresses 197
  - 13.2.1 NAT and IPv6 198
- 13.3 NAT Chains 198
- 13.4 NAT Actions 199
  - 13.4.1 Accept 199
  - 13.4.2 Add to Address List 199
  - 13.4.3 Destination NAT 199
  - 13.4.4 Jump 199
  - 13.4.5 Log 200
  - 13.4.6 Masquerade 200
  - 13.4.7 Netmap 200
  - 13.4.8 Passthrough 200
  - 13.4.9 Redirect 201
  - 13.4.10 Return 201
  - 13.4.11 Source NAT 201
- 13.5 Review Questions 202

    13.6 Review Answers 204

14 Wireless   205
    14.1 Wireless Protocols 205
    14.2 802.11 Wireless Standards 206
    14.3 Frequency Bands 206
    14.4 ISM 207
    14.5 U-NII 207
    14.6 DFS 207
    14.7 Channels 208
    14.8 Wireless Scanner 209
    14.9 Data Rates 212
    14.10 Multiplexing 212
    14.11 Chains 213
        14.11.1 Transmit Power 213
        14.11.2 Antenna Gain 215
        14.11.3 Noise Floor 215
    14.12 Wireless Link Configurations 217
        14.12.1 Access Point - Bridge Mode 218
        14.12.2 Station Mode 219
    14.13 Wireless Monitoring 220
        14.13.1 Registration Table 220
        14.13.2 Snooper 220
        14.13.3 CCQ 222
    14.14 Review Questions 224
    14.15 Review Answers 226

15 Wireless Security   227
    15.1 Wireless Interface Security Options 227
        15.1.1 Default Authenticate 227
        15.1.2 Default Forward 228
        15.1.3 Hide SSID 228
    15.2 Access List 228
    15.3 Connect List 230
    15.4 Encryption 231
        15.4.1 Encryption Algorithms 231
        15.4.2 WEP 231
        15.4.3 WPA & WPA2 Encryption 232
    15.5 Security Profiles 233
    15.6 WPS 234
        15.6.1 WPS Mode 234
        15.6.2 WPS Client 235
        15.6.3 WPS Accept 235
    15.7 Review Questions 236
    15.8 Review Answers 238

16 Troubleshooting Tools — 239
- 16.1 IP Scan — 239
- 16.2 MAC Scan — 240
- 16.3 Additional Scanning Tools — 241
- 16.4 Email — 241
  - 16.4.1 Email Usage — 242
- 16.5 MAC Server — 245
  - 16.5.1 MAC Server Settings — 245
  - 16.5.2 MAC Ping — 245
  - 16.5.3 MAC Telnet — 246
- 16.6 Netwatch — 246
- 16.7 Packet Sniffer — 247
- 16.8 Ping — 250
- 16.9 Ping Speed — 252
- 16.10 RoMON — 252
  - 16.10.1 Enable RoMON — 253
  - 16.10.2 RoMON Secrets — 253
  - 16.10.3 RoMON Interfaces — 253
  - 16.10.4 Discovery — 253
  - 16.10.5 Connecting via RoMON — 254
- 16.11 Telnet — 255
- 16.12 Traceroute — 256
  - 16.12.1 Traceroute Usage — 256
  - 16.12.2 Traceroute Limitations — 257
- 16.13 Bandwidth Test Server — 257
- 16.14 Bandwidth Test Client — 258
- 16.15 Flood Ping — 260
- 16.16 Review Questions — 262
- 16.17 Review Answers — 264

17 RouterOS Monitoring — 265
- 17.1 Graphs — 265
  - 17.1.1 Accessing Graphs — 265
  - 17.1.2 Configuring Graphs — 267
- 17.2 Interface Monitoring — 270
  - 17.2.1 Interface Statistics — 270
  - 17.2.2 Torch Tool — 272
  - 17.2.3 Interface Monitor-Traffic Tool — 274
  - 17.2.4 Traffic Monitor Tool — 274
- 17.3 Performance Monitoring — 274
  - 17.3.1 Console Resource Monitoring — 275
  - 17.3.2 Console CPU Monitoring — 275
  - 17.3.3 Profile Tool — 275
  - 17.3.4 CPU Graphs — 277
- 17.4 Event Monitoring — 277

		17.4.1 RouterOS Logs	277
		17.4.2 Interface Events	279
		17.4.3 Security Events	279
	17.5	SNMP	280
		17.5.1 SNMP Versions	280
		17.5.2 Community Strings	281
	17.6	Syslog	282
		17.6.1 Logging Actions	282
		17.6.2 Logging Rules	282
		17.6.3 Syslog Security	282
	17.7	Review Questions	284
	17.8	Review Answers	286

18 The Dude — 287

- 18.1 Dude Server . . . 287
- 18.2 Dude as a VM . . . 288
- 18.3 Creating a Virtual Machine . . . 289
  - 18.3.1 Name and Location . . . 289
  - 18.3.2 VM Generation . . . 290
  - 18.3.3 Memory . . . 291
  - 18.3.4 Virtual Network Connection . . . 292
  - 18.3.5 Install Virtual Hard Disk . . . 293
  - 18.3.6 Attach Additional Storage . . . 294
- 18.4 VM Integration Services . . . 295
- 18.5 Dude Configuration . . . 296
  - 18.5.1 Manage Storage . . . 296
  - 18.5.2 Manage Services . . . 297
- 18.6 Dude Client . . . 298
- 18.7 Auto-Discover . . . 299
- 18.8 SNMP . . . 299
- 18.9 Syslog . . . 302
- 18.10 Dude Client . . . 303
- 18.11 Devices . . . 304
  - 18.11.1 Device Types . . . 304
  - 18.11.2 Up . . . 306
  - 18.11.3 Partially Down . . . 307
  - 18.11.4 Down . . . 307
  - 18.11.5 Device Autodiscovery . . . 307
- 18.12 Agents . . . 308
- 18.13 Maps . . . 309
  - 18.13.1 Network Submaps . . . 309
  - 18.13.2 Adding Devices to Maps . . . 310
- 18.14 Links . . . 312
- 18.15 Performance Charts . . . 313
- 18.16 Review Questions . . . 315

18.17 Review Answers 317

Online Resources **319**

Preface

Introduction

The MikroTik platform is one of the most cost-effective routing and switching network products available today. It maintains a strong presence in the WISP market, and continues making inroads into organizations around the world. While consulting with organizations who need help implementing new networks and security, I'm always surprised by who I find running MikroTik. Consulting on MikroTik has introduced me to a WISP in the Midwestern US, a county government on the west coast of the United States, and a business office in Australia. There are many others as well, all recognizing the cost-effectiveness and growth possibilities around MikroTik's approach to networking hardware and software.

My first introduction to MikroTik was in 2011 by a friend I met in college. He was a high-level network engineer who was listening to me talk about the issues I was experiencing with a network at the time. He asked me if I'd heard of a brand called "MikroTik", and at the time I hadn't. Up until that point my network experience consisted entirely of products from large incumbent vendors. After I realized how inexpensive MikroTik routers were I bought one to try in the lab and was immediately hooked. For the last six years I've been helping organizations grow their networks quickly and affordably with MikroTik and I haven't looked back since.

What This Book Is

This book is a MikroTik learning aid and on-the-job reference that covers exam objectives[1] for the MikroTik Certified Network Associate (MTCNA) certification. The chapters in this book were developed around the January 22, 2016 version of the certification outline published by MikroTik [20]. This outline does not include some newer features introduced in later versions of RouterOS v6. However, some new features are covered in this book because they can impact security and best practice implementation.

---

[1] `https://www.mikrotik.com/download/pdf/MTCNA_Outline.pdf`

The MTCNA certification is targeted to,

> *Network engineers and technicians wanting to deploy and support corporate networks [and] client CPEs (WISPs and ISPs)* [20]

If that's you, or if you're supervising administrators using MikroTik then this is the right place to be.

What This Book Is Not

This book is not an introduction to basic networking or subnetting. You should already be familiar with the following concepts before attempting the MTCNA:

- Mainstream network protocols (TCP, UDP, ICMP, IP, etc.)
- Internet Protocol v4 (IPv4) subnetting and Variable-Length Subnet Masking (VLSM)
- The Open Systems Interconnect (OSI) Model
- Basic networking tools, including *ping*, *traceroute*, *telnet*, etc.

If you don't have a good grasp of these concepts an excellent place to start would be CompTIA's Network+® program or the ICND-1 portion of Cisco's CCNA® track. With a good grasp of the fundamentals you'll be able to leverage MikroTik and RouterOS to their full potential.

Using This Book

This book is organized around topics in the MTCNA outline and formatted to highlight important concepts, notes, "quick wins", and common tasks that I've encountered with my own networks and customers. I've done my best to capture these for you in easily-consumable sections and "blurbs". Additional information beyond the MTCNA outline is sometimes provided based on real-world experiences when building or auditing networks.

Commands are set apart and in a different font so you can easily distinguish what to enter at the command prompt. The following command sets the device hostname:

```
/system identity set name=router.manitonetworks.com
```

Longer commands are often split into two parts and may break from one line to the next:

```
/ip firewall filter
add chain=input protocol=tcp dst-port=80 action=accept comment="HTTP"
```

Notes call out important knowledge items or answers to frequently asked questions.

> **NOTE**: I am a note, please read me!

Warnings call your attention to commands or common mistakes that could cause loss of services or connectivity. Warnings may also highlight best practices that can protect your networks from security risks or non-compliance with common standards.

> **WARNING**: This command will reboot the router!

Thoughts

As you're reading through this book remember to think of networks as dynamic, moving things. Our networks can grow, shrink, and change over time as the organization changes. We should design networks for flexibility and growth, while always bearing in mind security needs and best practices.

Good luck in growing and securing your MikroTik networks, and thank you for taking the time to read my book. I hope you get more than you expected out of this resource and the motivation to continue learning more about MikroTik.

Network Security

The majority of this book is devoted to understanding and configuring MikroTik hardware and software set out in the MTCNA outline. However, just setting up a functional network is not enough; Networks and systems must be secure and customer data protected. Having a network with great performance but insufficient firewall rules could have a net-negative effect on an organization. Spam, ransomware infections, Denial of Service (DoS) attacks, botnet activity, and more are legitimate security concerns for everyone with internet-connected devices. Having your network co-opted into a Distributed DoS (DDoS)-for-hire or spam ring could cause you to be blacklisted by email and network providers. Ransomware infections via the network can mean financial and reputation loss, as well as possible legal and compliance issues.

CIA Triad

In this book when discussing security and best practice implementations we'll often reference the Confidentiality, Integrity, and Availability (CIA) Triad. Keeping networks operational and performant while maintaining CIA is the main role of both IT security and network professionals. Keep the three following sections in mind while progressing through the chapters in this book.

Confidentiality

The confidentiality of data is what comes to mind first for most people - is the data secure? We encrypt data and build defenses around our networks to protect their confidentiality. This is done with data at rest on computers and with data in-flight over encrypted Virtual Private Networks (VPNs) like Internet Protocol Security (IPSEC). Protecting the confidentiality of data is directly related to compliance standards like Health Insurance Portability and Accountability Act (HIPAA) and Payment Card Industry - Data Security Standard (PCI-DSS). Electronic Medical Record (EMR) privacy is protected in the United States by HIPAA, and credit card information is protected by PCI-DSS. Encrypting wireless networks, securing VPNs, and using Secure Shell (SSH) instead of Telnet are examples of maintaining *confidentiality*.

Integrity

Data integrity depends on whether or not that data has been modified, corrupted, or deleted. Attackers will often selectively or completely purge log events to cover their tracks. Malicious attackers could deliberately corrupt or modify production data on networked file shares so the data owner can't trust it. Ransomware attacks also violate the integrity of data that attackers are holding hostage. Controls built around networks maintain the integrity of the data passing over them. Securing access to MikroTik devices themselves so their configurations can't be tampered with also maintains *integrity*.

Availability

Networks should be usable by authorized people and network hosts to support an organization's mission or business. A DDoS attack or network bandwidth hog could cause regular users to lose access. When legitimate users and systems don't have access to network resources, either because of an attack or misconfiguration, availability has been compromised. Bandwidth throttling, traffic filtering, and performance monitoring are all activities that maintain a network's *availability*.

Defense In Depth

It's worthwhile to think of network appliances like MikroTik routers and firewalls as part of a larger, layered Defense-in-Depth (DiD) solution. With this approach to security, when an attacker is able to bypass one layer of protection they will hopefully be blocked by another. An example of DiD is having a firewall at the network edge and anti-virus or Host Intrusion Protection (HIP) software installed on network clients. A DiD network architecture will also include consolidated event monitoring and alerting.

This book walks you through implementing user controls, firewall rules, consolidated monitoring, and more. We'll build layers of security around your network and implement best practices from the beginning, while also exploring the domains in the MTCNA outline.

Chapter 1

MikroTik

1.1 The MikroTik Company

The MikroTik company was founded in 1996 and made its RouterOS software available in 1997. At the beginning the company focused on providing software to run on commodity hardware. In 2002 production of the RouterBOARD hardware platform began, combining RouterOS and in-house developed network appliances into a cohesive platform. The company is based in Latvia's capital city Riga, and a company summary published in 2016 indicated about 140 employees make up the company [6].

The company hosts meetings around the world called MikroTik User Meetings - MuMs for short - where professionals can meet with vendors, see upcoming products, and get official MikroTik training. Records on MikroTik's website show these meetings have taken place on all continents except Antarctica. RouterBOARD and RouterOS documentation is available online in wiki format, and numerous consultants and networking enthusiasts have established knowledge-bases online.

1.2 MikroTik Distribution

MikroTik does not sell directly to consumers but maintains relationships with a number of distributors who are well-known in the WISP industry. A list of distributors is available on MikroTik's website at the following URL:

```
https://routerboard.com/distributors
```

1.3 RouterOS Software

MikroTik's RouterOS network operating system is the "secret sauce" that brings advanced networking capabilities to physical and virtual routers. The RouterOS software platform is based on Linux, as of early 2017 the v3.3.5 kernel. It can run on both physical and virtual platforms and is very customizable in terms of software packages and capabilities. RouterOS software looks and acts the same regardless of platform, though some configuration options may be absent depending on the hardware installed.

If you can configure a smaller Small Office, Home Office (SOHO) router you already know some of the commands for configuring core routers like the Cloud Core Routers (CCRs). Being Linux-based allows administrators to run scripts and interact with the system at a lower level than some other platforms. With that being said, RouterOS doesn't expose a full Linux shell environment like 100% Linux instances running BIRD or other open source projects like VyOS. It's also not possible to implement your own non-MikroTik drivers or create your own software packages (p. 24)

1.4 MikroTik Resources

Additional resources are available to help you learn RouterOS features, engage with the community, and get help online. Knowing where to go for help, training, or system documentation is just as important as knowing commands and configuration steps. Participating in online communities can also be very rewarding and help you develop new skills.

1.4.1 MikroTik Newsletter

MikroTik periodically sends a newsletter out with new product and feature announcements, training schedules, and other important information. Current and past issues of the newsletter and summaries are available at the following URL:

```
https://wiki.mikrotik.com/wiki/MikroTik_News
```

Keep an eye on this page or subscribe to the email newsletter on the MikroTik website to keep up to date with the latest developments.

1.4.2 RouterOS Changelog

The RouterOS Changelog is a list of past changes in RouterOS releases. The Changelog for the Release Candidate software branch details features that may be implemented in future stable releases. Before upgrading to the latest RouterOS version or testing a Release Candidate branch feature it's a good idea to check the Changelog first at the following URL:

```
https://mikrotik.com/download/changelogs/
```

Sometimes breaking changes to certain features or packages are noted in the Changelog, so check before upgrading even when running the Stable software branch.

1.4.3 MikroTik Wiki

The MikroTik Wiki is the primary source of MikroTik and RouterOS documentation. It houses command and feature documentation, including example configurations for some common solutions. Updates to documentation keeps pace with software updates for the most part, and the pages are fairly easy to navigate. Comprehensive lists of command options and defaults are also available in the Wiki. Access the Wiki resource at the following URL:

```
https://wiki.mikrotik.com/
```

1.4.4 MikroTik Forum

The MikroTik Forum is an online space for interacting with the MikroTik community and RouterOS developers. News about future release and features are often posted, and community members can reach out to help from their peers and the vendor via forum threads. Access the MikroTik Forum at the following URL:

```
https://forum.mikrotik.com/
```

> **WARNING**: Before posting a device's configuration to the forum for peer assistance be sure to sanitize it. Remove any passwords, keys, public Internet Protocols (IPs), or other organization-specific information.

1.4.5 MikroTik User Meetings

MikroTik User Meetings (MUMs) are regular events where MikroTik users and vendors can meet, attend workshops, and view new products. MikroTik User Meetings (MUMs) also offer training and certification opportunities for MikroTik professionals. See the following URL for a list of current and upcoming meetings around the world:

```
https://mum.mikrotik.com/
```

1.4.6 Distributor and Consultant Support

Distributors and consultants often offer commercial support and resources for growing and maintaining MikroTik networks. Speak with your MikroTik distributor to learn what they offer in terms of engineering and support.

1.4.7 Reddit

I've had a great experience collaborating with other MikroTik peers on Reddit.com. The most active MikroTik-specific subreddit can be found at the following URL:

`https://www.reddit.com/r/mikrotik/`

As of this writing the /r/mikrotik community is fairly active and the moderators have been very responsive to questions and concerns. As MikroTik becomes more popular outside the WISP community it's appearing in other subreddits as well that have wider industry focuses. If you're a Reddit user take a look at these other URLs for industry-related discussions and the occasional MikroTik post:

- `https://www.reddit.com/r/networking/`
- `https://www.reddit.com/r/sysadmin/`
- `https://www.reddit.com/r/netsec/`

1.5 MikroTik Support

MikroTik provides support for RouterBOARD and RouterOS products via email. In my experience they have been very responsive in responding to bug reports and miscellaneous requests for documentation updates. With that being said, to get the best support possible you must provide the best information you have available about your issue. As anyone who has worked a helpdesk knows, vague reports and tickets don't generate the best responses.

1.5.1 Emailing Support

If you're experiencing strange behavior or think you've discovered a bug MikroTik engineers will most likely ask you to send an email to *support@mikrotik.com* with an attached *supout.rif* file. The Winbox *Make Supout.rif* button used to create the file is shown in Figure 1.1 and the command sub-window is shown to the right.

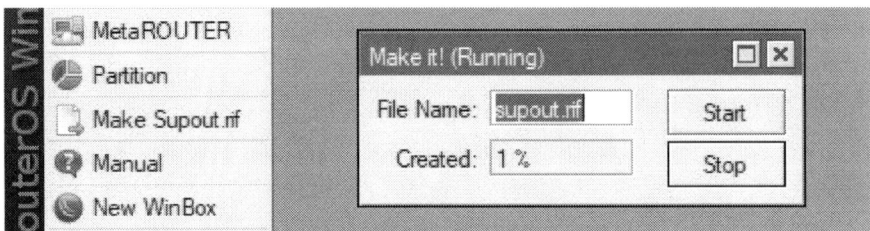

Figure 1.1: Making supout.rif

> **WARNING**: Only send your *supout.rif* file to MikroTik staff. Do not post the *supout.rif* file publicly on the MikroTik forum or elsewhere.

From the terminal a supout.rif file can also be created with the "*/system sup-output*" command. The new "*supout.rif*" file can now be copied off the device via File Transfer Protocol (FTP) or SSH, or by clicking and dragging via the "*File*" button in Winbox. Figure 1.2 shows the file listed at the Terminal using the "*/file print*" command.

```
[admin@MikroTik] > /system sup-output
created: 100%

[admin@MikroTik] > /file print
#  NAME              TYPE        SIZE      CREATION-TIME
0  flash             disk                  dec/31/1969 20:00:00
1  disk1             disk                  dec/31/1969 20:00:01
2  backup.rsc        script      6.0KiB    aug/04/2017 21:34:03
3  supout.rif        .rif file   523.2KiB  aug/06/2017 22:16:42
4  disk1/logs        directory             feb/02/2017 23:32:23
5  disk1/lost+...    directory             feb/02/2017 23:23:23
6  flash/skins       directory             dec/31/1969 20:00:02
7  flash/log.0...    .txt file   59        feb/20/2017 19:21:36
[admin@MikroTik] > _
```

Figure 1.2: Supout.rif File Print

1.5.2 Autosupout.rif File

While the *supout.rif* file is manually generated for troubleshooting and support purposes, another file exists that is generated automatically to assist support personnel. The *autosupout.rif* file is created automatically by the system when a software failure occurs. Sometimes failures of the software subsystems won't generate log entries that administrators can use, so *autosupout.rif* is created to fill that gap. The debug information in this file is only useful to RouterOS developers, and as of this writing there is no tool for viewing the internals of the file yourself. If your device is crashing and generating this file you should email *support@mikrotik.com*, describe your issue, and include the *autosupout.rif* file for the developers to examine.

1.5.3 Support Best Practices

If you're putting an email together for the support staff at MikroTik be sure to include the following information to help them understand your problem:

1. RouterBOARD model or Cloud Hosted Router (CHR) hypervisor
2. RouterOS software version number and channel
3. RouterBOOT firmware version number

This list comes from my own experiences working with MikroTik support. Having this information at-hand helps support staff get to work quickly and without additional emails back-and-forth asking for information. Consider the following questions as well when formatting a copy of your device configuration for support staff to examine:

- Do your firewall, Network Address Translation (NAT), Mangle, etc. rules have logical names?
- Have comments been added to address lists, rules, or other entries?
- If copying and pasting configuration lines into an email, are they neatly formatted and readable?

Getting the best support from any vendor starts with providing them the best information to start the process.

1.6 RouterBOARD

Since 2002 MikroTik has produced a wonderful diversity of equipment including routers, switches, and wireless infrastructure components. The RouterBOARD platform, introduced in 2002, puts the RouterOS software on MikroTik-branded hardware. Units range from small office routers with five Ethernet ports, up to fiber optic-based core routers with more than a dozen ports. There is a large variety of wireless products as well, including small indoor Access Points (APs) and large tower-based microwave back-haul units.

The RouterBOARD product line is powered by different processor architectures. While the RouterOS software can run directly on x86 and x86-64 platforms from Intel® and AMD® (x86 & x86_64), it's most often run on embedded systems using the following processor architectures:

- MIPSBE
- MIPSLE
- MMIPS
- SMIPS

- TILE
- Power PC (PPC)
- ARM

Many RouterBOARD units feature a Microprocessor without Interlocked Pipeline Stages (MIPS) architecture processor which is very popular for use in embedded devices like routers. The MIPS instruction set has been licensed to chip manufacturers like Qualcomm Atheros, Texas Instruments, and others who produce the chips. To view a specific device's architecture, memory, processor count, model name, and more use the *"/system resource print"* command as shown in Figure 1.3 on the following page:

```
[admin@MikroTik] > /system resource print
                  uptime: 5d13h55m16s
                 version: 6.39rc72 (testing)
              build-time: Apr/13/2017 11:56:11
        factory-software: 6.34.2
             free-memory: 36.5MiB
            total-memory: 64.0MiB
                     cpu: MIPS 24Kc V7.4
               cpu-count: 1
           cpu-frequency: 650MHz
                cpu-load: 7%
          free-hdd-space: 4.9MiB
         total-hdd-space: 16.0MiB
 write-sect-since-reboot: 1448
        write-sect-total: 42580
              bad-blocks: 0%
       architecture-name: mipsbe
              board-name: hAP ac lite
                platform: MikroTik

[admin@MikroTik] > _
```

Figure 1.3: System Resources

In the case of this router the MIPSBE chip is a *MIPS 24Kc* made by Qualcomm Atheros. The same information is available in Winbox under *System > Resources* as shown in Figure 1.4:

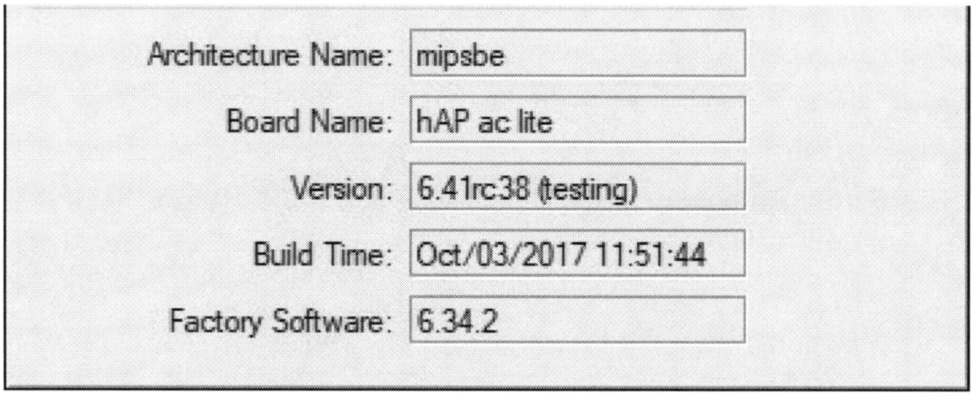

Figure 1.4: Winbox System Resources

Some of these processors, like MIPSBE, are single-core and made for SOHO environments. Others processors, including PPC and TILE, are used in larger models like the RB-1100AHx2 and CCRs. Most models are passively cooled and feature a single power supply. Higher-end models have active cooling and multiple hot-swap power supplies. RouterOS x86 installs can run on commodity server hardware from Dell, HPE, Trend Micro, and others. They then benefit from the server's built-in redundant cooling, power supplies, storage controllers, and more.

1.6.1 RouterBOARD Features

The RouterBOARD product line includes rack-mounted routers, desktop SOHO routers, and wireless devices. Some RouterBOARD devices can be expanded with Mini PCI (MPCI) radio modules, additional Random Access Memory (RAM), and storage. Many units in the RouterBOARD line begin with the "RB" model designation like the RB2011 and RB951. Newer models like the hEX and hAP aren't marketed with "RB" designation but it's still included in the model number. For example, the hEX model with Power Over Ethernet (POE) shown in Figure 1.5 is model number "RB960PGS":

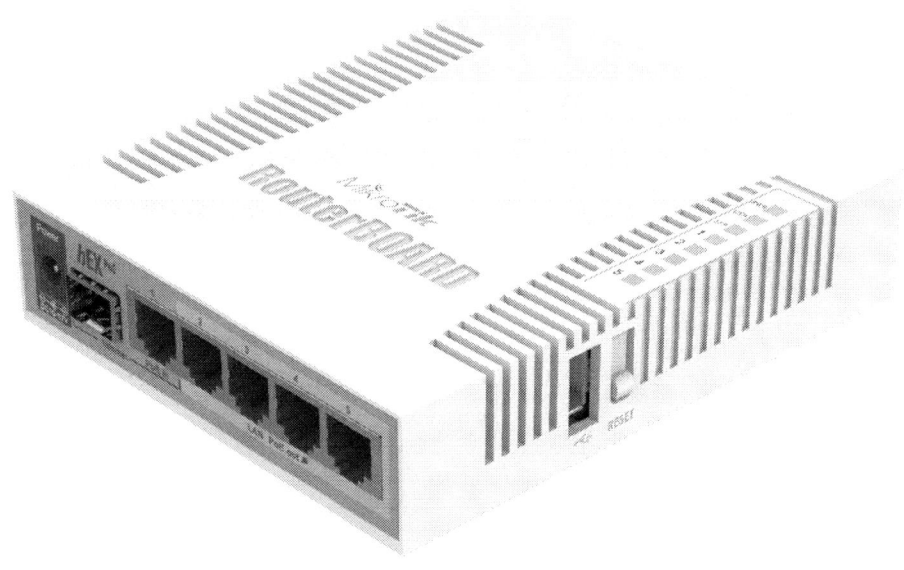

Image Credit: *MikroTik*
Figure 1.5: hEX POE (RB960PGS)

RouterBOARD units can also be purchased as mountable circuit board units for use in custom or specialized enclosures. An example of this type of unit is the RB493AH shown in Figure 1.6 on the following page. For outdoor and tower-mounted environments that can experience extremes in temperature, UV, humidity, or saltwater exposure a unit like this in a custom enclosure is often the best choice.

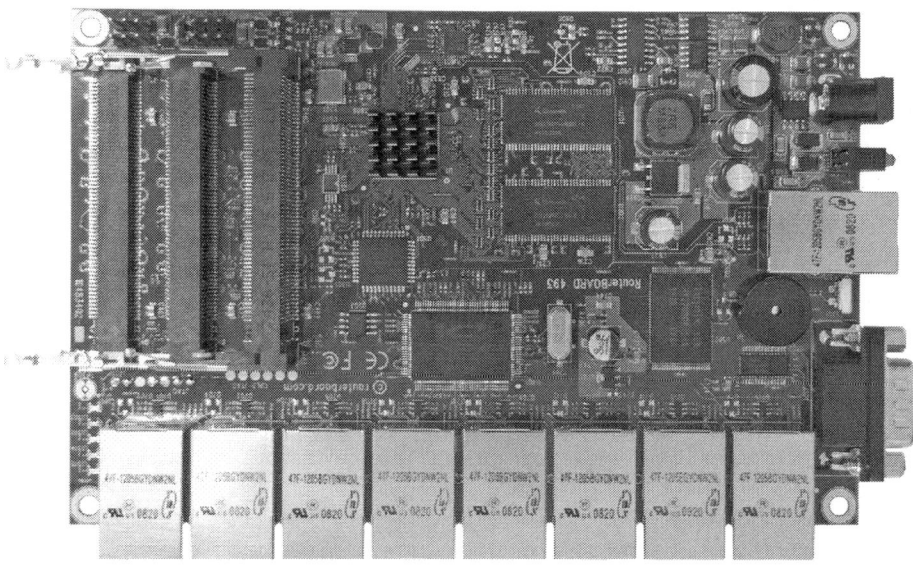

Image Credit: *MikroTik*
Figure 1.6: RB493AH Board

RouterBOARD models like the RB800-series can also accept "daughter boards" that add additional MPCI and Mini PCI-Express (MPCI-E) expansion ports. One of these boards is shown in Figure 1.7.

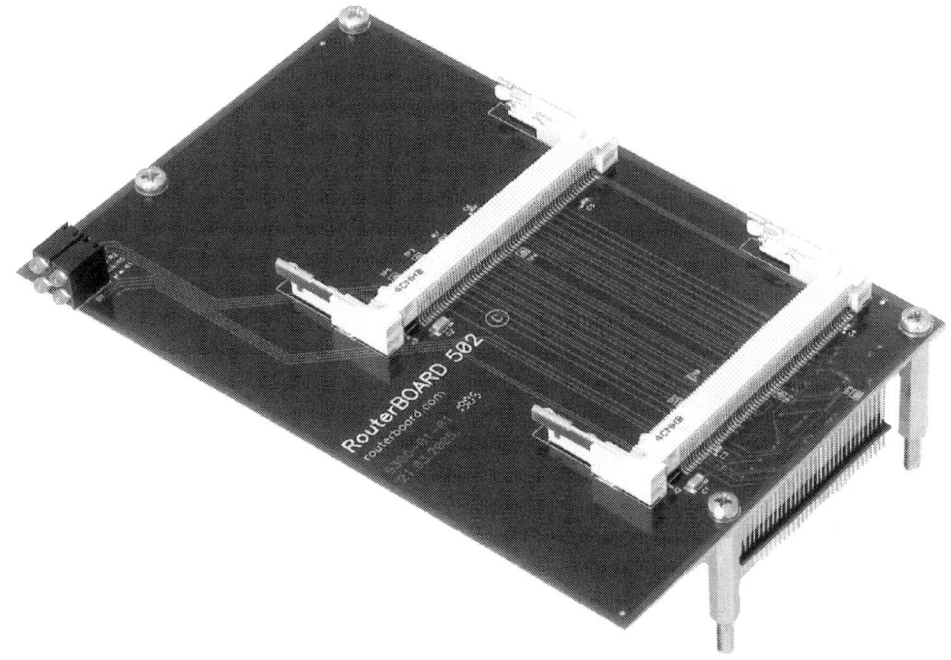

Image Credit: *MikroTik*
Figure 1.7: Daughter Board

With a daughter board installed plus MPCI cards like those shown on page 104 a custom case with additional antenna holes and mounts is typically the best option.

1.6.2 Cloud Core Router

The CCR product line was announced in 2012 to much excitement from the community. Many enterprise users had been asking for a platform with more robust processing that could operate in the network core and better handle full Border Gateway Protocol (BGP) routing tables. Based on the TILE architecture, CCR models that are current as of this writing feature 16, 36, or 72 processor cores. Most models also have expandable memory slots and come pre-configured with enough memory to support large routing tables, complex queues, and robust firewalls.

The CCR product line also includes devices that support SFP Plus (SFP+) fiber modules, redundant power supplies, and active cooling. Figure 1.8 shows some of the components inside a CCR model. Small Form-Factor Pluggable (SFP) ports are located in the bottom-left, and a large heatsink with fans and a shroud for active cooling in the middle:

Image Credit: *MikroTik*
Figure 1.8: MikroTik CCR Components

These features make it easier to introduce MikroTik into provider networks and the enterprise network core. The MikroTik CCR1016-12S-1S+ is pictured in Figure 1.9 on the following page and is a great example of both a CCR and a device that uses SFP fiber modules (p. 101):

Image Credit: *MikroTik*
Figure 1.9: MikroTik CCR1016-12S-1S+

Some CCR models support dual Power Supply Units (PSUs) as shown in Figure 1.10 for increased stability and hot-swap in case of failure. A replacement PSU is shown in Figure 1.11:

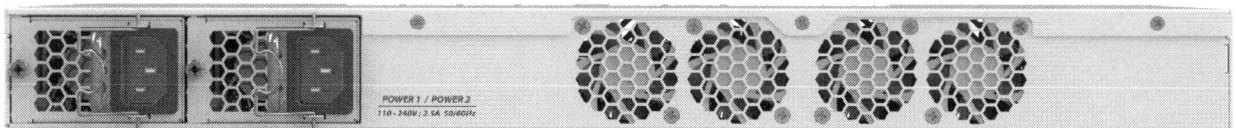

Image Credit: *MikroTik*
Figure 1.10: MikroTik CCR Reverse

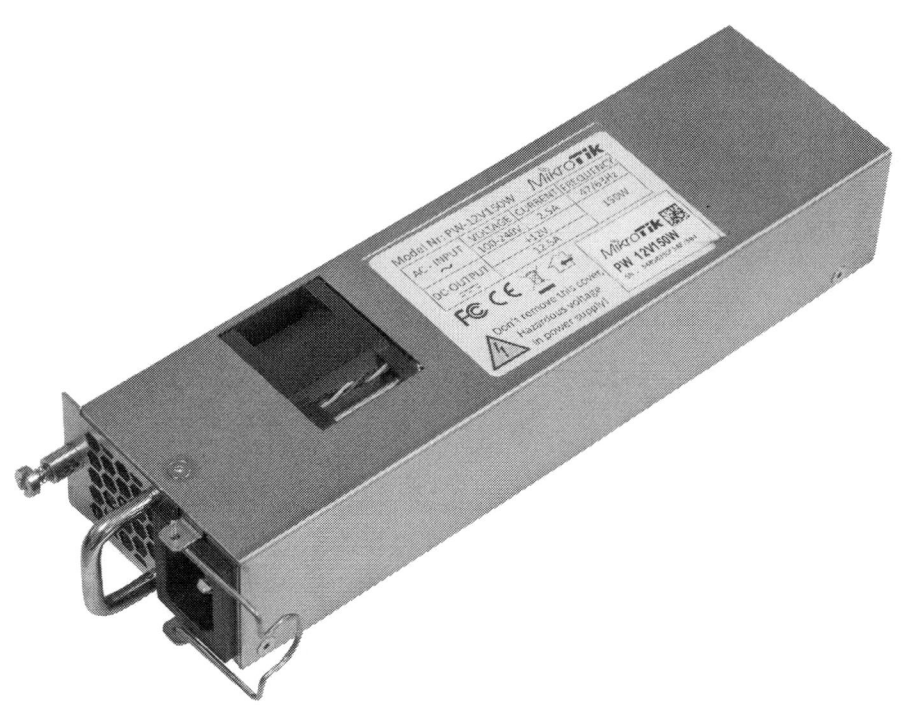

Image Credit: *MikroTik*
Figure 1.11: MikroTik Replacement PSU

1.6.3 Cloud Router Switch

The Cloud Router Switch (CRS) platform is MikroTik's higher-end switch product offering. Historically MikroTik did not offer larger network switches, though smaller "Smart Switch" units like the RB260-series shown in Figure 1.12 were available.

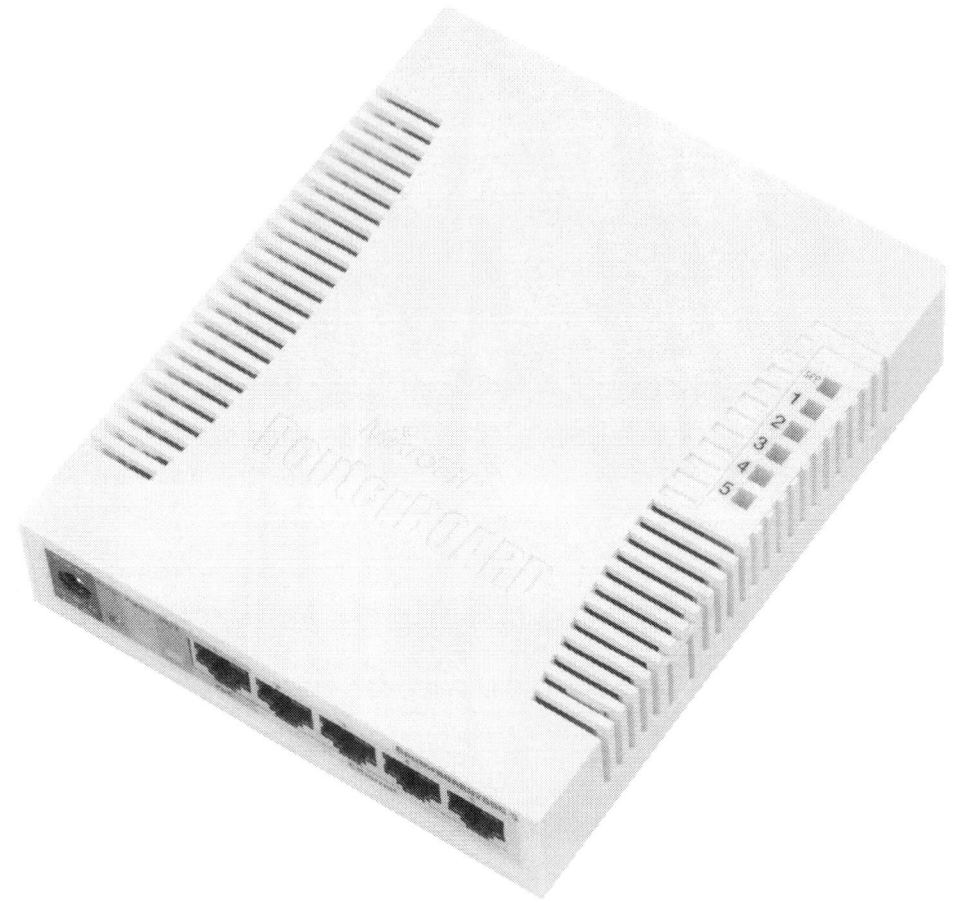

Image Credit: *MikroTik*
Figure 1.12: RB260GS Smart Switch

The larger CRS product line includes both desktop and rack-mounted switches that complement the other wireless and router offerings. This allows consumers to have a larger Layer 3 (L3) "smart switch" and enjoy the same RouterOS environment they are used to. An example of the CRS, a CRS226-24G-2S+RM, is shown in Figure 1.13 on the following page.

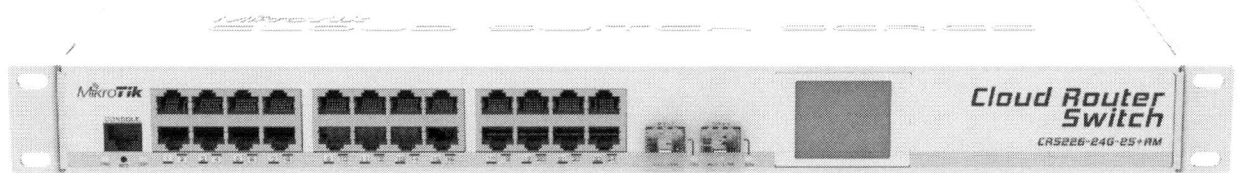

Image Credit: *MikroTik*
Figure 1.13: MikroTik CRS226-24G-2S+RM

Smaller switches like the RB260-series run a dedicated software release for switches called SwitchOS (SwOS). Larger switches like the CRS have the option of booting either to RouterOS or SwOS environments. The SwOS software features a web interface and is designed specifically for management of switching functionality. While the SwOS software is not part of the MTCNA outline it's worthy of mention here because of its continued use.

1.7 Cloud Hosted Router

The CHR is a pre-rolled virtual RouterOS installation. While the x86 version of RouterOS can be installed on bare metal servers or a hypervisor, the CHR is purpose-built for virtualization. It's distributed on the MikroTik download web page in virtual disk formats like *.vmdk* and *.vdi*. The CHR can run on virtualization platforms like VMware's vSphere®, Oracle VirtualBox, Microsoft Hyper-V, and other mainstream platforms. While the CHR is free to download and use, unlicensed CHR instances are limited to 1Mb/sec speed until a valid license key is entered. Figure 1.14 shows a CHR running in Microsoft Hyper-V:

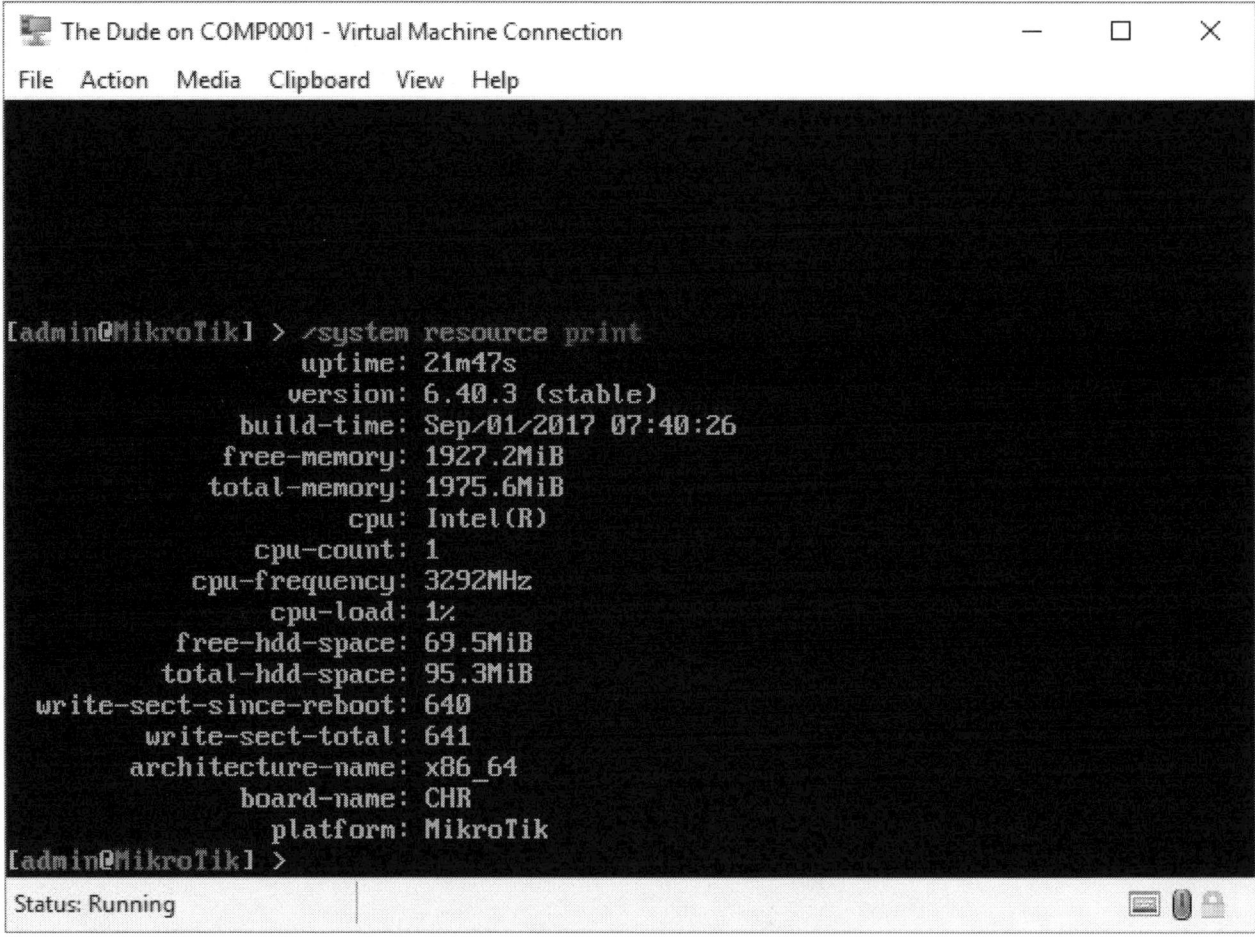

Figure 1.14: CHR Hyper-V Console

Since RouterOS runs on a Linux kernel the type of Virtual Machine (VM) in VirtualBox is "Linux", and the operating system is "Other Linux (64bit)". In Microsoft Hyper-V the VM type is simply a "Generation One" VM. The minimum hardware required to run the CHR includes the following [7]:

- 64-bit CPU with virtualization support
- 128 MB RAM
- 128 MB hard disk space

Figure 1.15 shows the virtual hardware (with IDE storage) assigned to a CHR running Dude monitoring software (ch. 18 on page 287):

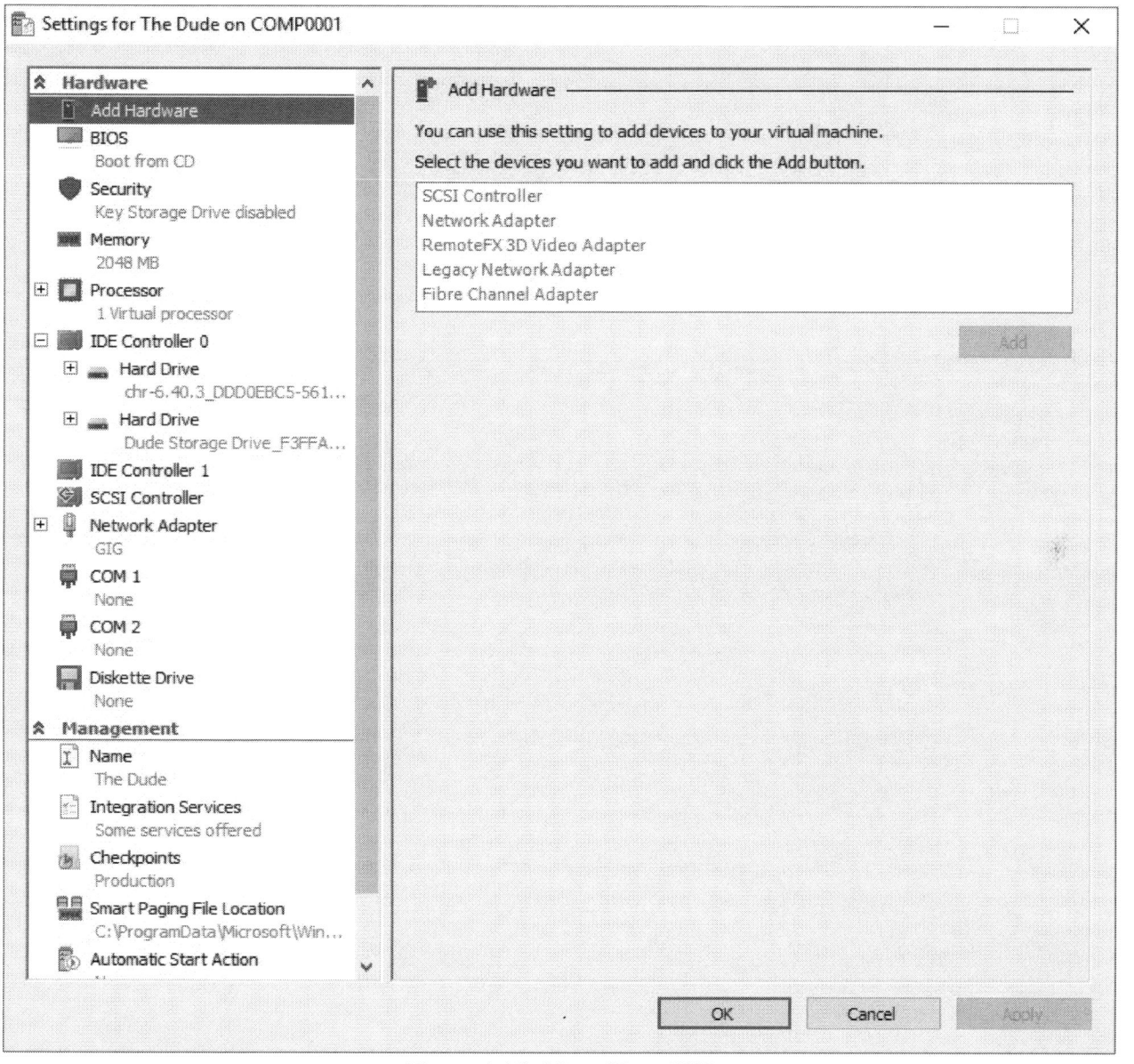

Figure 1.15: VirtualBox CHR

Some specific storage guidelines must also be observed [7]:

- The system installation drive has a maximum supported size of 16 GB
- The primary drive's physical or virtual storage controller must be *IDE*
- Secondary drive storage controllers can be SATA, SCSI, etc.

Once the CHR instance is installed and running you can take advantage of robust failover, snapshot, and portability features that enterprise virtualization makes available in the datacenter. Figure 1.16 illustrates the speed limit with a receive-only bandwidth test running between a physical RouterBOARD and a virtual CHR. The average speed reached in the test is only 1003.1 kbps:

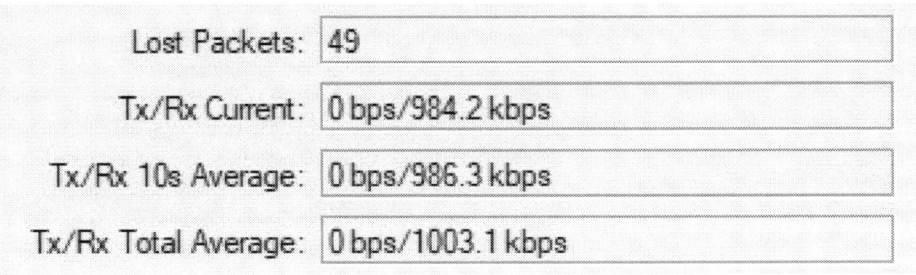

Figure 1.16: CHR Speed Limitation

1.8 RouterOS Licenses

As of this writing there are six active license levels, of which three can be purchased directly from MikroTik or a distribution partner [14]. Licenses don't expire, and software upgrades aren't limited by the vendor. However, it's not possible to change the license level once a purchased key has been entered. All RouterOS license levels are listed below:

- Level 0 - 24hr Trial
- Level 1 - Demo
- Level 2 - *Not Used*
- Level 3 - WISP Customer Premise Equipment (CPE)
- Level 4 - WISP *(Small)*
- Level 5 - WISP *(Large)*
- Level 6 - Controller

RouterBOARD devices come with an embedded license that cannot be transferred. Higher license levels can handle more concurrent tunnels, User Manager sessions, Hotspot users, and more. Levels four, five, and six also come with different durations of initial vendor support time. To view the license on your device use the "*/system license print*" command as shown in Figure 1.17 on the following page:

```
[admin@MikroTik] > /system license print
software-id: ABCD-1234
    nlevel: 4
  features:
[admin@MikroTik] > _
```

Figure 1.17: System License

The same information in Winbox can be accessed under *System > License*.

1.8.1 Level 0 Trial

Level zero licenses will reset the device after 24 hours and require re-installation to test for another day. RouterOS x86 installations have a level zero license by default for testing and proof-of-concept but the license can be upgraded in-place.

1.8.2 Level 1 Demo

Level one demo licenses can be requested for free via the MikroTik client portal at the following URL:

https://mikrotik.com/client/keyDemo

Unlike level zero trial keys, the demo doesn't expire after 24 hours. However, there are a number of stipulations to running a device at this level. See the URL above for more information on these restrictions applied to demo license keys:

- Limited connections for tunnels like PPTP, EoIP, etc.
- No wireless support
- No included version upgrades
- No included support from MikroTik
- Not eligible for resale

1.8.3 Level 2

Level two is no longer used in modern RouterOS versions [14]. Very old MikroTik models still in production may be utilizing a level two license but it won't be found on MikroTik hardware typically deployed in modern networks.

1.8.4 Level 3

Level three licensed devices cannot function as Wireless Access Points because they are only licensed to work as CPEs. This is a cost-effective license for WISPs with many smaller CPE radios in the field that only need to join the WISP network to provide connectivity for customers. This level isn't available to individuals for purchase on MikroTik's website, though it is available for volume purchasers.

1.8.5 Levels 4 and 5

Levels four and five licensed routers can function as infrastructure devices and APs in WISP and Enterprise environments. Hotspot users, tunnels, and other features are limited in their quantity depending on the license level [14]. For example, Level 4 licenses can support up to 200 PPPoE, L2TP, and PPTP tunnels. Level 5 licenses can support up to 500 of those tunnels. For a list of specific features and limitations see the following URL:

```
https://wiki.mikrotik.com/wiki/Manual:License#License_Levels
```

1.8.6 Level 6

Level six licensed devices are often installed as core routers or tunnel aggregation devices. They are licensed for an *unlimited* number of tunnels, hotspot users, and more [14]. At this level hardware capacity of the device becomes the limiting factor. Many organizations handling a lot of users or tunnels choose to deploy routers with this license level on dedicated servers with high-end network interface cards installed.

1.8.7 CHR License

The CHR virtual image is licensed out-of-the-box as a fully functional router. However, until a valid license key is entered all interfaces are limited to 1Mb/sec speeds. Unlike level zero licenses the CHR image doesn't reset after a 24hr period but it still retains the speed limit. The output of *"/system license print"* shows the license Level as *"free"* in Figure 1.18:

```
[admin@MikroTik] > /system license print
system-id: abc123xyz
    level: free
[admin@MikroTik] > _
```

Figure 1.18: CHR License Print

The same information can be viewed in Winbox for the CHR under *System > License*. The free CHR license is good for proof-of-concept virtual installations and learning RouterOS. Another advantage to running CHR devices virtually is that snapshots and Open Virtualization Archive (OVA) / Open Virtualization Format (OVF) exports can be made prior to big system changes. Before going live you can purchase the amount of keys you need and license the CHR devices in-place without re-installing.

1.9 Review Questions

1. Which file is manually generated to assist MikroTik when investigating possible bugs?

    (a) supout.rif

    (b) support.rif

    (c) supout.txt

    (d) autosupout.rif

2. Which document outlines updates in new RouterOS releases?

    (a) RouterBoard product sheets

    (b) Changelog

    (c) MikroTik MuMs

    (d) Release Candidate

3. RouterOS and command documentation is located where?

    (a) RouterOS.com

    (b) MikroTik Subreddit

    (c) MikroTik Forum

    (d) MikroTik Wiki

4. What is the software that powers MikroTik products?

    (a) RouterNOS

    (b) RouterBoard

    (c) RouterOS

    (d) RouterBOOT

5. Which MikroTik product is designed to run in a virtualized environment?

    (a) CHR

    (b) CCR

    (c) CRS

    (d) RouterBoard

6. What speed is the CHR limited to until a valid license is input?

    (a) 1000Mb/sec

    (b) 100Mb/sec

    (c) 10Mb/sec

    (d) 1Mb/sec

7. Which line of RouterBoard models is most appropriate for large enterprises or service providers?

    (a) CHR

    (b) CCR

    (c) CRS

    (d) RB-951

8. How long do you have to enter a valid license key on an x86 installation?

    (a) 24 hours

    (b) 48 hours

    (c) 7 days

    (d) 30 days

9. What is the minimum amount of RAM required to run a CHR?

    (a) 64 MB

    (b) 128 MB

    (c) 256 MB

    (d) 512 MB

10. What command will output the license level and product key in RouterOS?

    (a) /show system license

    (b) /system key print

    (c) /license print

    (d) /system license print

1.10 Review Answers

1. Which file is manually generated to assist MikroTik when investigating possible bugs?

   A – supout.rif (p. 4)

2. Which document outlines updates in new RouterOS releases?

   B – Changelog (p. 2)

3. RouterOS and command documentation is located where?

   D – MikroTik Wiki (p. 3)

4. What is the software that powers MikroTik products?

   C – RouterOS (p. 2)

5. Which MikroTik product is designed to run in a virtualized environment?

   A – CHR (p. 14)

6. What speed is the CHR limited to until a valid license is input?

   D – 1Mb/sec (p. 14)

7. Which line of RouterBoard models is most appropriate for large enterprises or service providers?

   B – CCR (p. 10)

8. How long do you have to enter a valid license key on an x86 installation?

   A – 24 hours (p. 17)

9. What is the minimum amount of RAM required to run a CHR?

   B – 128 MB (p. 14)

10. What command will output the license level and product key in RouterOS?

    D – /system license print (p. 17)

Chapter 2

RouterOS Software

RouterOS is the network operating system that powers physical and virtual MikroTik devices. Upgrading, downgrading, managing software packages, and making configuration changes are typical parts of any MTCNA candidate's duties. Fortunately, RouterOS looks and feels much the same across different networks and devices. As long as you have a good working knowledge of how RouterOS functions, you can work at a WISP, an MSP, or in an enterprise that uses MikroTik and feel at-home.

2.1 RouterOS Installations

RouterOS and its components arrive in a number of formats for MikroTik users:

- Pre-installed on RouterBOARD units
- Pre-packaged in virtual hard disk files
- *.iso* images
- *.npk* software packages

Regardless of the installation, type functionality is largely the same from a network administrator's perspective. This makes RouterOS skills very portable across platforms and organizations.

2.1.1 Pre-Installed RouterOS

The pre-installed copy of RouterOS on each RouterBOARD is ready to go immediately without any further installation or licensing. The license level can be raised if necessary to enable additional functionality. To view the license level use the *"/system license print"* command, shown in Figure 2.1 on the next page for a pre-installed RouterBOARD unit:

```
[admin@MikroTik] > /system license print
 software-id: ABCD-1234
      level: 4
   features:
[admin@MikroTik] > _
```

Figure 2.1: Showing Pre-Installed License

2.1.2 RouterOS Virtual Hard Disks

The CHR is available pre-loaded in virtual hard disk, RAW disk, and OVA formats. Access these files for your respective virtualization platform from the MikroTik download page at the following URL:

https://www.mikrotik.com/download

As of early 2017, downloadable file formats include the following:

- VHDX (Microsoft Hyper-V)
- VMDK (VMware products, Oracle VirtualBox)
- VDI (Oracle VirtualBox)
- Raw Disk Image

A CHR VM is easily brought online by adding the basic Linux-compatible virtual hardware, attaching the Virtual Hard Disk (VHD), and booting the VM. In chapter 18 on page 287 there are step-by-step directions for creating a CHR VM in Microsoft Hyper-V.

2.2 RouterOS Packages

MikroTik routers all come with the default set of packages for doing basic routing and other functions. Additional packages can be installed to extend functionality with more advanced features like Multiprotocol Label Switching (MPLS), Internet Protocol v6 (IPv6), CALEA[1], etc. By default, the *system* package is always checked (and cannot be unchecked) during an installation, and other packages can be selected as shown in Figure 2.2 on the following page:

---

[1]United States Communications Assistance for Law Enforcement Act

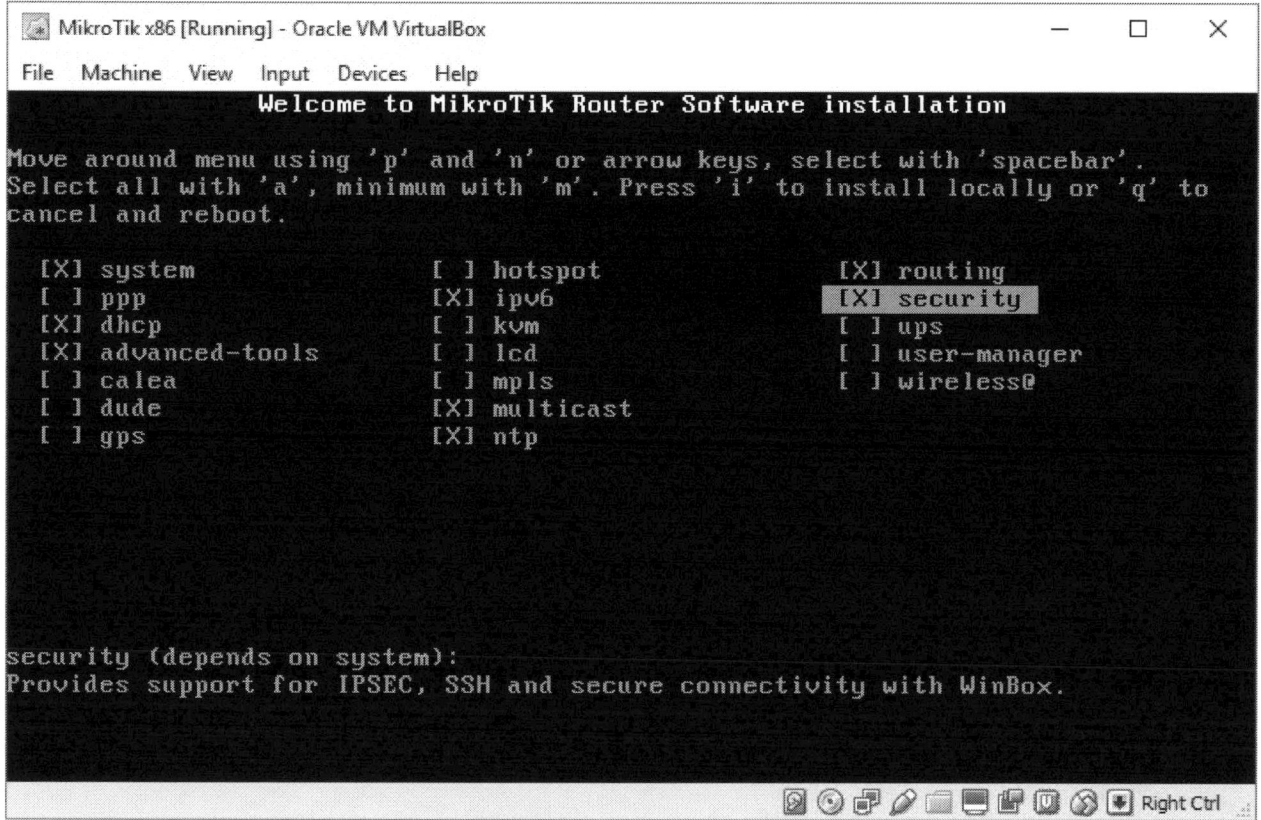

Figure 2.2: Package Selection

Each package includes different software capabilities for the router. These packages are available and include the following features:

1. Advanced Tools: Network monitoring, IP scanning, Wake on LAN (WOL), and more complex Ping tools.

2. Communications Assistance for Law Enforcement Act (CALEA): Tools for collecting subscriber data pursuant to the Communications Assistance for Law Enforcement Act in the United States.

3. Dynamic Host Configuration Protocol (DHCP): This package allows the router to run as a DHCP client, server, and relay.

4. GPS: MikroTik devices can use an attached Global Positioning System (GPS) receiver to get position and time updates with this package.

5. Hotspot: Includes software to run a paid captive portal for public network access.

6. IPv6: All the software needed to run an IPv6 router.

7. MPLS: This package allows the router to participate in MPLS switching, including Virtual Private LAN Service (VPLS) tunnels.

8. Multicast: With this package a router can rum Protocol Independent Multicast (PIM) and Internet Group Management Protocol (IGMP) proxying.

9. Network Time Protocol (NTP): The router can run as an NTP client or server with this package.

10. OpenFlow: Provisional support for the OpenFlow Software Defined Network (SDN) standard is included in this package. It should be noted that support for OpenFlow is still in limbo at this point while SDN technology evolves in the market.

11. Point-to-Point Protocol (PPP): The router can run PPP, Point-to-Point Tunnel Protocol (PPTP), Layer Two Tunneling Protocol (L2TP), and PPP over Ethernet (PPPoE) server and client services with this package.

12. RouterBOARD: This package has hardware-specific functionality for RouterBOOT and RouterBOARD management.

13. Routing: Dynamic routing including Open Shortest Path First (OSPF), Routing Information Protocol (RIP), BGP, and more. RouterOS can run without this package as long as only static routes are used.

14. Security: This package includes software for IPSEC, SSH, and other encrypted connections.

15. System: This is the bare-bones software component for RouterOS. Includes basic functionality like static routing, telnet, firewalling, Domain Name Service (DNS), bridging, etc. This package is always installed and necessary, regardless of the RouterOS instance type.

16. UPS: This package allows a router to communicate with APC-brand UPS units.

17. User Manager: When using a Hotspot, the User Manager package allows for more centralized administration.

18. Wireless: This package provides support for wireless interfaces and connections.

MikroTik assembles individual packages together into "rollup" packages for RouterOS instances on different platforms. For example, the *routeros-x86* package includes the following individual packages:

- System
- Hotspot
- Wireless
- PPP
- Security
- MPLS
- Advanced Tools
- DHCP
- RouterBOARD
- IPv6
- Routing

For more information about each package and links to relevant resources visit the MikroTik package documentation page at the following URL:

```
https://wiki.mikrotik.com/wiki/Manual:System/Packages
```

2.2.1 Installed Packages

The "*/system package print*" command lists all installed packages, including their version and the current status. The results, with some packages already disabled and marked with an "*X*", are shown in Figure 2.3:

```
[admin@MikroTik] > /system package print
Flags: X - disabled
 #   NAME              VERSION         SCHEDULED
 0   routeros-mipsbe   6.39rc76
 1   system            6.39rc76
 2 X ipv6              6.39rc76
 3   wireless          6.39rc76
 4 X hotspot           6.39rc76
 5   dhcp              6.39rc76
 6   mpls              6.39rc76
 7   routing           6.39rc76
 8 X ppp               6.39rc76
 9   security          6.39rc76
10   advanced-tools    6.39rc76
11   multicast         6.39rc76

[admin@MikroTik] > _
```

Figure 2.3: Installed Packages

The same information is available in Winbox under *System > Packages* as shown in Figure 2.4. There is easy access to buttons on the same screen for package enabling and disabling, downgrades, and installation checking.

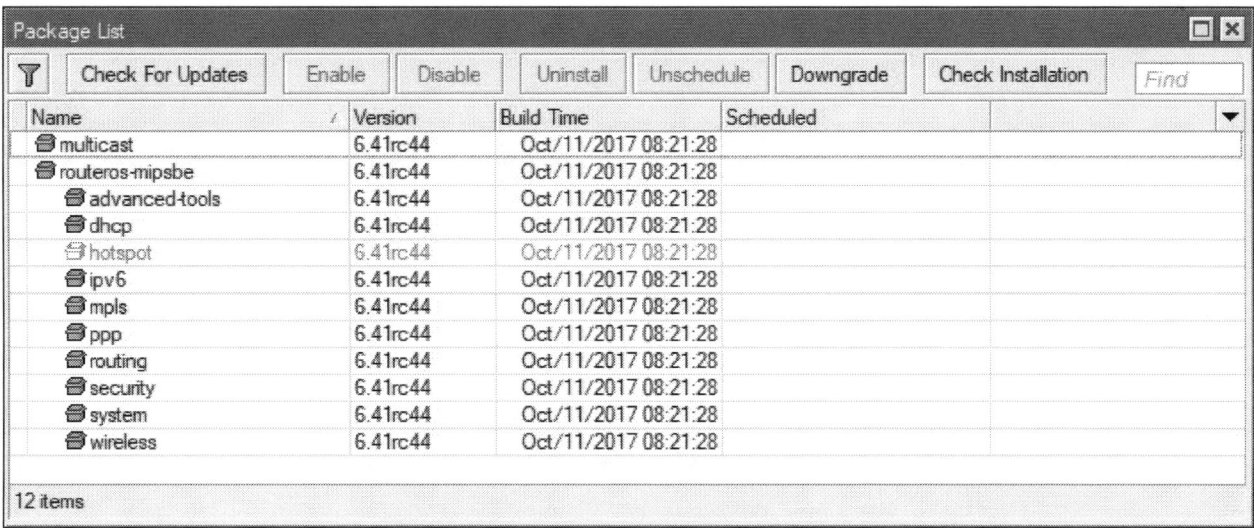

Figure 2.4: System Packages, Winbox

2.2.2 Package Format

Packages are downloaded in a compressed Zip file and extracted into a directory with individual package files. Each package is an *.npk*-format file that is digitally signed by MikroTik. As of late 2017 it is not possible to generate your own packages for RouterOS or easily view the contents of existing package files. It is also not possible to upload custom or proprietary drivers for third-party hardware.

2.2.3 Downloading Packages

Download additional packages if you need their featured capabilities (p. 25) from the MikroTik download page at the following URL:

`https://mikrotik.com/download`

The downloaded package files can be dragged into the Winbox *File* window or uploaded via FTP or SSH. A reboot of the device will force RouterOS to detect and install the newly-uploaded files. Once packages are installed the built-in package manager can update them in-place. Consult the guidance on package releases in the next section to ensure you're using the software branch that's right for your networks.

2.3 RouterOS Releases

Four RouterOS software branches are available for download on the MikroTik download page. Each of the following release branches has its place in enterprise and provider networks:

- Current
- Bugfix Only
- Legacy
- Release Candidate (RC)

For many MikroTik users the current branch will always be the most appropriate.

2.3.1 Current

The current branch is the latest stable version of RouterOS. This includes the latest tested features, bugfixes, and patches. It is recommended for production environments that you run the current software branch available for your devices. Be sure to test the new version first on non-production devices before widespread implementation when upgrades for this branch are available.

2.3.2 Bugfix Only

The bugfix only branch for a given release is a roll-up of bug fixes with none of the additional functionality that has been subsequently released. If you're stuck on a particular release for whatever reason and can't upgrade but still require a bug fix then this is the release for you.

2.3.3 Legacy

The legacy branch is a past milestone release that was considered stable at the time. While it was stable at the time of release, this branch does not receive any bug fixes. Compatibility issues with hardware, known issues with a particular architecture, or other unique circumstances could warrant use of the Legacy branch. Running this branch in production would be a last resort and you should engage MikroTik support in the meantime. Unless there is a very specific reason to remain on the legacy branch it's recommended you upgrade to current.

2.3.4 Release Candidate

The Release Candidate (RC) branch is for those who want to test "bleeding edge" software features and improvements. This branch is meant for testing only, and it is not officially supported for production use like the current branch is. The RC branch should not be run in production networks outside of limited, well-controlled tests. Typically the MikroTik staff will announce new RC versions on the forum and ask for feedback from those doing testing. If you deploy RC for testing in your networks and discover a bug you should report it in the forum thread so it can be addressed.

2.4 Updating RouterOS

It's important to keep abreast of changes in the Changelog (p. 2) and subscribe to the MikroTik newsletter (p. 2) for the latest information about software updates and features. Attackers won't hesitate to take advantage of bugs or other vulnerabilities in outdated software. Keeping RouterOS updated is another layer in your DiD security strategy.

2.4.1 Check for Updates

Checking for software updates is easy, but the upgrade process requires a few things to be configured first:

1. Internet connectivity
2. Available DNS server(s)
3. Correct software release channel

The first two items should be easy, especially if you're using the default configuration with a DHCP client running on *ether1*. To check for updates first verify that your device is set to the right branch with the *"set channel=..."* command. Once the release channel is set, kick off the step that checks for available updates. An example of the entire task using the *release-candidate* channel is shown in Figure 2.5:

```
[admin@MikroTik] > /system package update
[admin@MikroTik] /system package update> set channel=release-candidate
[admin@MikroTik] /system package update> check-for-updates
         channel: release-candidate
 current-version: 6.41rc9
  latest-version: 6.41rc9
          status: System is already up to date

[admin@MikroTik] /system package update> _
```

Figure 2.5: Checking for Updates

To run this process with the current branch the *"set channel=current"* command modifies that option. In this case no update is available for the RC software release. The example in Figure 2.6 shows a new version available in the RC branch:

```
[admin@MikroTik] > /system package update check-for-updates
         channel: release-candidate
 current-version: 6.38.5
  latest-version: 6.39rc72
          status: New version is available

[admin@MikroTik] > _
```

Figure 2.6: New Version Available

The equivalent functionality can be found in Winbox under *System > Packages* as shown in Figure 2.7 on the following page:

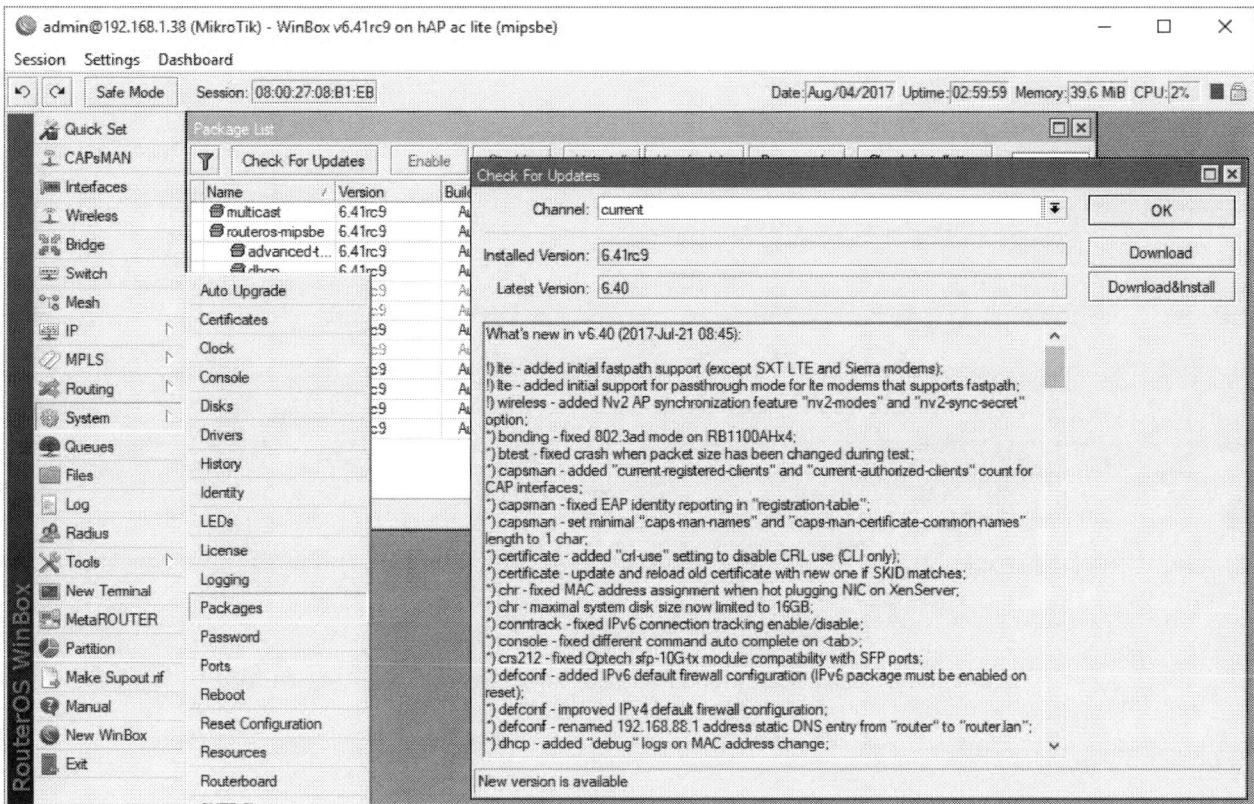

Figure 2.7: Checking for Updates, Winbox

In Figure 2.7 the current software loaded is from the Release Candidate branch but the Current branch is selected. For that reason the "*Download & Install*" button is clickable even though the Current software version is lower than the RC version. Running "*check-for-updates*" at the console or clicking the "Check for Updates" button will reach out to the MikroTik download servers and check for any available updates.

2.4.2 Upgrading Software

The following commands will download updated packages for your branch over the internet and install them:

```
/system package update download
/system reboot
```

This first command downloads packages but does not install them automatically. A device reboot is required to install the packages and finish the upgrade. In Winbox clicking the *Download & Install* button shown in Figure 2.7 downloads and automatically reboots the device to complete installation. If a device doesn't have internet access you can upload *.npk* package files using SSH or FTP. Once the packages have been uploaded use the following command to finish the upgrade process:

```
/system package update install
```

> **WARNING**: This command will reboot the device without asking for further confirmation. The device will remain offline for approximately one minute while the process completes.

2.4.3 Downgrading Software

If for whatever reason a software update causes issues on a device it can always be downgraded to a previous version. Upload the older *.npk* files to the router then click the *Downgrade* button shown in Figure 2.8:

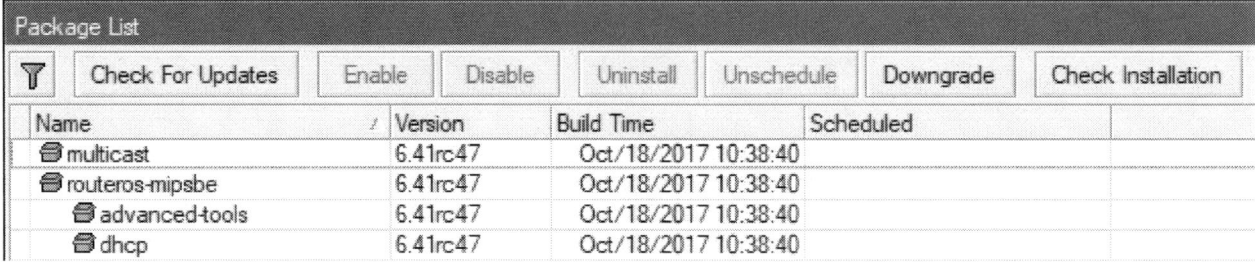

Figure 2.8: Winbox Package Downgrade Button

RouterOS will then ask for confirmation of the downgrade and system reboot:

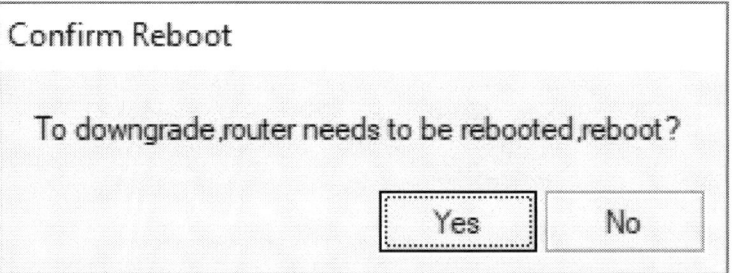

Figure 2.9: Winbox Downgrade Confirmation

The router will reboot and re-install the older packages that were uploaded.

2.4.4 Disabling RouterOS Packages

Not all packages will be used on every MikroTik device in your network. With that in mind, a good best practice to follow is disabling or removing any packages you don't need. For example, if you're not using IPv6 addresses then the *ipv6* package isn't needed. Use the following command to disable a package not currently in use e.g. *ipv6*:

```
/system package disable ipv6
```

Once that command is run if you run *"/system package print"* again the status of the IPv6 package will be *"scheduled for disable"* as shown in Figure 2.10:

```
[admin@MikroTik] > /system package disable ipv6
[admin@MikroTik] > /system package print
Flags: X - disabled
 #   NAME              VERSION     SCHEDULED
 0   routeros-mipsbe   6.39rc72
 1   system            6.39rc72
 2   ipv6              6.39rc72    scheduled for disable
 3   wireless          6.39rc72
 4 X hotspot           6.39rc72
 5   dhcp              6.39rc72
 6   mpls              6.39rc72
 7   routing           6.39rc72
 8 X ppp               6.39rc72
 9   security          6.39rc72
10   advanced-tools    6.39rc72
11   multicast         6.39rc72
[admin@MikroTik] > _
```

Figure 2.10: Disabled Package

Reboot the device and the package will automatically be disabled. In Figure 2.10 the *hotspot* and *ppp* packages had already been disabled, and that's how *ipv6* will appear after a reboot. Re-enabling packages works much the same way. To re-enable the *ipv6* package use the following commands:

```
/system package enable ipv6
/system reboot
```

2.5 RouterBOOT Firmware

Once a RouterBOARD is powered on, the RouterBOOT environment is the first to load. Per MikroTik's RouterBOOT documentation[2],

> "RouterBOOT is responsible for starting RouterOS in RouterBOARD devices."

Periodically MikroTik publishes updates to the RouterBOOT software that can be installed via the built-in upgrade commands. First find the current firmware version using the command in Figure 2.11:

```
[admin@MikroTik] > /system routerboard print
      routerboard: yes
            model: RouterBOARD 952Ui-5ac2nD
    serial-number: 6CBA06ED497F
    firmware-type: qca9531L
factory-firmware: 3.29
current-firmware: 3.41
upgrade-firmware: 3.41
[admin@MikroTik] > _
```

Figure 2.11: RouterBOARD Firmware Version

In this case the "*current-firmware*" version is the same as the "*upgrade-firmware*", meaning no upgrades are available. If the device were power-cycled with the reset button pressed for a few seconds the unit would revert to the "*factory-firmware*" loader version for device recovery. As of this writing it's not possible to upgrade the *factory-firmware* version that's installed.

When a firmware update is available for the *current-firmware* version the "*/system routerboard upgrade*" command downloads and installs it. However, the installation won't fully take effect until the device is rebooted. This makes firmware upgrades safe to do while in production but the reboot caveat still applies.

---

[2]https://wiki.mikrotik.com/wiki/Manual:RouterBOOT

2.6 Review Questions

1. Which software bootstraps the RouterOS environment?

    (a) RouterBOOT

    (b) RouterBIOS

    (c) NetBOOT

    (d) MikroTik IOS

2. What is the most appropriate RouterOS release channel for production router devices?

    (a) RouterOS v6

    (b) Bugfix

    (c) Release Candidate

    (d) Current

3. What file format are RouterOS packages contained in?

    (a) .pkg

    (b) .npk

    (c) .deb

    (d) .tar

4. What command would disable the IPv6 package in RouterOS?

    (a) */system software disable ipv6*

    (b) */system package disable ipv6*

    (c) */system running disable ipv6*

    (d) */system os disable ipv6*

5. What service must be available for RouterOS to check for updates?

    (a) DNS

    (b) DHCP

    (c) FTP

    (d) SFTP

6. You can create and upload your own *.npk* files for RouterOS.

    (a) True

    (b) False

7. What is the most appropriate RouterOS release channel for bench-testing new features?

    (a) RouterOS v6

    (b) Bugfix

    (c) Release Candidate

    (d) Current

8. Which CHR virtual hard disk format would be used on Microsoft Hyper-V?

    (a) ISO

    (b) Raw Disk Image

    (c) OVF

    (d) VHDX

9. A reboot is required to complete an update of RouterOS.

    (a) True

    (b) False

10. It's possible to update the *factory-firmware* version of RouterBOOT.

    (a) True

    (b) False

2.7 Review Answers

1. Which software bootstraps the RouterOS environment?

   A – RouterBOOT (p. 34)

2. What is the most appropriate RouterOS release channel for production router devices?

   D – Current (p. 28)

3. What file format are RouterOS packages contained in?

   B – .npk (p. 28)

4. What command would disable the IPv6 package in RouterOS?

   B – */system package disable ipv6* (p. 33)

5. What service must be available for RouterOS to check for updates?

   A – DNS (p. 30)

6. You can create and upload your own *.npk* files for RouterOS.

   B – False (p. 28)

7. What is the most appropriate RouterOS release channel for bench-testing new features?

   C – Release Candidate (p. 29)

8. Which CHR virtual hard disk format would be used on Microsoft Hyper-V?

   D – Virtual Hard Disk (VHDX) (p. 24)

9. A reboot is required to complete an update of RouterOS.

   A – True (p. 31)

10. It's possible to update the *factory-firmware* version of RouterBOOT.

    B – False (p. 34)

Chapter 3

Defaults

The default configurations of RouterOS devices is fairly straightforward and consistent across devices. On smaller RouterBOARD devices meant for the SOHO environment there will be a NAT rule and firewall rules to allow traffic out and block traffic inbound. Larger devices like the CCR line have a default IP address but no firewall or NAT rules and technicians are expected to apply usable configurations.

To view the default configuration at the console use the following command:

```
/system default-configuration print
```

The output is quite long and will display one page at a time. It also includes scripting logic to selectively apply configurations depending on the hardware installed in the platform and other factors. Use the spacebar to page through the configuration lines, and once you're done use the "*Q*" key to quit.

3.1 Credentials

The default credentials for accessing MikroTik devices are easy to remember:

- Username: *admin*
- Password: *No Password*

A prudent administrator should create a complex password for the *admin* user before configuring anything else. Best practices for networks requiring heightened security may require that the default account be disabled in favor of individual administrator accounts. This would meet the PCI-DSS requirement outlining the use of shared accounts [3, p. 13]:

> "Do not use group, shared, or generic IDs, passwords, or other authentication methods..."

Having unique accounts for each person logging into the device enables *accountability* for changes made on devices in the organization. See page 83 for the commands to create, update, and remove router credentials.

3.2 Interfaces

On many RouterOS devices for the SOHO environment[1] the first Ethernet interface (*ether1*) is configured as the Wide Area Network (WAN) port. Ethernet ports *ether2* and beyond are pre-configured for Local Area Network (LAN) access. This kind of configuration makes implementing MikroTik in smaller branch and home offices fairly plug-and-play. MikroTik Switch Chip documentation[2] shows the exact default configuration for each model. On larger devices targeted for enterprises and service providers there is little or no default configuration. On these units it's expected that a more custom network configuration will be implemented.

3.3 Local Area Network Addresses

The default IP address and network is the same for all MikroTik products that arrive pre-addressed:

- IP Address: 192.168.88.1
- Subnet Mask: 255.255.255.0 (/24)
- Network Address: 192.168.88.0
- Broadcast Address: 192.168.88.255

Using the *192.168.88.0/24* network is distinct to MikroTik devices and should be committed to memory. Plugging a DHCP client into *ether2* and beyond puts that host on the 192.168.88.0/24 network. The DHCP lease assigned to each LAN host will also point to the MikroTik router as the default gateway and DNS server.

> **NOTE**: Virtual routers like the CHR and x86 instances do not have pre-configured addresses.

3.4 Dynamic Addresses

Most RouterOS devices are configured with a DHCP client on the first Ethernet interface and a DHCP server running on the others. Larger devices may not have these default configurations but creating them doesn't take long.

---

[1] RB700 and 900-series, hAP models, etc.
[2] https://wiki.mikrotik.com/wiki/Manual:Switch_Chip_Features

3.4.1 WAN DHCP Client

A DHCP client runs on *ether1* by default on RouterBOARD units, requesting a dynamic IP address from the upstream service provider. For most home-based users and typical business broadband connections this is the only configuration needed to get the router connected to the ISP. An example of the default client is shown in Figure 3.1:

```
[admin@MikroTik] > /ip dhcp-client print detail
Flags: X - disabled, I - invalid
 0   ;;; defconf
interface=ether1 add-default-route=yes default-route-distance=1 use-peer-dns=
   yes use-peer-ntp=yes dhcp-options=hostname,clientid status=bound address
   =192.168.1.38/24 gateway=192.168.1.1 dhcp-server=192.168.1.1 primary-dns
   =8.8.8.8 secondary-dns=8.8.4.4 expires-after=12h47m39s
[admin@MikroTik] > _
```

Figure 3.1: Default WAN DHCP Client

In Winbox the DHCP Client is located under *IP > DHCP Client*. The *Use Peer DNS* option is set to *yes* so the router itself can query DNS and function as a local caching server for LAN clients. The *Add Default Route* option is also set to *yes*, because it's assumed the upstream ISP connection is the only connection outbound. Multi-homed router configurations may need to change this last option.

Virtual CHR instances come with a DHCP client configured and enabled automatically on interface *ether1*. This could be used as a WAN connection to an upstream provider, or to automatically configure a local address for a service like The Dude (p. 287).

3.4.2 LAN DHCP Server

A DHCP server runs by default on most RouterBOARD routers, assigning IP addresses in the 192.168.88.0/24 network with 192.168.88.1 as the gateway. The router uses itself as a caching DNS server and assigns the *192.168.88.1* address as the local DNS server by default. With *ether2* through *ether5* and the Wireless LAN (WLAN) interfaces all bridged together it makes smaller routers fairly turn-key. DHCP is covered more in-depth on page 116.

It should be noted on CHR instances running as a VM there is no default DHCP server running and no local 192.168.88.1/24 address assigned.

3.5 Firewall

A number of firewall rules exist to protect most RouterBOARD devices as soon as they come online. They can protect the device from spurious connections from the outside, though the lack of a complex default password still creates a vulnerability. CHR instances have no default firewall rules configured at all. The Firewall is covered more in-depth on page 173. On devices that do have default firewall rules the following sections give an overview of the traffic that's allowed.

3.5.1 Forward Traffic

By default, connections are allowed outbound *through* the router via the default NAT *masquerade* rule. This traffic is allowed from all local networks both wired and wireless. Traffic inbound to the WAN port that is not part of an already established outbound connection is dropped to prevent an attacker from spoofing traffic to your internal networks. NAT rules are covered more in Chapter 13 on page 195.

3.5.2 Input Traffic

Connections inbound on the WAN port that haven't been initiated outbound previously are blocked. This stops port scans and other types of reconnaissance from succeeding. Connections to the router from internal networks are allowed, allowing network administrators easy access via Winbox, SSH, etc. However, one exception is made in default firewall rules for Internet Control Message Protocol (ICMP) traffic, allowing anyone to send an ICMP Echo (*ping*) to the device. While this can be helpful for bootstrapping a router or troubleshooting, compliance standards like PCI-DSS do not allow for these kind of connections from external hosts.

3.5.3 Output Traffic

By default, connections are allowed outbound from the router itself to upstream resources like DNS and NTP servers. No active filtering is configured by default for traffic matching the *Output* chain (p. 177).

3.5.4 NAT

The router will NAT Traffic headed outbound to the Internet via the *ether1* interface by default. All traffic will appear to originate from the publicly routable address, either statically assigned or dynamically IP assigned by the ISP.

3.6 IP Services

RouterOS instances run a number of services right out-of-the-box. This makes routers very accessible right out-of-the-box but can also have security implications. A production device should have unsecure protocols like Hypertext Transfer Protocol (HTTP) and FTP turned off in favor of more secure protocols like HTTP Secure (HTTPS) and SSH. Table 3.1 lists network services - other than routing protocols - that RouterOS runs. Most services are enabled by default and some service pruning is required to secure your devices.

Service	Protocol	Port	Default Enabled
API	TCP	8728	X
API-SSL	TCP	8729	X
Bandwidth Test Server	TCP	2000	X
DNS	TCP, UDP	53	
FTP	TCP	20, 21	X
NTP	UDP	123	
SNMP	UDP	161	
SSH	TCP	22	X
Telnet	TCP	23	X
UPnP	TCP	2828	
Winbox	TCP	8291	X
WWW	TCP	80	X
WWW-SSL	TCP	443	X

Table 3.1: IP Services

3.7 Review Questions

1. Telnet is enabled by default and can be used to administer RouterOS devices.

    (a) True

    (b) False

2. Which technology is used to allow internal hosts to connect to the internet via a single publicly-routable IPv4 address?

    (a) GRE

    (b) NAT

    (c) IP Helper

    (d) SLAAC

3. What is the password for the default *admin* RouterOS user?

    (a) *mikrotik*

    (b) *admin*

    (c) No password

    (d) *router*

4. Which Network ID does a default installation of RouterOS use for the LAN?

    (a) 192.168.88.0

    (b) 192.168.88.1

    (c) 192.168.1.0

    (d) 192.168.1.1

5. Which interface on a SOHO router is typically configured to be the WAN out-of-the-box?

    (a) ether3

    (b) ether2

    (c) ether1

    (d) ether0

6. How is the IPv4 address assigned on the WAN interface for a RouterBOARD with the default configuration?

    (a) SLAAC

    (b) DHCP

    (c) BOOTP

    (d) PXE

7. Which NAT action is used to translate traffic out to the ISP using a single public IP address?

    (a) Mangle

    (b) DST-NAT

    (c) Masquerade

    (d) SRC-NAT

8. What dynamic address will be handed out to the first DHCP client that requests it from a default RouterOS installation?

    (a) 192.168.1.2

    (b) 192.168.88.1

    (c) 192.168.88.0

    (d) 192.168.88.254

9. Output-type traffic is filtered by default in the firewall.

    (a) True

    (b) False

10. Which protocol is permitted inbound to the router on all interfaces by default?

    (a) UDP

    (b) GRE

    (c) TCP

    (d) ICMP

3.8 Review Answers

1. Telnet is enabled by default and can be used to administer RouterOS devices.

    A – True

2. Which technology is used to allow internal hosts to connect to the internet via a single publicly-routable IPv4 address?

    B – NAT

3. What is the password for the default *admin* RouterOS user?

    C – No password

4. Which Network ID does a default installation of RouterOS use for the LAN?

    A – 192.168.88.0

5. Which interface on a SOHO router is typically configured to be the WAN interface out-of-the-box?

    C – ether1

6. How is the IP address assigned on the WAN interface for a RouterBOARD with the default configuration?

    B – DHCP

7. Which NAT action is used to translate traffic out to the ISP using a single public IP address?

    C – Masquerade

8. What dynamic address will be handed out to the first DHCP client that requests it from a default RouterOS installation?

    D – 192.168.88.254

9. Output-type traffic is filtered by default in the firewall.

    B – False

10. Which protocol is permitted inbound to the router on all interfaces by default?

    D – ICMP

Chapter 4

Accessing the Router

There are more than a few ways of accessing and configuring MikroTik devices. Methods range from command line to web access, desktop access with Winbox, and even an Application Program Interface (API). With command structure being consistent throughout the platform it makes administration easy once technicians are familiar with commands.

4.1 Access Methods

RouterBOARD devices can be accessed and configured in a few different ways. In fact, you don't even have to configure an IP address on a device to get access to it on the network. Devices can be configured via graphical interfaces or via Command Line Interface (CLI). Here are the methods of accessing RouterBOARD devices and virtual RouterOS instances:

- Serial Port (select models)
- LCD Touch Screen (select models)
- Telnet
- SSH
- Webfig (HTTP & HTTPS)
- Winbox
- MAC Winbox
- API & API-SSL

All these methods give you access to create, update, and remove configuration options. Winbox and Webfig can easier to use than the others for technicians that aren't comfortable with the CLI environment. As of this writing there are some options available from the command line that haven't been integrated into Winbox or Webfig. Fortunately there aren't many, but be aware that it does happen.

For more advanced enterprises and service providers it's also possible to centralize management of RouterOS via orchestration software like Ansible, Puppet, and Chef.

4.2 Serial Port

The hardware serial port allows you access the device directly and recover it if needed. A null-modem type cable is required to connect to the device from a computer. Software like Microsoft's HyperTerminal[1] or PuTTY[2] in "Serial" mode are required to interact with the console. For CRS and RB-2011 devices a "Cisco-style" RJ-45 to DB-9 connection is required, but those cables are cheap and most network administrators have one squirreled away from working with other vendors' equipment. The default serial line configuration is as follows:

- Baud Rate: 9600
- Data Bits: 8
- Parity: None
- Stop Bits: 1
- Flow Control: None

4.3 LCD Touchscreen

Some RouterBOARD models like the RB-2011, CCR, and CRS feature an Liquid Crystal Display (LCD) touchscreen on the front or top of the device. This screen can be used to monitor interface traffic and do basic configurations like changing IP addresses. By default, the LCD screen is Personal Identification Number (PIN)-protected, but the default PIN is "1234". For security reasons this PIN should be changed, or the LCD screen should be set to "read-only" using the following commands:

```
/lcd
set pin=1739
set read-only-mode=yes
```

In read-only mode the PIN does not apply. A non-default PIN should always be set in case the LCD is taken out of read-only mode in the future. An example of the LCD touchscreen from the front of the RB2011 is shown in Figure 4.1 on the following page. Another example was shown on the front of a CCR model in Figure 1.9 on page 11.

---

[1] Last supported in Windows XP
[2] Other clients like SecureCRT work well too, but for the purposes of this book PuTTY is the preferred client

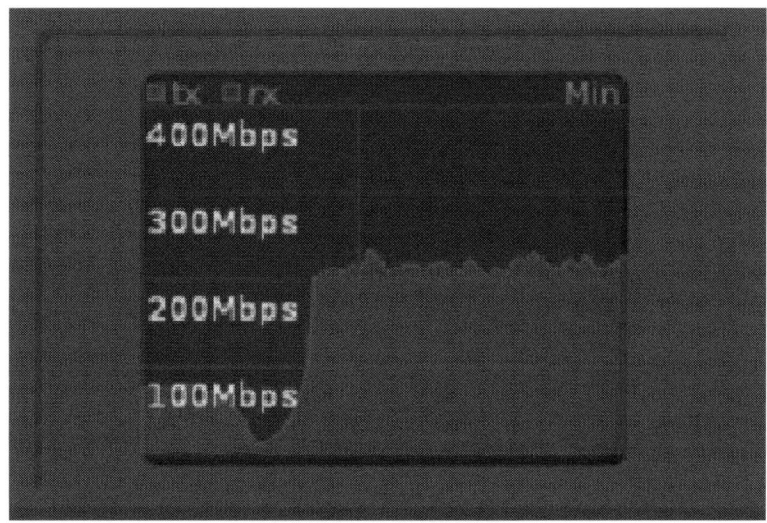

Image Credit: *MikroTik*
Figure 4.1: LCD Screen

4.4 Telnet

Like in many systems Telnet is available for command line configuration, though it is not a secure protocol. All usernames and passwords are sent in plain-text and easy to sniff with tools like Wireshark or Cain & Abel. When possible disable Telnet and use SSH instead. If Telnet must be used for whatever reason it should be isolated to a dedicated Virtual LAN (VLAN) or management network. Disable Telnet if possible with the commands shown in Figure 4.2:

```
[admin@MikroTik] > /ip service
[admin@MikroTik] /ip service> set telnet disabled=yes
[admin@MikroTik] /ip service> print where name=telnet
Flags: X - disabled, I - invalid
 #     NAME     PORT     ADDRESS          CERTIFICATE
 0 XI  telnet   23
[admin@MikroTik] /ip service> _
```

Figure 4.2: Disabling Telnet Service

4.5 Secure Shell

SSH gives technicians the ability to administer a router from the command line securely. SSH should be used in lieu of Telnet whenever possible. It's also possible to securely transfer files over an SSH connection, and orchestration software like Ansible uses SSH for connections. As secure as SSH is, it's recommended that you enable more robust encryption ciphers using the following command:

```
/ip ssh set strong-crypto=yes
```

This setting helps satisfy the PCI-DSS requirement number 8.2.1 [3, p. 12]:

> "Using strong cryptography, render all authentication credentials... unreadable during transmission..."

With this setting in place the "*/ip ssh print*" command verifies the new settings as shown in Figure 4.3:

```
[admin@MikroTik] > /ip ssh print
        forwarding-enabled: no
always-allow-password-login: no
              strong-crypto: yes
              host-key-size: 2048
[admin@MikroTik] > _
```

Figure 4.3: SSH Strong Crypto Enabled

Some organizations beholden to higher security standards require that SSH keys be regenerated on a regular basis, and that default keys in-place when a unit is delivered aren't used in production. Figure 4.4 shows the commands for regenerating random SSH encryption keys:

```
[admin@MikroTik] > /ip ssh regenerate-host-key
This will regenerate current SSH host keys (changes will take affect only
    after service restart or reboot), yes? [y/N]:
y
16:43:19 echo: ssh,critical SSH host key regenerated, reboot or service
    restart required!
[admin@MikroTik] > /system reboot
```

Figure 4.4: Regenerating SSH Keys

After the system reboots the new keys will be used for all SSH connections.

4.6 Winbox

Winbox is a MikroTik-specific program for Microsoft Windows that allows routers to be configured and monitored remotely. The program can also be used on Linux with the WINE emulator but that isn't officially supported by MikroTik. The Winbox program can be downloaded from the MikroTik website and it is updated fairly often to accommodate new commands and features. By default, the Winbox application connects to RouterOS devices on Transmission Control Protocol (TCP) port 8291 and connections are secure.

A convenient feature of Winbox is that it can discover MikroTik devices on the local network via Neighbor Discovery. Nearby devices that were discovered are shown in the *Neighbors* tab in Figure 4.5. Login profiles for multiple devices can be saved to help you easily administer multiple devices[3].

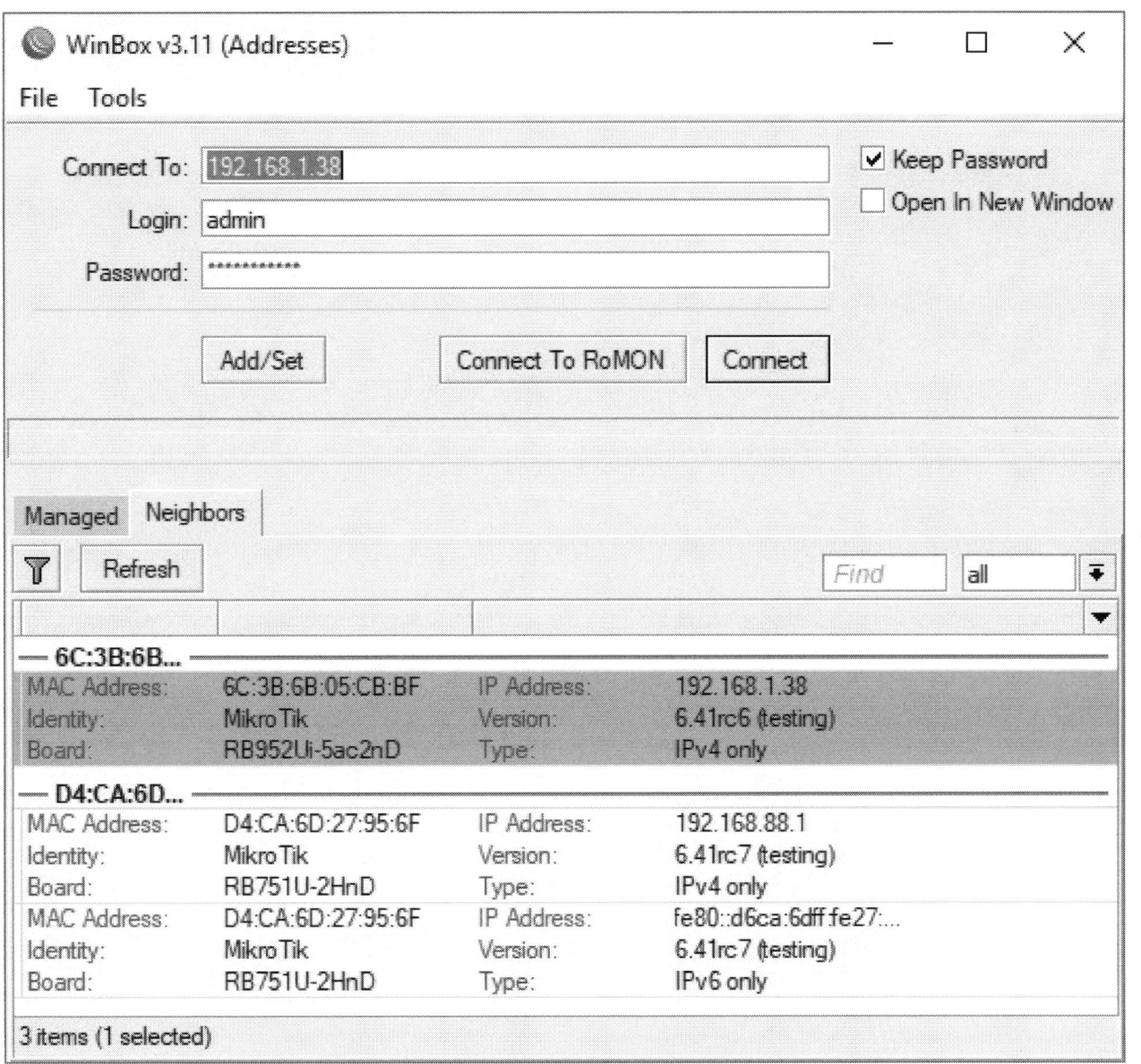

Figure 4.5: Winbox Login

The Winbox application looks much like the Webfig interface shown in Figure 4.9 on page 55 - if you can use one you can use the other. Once authenticated in Winbox the main window will load, giving you access to configure the device as shown in Figure 4.6 on the next page:

---

[3]In networks with heightened security or compliance requirements saving credentials in Winbox may not be allowed.

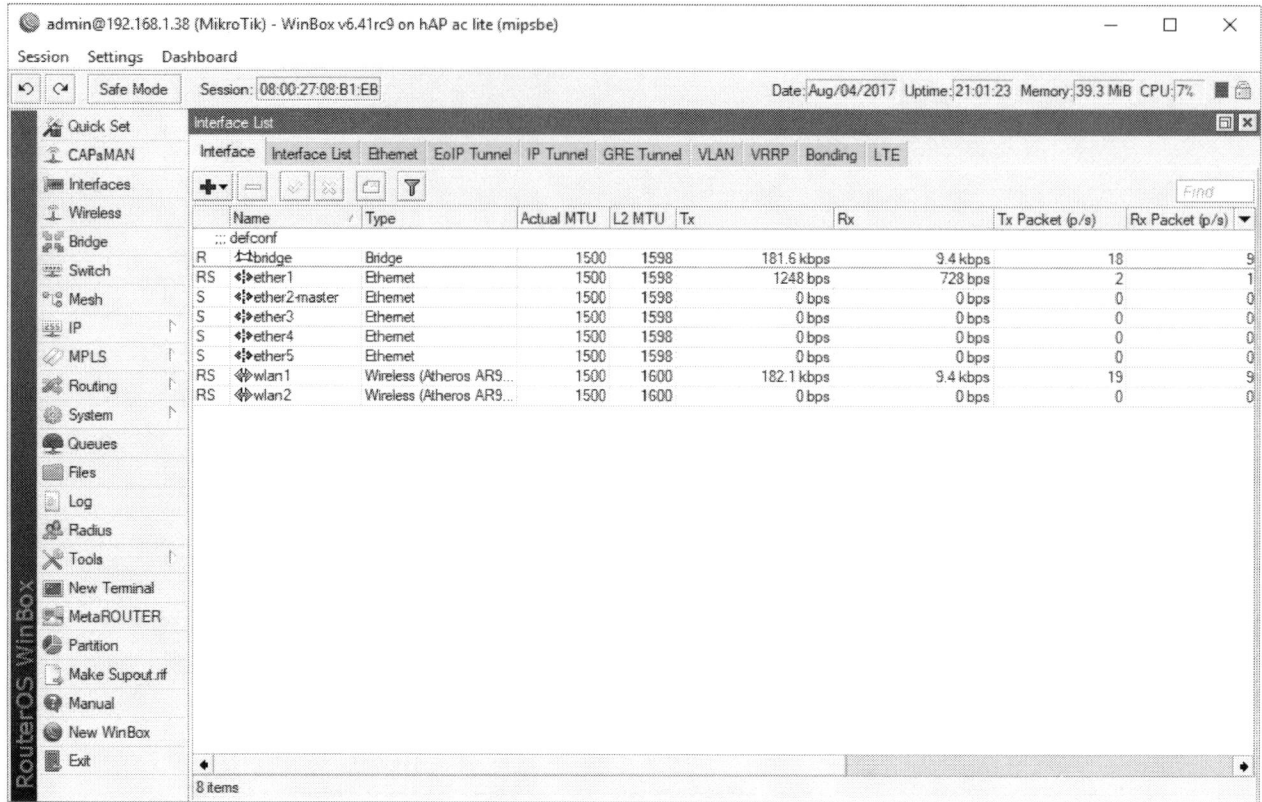

Figure 4.6: Winbox

When new functionality is added to RouterOS an update to Winbox is sometimes necessary. In recent versions of Winbox a built-in updater was added to the login window shown in Figure 4.7:

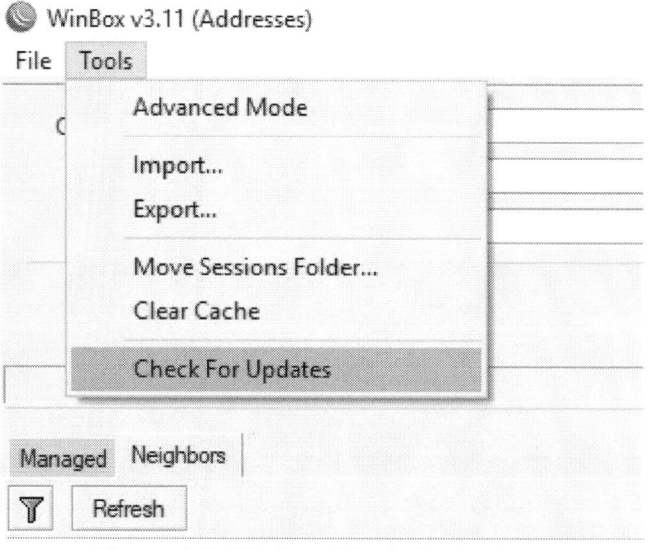

Figure 4.7: Winbox Check for Updates

4.7 Winbox Device Access

Use the following steps to connect to a RouterBOARD device running the default configuration with Winbox:

1. Download the Winbox program from the MikroTik download page at the following URL:

    https://mikrotik.com/download

2. Power on the RouterBOARD unit, giving it about ten seconds to boot
3. Verify the laptop or desktop host you'll be using is set to receive a DHCP address
4. Connect the host's network interface to *ether2* on the RouterBOARD unit, or,
5. If using a wireless connection select the MikroTik wireless network that corresponds with the Media Access Control (MAC) address on the manufacturer's sticker
6. Verify your host has been assigned a dynamic IP in the 192.168.88.0/24 network
7. Open Winbox and select the *Neighbors* tab
8. Double-click the discovered RouterBOARD device, or if necessary click the *Refresh* button and then select the device
9. Enter *admin* for the username and nothing for the password
10. Click *Connect*
11. In the new window click the *Terminal* button in the lower-left to open a console for the following steps

The first thing an administrator should do after logging in is set a reasonably complex password for the *admin* account. Use the following command to update the password for the *admin* account:

```
/user set admin password=abc123!
```

Another best practice is to rename the account to help prevent password guessing attacks. Rename the *admin* account using the following command:

```
/user set admin name=tyler comment="Tyler Hart"
```

While renaming the *admin* account isn't a perfect defense against brute force and password guessing attacks it can be a good part of an overall DiD strategy.

4.8 MAC Winbox

MAC Winbox provides the same functionality as regular Winbox but it can connect to devices without an IP address. This works really well for higher-end MikroTik devices that don't come pre-configured with an IP address. Not needing an IP address can also be a life-saver when an administrator accidentally deletes the wrong IP address. Refer to the Safe Mode section on page 70 for another failsafe measure to take when configuring devices remotely.

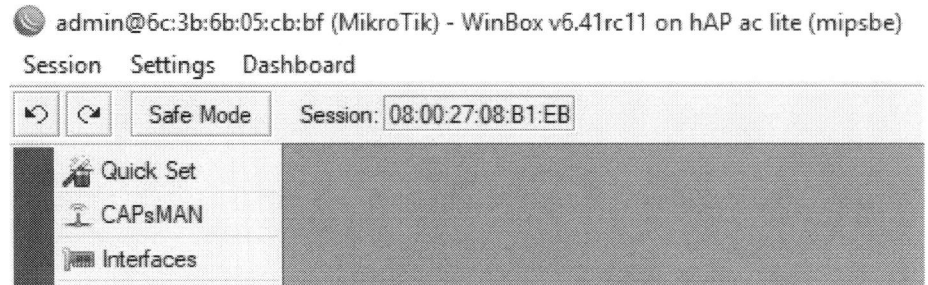

Figure 4.8: MAC Winbox

The only downside to connecting to a device via MAC Winbox is that you must be on the same network segment as the device. It's not possible to reach a device via MAC address across different networks without a Layer 2 tunnel like Ethernet Over IP (EoIP) or Proxy Address Resolution Protocol (ARP) running.

4.9 Webfig

All RouterOS devices can be configured via a web browser using Webfig. The web interface listens for connections on TCP ports 80 and 443. Use the following URL to access Webfig for a router running the default configuration:

```
http://192.168.88.1
```

An example of a typical Webfig screen is shown in Figure 4.9 on the following page:

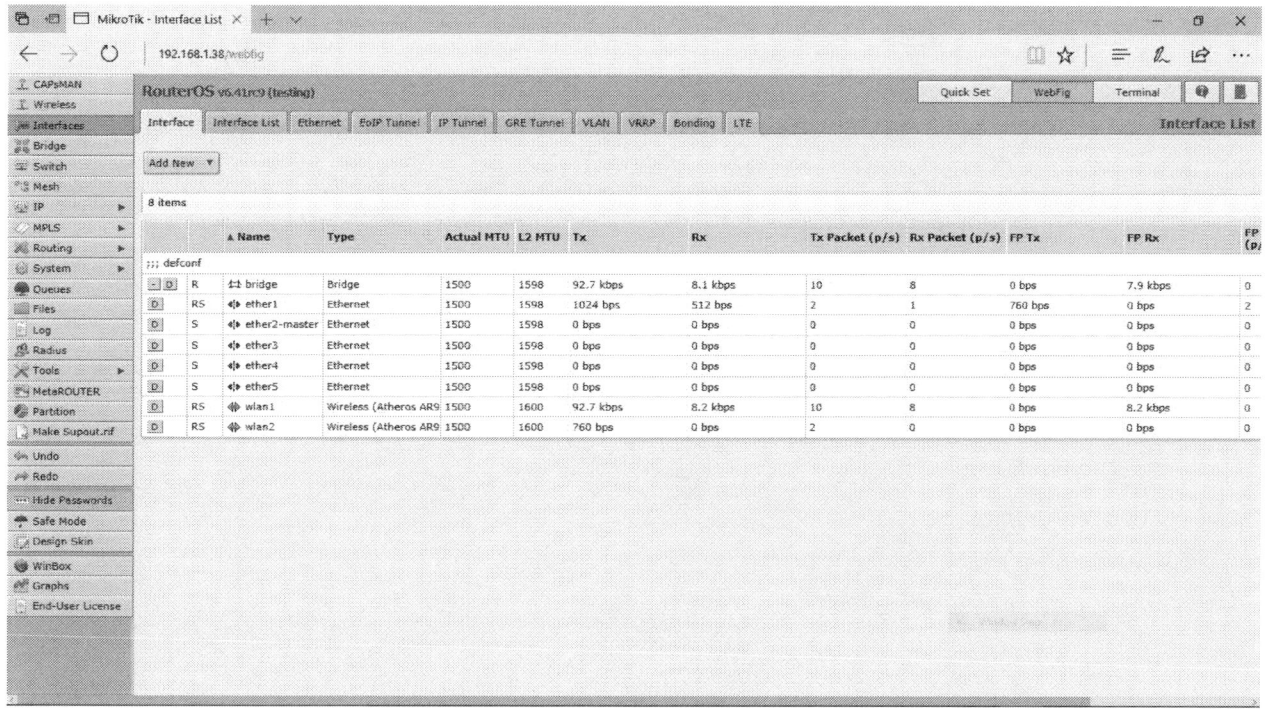

Figure 4.9: Webfig

> **WARNING**: The secure HTTPS Webfig interface should be used in lieu of the less-secure HTTP interface.

The Webfig interface features a few links that Winbox doesn't have. In the lower-right portion of the screen is a link to the device graphs accessible with the web browser. There is also a "Winbox" link that directs you to the MikroTik download page's latest stable version of the program.

4.10 API

The RouterOS API allows an administrator to make changes to device configurations programmatically. The unsecure API and secure API-Secure Socket Layer (SSL) services run on TCP port 8728 and 8729, respectively. Having an API available means repetitive operations can be scripted, and automated commands can be run regularly to verify settings and performance. The MikroTik Wiki provides links to API examples for C++, C#, PHP, Python, Go, and more[4].

> **WARNING**: Access to the API should be protected just like Telnet or SSH access. If not actively in use the API services should be disabled.

---

[4]https://wiki.mikrotik.com/wiki/Manual:API#External_sources

4.11 FTP

While FTP cannot be used to remotely configure the router it can be used to upload and download files. Like Telnet, FTP sends all authentication in the clear (unencrypted) and should not be the first choice for moving files. For securely transferring files it's recommended that SSH be used instead, and all modern FTP clients like FileZilla support secure file transfers. Disabling FTP also satisfies Infrastructure Router STIG Finding V-14668[5]. Disable FTP with the following commands:

```
/ip service
set ftp disabled=yes
```

---

[5]https://www.stigviewer.com/stig/infrastructure_router/2016-07-07/finding/V-14668

4.12 Review Questions

1. Which remote access and configuration protocol sends traffic "in the clear" without encryption?

    (a) Telnet

    (b) Winbox

    (c) SSH

    (d) MAC

2. What is the default baud rate for serial ports?

    (a) 512

    (b) 112800

    (c) 1024

    (d) 9600

3. 16 data bits are used by default for serial port connections.

    (a) True

    (b) False

4. Which feature allows routers to be configured programmatically via Python, PHP, and other languages?

    (a) FTP

    (b) API

    (c) Webfig

    (d) MAC Winbox

5. Which step(s) are recommended for allowing secure monitoring of devices via LCD screens?

    (a) Set the LCD to read-only

    (b) Disable the LCD

    (c) Configure a non-default PIN

    (d) Change the baud rate

6. Which port and protocol does SSH run on by default?
    (a) TCP port 21
    (b) UDP port 20
    (c) TCP port 23
    (d) TCP port 22

7. What is the default PIN for LCD touchscreens?
    (a) 9999
    (b) 4321
    (c) 0000
    (d) 1234

8. Which SSH option enables more robust encryption algorithms?
    (a) *strong-crypto*
    (b) *robust-crypto*
    (c) *secure-crypto*
    (d) *high-crypto*

9. Which feature allows you to connect to a RouterBOARD without first assigning an IP address?
    (a) Webfig
    (b) MAC Address
    (c) MAC Winbox
    (d) SSH

10. Unencrypted connections to Webfig can be made via TCP port 8080.
    (a) True
    (b) False

4.13 Review Answers

1. Which remote access and configuration protocol sends traffic "in the clear" without encryption?

   A – Telnet

2. What is the default baud rate for serial ports?

   D – 9600

3. 16 data bits are used by default for serial port connections.

   B – False

4. Which feature allows routers to be configured programmatically via Python, PHP, and other languages?

   B – API

5. Which step(s) are recommended for allowing secure monitoring of devices via LCD screens?

   A and C – Set the LCD to read-only and configure a non-default PIN

6. Which port and protocol does SSH run on by default?

   D – TCP port 22

7. What is the default PIN for LCD touchscreens?

   D – 1234

8. Which SSH option enables more robust encryption algorithms?

   A – *strong-crypto*

9. Which feature allows you to connect to a RouterBOARD without first assigning an IP address?

   C – MAC Winbox

10. Unencrypted connections to Webfig can be made via TCP port 8080.

    B – False

Chapter 5

Configuring RouterOS

Network administrators coming from a background in other platforms can find the MikroTik command structure a bit different. However, after using RouterOS for a bit and getting to know the command structure it quickly makes sense. Winbox, Webfig, and the console are all organized around the same command structure so the knowledge you gain in this chapter is extremely portable. This chapter teaches you how RouterOS uses commands and shortcuts, then walks you through basic configurations like the hostname and DNS so you can practice using them. The sections on structure, shortcuts, moving up and down the hierarchy, and more are equally applicable to other commands like those for the firewall or queues.

5.1 Command Structure

Commands and configuration options in RouterOS are organized in a hierarchical fashion starting with a top-level category and moving down the command options. The command tree begins with an optional backslash ("/"), then the category. For example, */ip* and */routing* are a top-level categories. Below the */ip* level you'll also find *address*, *firewall*, *route*, and more. Commands are structured in a hierarchical manner, with "/" at the top, then categories, a command, and then options and settings. The following example shows the full length of the command that sets the router's hostname:

```
/system identity set name=router.manitonetworks.com
```

The command in the example features these components:

1. Top-level slash (optional)
2. Category (*system*)
3. Sub-category (*identity*)
4. Action (*set*)
5. Option (*name=router.manitonetworks.com*)

Like in many other platforms command keywords can be shortened so long as no other commands match the shortened input. The "/" is also optional if you're already at the top of the command hierarchy. All of the following commands do the same thing as the example shown above:

```
/sys id set name=router.manitonetworks.com
sys id set name=router.manitonetworks.com
system identity set name=router.manitonetworks.com
```

It's up to you how to enter commands and whether or not to use the shortened versions of the command components, the result is functionally the same.

5.1.1 Moving Up and Down Commands

With the command structure being hierarchical it's possible to move up and down command levels so you don't have to type the entire string of text each time. For example, if adding multiple firewall filter rules you can save a lot of typing by moving down the command structure into "*/ip firewall*" as shown in Figure 5.1:

```
[admin@MikroTik] > /ip firewall filter
[admin@MikroTik] /ip firewall filter> add chain=input...
[admin@MikroTik] /ip firewall filter> add chain=forward...
[admin@MikroTik] /ip firewall filter> add chain=output...
```

Figure 5.1: Moving Command Location

Note the change in the prompt from the first to second lines in Figure 5.1. Once the administrator has moved further down the command hierarchy it's no longer necessary to type in "*/ip firewall filter*" for each command. It's possible to move up the command hierarchy by using the ".." command as shown in Figure 5.2:

```
[admin@MikroTik] > /ip
[admin@MikroTik] /ip> firewall
[admin@MikroTik] /ip firewall> filter
[admin@MikroTik] /ip firewall filter> ..
[admin@MikroTik] /ip firewall> ..
[admin@MikroTik] /ip> ..
[admin@MikroTik] > _
```

Figure 5.2: Moving Up Commands

Again note the prompt changes from one level to the next all the way back up to the root of the command hierarchy. To move all the way back up to the top of the command hierarchy simply use the "/" command shown in Figure 5.3 on the following page:

```
[admin@MikroTik] > /ip firewall filter
[admin@MikroTik] /ip firewall filter> add chain=input...
[admin@MikroTik] /ip firewall filter> add chain=foward...
[admin@MikroTik] /ip firewall filter> add chain=output...
[admin@MikroTik] /ip firewall filter> /
[admin@MikroTik] > _
```

Figure 5.3: Using Slash

5.2 Shortcuts and Help

The [TAB] key, [?] key, and different colored text at the terminal make the job of administering a router from the CLI easier and more consistent. If you forget the function of the different shortcut or help keys you can always refer to the default command line banner message shown in Figure 5.4:

```
  MMM       MMM       KKK                            TTTTTTTTTT       KKK
  MMMM     MMMM       KKK                            TTTTTTTTTT       KKK
  MMM MMMM MMM  III   KKK  KKK   RRRRRR     OOOOOO       TTT     III  KKK  KKK
  MMM  MM  MMM  III   KKKKK      RRR  RRR  OOO  OOO      TTT     III  KKKKK
  MMM      MMM  III   KKK KKK    RRRRRR    OOO  OOO      TTT     III  KKK KKK
  MMM      MMM  III   KKK  KKK   RRR  RRR   OOOOOO       TTT     III  KKK  KKK

  MikroTik RouterOS 6.41rc47 (c) 1999-2017       http://www.mikrotik.com/

  [?]             Gives the list of available commands
  command [?]     Gives help on the command and list of arguments

  [Tab]           Completes the command/word. If the input is ambiguous, a
     second [Tab] gives possible options

  /               Move up to base level
  ..              Move up one level
  /command        Use command at the base level
  [admin@MikroTik] > _
```

Figure 5.4: Default Banner Message

5.2.1 Console Colors

In colorize terminal session or in the Winbox Terminal command components will be colored. To see the colors in a third-party SSH client like PuTTY, KiTTY, or WinSCP ensure that the option allowing the terminal to specify colors in enabled. Figure 5.5 on the next page shows the configuration in PuTTY:

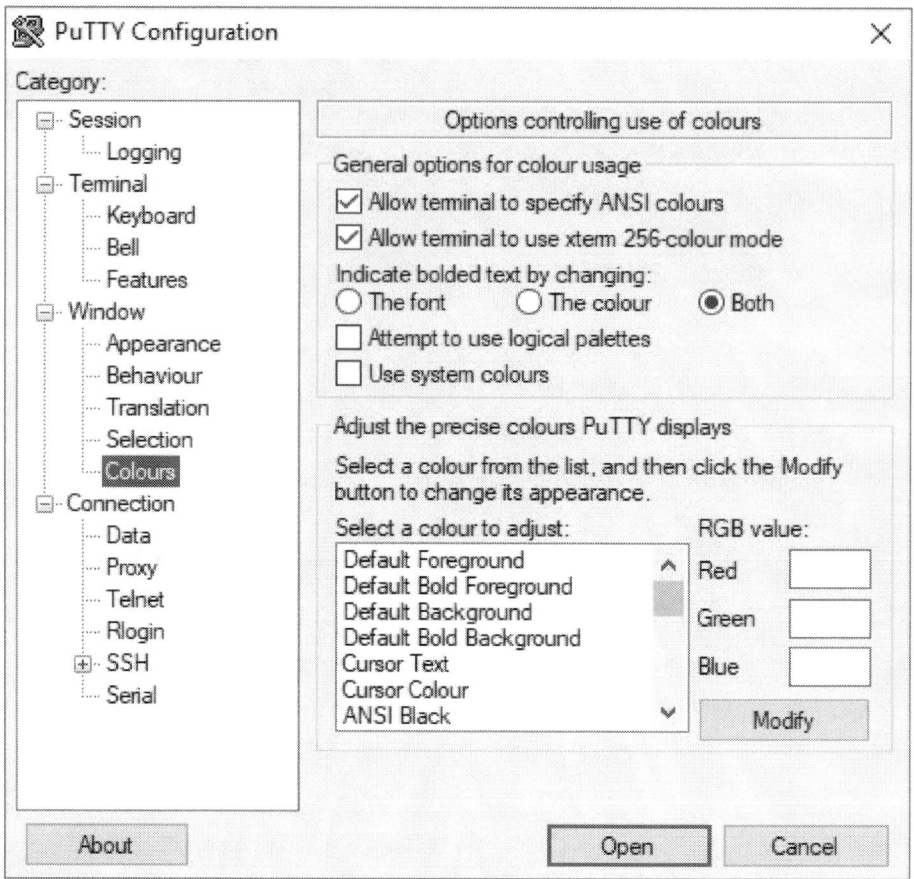

Figure 5.5: PuTTY Terminal Color Settings

The following three colors are used in RouterOS:

- Blue: Categories and sub-categories (*/ip firewall filter...*)
- Fuchsia: Executable commands (*add*, *set*, *remove*, etc.)
- Green: Options and their settings (*name=...*)

5.2.2 Tab Key

Using the Tab key at the console will auto-complete partially typed commands. This works just like on Linux systems like Red Hat® Enterprise Linux and Ubuntu® Linux. Having the option to "tab" through a command speeds up CLI usage considerably. It can also help you move down through sets of options if you don't know them from memory. The behavior of the Tab key depends on if there is a space in the command and how many commands match the partial input.

Single Tab

An excellent example of single-tab usage is the letter "l" and a single [Tab] with no space between them as shown in Figure 5.6:

```
[admin@Mikrotik] > l[Tab]
...
[admin@Mikrotik] > log _
```

Figure 5.6: Single Tab Results

Since there is only one command that starts with an "*l*" RouterOS auto-completes the command ("*/log*") and advances the cursor. Another usage of the [Tab] key would be entering the same command with a single space between them as in the following example:

```
admin@Mikrotik > l [Tab]
```

Since only one command starts with an "l" and a space was entered all sub-commands of "*log*" are listed and the console advances the cursor. An example of this behavior is shown in Figure 5.7:

```
[admin@MikroTik] > l [Tab]
debug   error   find   info   print   warning
[admin@MikroTik] > l _
```

Figure 5.7: Single Tab with Space

> **NOTE**: Tab key output does not include explanations of the available commands - that is covered by the '?' key on page 66.

Double-Tab

Using a double-Tab will perform the following actions:

1. Auto-complete the command if possible, or,
2. List all sub-commands available (if auto-complete not possible), and,
3. Advance the cursor forward

Using a double-Tab can make for especially fast, efficient CLI execution. The results of a successful double-Tab are shown in Figure 5.8 on the next page with the command auto-completed and sub-commands listed:

```
[admin@MikroTik] > /ip fi[Tab][Tab]
    address-list  calea  connection  filter  layer7-protocol  mangle  nat  raw
    service-port  export
[admin@MikroTik] > /ip firewall _
```

Figure 5.8: Double-Tab Result

5.2.3 Question Mark Key

The question mark key will show you lists of available commands and options *with explanations*, but it doesn't auto-complete your entries. Become familiar with both Tab and Question Mark keys because they are both useful in their own ways. The results of using a question mark with */ip firewall* are shown in Figure 5.9:

```
[admin@MikroTik] > /ip firewall ?
Firewall allows IP packet filtering on per packet basis.

.. -- go up to ip
address-list --
calea --
connection -- Active connections
export -- Print or save an export script that can be used to restore
    configuration
filter -- Firewall filters
layer7-protocol --
mangle -- The packet marking management
nat -- Network Address Translation
raw --
service-port -- Service port management
...
[admin@MikroTik] > _
```

Figure 5.9: Question Mark Results

Sub-categories of commands aren't given a description, but adding them to the command and using the Question Mark again will describe those commands further down the hierarchy.

> **NOTE**: As of this writing not all commands available at the console have menu items in Winbox or Webfig, so using the Question Mark can help you discover these "hidden" features.

5.2.4 HotLock

When enabled the HotLock feature will auto-complete commands as they are typed at the CLI. The [CTRL+V] keystroke then pressing [Enter] turns this feature on. Because it shares the same keystroke as the "Paste" functionality in Microsoft Windows and other operating systems many technicians discover this feature by mistake. However, without pressing [Enter] nothing will happen no matter how many times you use [CTRL+V]. Once all keys have been pressed the prompt will change to ">>", indicating the new CLI mode as shown in Figure 5.10:

```
[admin@MikroTik] > [CTRL+V][Enter]
[admin@MikroTik] >> _
```

Figure 5.10: Turning on HotLock

A good example of HotLock usage is when "*/ip f*" is auto-completed to "*/ip firewall*" on-the-fly because it's the only matching entry. Just like when turning the feature on, you must use both [CTRL+V] and [Enter] to turn it off.

5.2.5 Clearing the Screen

If the console screen becomes full distracting output you can use the [CTRL+L] keystroke to clear the screen. This only clears the screen and does not clear the command history so the up and down keys can still be used to repeat commands. To clear the command history see the example on page 67.

5.3 Command History

The system keeps a history of commands executed at the console which can be accessed via the Up and Down keys. Commands can also be un-done and re-done, and a running history of changes is available.

5.3.1 Viewing Command History

The "*/system history print*" command shows a summary of recent configuration changes made on the system and which user performed them. An example is shown in Figure 5.11 on the next page where *admin* recently modified routes, changed the hostname, and made other changes:

```
[admin@router.lan] > /system history print
Flags: U - undoable, R - redoable, F - floating-undo
ACTION                         BY        POLICY
U system identity changed      admin     write
U route removed                admin     write
U route removed                admin     write
U route removed                admin     write
U route added                  admin     write
U route added                  admin     write
U route added                  admin     write
U traffic flow target added    admin     write
U item added                   admin     write

[admin@router.lan] > _
```

Figure 5.11: System History

5.3.2 Rolling Back Commands

While not all changes can be rolled back with the "*/undo*" command most configuration changes can be easily undone. Figure 5.12 shows the latest command (a system identity change) being un-done.

```
[admin@router.lan] > /undo
[admin@MikroTik] > /system history print
Flags: U - undoable, R - redoable, F - floating-undo
ACTION                         BY        POLICY
R system identity changed      admin     write
U route removed                admin     write
...
[admin@MikroTik] > _
```

Figure 5.12: Command Undo Results

Note the change in the prompt after the "*/undo*" command was sent, and that the system identity change line's flag has been shifted from "U" (undo-able) to "R" (redo-able). Running the "*/redo*" command puts the original configuration change back in place.

5.3.3 Clearing Command History

To clear the console history and make previous commands unavailable via the Up and Down keys use the following command:

```
/console clear-history
```

While this removes past commands from an administrator's console it does not remove them from "*/system history*", and commands can still be undone or redone.

> **NOTE**: Clearing the history after entering commands with sensitive information in them like passwords and wireless keys can help keep networks secure and protect *confidentiality*.

5.4 Quick Set

RouterOS comes with "Quick Set" functionality to configure devices with boilerplate settings. Using this feature will set up devices in a way that is appropriate for most home networks or remote home teleworkers. Settings include the following:

1. WAN DHCP client or static addressing
2. LAN IP and subnet mask
3. LAN DHCP server
4. LAN NAT settings

Access to Quick Set is available via Webfig and shown in Figure 5.13:

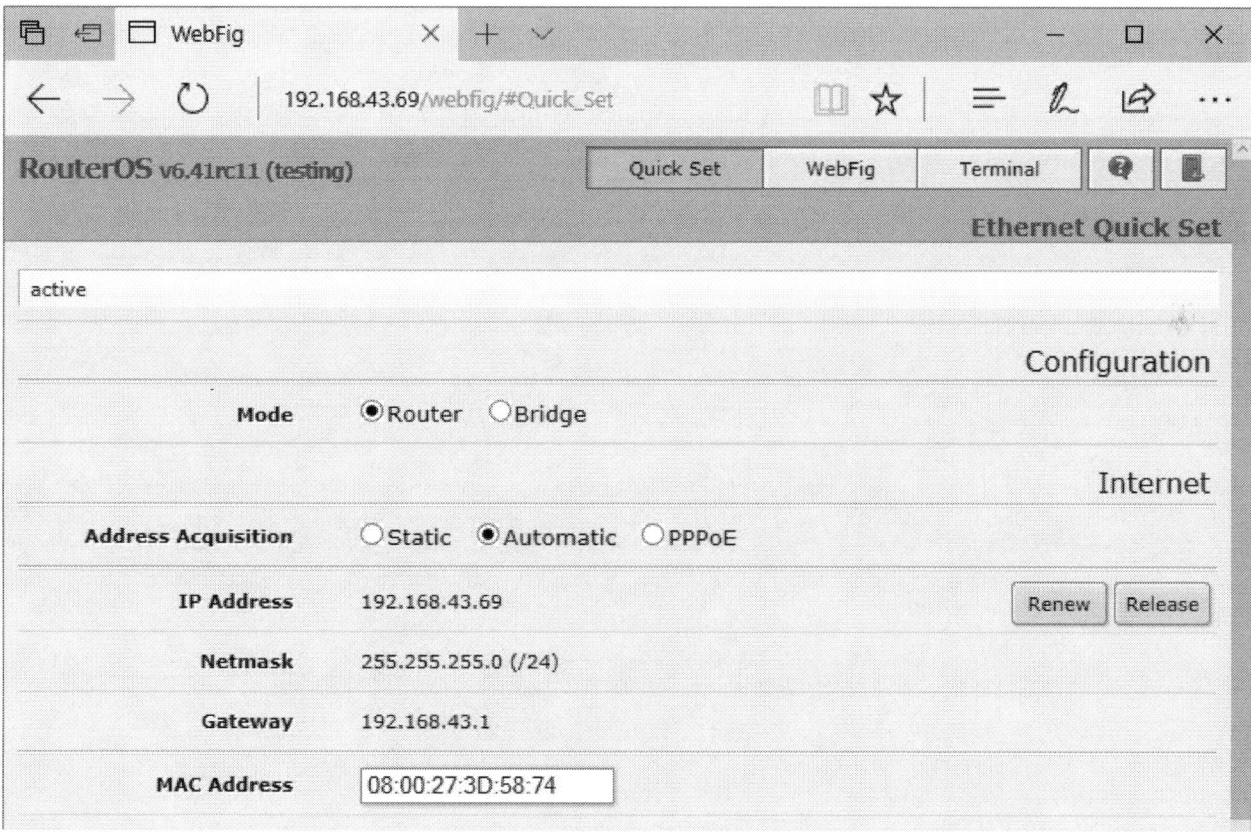

Figure 5.13: Quick Set Configuration

Clicking the "*Apply*" button at the bottom of the page resets the router's configuration and puts the Quick Set options in place. While this feature is useful for bootstrapping a device configuration it doesn't apply security configurations like pruning IP services, non-default Simple Network Management Protocol (SNMP) Communities, etc.

5.5 Safe Mode

RouterOS has some built-in capabilities to protect you from locking yourself out of a device. The easiest way to ensure your on-going access while making changes is to utilize Safe Mode. If for whatever reason your session with a device in Safe Mode is cut off abnormally the router will revert any changes that were made since Safe Mode was started. Enter Safe Mode by using the [CTRL+X] keystroke at the CLI. The prompt will change to reflect that you're now in the new mode, as shown in Figure 5.14:

```
[admin@MikroTik] > [CTRL+X]
[Safe Mode taken]
[admin@MikroTik] <SAFE> _
```

Figure 5.14: CLI Safe Mode

Changes can be made but they won't be saved unless you use the [CTRL+X] keystroke a second time. If you use the [CTRL+D] exit keystroke or if the connection is cut off prematurely the device will revert changes made while in Safe Mode. Exiting Safe Mode properly with the second keystroke at the console results in a "*[Safe Mode released]*" message. The prompt will also change back to the typical "non-SAFE" formatting.

Winbox also features Safe Mode, with the Safe Mode button shown selected in Figure 5.15:

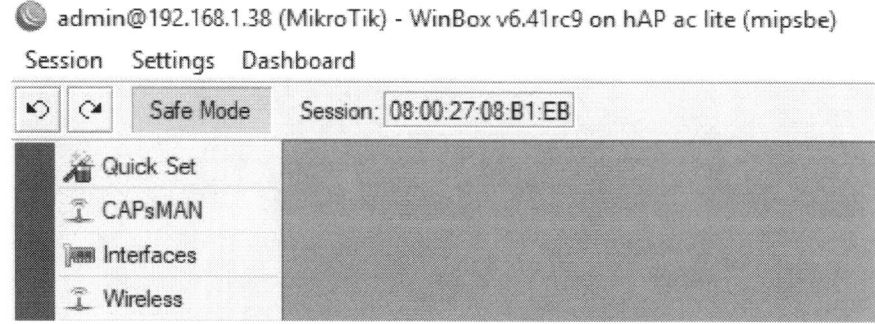

Figure 5.15: Winbox Safe Mode

Clicking the Safe Mode button grays out the box and places you in Safe Mode. Clicking the button again takes you out of Safe Mode and leaves changes applied. If you make Winbox changes in Safe Mode and then try to quit without exiting Safe Mode first a confirmation dialog opens as shown in Figure 5.16 on the following page:

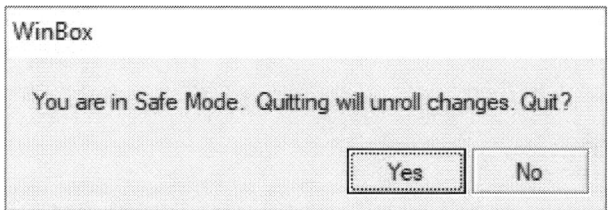

Figure 5.16: Winbox Safe Mode Quit

Think of Safe Mode as your "get out of jail free card" if you cut yourself off from a remote device.

5.6 System Hostname

The default hostname for every router is simply *"MikroTik"*. As your organization grows and brings more RouterOS devices online it's important to uniquely identify each router and switch. Each device should have a hostname that is unique and readily identifiable. Use the *"/system identity ..."* command in Figure 5.17 to update the hostname for each device:

```
[admin@MikroTik] > /system identity set name=router.lan
[admin@router.lan] > _
```

Figure 5.17: Setting System Hostname

Having good hostnames in place does the following for an organization:

- Eases device inventory processes
- Improves device monitoring maps in The Dude (p. 287)
- Quickly identifies devices while troubleshooting
- Bring new administrators up-to-speed faster on the network topology

5.7 Login Banner

Most compliance standards require some type of login banner that displays a message at the console when a user attempts to log in. Some countries and jurisdictions give different legal weight to these notices, but it's still a best practice to add a banner to your device provisioning process. First, set the empty banner to be displayed at login:

```
/system note set show-at-login=yes
```

Then set the contents of the banner message. This should be something that clearly states access to the router is for authorized administrators only and that access is monitored. Consult with a legal professional in your area for the appropriate verbiage. The following command sets a very basic banner message:

```
/system note
set note="Company, Inc. authorized administrators only. Access to this device
    is monitored. Unauthorized access is prohibited, and may result in
    prosecution."
```

5.8 Time Zone and Clock

By default the time zone and Daylight Savings Time (DST) preference are not configured on RouterOS devices. Figure 5.18 shows the baseline configuration for the time zone and other system clock settings:

```
[admin@MikroTik] > /system clock print
                time: 06:28:57
                date: aug/15/2017
time-zone-autodetect: yes
      time-zone-name: manual
          gmt-offset: +00:00
          dst-active: no
[admin@MikroTik] > _
```

Figure 5.18: Default Time Settings

Production RouterOS devices and virtual machines must have their time zones and DST configuration set correctly. In my case I'm the United States' Eastern time zone and we do observe DST in this region. The following commands set the time zone and DST is configured automatically:

```
[admin@MikroTik] > /system clock set time-zone-name=US/Eastern
[admin@MikroTik] > /system clock print
                time: 02:33:32
                date: aug/15/2017
time-zone-autodetect: yes
      time-zone-name: US/Eastern
          gmt-offset: -04:00
          dst-active: yes
[admin@MikroTik] > _
```

Figure 5.19: Configuring Time Zones

Once the time zone is set the NTP configuration on page 73 can effectively change the system clock and update it without manual intervention.

> **NOTE**: Many organizations set their infrastructure device time zones to *UTC* so that all timestamps match across devices and don't have to be adjusted for local time when doing log analysis. This isn't required but it does help if your organization spans multiple time zones or regions that observe DST differently.

5.9 Network Time Services

RouterOS does not synchronize time from upstream NTP servers by default as of this writing. The baseline configuration is shown in Figure 5.20:

```
[admin@MikroTik] > /system ntp client print
         enabled: no
     primary-ntp: 0.0.0.0
   secondary-ntp: 0.0.0.0
server-dns-names:
            mode: broadcast
[admin@MikroTik] > _
```

Figure 5.20: Default NTP Configuration

In this state the device relies on the manually configured date and time which is subject to clock drift as days, weeks, and months go by. Many RouterBOARD units also do not have a real-time clock unit onboard with a backup battery. Therefore, power events that reset the unit also reset the system clock.

The security of network devices and accuracy of system logs depend on having updated clocks on network devices. Accurate timestamps in device logs helps enforce *accountability* for network administrators who are making changes in production networks. Accurate time is so important that PCI-DSS has a line-item specifically for this configuration [3, p. 17]:

> "Using time-synchronization technology, synchronize all critical system clocks and times and ensure that the following is implemented... Critical systems have the correct and consistent time."

Configure NTP time synchronization using the following commands:

```
/system ntp client
set enabled=yes server-dns-names=time.google.com,0.pool.ntp.org
```

If dedicated NTP servers are used in the organization they can be specified by IP using the "*primary-ntp*" and "*secondary-ntp*" options. The RouterOS device will synchronize its time with the servers specified above in the "*server-dns-names=...*" option and adjust the system clock. The result is shown in Figure 5.21 on the next page:

```
[admin@MikroTik] > /system ntp client print
          enabled: yes
      primary-ntp: 0.0.0.0
    secondary-ntp: 0.0.0.0
 server-dns-names: time.google.com,0.pool.ntp.org
             mode: unicast
    poll-interval: 8m32s
    active-server: 204.2.134.163
 last-update-from: 204.2.134.163
last-update-before: 2m1s930ms
  last-adjustment: 698us
[admin@MikroTik] > _
```

Figure 5.21: Updated NTP Configuration

5.10 Configuration Management

It's extremely important to have good working copies of device configurations in case of system failure. Having a ready-spare device is important but without a backup configuration it's just a blank slate. That could mean spending hours re-configuring the device by hand before network services are restored. Back-up device configurations are an important component of any disaster recovery and business continuity (DR & BC) plan. It's also important to verify the following for disaster recovery:

1. Administrators know where device backups are located and have ready access

2. Backups are tested and confirmed regularly *before* a disaster strikes

3. An accurate measurement of the time-to-restore (TTR) is known so it can be given to the organization's leadership and customers during a disaster

5.10.1 Device Backup

The "*/system backup*" utility creates a *binary backup file* of the router's full configuration. This includes MAC addresses and other platform and model-specific information. Since the binary file is so granular it's meant to only be restored on the original device. Since backups of this type contain sensitive information they are encrypted by default if your RouterOS user is password-protected. The "*password*" command option will also indicate to the system that the file should be encrypted. Use the following example command to create the binary backup file:

```
/system backup save name=config
```

Backup files are automatically created with a ".*backup*" file extension. The "*/file print*" command lists files on the router, and the "*where type=backup*" option trims the output to only the files we're looking for. Figure 5.22 on the following page shows the file successfully created and listed on the system's storage.

```
[admin@MikroTik] > /system backup save name=config
Saving system configuration
Configuration backup saved
[admin@MikroTik] > /file print where type=backup
 # NAME                TYPE       SIZE    CREATION-TIME
 0 config.backup       backup     151.1KiB sep/06/2017 20:17:50
[admin@MikroTik] > _
```

Figure 5.22: Creating Device Backup File

5.10.2 Device Restore

Just as important as backing up a device's configuration is testing your restore capabilities and procedures. This will give you the chance to revise procedures as necessary and identify any training that needs to occur. Should you ever need to restore from backup just upload the file created in Figure 5.22 and use the following command:

```
/system backup load name=config.backup
```

The router will verify you want to restore and reboot, then the rest will be handled automatically. An example of a device backup file being used for restore is shown in Figure 5.23:

```
[admin@MikroTik] > /system backup load name=config.backup
password: *********
Restore and reboot? [y/N]:
y
Restoring system configuration
System configuration restored, rebooting now
[admin@MikroTik] > _
```

Figure 5.23: Restoring From Backup

Whatever Winbox or other remote sessions that are currently open will be terminated a few seconds after confirming the reboot. Typically RouterBOARD devices will restart, restore the configuration, and come back online within a minute. RouterOS-based virtual machines can sometimes come back online even faster.

5.10.3 Configuration Export

Unlike the "*/system backup*" command that creates a binary file the "*export*" command produces *human-readable text*. Files are exported in *.rsc* format and can be executed directly by RouterOS, or commands can be copy-pasted individually to a terminal. Despite being in *.rsc* format the exported configuration files can be opened and edited in text editors like Notepad++, Vin and Nano on Linux, or Notepad on Microsoft Windows. Running the "*export*" command from the top of the command hierarchy ("*/export...*") exports *most* of the device configuration:

```
/export file=backup
```

Router users, passwords, and groups are not included in configuration exports. To export groups and users (but still no passwords) use the *"/user export file=... verbose"* command. The resulting *backup.rsc* file can now be found in Winbox by clicking the *Files* button, as shown in Figure 5.24:

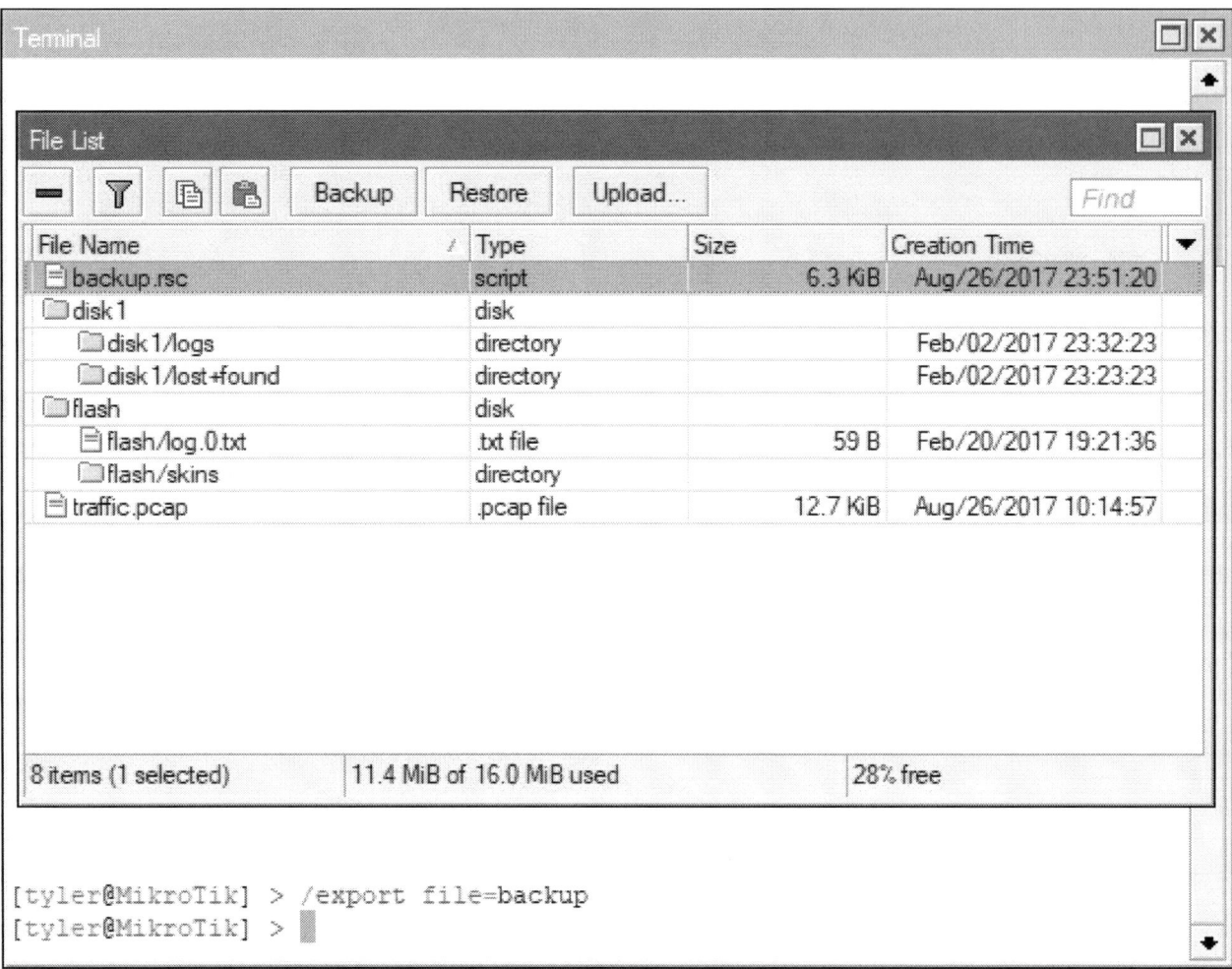

Figure 5.24: Configuration Export File

Using the following command exports only the firewall configuration:

```
/ip firewall export file=firewall_backup
```

The configuration export command is flexible so you can copy as much or little of the device configuration as you'd like. This is especially helpful when creating templates for MikroTik device rollouts happening en masse.

5.10.4 Hide Sensitive

The *hide-sensitive* option ensures that sensitive information like wireless encryption keys aren't included in the plaintext *.rsc* file. This doesn't mean that configuration files don't need to be stored securely but it can be a component of your security plan. Regardless of whether you use this option router user passwords still aren't exported.

5.10.5 Configuration Restore

If after making changes you want to revert back to a previously saved configuration file simply click the *Restore* button shown in Figure 5.25:

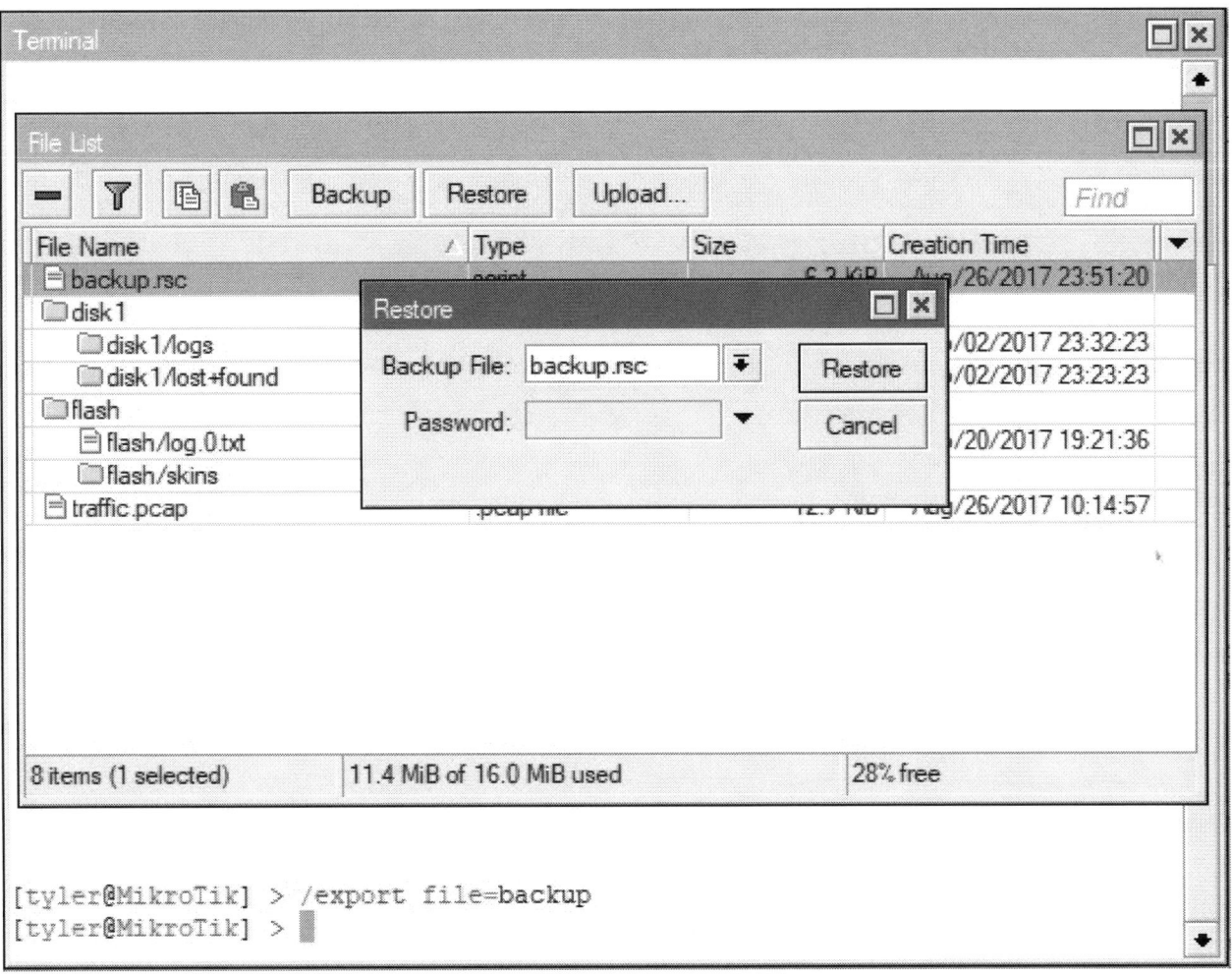

Figure 5.25: Configuration Export Restore

The following command restores from the *backup.rsc* file created above:

```
/import backup.rsc
```

This type of restore operation doesn't force a reboot like the binary restore did on page 75 but it may cause some clients and networks to disconnect. The effect on your network will depend on what settings are being reverted by the configuration restore.

5.11 Using USB Storage

Almost all RouterBOARD models come with a built-in USB port for connecting GPS devices or wireless modems. These ports can also be used to attach USB thumb drives for backup storage. If the onboard flash storage were to fail you could still retrieve backup configuration copies from the USB storage. Insert a thumb drive then use the command shown in Figure 5.26:

```
[admin@MikroTik] > /disk print
# NAME          LABEL          TYPE    DISK            FREE        SIZE
0                              unknown USB 2.0 FD                  3864.0MiB
[admin@MikroTik] > _
```

Figure 5.26: List Disks

Format the attached storage with the command shown in Figure 5.27:

```
[admin@MikroTik] > /disk format-drive 0 label=Backup file-system=fat32
formatted: 23%
-- [Q quit|D dump|C-z pause]
```

Figure 5.27: Formatting USB Storage

In this case the *fat32* option is used because the thumb drive becomes readable and writable by Microsoft, Linux, and Apple hosts. The *ext3* file system is used on page 296 for Dude monitoring data storage where portability isn't as important as performance. In Winbox click the *Files* button and a new "Disk1" entry should appear. The "/disk print" command will also list the new storage details as shown in Figure 5.28:

```
[admin@MikroTik] > /disk print
# NAME          LABEL          TYPE    DISK            FREE        SIZE
0 disk1         BACKUP         fat32   USB 2.0 FD      3803.2MiB   3864.0MiB
[admin@MikroTik] > _
```

Figure 5.28: Listing Formatted USB Storage

Use the steps to create a device backup file on page 74, then in the Winbox *Files* window click-and-drag the backup file to the *disk1* directory.

5.12 Device Reset

Devices that are being used for bench-testing, networking labs, or other non-production roles often need settings completely reset. This can be done quickly and easily with the "*/system reset-configuration ...*" command. The reset command has options for keeping credentials already in-place and default settings after the reset. To completely "nuke" a device and remove all configuration items use the command shown in Figure 5.29:

```
[admin@MikroTik] > /system reset-configuration keep-users=no no-defaults=
yes
Dangerous! Reset anyway? [y/N]:
y
System configuration will be reset
```

Figure 5.29: Complete Device Reset

After entering "*y*" at the console the system immediately reboots and wipes all configuration settings. It reverts back to having no IP addresses assigned and has the default "*admin*" user with no password. To see what's in the default configuration for each RouterOS instance before doing a complete reset run the "*/system default-configuration print*" command.

5.13 Review Questions

1. Which console command will list all sub-commands and brief description for each?

    (a) Question Mark

    (b) Tab

    (c) Double Tab

    (d) Tilde

2. Which command moves up the command hierarchy at the console?

    (a) .

    (b) ..

    (c) ...

    (d) _

3. Which mode rolls back changes made in the current session if it's disconnected unexpectedly?

    (a) Command Mode

    (b) Commit Mode

    (c) Enable Mode

    (d) Safe Mode

4. Which option makes DNS services available on the router to internal and external network hosts?

    (a) allow-remote-requests=yes

    (b) allow-dns=yes

    (c) drop-remote-requests=no

    (d) remote-name-query=yes

5. Which feature puts basic, default settings in place that work for most SOHO environments?

    (a) Factory reset

    (b) Quick Set

    (c) Default Set

    (d) Mainboard Jumper

6. What protocol updates a router's data and time?

    (a) ICMP

    (b) IGMP

    (c) NTP

    (d) SMTP

7. The "*/system export*" command creates a binary backup file for a router.

    (a) True

    (b) False

8. What will RouterOS use DNS servers for?

    (a) Locating MikroTik update servers

    (b) Pinging well-known domain names for troubleshooting

    (c) Resolving IP addresses for domain names used in address lists

    (d) All of the above

9. Which security group is appropriate for analysts who need to view logs but not change configurations?

    (a) Full

    (b) Write

    (c) Read

    (d) Read-Only

10. Which command sets the router's host name to "*router.lan*"?

    (a) */system hostname set name=router.lan*

    (b) */system name set name=router.lan*

    (c) */system identity set name=router.lan*

    (d) */system prompt set name=router.lan*

5.14 Review Answers

1. Which console command will list all sub-commands and brief description for each?

    A – Question mark (p. 66)

2. Which command moves up the command hierarchy at the console?

    B – Double-stop (..) (p. 62)

3. Which mode rolls back changes made in the current session if it's disconnected unexpectedly?

    D – Safe Mode (p. 70)

4. Which option makes DNS services available on the router to internal and external network hosts?

    A – *allow-remote-requests=yes* (p. 131)

5. Which feature puts basic, default settings in place that work for most SOHO environments?

    B – Quick Set (p. 69)

6. What protocol updates a router's data and time?

    C – NTP (p. 73)

7. The "*/system export*" command creates a binary backup file for a router.

    B – False (p. 74)

8. What will RouterOS use DNS servers for?

    D – All of the above (p. 130)

9. Which security group is appropriate for analysts who need to view logs but not change configurations?

    D – Read (p. 90)

10. Which command sets the router's host name to "*router.lan*"?

    C – */system identity set name=router.lan* (p. 71)

Chapter 6

Managing Users

Users have the ability to log in to the device directly, monitor device performance, make settings changes, and list configured settings and options. Users are granted permissions by having a membership in a group. There are three default groups and one administrative user pre-configured on RouterOS.

This chapter is placed ahead of the others that include managing interfaces and addresses because basic user security should be implemented before bringing a RouterOS device onto production networks. Feel free to continue using the default account with no password in lab environments or when pre-staging devices prior to deployment. However, be sure to secure the default RouterOS account before putting a MikroTik device on local networks or connecting it to the internet.

6.1 Default Admin User

The default, built-in RouterOS user has the following credentials:

- Username: admin
- Password: *No password*

This default *admin* user is standard across all RouterOS instances both physical and virtual. List all users configured locally on a device with the "*/user print*" command as shown in Figure 6.1 on the next page and you'll find the *admin* user:

```
[admin@MikroTik] > /user print
Flags: X - disabled
 #   NAME      GROUP     ADDRESS        LAST-LOGGED-IN
 0   ;;; system default user
     admin     full                     jun/06/2017 22:36:24
 1   ;;; Tyler Hart
     tyler     full
[admin@MikroTik] > _
```

Figure 6.1: Listing Users

It's very important that a strong password is set for the default *admin* user to protect a device's *confidentiality*. Putting a device on a production network with the default credentials in place violates best practices and could lead to a data breach.

6.2 User Best Practices

Before covering how to create and manage users it's important to have a good grasp of best practices for user management. Mishandling of users and credentials generate some of the most typical audit "hits" in many organizations. Fortunately, there are well-defined and freely-available standards for managing user access to devices like MikroTik routers and switches.

6.2.1 Least-Privilege

RouterOS users should only be assigned the permissions necessary to perform their duties. Granting more permissions than are needed could lead to a network breach, or to a misconfiguration by an untrained administrator. The Infrastructure Router STIG [1, Vul. ID V-3057] reinforces the requirement for least-privilege user permissions:

> "Configure authorized accounts with the least privilege rule. Each user will have access to only the privileges they require to perform their assigned duties."

Use the built-in groups or create your own custom groups (p. 89) to automate application of permissions.

6.2.2 Nonrepudiation

Each person with access to a MikroTik router, switch, wireless AP, etc. should have and use their own credentials. PCI-DSS guidance [3, p. 12] states the following for organizations that accept debit or credit payment cards:

> "8.1.1 Assign all users a unique ID before allowing them to access system components or cardholder data."

If an organization doesn't process payment card transactions this is still a good best practice to follow. Credentials on each device should be audited periodically as well. This supports the principle of "nonrepudiation", meaning that when someone does something with their own credentials it can't later be denied. The use of shared accounts violates this principle because there is no way to tell who used those credentials. When trying to find who is responsible for an incident involving a shared account, any one person could claim it was caused by someone else. This is especially problematic when investigating a possible hacking incident, data breach, or violation of change control procedures that takes down a network.

6.2.3 Accountability

When each person has their own credentials and uses them on every device it's possible to hold people in the organization accountable for their actions and changes. Log entries for those individual accounts across MikroTik devices can then answer the following questions:

1. Who attempted to authenticate to a device?
2. What system did the user attempt to authenticate from?
3. When did the attempt occur?
4. Was the attempt successful?
5. What changes did the user make while logged in?
6. When did the user finally log out?

With shared accounts it's possible to see when authentication occurred and from what system. It's also possible to see what changes were made, but it's difficult to know who the person was behind the keyboard and hold them accountable.

6.2.4 Passwords and Comments

Each user's credentials should have a robust password and a comment that easily links the credential to its owner. Set a robust password for the *admin* user with the following command:

```
/user set admin password=abc123!
```

Each user can update their own command as well once they've authenticated to a RouterOS device. Figure 6.2 on the next page shows the *admin* user updating their own password directly from the console:

```
[admin@MikroTik] > password
old-password: *********
new-password: *********
confirm-new-password: *********

[admin@MikroTik] > _
```

Figure 6.2: User Updating Password

The command to reset a user's own password is available from the root of the command prompt or from any location when using the "*/password*" command. Bear in mind these best practices for password management:

- Choose a unique password instead of recycling something used previously
- Don't use names, places, or dates that could be found by an attacker snooping on social media or an organization's website
- Use a password manager to securely share passwords if necessary
- Document emergency backup account passwords and store them in tamper-evident envelopes in a known, secure location

Set each user's full name as a comment for easier auditing with the following commands:

```
/user set tyler comment="Tyler Hart"
/user set admin comment="Emergency use only"
```

Note that in the two commands above each comment string is enclosed inside double quotes. These are necessary because both comments have text with spaces. Without the double quotes RouterOS has no way to know when the string of text ends. Comments that are only one word don't require any punctuation as shown in the following commands:

```
/user set tyler comment="Tyler Hart"
/user set tyler comment=Hart
```

The command to set a password for the admin user also did not use quotes because there is no space in the password being set.

6.2.5 Rename Admin Account

The default *admin* user is well-known across the industry and there are many freely-available tools for password guessing attacks targeting default accounts. Renaming the *admin* account creates another layer in the DiD strategy for securing RouterOS devices. Rename the built-in *admin* account with the following command:

```
/user set admin name=tikadmin
```

6.3 User Operations

Each network administrator or analyst should have their own credentials so configuration changes and events can be audited and traced back to a source. Router and switch users should also be periodically audited to ensure backdoor accounts haven't been created or old accounts don't remain. Security best practices recommend that credentials be disabled or deleted if an administrator leaves an organization or is suspended. This ensures that a disgruntled administrator can't sabotage a device after their employment ends.

6.3.1 Creating Users

Create an admin-level user with the following command:

```
/user add name=tyler group=full comment="Tyler Hart" password=abc123!
```

The *"group=full"* option gives the new user rights to do everything on that particular router. Only administrators who need that set of permissions should have them assigned. See page 90 for directions on creating custom groups with specific permissions for those who don't require full rights. Users credentials can be restricted to specific networks or addresses with the *address* option. The following command creates the same user as above, but only allows it to be used from *192.168.88.199*:

```
/user add name=tyler group=full comment="Tyler Hart" password=abc123! address
   =192.168.88.199
```

6.3.2 Disabling and Enabling Users

User credentials can be disabled without removing them entirely from the device. Disable the user *"tyler"* with the following command:

```
/user disable tyler
```

The credential will still exist but it can't be used for authentication while disabled. If a session using the credential is currently open when the user is disabled it will remain open until disconnected. The command in Figure 6.3 on the next page lists currently open user sessions:

```
[admin@MikroTik] > /user active print
Flags: R - radius, M - by-romon
 #   WHEN                   NAME    ADDRESS        VIA
 0   oct/15/2017 14:13:26   admin                  console
 1   oct/15/2017 14:54:26   admin   192.168.1.40   dude
 2   oct/15/2017 14:58:15   admin   192.168.1.40   winbox
 3   oct/15/2017 16:59:50   admin   192.168.1.40   telnet

[admin@MikroTik] > _
```

Figure 6.3: Active Users

Users can be re-enabled using the "*enable*" command:

```
/user enable tyler
```

6.3.3 Removing Users

Once an administrator or other user is no longer with an organization they should be removed from all devices that they were given access to. PCI-DSS [3, p. 12] has this to say about removing access for terminated users:

> "*8.1.3 Immediately revoke access for any terminated users.*"

Delete the user *tyler* with the "*remove*" command:

```
/user remove tyler
```

> **WARNING**: No further confirmation is requested and the user will be immediately removed. This action can be undone using the "*/undo*" command. See page 68 for guidance on rolling back commands.

All the same user management commands above can be done from the command line in Winbox using the plus, minus, check, and "X" buttons. The user management dialog is shown in Figure 6.4 on the following page:

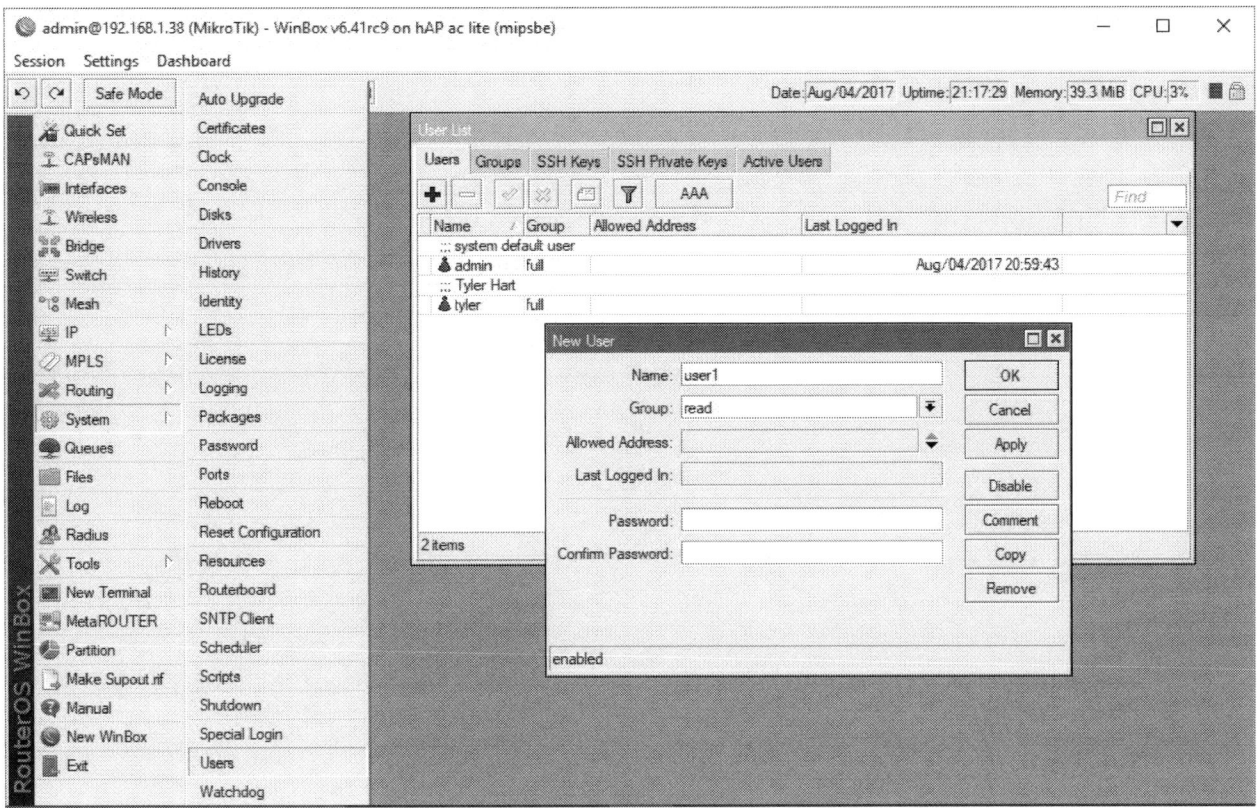

Figure 6.4: Winbox User Management

6.4 Groups

User groups determine which permissions the group members have on a device. Three groups are configured by default:

- Full
- Read
- Write

Full Group

Members of the Full group can make configuration changes on the device, add and remove users, change packages, and all other tasks. Only users with network administration experience and a genuine organizational need should be granted Full group access. Examples of these types of users include the following:

- Senior network administrators
- Network administrators responsible for creating device credentials

- Technicians actively managing User Manager or Hotspot functionality[1]

6.4.1 Read Group

The Read group allows its members to view device configurations and performance but not save changes. Network and security analysts, system administrators who need to see network service status, and others can safely have access via the Read group without worry they can change things.

- Network analysts responsible for basic troubleshooting and performance monitoring
- Network security analysts responsible for log monitoring and analysis, as well as network compliance scanning

6.4.2 Write Group

The Write group has the same permissions as the Full group except for the rights to log in via FTP, manage users, and work with The Dude. This group is appropriate for the following types of users:

- Network administrators who are responsible for maintaining and troubleshooting networks
- Experienced network analysts working with administrators

6.4.3 Custom Groups

The three default groups cannot be removed but you can create your own custom groups. Users can only be a member of one group so if the three default groups don't meet your security needs create a custom group with the necessary permissions. A custom group can be especially useful for new network administrators that should be able to make minimal changes and monitor devices but not perform tasks that could break a device's configuration.

The following commands create a custom group that allows a user to read non-sensitive configuration information, transfer files via FTP, and log in via Winbox for monitoring:

```
/user group
add name="Network Analysts" policy=winbox,ftp,read,!sensitive
```

The exclamation point in front of "*sensitive*" indicates "*not sensitive*", meaning the analyst users can't see wireless or IPSEC keys, user manager credentials, etc. More experienced analysts could also be put in the same type of group that also has the "*reboot*" option added if the organization is comfortable with those users being able to reboot devices.

---

[1] Both User Manager and Hotspot are beyond the scope of the MTCNA.

6.5 Active Users

To view users currently logged in to a device use the *"/user active print"* command. For a list of users currently logged in, their source IP, login service and time, and user group use the *"detail"* option shown in Figure 6.5:

```
[admin@MikroTik] > /user active print detail
Flags: R - radius, M - by-romon
 0   when=mar/28/2017 09:25:50 name="admin" address=192.168.88.253 via=winbox
     group=full
```

Figure 6.5: Printing Active Users

6.6 Further Reading

RouterOS devices can consolidate Authentication, Authorization, and Accounting (AAA) with the use of a separate Remote Authentication Dial-In User Service (RADIUS) server. This allows administrators to use the same credentials across the entire network. The RADIUS server can also implement password policies for length, complexity, age, and more. Authentication and accounting logs are stored in one location as well which makes auditing easier. This configuration can be quite complex and is beyond the scope of the MTCNA. The MikroTik Security Guide, Second Edition, by Tyler Hart provides step-by-step instructions for configuring RADIUS on a FreeRADIUS or Microsoft Windows NPS server.

6.7 Review Questions

1. The name of the default RouterOS user is *administrator*.

   (a) True

   (b) False

2. It's considered a best practice to rename the built-in default account.

   (a) True

   (b) False

3. Which default user group is appropriate for junior network analysts?

   (a) Full

   (b) Write

   (c) Read

   (d) All

4. Which command lists users currently logged in?

   (a) */user print*

   (b) */user active print*

   (c) */print user active*

   (d) */show user active*

5. Which default user group is appropriate for senior network administrators?

   (a) Full

   (b) Write

   (c) Read

   (d) All

6. The "*/user remove...*" command can be undone.

   (a) True

   (b) False

7. Accountability includes what permissions are assigned to a user.

    (a) True

    (b) False

8. Which protocol can be used to authenticate credentials to a centralized database?

    (a) PIM

    (b) IGMP

    (c) SNMP

    (d) RADIUS

9. Users can be restricted to only logging in via certain addresses without the use of firewall filter rules.

    (a) True

    (b) False

10. Which actions are appropriate for a user account belonging to an administrator that was recently terminated?

    (a) Leave account intact

    (b) Disable account

    (c) Remove account

    (d) Rename account

6.8 Review Answers

1. The name of the default RouterOS user is *administrator*.

    B – False (p. 83)

2. It's considered a best practice to rename the built-in default account.

    A – True (p. 86)

3. Which default user group is appropriate for junior network analysts?

    C – Read (p. 90)

4. Which command lists users currently logged in?

    B – */user active print* (p. 91)

5. Which default user group is appropriate for senior network administrators?

    A – Full (p. 89)

6. The "*/user remove...*" command can be undone.

    A – True (p. 88)

7. Accountability includes what permissions are assigned to a user.

    B – False (p. 85)

8. Which protocol can be used to authenticate credentials to a centralized database?

    D – RADIUS (p. 91)

9. Users can be restricted to only logging in via certain addresses without the use of firewall filter rules.

    A – True (p. 87)

10. Which actions are appropriate for a user account belonging to an administrator that was recently terminated?

    B and C – Disable account and Remove account (p. 88)

Chapter 7

Interfaces

Managing interfaces is a critical skill for any MTCNA candidate. Knowing how to configure, monitor, create, and enable or disable interfaces is important for day-to-day RouterOS operations.

7.1 Interface Types

RouterOS supports many different kind of network interfaces both physical and logical. Physical interfaces include the following:

- Ethernet (Onboard Copper, SFP & SFP+ modules)
- Wireless (Integrated or MPCI / MPCI-E card)
- Cellular 3G / 4G / 4G LTE (either USB dongle or MPCI / MPCI-E card)

Logical interface types include (but are not limited to) the following:

- VLANs
- Tunnels (Generic Route Encapsulation (GRE), EoIP, IP-IP (IP-IP), PPP, etc)
- Virtual Router Redundancy Protocol (VRRP)
- Bridges
- Virtual Ethernet
- VPLS

Other types of virtual interfaces exist but they are either covered by more advanced certification outlines or are only used in very specialized configurations. The default generic settings for most interfaces are as follows:

- Interface: Enabled
- Duplex: Auto Negotiate

- Speed: Auto Negotiate
- ARP: Enabled (if applicable)
- Bandwidth: Unlimited
- Flow Control: Off (if applicable)
- MTU: 1500

These are fairly typical settings that don't require modification to work in most networks.

7.2 Interface Listing Commands

To list all interfaces present on RouterOS devices use the following command:

```
/interface print
```

An example of a factory-default configured router's interfaces is shown in Figure 7.1:

```
[admin@MikroTik] > /interface print
Flags: D - dynamic, X - disabled, R - running, S - slave
 #      NAME              TYPE       ACTUAL-MTU  L2MTU
 0      ether1            ether          1500     1600
 1    S ether2-master     ether          1500     1598
 2    S ether3            ether          1500     1598
 3    S ether4            ether          1500     1598
 4    S ether5            ether          1500     1598
 5   RS wlan1             wlan           1500     1600
 6   R  ;;; defconf
bridge                    bridge         1500     1598
[admin@MikroTik] > _
```

Figure 7.1: Default RouterBOARD Interfaces

To see the total count of interfaces on a device use the *"count-only"* option as shown in Figure 7.2:

```
[admin@MikroTik] > /interface print count-only
8
[admin@MikroTik] > _
```

Figure 7.2: Interface Count Command

In this instance the device has a total of eight interfaces. To see a count of wireless interfaces use a *'where type="wlan"'* clause as shown in Figure 7.3 on the following page:

```
[admin@MikroTik] > /interface print count-only where type="wlan"
2
[admin@MikroTik] > _
```

Figure 7.3: Wireless Interface Count Command

7.3 Interface Statistics

The "*/interface print stats where running*" command shown in Figure 7.4 shows packets transmitted and received on each interface, as well as any errors.

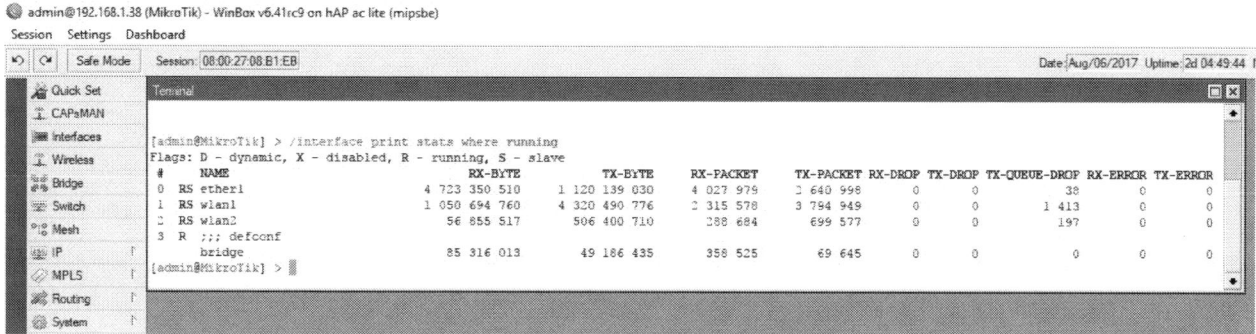

Figure 7.4: Running Interface Statistics

To continuously monitor interfaces from the console use the "*/interface print stats follow where running*" command. The [CTRL+C] keystroke ends the continuous monitoring started with the "*follow*" keyword.

7.4 Ethernet Interfaces

Typically *ether1* is configured by default with a DHCP client to request a dynamic IP address. *Ether2* and beyond are often bridged together using the *Master Port* option for convenience, giving local devices access to the same network. With the default configuration applied on SOHO devices the *ether2* interface is named *ether2-master*, specifically indicating this configuration. Devices like the RB7xx and RB9xx use *ether2* as the master port, with *ether3* through *ether5* pointing to *ether2* as master. An example is shown in Figure 7.5 on the next page:

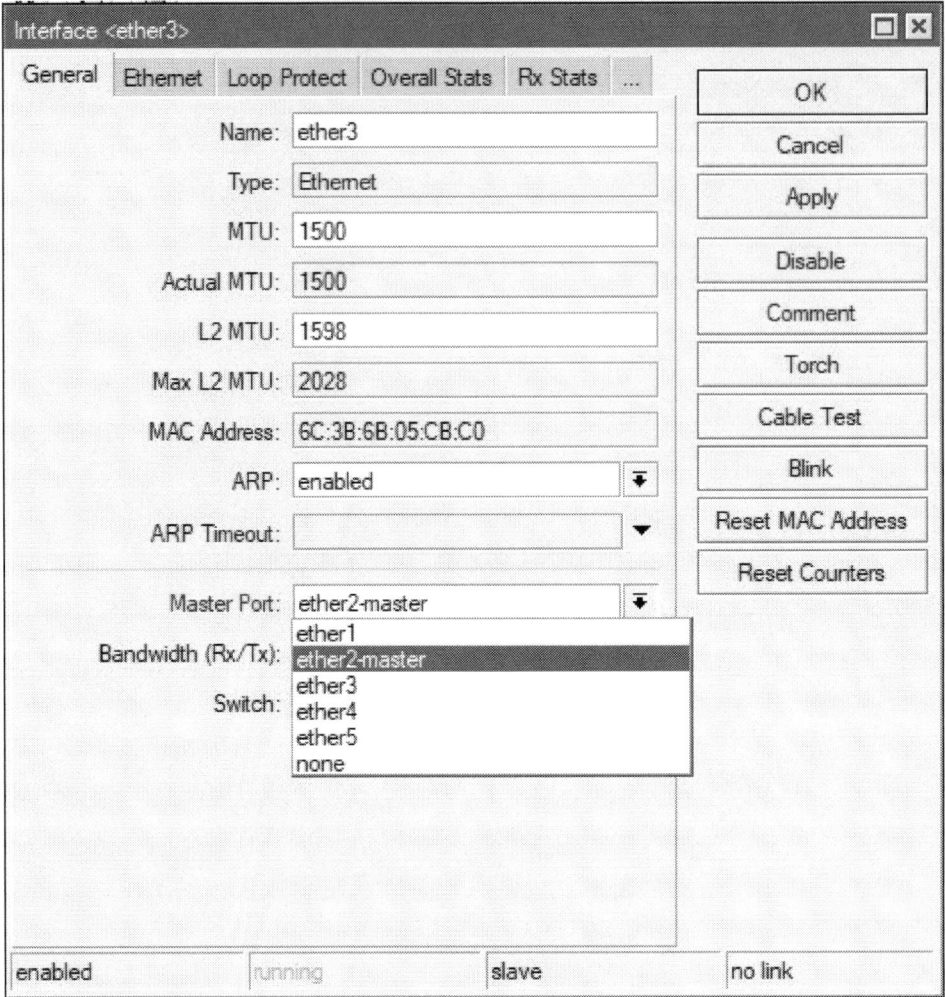

Figure 7.5: Master Port

NOTE: The *Master Port* setting on *ether2* will be *None* because *ether2* is the master port.

```
[admin@MikroTik] > /interface ethernet print brief
Flags:  X — disabled,  R — running,  S — slave
 #    NAME            MTU    MAC-ADDRESS        ARP       MASTER-PORT      SWITCH
 0 R  ether1          1500   6C:3B:6B:05:CB:BE  enabled   none             switch1
 1 RS ether2-master   1500   6C:3B:6B:05:CB:BF  enabled   none             switch1
 2 RS ether3          1500   6C:3B:6B:05:CB:C0  enabled   ether2-master    switch1
 3 RS ether4          1500   6C:3B:6B:05:CB:C1  enabled   ether2-master    switch1
 4 RS ether5          1500   6C:3B:6B:05:CB:C2  enabled   ether2-master    switch1
[admin@MikroTik] > _
```

Figure 7.6: Ethernet Interfaces

7.5 Power Over Ethernet

POE allows one Ethernet device to power another. Many RouterBOARD models are able to power other devices or be powered themselves by POE-capable Ethernet connections. Often wireless models like the SXT mounted up on a tower are powered by a POE switch or injector below.

7.5.1 POE Modes

Ports on POE-capable devices can operate in three modes:

- Auto On
- Forced On
- Off

The default mode in modern RouterOS releases is "*Auto On*". When an Ethernet port is providing POE power the color of the activity LED turns to red. To view the status of all POE ethernet ports use the command shown in Figure 7.7:

```
[admin@MikroTik] > /interface ethernet poe print detail
0 name="ether5" poe-out=auto-on poe-priority=10 power-cycle-ping-enabled=no
   power-cycle-interval=none
[admin@MikroTik] > _
```

Figure 7.7: Listing POE Status

WARNING: Verify that devices attached to POE ports are POE-compatible before using the "*Forced On*" mode.

To watch POE transition when a device is plugged in use the "*monitor*" command shown in Figure 7.8:

```
[admin@MikroTik] > /interface ethernet poe monitor ether5
         name: ether5
      poe-out: auto-on
poe-out-status: powered-on
-- [Q quit|D dump|C-z pause]
```

Figure 7.8: Monitoring POE Status

7.5.2 POE Priority

Each POE-capable port is assigned a priority number. Zero is the highest priority, 99 is the lowest. The default priority value for POE ports is 10 as shown in Figure 7.7 on the previous page. If the RouterBOARD unit detects an over-current condition the ports with the lowest priority will have POE output disabled first. RouterOS checks for over-current conditions every six seconds [16]. This protects the RouterBOARD device while also ensuring that upstream POE devices remain online if possible.

7.5.3 Power-Cycle POE

A very convenient feature in RouterOS is the ability to power-cycle POE ports. This action forces a reboot of the device on the other end of the connection. The example in Figure 7.8 on the previous page showed *ether5* as a POE port. The following command would force a power-cycle of ten seconds for whatever device is being powered by port *ether5* on the RouterBOARD:

```
/interface ethernet poe power-cycle ether5 duration=10s
```

In lieu of a POE-capable model that can output power a MikroTik POE injector shown in Figure 7.9 on the following page can be used. These are low-cost units that can be installed with very minimal downtime. The injector is placed in-line with a copper CAT-5/6 cable between devices and only outputs power from the upstream port.

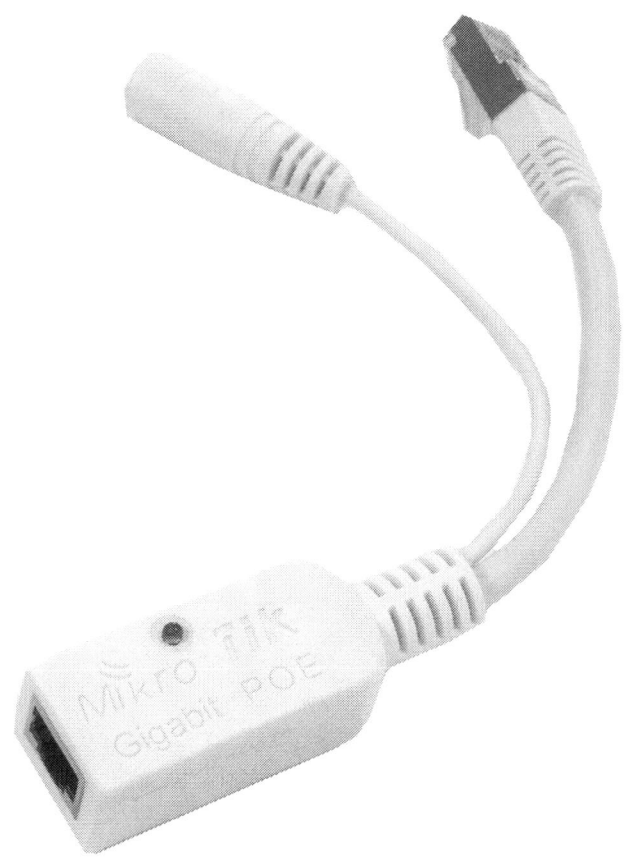

Image Credit: *MikroTik*
Figure 7.9: MikroTik POE Injector

Unfortunately these injectors can't be remotely power-cycled like the RouterBOARD POE ports in the previous example. It's also important that the injectors have stable, reliable power inputs. Surges during lightning strikes or brown-outs could not only damage the injector but also cause the device getting power further down the line to go offline and require an on-site technician visit.

7.6 SFP Modules

SFP and SFP+ modules allow organizations to use copper and fiber optic cables of different standards with a module that plugs into an industry-standard port. When cabling is upgraded the routers and switches don't need to be replaced. Instead, simply upgrading the SFP or SFP+ modules to those that work with the new cabling is all that's required. These interfaces that accept these modules are numbered the same as Ethernet ports and have the same default configurations. SFP+ interfaces facilitate faster 10 Gb/sec connections to higher-end RouterBOARD units like the CCR. Ports are named "*sfp1*", "*sfp2*", "*sfp3*", etc. A copper Ethernet SFP module is shown in Figure 7.10 on the next page, and a fiber optic SFP module is shown in Figure 7.11 on the next page:

Image Credit: *MikroTik*
Figure 7.10: Copper SFP Module

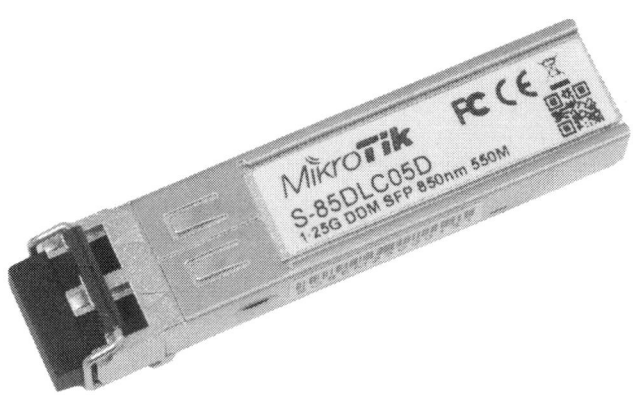

Image Credit: *MikroTik*
Figure 7.11: Fiber Optic SFP Module

On older devices with optics built-in to the unit when a port "died" it simply couldn't be used anymore. With SFP-based connections the module can simply be replaced or upgraded. For organizations that rely heavily on fiber optic connections using different SFP modules also allows for mix-and-match fiber deployment between devices. Cheaper multi-mode fiber can be deployed for short-range cable runs, while the more expensive single-mode can be used for longer runs.

Use the following command to view the SFP module status for port *sfp1*:

```
/interface ethernet monitor sfp1
```

This command will display extended information about the SFP module detected in the *sfp1* port. This includes the module's vendor name, part number, serial number, and fault status.

Another option for linking devices with high-speed connections is using pre-fabricated Direct Attach Cables (DACs). These are high-speed links typically one to five meters long with SFP or SFP+ modules and cable combined into one unit. An example of a DAC is shown in Figure 7.12:

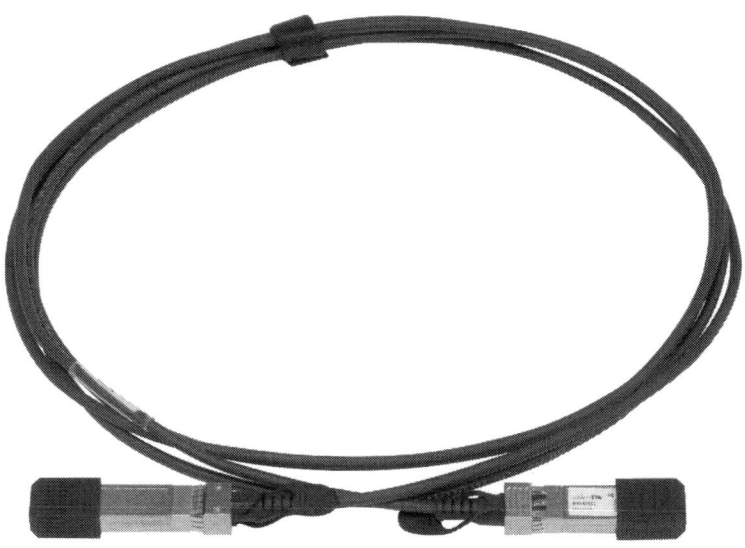

Image Credit: *MikroTik*
Figure 7.12: MikroTik DAC

These are very cost-effective units for connecting devices with high-speed links but the modules at each end cannot be removed from the cable and reused. They are also limited in length with only enough distance to go between devices in the same rack or racks immediately adjacent to one another.

7.7 Wireless

SOHO MikroTik devices with wireless network interfaces often have bridged connections between wired and wireless networks. With this default configuration all interfaces, except *ether1* running as the WAN port, are part of the same LAN. For most small networks this is all the configuration they ever need. Having wired and wireless connections bridged also allows streaming to wireless devices like Apple TV® or Google Chromecast® from wired hosts. Additional Mini PCI / Mini PCI-Express wireless add-on cards will have no default configuration. An example of these add-on cards is shown in Figure 7.13 on the next page:

Image Credit: *MikroTik*
Figure 7.13: Mini PCI-Express Wireless Radio

These interfaces generally use external antennas (three connectors shown above) that also need their gain (measured in Decibels (dBs)) set in the card's wireless configuration. Wireless configuration and interfaces are covered more in-depth later in the book.

7.8 Bridge Interfaces

Bridges are hardware or software components that combine OSI layer two (data link) network segments. In RouterOS bridges are implemented in software for combining separate interfaces into the same network. As of this writing an implementation of bridging in hardware is available in the *Release Channel* software branch but isn't ready yet for general release. Once hardware bridging is released it will improve bridged network performance and lower the processing resource overhead on physical RouterBOARD units.

A bridge can also be used as a virtual loopback interface for running OSPF, MPLS, or other protocols. This allows physical interfaces attached to the bridge to go up or down and not affect the protocol because the virtual interface remains online. This kind of virtual loopback implementation will be covered more in the Routing chapter on page 137.

To connect physical networks together via a virtual bridge only requires a few steps:

1. Create the bridge interface
2. Configure features on the bridge (Fast Forward, etc.)
3. Add ports to the bridge

The following sections will walk you through the steps above.

7.8.1 Creating Bridges

The only thing required to create a typical bridge interface is a very short command:

```
/interface bridge
add name="LAN Bridge" comment=LAN
```

This new bridge is an isolated interface with no IP addresses and no network traffic in or out.

7.8.2 Fast Forward

As of RouterOS 6.39 the new *Fast Forward* feature is available. This speeds up connections on bridges with two or more interfaces attached. To enable Fast Forward on a new bridge as it's created use the "*fast-forward=yes*" option shown in the following example:

```
/interface bridge
add name="LAN Bridge" comment=LAN fast-forward=yes
```

7.8.3 Adding Ports

Assume for this example that on a router ports *ether2* and *ether3* should be joined together into a single broadcast domain (bridged). The easiest way to link the attached network segments is to bridge the ports. First create a bridge, then add the two ports with the following commands:

```
/interface bridge
add name="LAN Bridge" comment=LAN fast-forward=yes

/interface bridge port
add interface=ether2 bridge="LAN Bridge"
add interface=ether3 bridge="LAN Bridge"
```

At this point the hosts connected to *ether2* and *ether3* belong to the same broadcast domain. After being added to the bridge those physical interfaces run in "Slave" mode. In Winbox the ports will display with an "R" and "S" status, indicating *Running* and *Slave* statuses, respectively. In Figure 7.14 on the next page a bridge interface is running along with Ethernet ports. *Ether1* is not a member of the bridge, so it's running ("R") and not in slave mode. *Ether2* and *ether4* are both connected *and* members of the bridge so their statuses are both "RS". Interface *ether3* is part of the bridge but not connected so it only shows as "S". Both wireless interfaces *wlan1* and *wlan2* are part of the bridge, so in this configuration wireless and wired hosts are part of the same broadcast domain.

```
[admin@MikroTik] > /interface print
Flags: D - dynamic, X - disabled, R - running, S - slave
 #      NAME              TYPE
 0   R  ether1            ether
 1   RS ether2-master     ether
 2   S  ether3            ether
 3   RS ether4            ether
 4   R  ether5            ether
 5   RS wlan1             wlan
 6   RS wlan2             wlan
 7   R  bridge            bridge
[admin@MikroTik] > _
```

Figure 7.14: Interface Running, Slave Status

7.8.4 Removing Bridge Ports

For whatever reason if you wanted to break the network back apart you can either delete the bridge interface entirely or remove individual interfaces from it.

> **WARNING**: When deleting a bridge, RouterOS will not ask you to confirm the removal if other interfaces are attached. It is considered good practice to remove bridged ports, then remove the bridge itself.

First list the ports attached to bridges and selectively remove them as shown in Figure 7.15:

```
[admin@MikroTik] > /interface bridge port print
Flags: X - disabled, I - inactive, D - dynamic
 #     INTERFACE         BRIDGE    PRIORITY    PATH-COST    HORIZON
 0 I   ;;; defconf
       ether2-master     bridge    0x80        10           none
 1     ;;; defconf
       wlan1             bridge    0x80        10           none
[admin@MikroTik] > /interface bridge port remove 0
```

Figure 7.15: Removing Bridge Ports

7.8.5 Removing Bridges

Removing a bridge is simple, but be careful to verify you're deleting the right bridge first. Use the command in the following example to remove a bridge:

```
/interface bridge remove "bridge"
```

Any network addresses, firewall rules, or other policies referencing the now-deleted bridge will appear in Winbox highlighted red because they are now invalid.

7.9 Interface MTU

An interface's Maximum Transmission Unit (MTU) is the maximum size of an Layer 2 (L2) frame or L3 packet that can be sent without fragmenting it first. By default, the MTU for L3 communications is 1500, though the L2 MTU is often higher. This is in-line with other vendors in the industry and allows for plug-and-play network operation. Larger frames known as "Jumbo Frames" can be around 9000 bytes depending on vendor implementation and hardware limitations. The current MTU values set for *ether1* on a smaller RouterBOARD are shown in Figure 7.16:

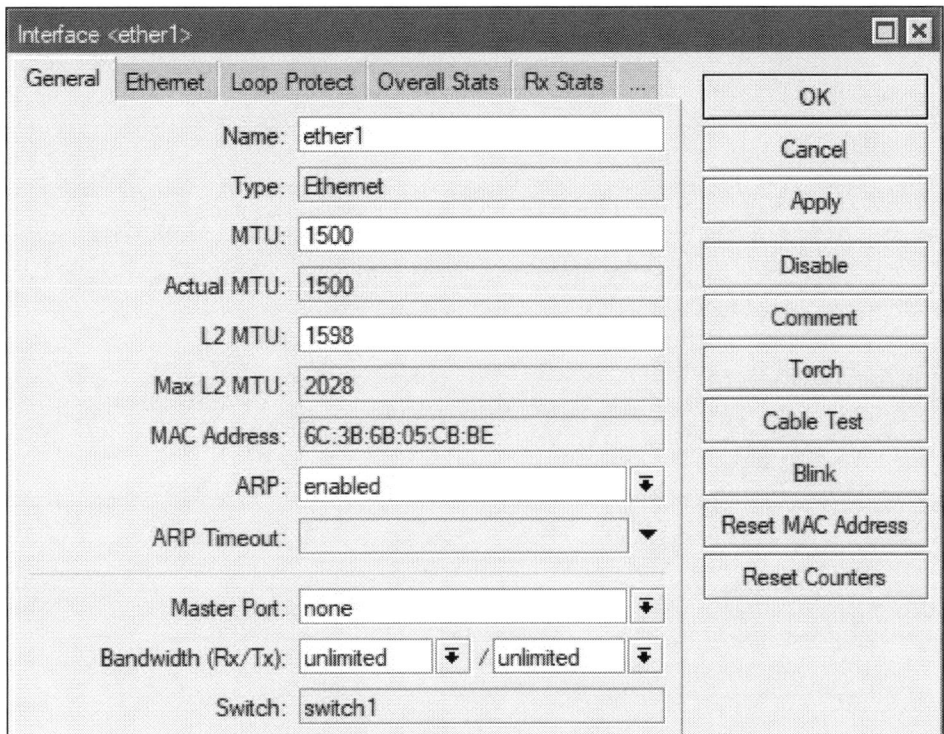

Figure 7.16: Interface MTU

The same information is available from the console with the "*/interface ethernet print detail*" command. In the past there were efficiency gains to be found by using Jumbo Frames because processing power in routers and switches was limited. Modern networks can recognize some gains by using Jumbo Frames but they are typically modest. There can also be significant administrative overhead incurred because all devices using Jumbo Frames or in the network path of those frames must have their interface MTUs adjusted.

RouterBOARD interfaces can support larger frames but different models have their own limitations. For example the higher-end CCR1036 can support a 10226 byte MTU but the smaller RB951 can only supports 4074 bytes[1] Figure 7.17 on the next page shows the maximum MTU for an RB751 port as 2290 bytes.

---

[1] https://wiki.mikrotik.com/wiki/Manual:Maximum_Transmission_Unit_on_RouterBoards#MAC.2FLayer-2.2FL2_MTU

7.10 State

Interfaces are enabled by default, but those that are unused should be disabled for security. To view interfaces that are actively running use the command shown in Figure 7.17:

```
[admin@MikroTik] > /interface print where running
Flags: D - dynamic, X - disabled, R - running, S - slave
 #    NAME       TYPE     ACTUAL-MTU  L2MTU   MAX-L2MTU
 0   RS wlan1    wlan     1500        1600    2290
 1    R  ;;; defconf
 bridge          bridge   1500                1598
[admin@MikroTik] > _
```

Figure 7.17: List Running Interfaces

Use the "!" symbol to list all types of interfaces that aren't running as shown in Figure 7.18:

```
[admin@MikroTik] > /interface print where !running
Flags: D - dynamic, X - disabled, R - running, S - slave
 #     NAME             TYPE     ACTUAL-MTU  L2MTU   MAX-L2MTU
 0     ether1           ether           1500  1600        4076
 1   S ether2-master    ether           1500  1598        2028
 2   S ether3           ether           1500  1598        2028
 3   S ether4           ether           1500  1598        2028
 4   S ether5           ether           1500  1598        2028
[admin@MikroTik] >
```

Figure 7.18: List Offline Interfaces

7.11 Duplex

Ethernet interfaces can run in full and half-duplex. Full duplex connections allow simultaneous Transmit (TX) and Receive (RX). Half duplex connections require TX and RX to happen in-turn. 802.11 wireless connections are half-duplex, though some implementations can use multiple antennas to achieve simultaneous TX and RX. The command in Figure 7.19 on the following page shows the duplex settings and current speed for *ether1*:

```
[admin@MikroTik] > /interface ethernet monitor ether1
                name: ether1
              status: link-ok
     auto-negotiation: done
                rate: 100Mbps
          full-duplex: yes
      tx-flow-control: no
      rx-flow-control: no
          advertising: 10M-half,10M-full,100M-half,100M-full
link-partner-advertising: 10M-half,10M-full,100M-half,100M-full
-- [Q quit|D dump|C-z pause]
```

Figure 7.19: Interface Monitor, Duplex Status

If you suspect a duplex mismatch on a network link use the "*monitor*" keyword to view the "*link-partner-advertising*" attribute as it changes.

7.12 Flow Control

Flow control allows an ethernet device receiving more traffic than it can handle to send a "Pause" frame. That particular frame requests the device at the other end of the connection to temporarily stop transmitting. By default, this feature is disabled on RouterOS ethernet interfaces as shown in Figure 7.19 under the *tx-flow-control* and *rx-flow-control* options. Interfaces that are set to auto-negotiate speed and duplex will also negotiate flow control settings [9], so RX and TX flow control settings rarely have to be changed. If you're manually setting speed and duplex and wish to enable this feature set the *tx-flow-control* and *rx-flow-control* options to "*auto*". Use the following commands to list interfaces that have observed "pause" frames to see if flow control is necessary in your networks:

```
/interface ethernet
print stats where rx-pause!="0"
print stats where tx-pause!="0"
```

If no interfaces are listed then your router will most likely not benefit from enabling flow control. If interfaces have observed these frames it's a good idea to begin troubleshooting which devices are acting as bottlenecks on the network.

7.13 Spanning Tree Protocol

Spanning Tree Protocol (STP) protects networks and hosts from broadcast storms created by looped connections between two devices. Devices running STP discover network paths between each other and elect a root bridge. By default, physical and virtual Ethernet-like interfaces are set to run Rapid STP (RSTP) [8] and have a default spanning tree cost of 32768. Figure 7.20 on the next page shows the defaults applied to a new bridge interface being created:

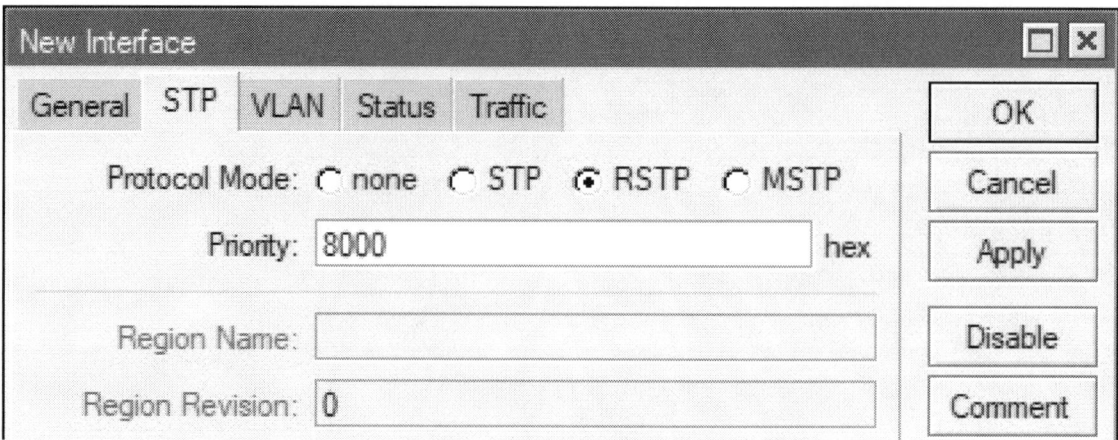

Figure 7.20: Spanning Tree Default Settings

The STP priority is shown as "8000" in hexadecimal, which is "32768" in Base-10. The "Region Name" option is only used when Multiple STP (MSTP) is implemented.

While not strictly required, it's recommended that some version of STP be run on Ethernet-like interfaces to prevent the problems associated with a switching loop. This is especially true if network users plug their own devices in or move frequently, or if networks are expanded with small switches or hubs. The following Spanning Tree modes are supported:

- STP
- RSTP
- MSTP (*Release Candidate* software branch as of this writing)
- None

The typical STP protocol is sometimes known as "vanilla STP". It's the original version of STP and is almost universally supported by all vendors. Although well-supported, it can take a long time (more than 30 seconds) for a STP network to converge. This long amount of time lead to the development of RSTP which converges much faster. RSTP also enjoys almost universal support amongst all major vendors. MSTP extends STP and RSTP, allowing for multiple instances of the protocol to run on the same physical network. This is especially useful when networks are segmented with VLANs, because each VLAN can have its own instance and take advantage of redundant network paths. As of this writing the configuration of MSTP is beyond the scope of the MTCNA certification.

7.13.1 Configuring STP

To set the Spanning Tree mode on a bridge (in this case to *rstp*) use the following commands:

```
/interface bridge
set "LAN Bridge" protocol-mode=rstp
```

Changes to the Spanning Tree configuration of an interface can cause a brief interruption of network traffic as the protocol reconverges.

7.14 Cable Test

RouterOS features a little-known piece of functionality for testing Ethernet network links. An example of a known-good cable testing good is shown in Figure 7.21:

```
[admin@MikroTik] > /interface ethernet cable-test ether5
    name: ether5
  status: link-ok
-- [Q quit|D dump|C-z pause]
```

Figure 7.21: Cable Test - Good

An example of a partially broken cable is shown in Figure 7.22 where some of the wire pairs were cut:

```
[admin@MikroTik] > /interface ethernet cable-test ether5
        name: ether5
      status: no-link
 cable-pairs: normal:?,shorted:0,normal:?,normal:?
-- [Q quit|D dump|C-z pause]
```

Figure 7.22: Cable Test Bad

While this type of tool won't certify a copper Ethernet link like a dedicated cable tester it will service for field-testing links. To test optical fiber a dedicated tool like an Optical Time-Domain Reflectometer (OTDR) is still required.

7.15 Physical Security

If a network port is not in use on a device it's considered a best practice to disable it. This helps prevent an attacker with local access to a device from gaining a network presence. With unused ports disabled an attacker would have to disconnect a live connection, hopefully drawing the attention of users and network administrators. PCI-DSS requires implementation of physical security, including logical controls like shutting down ports [3, p. 14]:

> "Implement physical and/or logical controls to restrict access to publicly accessible network jacks."

Use the following command to disable unused ports *ether4* and *ether5*:

```
/interface set ether4,ether5 disabled=yes
```

7.16 Review Questions

1. Which *print* command option shows interface statistics in real-time?

    (a) *follow*

    (b) *monitor*

    (c) *print*

    (d) *blink*

2. What is the default duplex setting for ethernet interfaces?

    (a) Half

    (b) Full

    (c) Multi

    (d) Auto

3. What is the default MTU value for ethernet interfaces?

    (a) 1024

    (b) 1500

    (c) 1600

    (d) 1900

4. On most SOHO-oriented RouterBOARD models, which interface is designated as the master port under the default configuration?

    (a) ether4

    (b) ether3

    (c) ether2

    (d) ether1

5. What metric does POE use to determine which ports remain on in an over-current condition?

    (a) AD

    (b) Weight

    (c) Priority

    (d) MAC

6. The following commands are used:
```
/interface bridge
add name="LAN Bridge" comment="My bridge"
```
Which ports will be assigned by default to the new bridge?

   (a) None

   (b) ether1, ether2

   (c) LAN Bridge, ether1

   (d) LAN Bridge, ether2

7. What type of physical link has two SFP or SFP+ modules integrated into a high-speed connection?

   (a) NAC

   (b) CAC

   (c) MAC

   (d) DAC

8. What OSI layer do bridges operate on primarily?

   (a) Layer 1

   (b) Layer 2

   (c) Layer 3

   (d) Layer 4

9. Which type of interfaces allow 10 Gb fiber connections to CCR routers?

   (a) SFP+

   (b) SFP

   (c) MPCI

   (d) MPCI-E

10. Which type(s) of expansion module adds wireless network interfaces to a router?

    (a) MPCI

    (b) MPCI-E

    (c) DAC

    (d) SFP

7.17 Review Answers

1. Which *print* command option shows interface statistics in real-time?

   A – *follow* (p. 97)

2. What is the default duplex setting for ethernet interfaces?

   D – Auto (p. 95)

3. What is the default MTU value for ethernet interfaces?

   B – 1500 (p. 95)

4. On most SOHO-oriented RouterBOARD models, which interface is designated as the master port under the default configuration?

   C – ether2 (p. 98)

5. What metric does POE use to determine which ports remain on in an over-current condition?

   C – Priority (p. 100)

6. Which ports will be assigned by default to the new bridge?

   A – None (p. 105)

7. What type of physical link has two SFP or SFP+ modules integrated into a high-speed connection?

   D – DAC (p. 103)

8. What OSI layer do bridges operate on primarily?

   B – Layer 2 (p. 104)

9. Which type of interfaces allow 10 Gb fiber connections to CCR routers?

   A – SFP+ (p. 101)

10. Which type(s) of expansion module adds wireless network interfaces to a router?

    A and B – MPCI and MPCI-E (p. 103)

Chapter 8

Addresses

Whether you're assigning addresses dynamically or statically it's important to understand how they work, how to add them, and how to view assigned addresses. It's especially important to understand how subnetting works if you're in an environment like a WISP that has a lot of point-to-point connections between larger pools of customer addresses.

8.1 Static Addresses

Static IP addresses are easily added to physical and virtual interfaces. The following command is an example, adding *192.168.200.1/24* to interface *ether5*:

```
/ip address
add address=192.168.200.1/24 interface=ether5
```

Administrators who aren't comfortable enough with subnetting to use the Classless Inter-Domain Routing (CIDR) mask in the address can also specify the long-form subnet mask:

```
/ip address
add address=192.168.200.1 netmask=255.255.255.0 interface=ether5
```

Comments should always be added to IP addresses, particularly if addresses for both production and testing are in use:

```
/ip address
add address=192.168.200.1/24 interface=ether5 comment=DMZ
add address=192.168.17.1/24 interface=ether6 comment=Workbench
```

Multiple IP addresses can be added to the same interface. This is often done when an organization has been assigned a block of static public addresses and only given one hand-off from the upstream provider. The organization can then configure NATing from the public internet to internal Demilitarized Zone (DMZ) servers. The following commands add multiple public addresses from a /28 IP block to *ether1*:

```
/ip address
add address=172.16.195.17/28 interface=ether1 comment="HTTP Server"
add address=172.16.195.18/28 interface=ether1 comment="Email Server"
add address=172.16.195.19/28 interface=ether1 comment="CRM Server"
```

To view static addresses only the example command shown in Figure 8.1 uses "... *where !dynamic*" to filter results on a small lab router:

```
[admin@MikroTik] > /ip address print where !dynamic
Flags: X - disabled, I - invalid, D - dynamic
 #    ADDRESS            NETWORK          INTERFACE
 0    ;;; Production LAN
      192.168.88.1/24    192.168.88.0     bridge
 1    ;;; BGP Lab LAN
      192.168.1.2/24     192.168.1.0      ether5
[admin@MikroTik] > _
```

Figure 8.1: Printing Static Addresses

8.2 Dynamic Addresses with DHCP

With DHCP on RouterOS there is the typical enterprise functionality plus a few features that bring something extra. On the RouterOS platform DHCP can run in three roles:

- Server
- Client
- Relay

There is also the option to not run DHCP at all and instead leave that to another device like a Windows Active Directory Domain Controller (DC) or an ISC DHCP server.

8.2.1 DORA Exchange

DHCP works the same as on any other platform, with dynamic IP addresses requested and assigned via the *DORA* process:

- **D**iscovery (Client)
- **O**ffer (Server)
- **R**equest (Client)
- **A**cknowledge (Server)

First, clients send out a broadcast looking for DHCP servers. Second, any DHCP server receiving the broadcast will reply with an offer if addresses are available. Third, the client can then request an IP address that was offered. Finally, the DHCP server that received the request acknowledges the address has been set aside for that client. From this point on the client will use the assigned dynamic address until the lease expires. It's possible to see most the DORA process in the RouterOS log if DHCP logging is enabled with the following command:

```
/system logging add action=memory topics=dhcp
```

Be sure to disable or remove this configuration once you're done observing DHCP behavior on the device.

8.2.2 DHCP Server

To use a RouterOS device as a DHCP server there are three things that must be configured:

- Client IP Pool
- DHCP Network
- DHCP Server Instance

8.2.3 Client IP Pool

The client IP pool is simply a range of addresses that the DHCP server can assign to clients. RouterBoards are configured with a local IP address of 192.168.88.1/24 and an IP pool of *192.168.88.10-192.168.88.254*. The first client to request an address would be assigned 192.168.88.254/24, the next client 192.168.88.253/24, and so on. This will happen until either all clients have an address or the pool is exhausted.

It's possible to configure a secondary pool to prevent exhaustion, but proper network design and segmentation should prevent that from happening. Shortening the client address lease times can also help free up addresses in the pool. Use the following command to create an IP pool for DHCP clients to utilize:

```
/ip pool
add name=192.168.88.0 ranges=192.168.88.10-192.168.88.254
```

It's also possible to use multiple pools in a subnet and point one to another with the *next-pool* option. This helps when working around reserved IP addresses in the middle of a scope that cannot be changed for whatever reason. Use the following commands to create two pools and point the first to the second:

```
/ip pool
add name=192.168.88.10 ranges=192.168.88.10-192.168.88.100 next-pool
    =192.168.88.150
add name=192.168.88.150 ranges=192.168.88.150-192.168.88.254
```

There is one interesting thing to note about RouterOS DHCP servers - addresses are handed out in reverse order beginning at the *last address* in the pool. Most DHCP servers on other platforms either assign addresses randomly or start at the first address in the pool and count up. Functionally there is no difference in the order addresses are handed out. However, I note this here because some network administrators panic after seeing a lease at the end of the scope, thinking they've already run out of addresses when that isn't the case.

8.2.4 DHCP Networks

A DHCP network ties together settings like DNS servers, the gateway, NTP servers, and option sets that clients need. The first setting (*address*) ties network options to a subnet. For example, the following command fragment would configure options for the 192.168.88.0/24 network:

```
/ip dhcp-server network
add address=192.168.88.0/24...
```

Adding additional options makes the clients functional on a network. The following command configures the gateway address and DNS servers for clients on the 192.168.88.0 network:

```
/ip dhcp-server network
add address=192.168.88.0/24 dns-server=8.8.8.8,8.8.4.4 gateway=192.168.88.1
```

DHCP Server Instance

A DHCP instance runs on a physical or virtual interface and listens for client broadcasts. The DHCP instance brings together the IP pool already configured and the DHCP network. Add a DHCP server instance on interface *ether2*, and specify the *192.168.88.0 pool* with a lease time of *8 hours* using the following commands:

```
/ip dhcp-server
add interface=ether2 address-pool=192.168.88.0 lease-time=8h name=192.168.88.0
    disabled=no
```

Note the extra option and setting "*disabled=no*" which are required because by default DHCP instances are disabled unless otherwise set.

8.2.5 Leases

The default lease duration in up-to-date releases of RouterOS is ten minutes. This can easily be increased, though in the industry it's considered unusual to have DHCP leases longer than 24 hours. On networks with only a few IP addresses remaining in the pool having long lease times could cause address exhaustion when new devices are brought online. Having a shorter lease time allows addresses to "churn" more often in the pool and be free for other clients to use.

Once a client has been offered and accepted an address it will appear in the *DHCP Leases* list. RouterOS tracks the following information for leases:

1. The client IP address assigned
2. Client MAC address corresponding to the lease
3. Remaining lifetime of the address lease
4. Client hostname (if available)

Use the following command to view active DHCP leases on the router:

```
/ip dhcp-server lease print
```

Abbreviated CLI output of the "*/ip dhcp-server lease print*" command is shown in Figure 8.2:

```
[admin@MikroTik] > /ip dhcp-server lease print
Flags: X - disabled, R - radius, D - dynamic, B - blocked
#   ADDRESS           MAC-ADDRESS         HOST-NAME   SERVER    STATUS
0   192.168.88.151    AC:18:26:4B:02:4A   EPSON       defconf   bound
1 D 192.168.88.139    60:45:BD:51:85:08   xbox        defconf   bound
2 D 192.168.88.136    2C:0E:3D:11:CA:C9   Android     defconf   bound
3 D 192.168.88.253    74:C6:3B:64:05:89   Desktop     defconf   bound
4 D 192.168.88.148    E8:4E:06:43:FD:6B   Computer    defconf   bound
5 D 192.168.88.131    08:00:27:95:85:2B               defconf   bound
6 D 192.168.88.122    6C:AD:F8:32:30:AB   Chromecast  defconf   bound
7 D 192.168.88.121    CC:95:D7:00:3F:85               defconf   bound
8 D 192.168.88.120    2C:0E:3D:0F:6E:9B   Samsung     defconf   bound
9 D 192.168.88.119    BC:83:85:10:04:B6   Laptop      defconf   bound
[admin@MikroTik] > _
```

Figure 8.2: DHCP Leases

It's possible to make a lease static so every time a client with a particular MAC requests an address it will get the same address. In Winbox simply right-click on a lease and select "Make Static" as shown in Figure 8.3 on the next page:

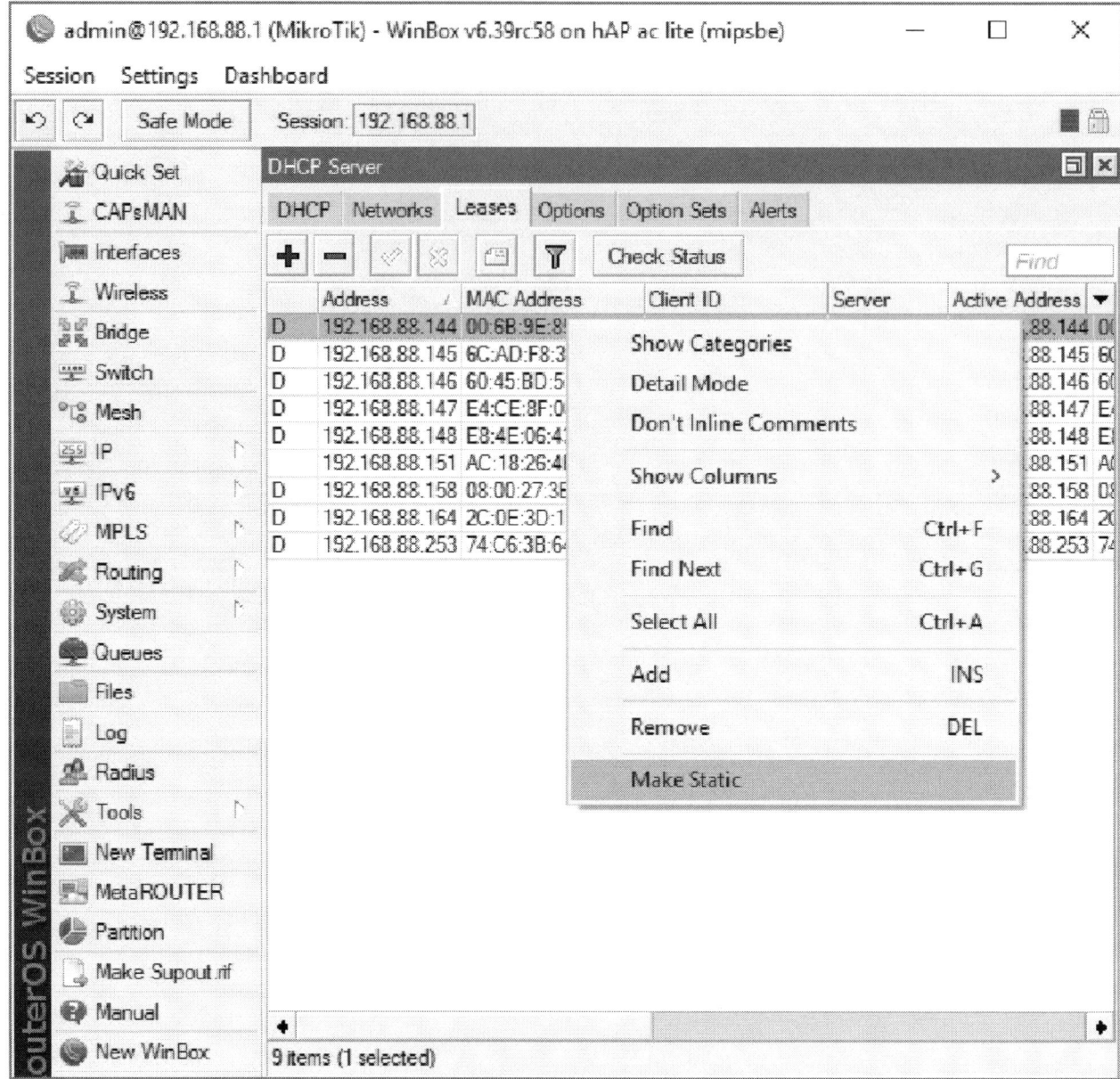

Figure 8.3: DHCP Make Static

> **NOTE**: Using static leases can be especially useful for printers. See page 122 for more information.

Marking a DHCP lease as static can be done at the command line as well. In this example the lease numbered as seven is set to static:

```
/ip dhcp-server lease make-static 7
```

To see all DHCP leases marked as static run the following command:

```
/ip dhcp-server lease print where !dynamic
```

> **NOTE**: The "!" symbol means "NOT" - this command could be read as "...lease print where NOT dynamic".

8.2.6 DHCP Options

DHCP Options set addressing and system details for DHCP clients. Every attribute assigned to DHCP clients is an option even if network administrators aren't aware of it. Most networking professionals are used to setting options like DNS servers and the gateway address but there are a lot more available. Not all clients can or do use all DHCP options. For example, Microsoft Windows clients don't use NTP options to automatically synchronize clocks even when the option is correctly set. Instead Microsoft Windows clients use Active Directory or static time options. A full list of options can be found in the Internet Engineering Task Force (IETF) RFC 2132 document at the following URL:

`https://tools.ietf.org/html/rfc2132`

The Internet Assigned Numbers Authority (IANA) also maintains a list of DHCP and Bootstrap Protocol (BOOTP) options at the following URL:

`https://www.iana.org/assignments/bootp-dhcp-parameters/bootp-dhcp-parameters.xhtml`

Some of the most common options include those in this list from Microsoft [5]:

- Option 1: Subnet mask
- Option 3: Router
- Option 6: DNS servers
- Option 15: Domain name
- Option 51: Lease time (seconds)

Using DHCP Options

To use DHCP options they first must be created then assigned to a DHCP server instance. Options can be assigned to an instance individually or they can be aggregated into sets. Two DHCP options are created in Figure 8.4 on the next page. The first options sets the NTP servers and the second sets the time zone:

```
[admin@MikroTik] > /ip dhcp-server option
[admin@MikroTik] /ip dhcp-server option> add name="pool.ntp.org" code="42"
   value="'0.pool.ntp.org,1.pool.ntp.org'"
[admin@MikroTik] /ip dhcp-server option> add name="Eastern Time" code="101"
   value="'America/New_York'"
[admin@MikroTik] > _
```

Figure 8.4: Creating DHCP Options

NOTE: Microsoft Windows clients do not use the NTP options specified and instead rely on Active Directory servers for accurate time updates. Setting the DHCP option will have no effect on workstations joined to a Windows domain.

8.2.7 Managing Static Addresses with DHCP

Once a network has grown beyond a certain point it becomes difficult to assign, change, and document static IP addresses. Considering the amount of routers, switches, printers, Wireless Access Points (WAPs), and more in a typical network the task can quickly get out of hand. Instead of entering static IP addresses on each device manually, an easier option is to let DHCP do it for you. Handing out static addresses with a protocol meant for dynamic addressing seems counter-intuitive but there are a few quick-wins that are easily recognized once you start using this strategy.

Pre-Staging IP Addresses

It's possible to pre-stage a device IP if you know the device's MAC address ahead of time. You can create a static DHCP reservation using the MAC, so when the device is plugged in it will immediately get the IP you want. Many vendors and Value-Added Resellers (VARs) will give you a list of serial numbers and MAC addresses prior to drop-shipping new devices to a location. This following example command reserves *192.168.88.119* for a printer with the MAC address *00:11:22:AA:BB:CC*:

```
/ip dhcp-server lease
add address=192.168.88.119 lease-time=8h mac-address=00:11:22:AA:BB:CC comment
   ="Accounting check printer"
```

Whenever that device is plugged in it will get an IP address of 192.168.88.119 with an 8 hour lease.

NOTE: Use descriptive comments to clearly identify address reservations and be specific. Comments like "Printer1", "Printer2", or "Printer26" aren't helpful long-term.

Limit Remote On-Site Trips

Pre-staging leases means you don't need a network administrator on-site to configure the IP address or network options. Simply have someone else plug the device in and DHCP will take care of the rest. This DHCP strategy can also save on shipping costs if devices would have to be sent via a main office first for configuration. The IP address of a device can also be changed easily with little or no downtime. Simply update the static DHCP reservation with the new address and the next renewal will push the change to the device.

Seamless Re-Addressing

Couple updated lease reservations with coordinated DNS record updates for the device and you can seamlessly re-IP devices on a network. It's possible to update other settings like DNS servers, the default gateway, NTP servers, and more without logging into the device. Just set the DHCP network options and either wait for the lease renewal or remotely reboot the device.

8.2.8 DHCP Client

MikroTik routers can be DHCP clients just as easily as servers. A DHCP client is normally configured when a router is pulling a dynamic IP and gateway from an upstream service provider. Some ISPs also hand out static IP addresses using DHCP, via a static lease using the client's MAC address. DHCP clients can be configured on a per-interface basis, with a few options to tune how routing occurs. The following command is used to add a DHCP client to interface *ether1*:

```
/ip dhcp-client
add interface=ether1 disabled=no comment="ISP WAN"
```

A boilerplate DHCP client is now configured that will pull down an IP address, gateway router IP, and DNS IP addresses. There are a few options that can be configured along with the interface and whether the client is disabled:

- *add-default-route*
- *use-peer-dns*
- *use-peer-ntp*

These three options are enabled by default, and being able to turn them off allows you to tune your DNS, NTP, and routing configuration to your needs. Having two DHCP clients with both setting a default route could obviously cause issues, so one client would most likely have "*add-default-route=no*" set. If you are using DNS servers other than those your ISP provides you can set "*use-peer-dns=no*" and configured your own instead. Figure 8.5 on the next page shows an active DHCP client and it's assigned options:

```
[admin@MikroTik] > /ip dhcp-client print detail
Flags: X - disabled, I - invalid
 0   ;;; defconf
     interface=ether1 add-default-route=yes default-route-distance=1 use-peer-
     dns=yes use-peer-ntp=yes dhcp-options=hostname,clientid status=bound
     address=a.b.c.d/x gateway=a.b.c.d dhcp-server=172.16.52.1/24 primary-dns
     =8.8.8.8 secondary-dns=8.8.4.4 expires-after=17h56m3s
[admin@MikroTik] > _
```

Figure 8.5: Active DHCP Client

8.3 Point-to-Point Addresses

For direct links between devices RouterOS supports two different types of IPv4 addressing.

- /30 addresses
- /32 addresses

The older and more typical /30 subnets can easily be used to create point-to-point networks. Unfortunately for each /30 network there are two "wasted" addresses for both the Network and Broadcast IPs. Using the older point-to-point addresses does have some advantages:

- Compatible with legacy network equipment
- No additional route entries are needed

8.3.1 Legacy /30 Addressing

Figure 8.6 shows a typical topology using 255.255.255.252 (/30) subnet masks. Each point-to-point link is its own subnet, complete with a network, host, and broadcast addresses.

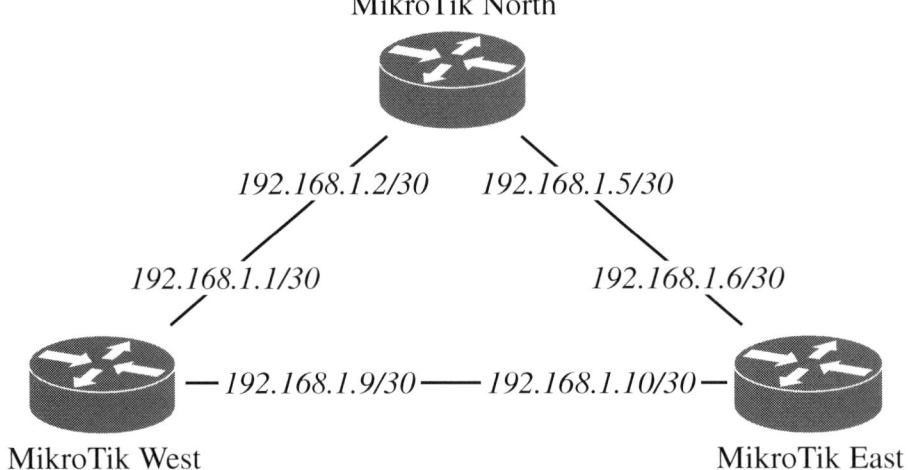

Figure 8.6: /30 Point-to-Point Addressing

No additional route entries are needed like in the following sections for one router to communicate with another across a link. However, the following IP addresses are "wasted" and can't be assigned to interfaces:

- Network Addresses: 192.168.1.0/30, 192.168.1.4/30, 192.168.1.8/30
- Broadcast Addresses: 192.168.1.3/30, 192.168.1.7/30, 192.168.1.11/30

8.3.2 Modern /32 Addressing

Usage of /32 IPs eliminates the "waste" of network and broadcast addresses in /30 networks. Unfortunately, this implementation requires additional administrative overhead for managing routes. An example network topology using /32 addresses is shown in Figure 8.7:

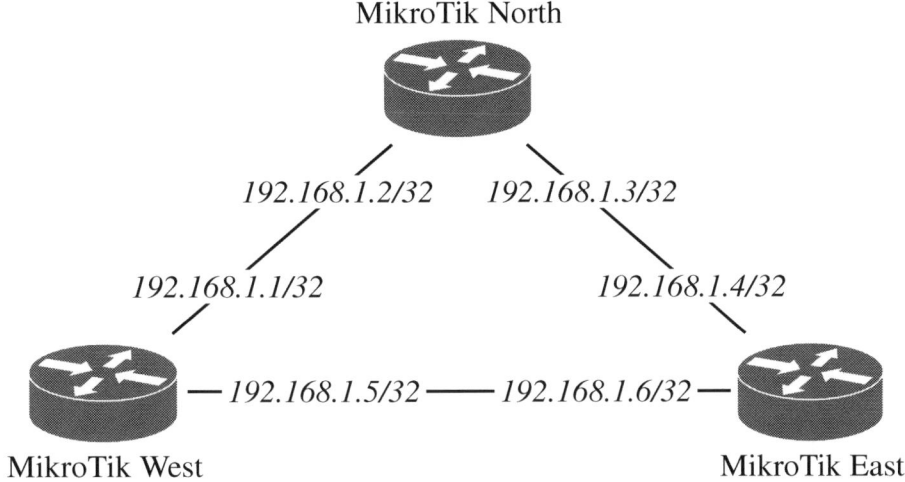

Figure 8.7: /32 Point-to-Point Addressing

Simply configuring the addresses on the interfaces isn't enough to make the /32 addressing work. Each router needs a route pointing to the other device IP via that interface. This can be accomplished via static route entries or dynamic routes via OSPF, RIP, or another routing protocol. The following commands implement the more address-efficient /32 addresses with static routes.

8.3.3 West Router Configuration

The link from West to North is on *ether1*. The link from West to East is on *ether2*. Add the IP addresses and routes with the following commands:

```
/ip address add interface=ether1 address=192.168.1.1/32
/ip address add interface=ether2 address=192.168.1.5/32
/ip route add dst-address=192.168.1.2 gateway=ether1
/ip route add dst-address=192.168.1.6 gateway=ether2
```

8.3.4 North Router Configuration

The link from North to West is on *ether1*. The link from North to East is on *ether2*. Add the IP addresses and routes with the following commands:

```
/ip address add interface=ether1 address=192.168.1.2/32
/ip address add interface=ether2 address=192.168.1.3/32
/ip route add dst-address=192.168.1.1 gateway=ether1
/ip route add dst-address=192.168.1.4 gateway=ether2
```

8.3.5 East Router Configuration

The link from East to North is on *ether1*. The link from East to West is on *ether2*. Add the IP addresses and routes with the following commands:

```
/ip address add interface=ether1 address=192.168.1.4/32
/ip address add interface=ether2 address=192.168.1.6/32
/ip route add dst-address=192.168.1.3 gateway=ether1
/ip route add dst-address=192.168.1.5 gateway=ether2
```

While this whole configuration required extra steps for routes it uses a total of six IP addresses instead of twelve. For an equivalent */30* configuration three IPs would have been used for a network address and another three for broadcast. Organizations that have a lot of point-to-point links like WISPs can realize substantial savings in addresses using */32* configurations.

8.4 MAC Addresses

Physical addressing at the OSI Data Link layer is done with MAC addresses. All physical interfaces having a globally unique address, each with six total hexadecimal octets. The first three octets are set aside for the Organizationally Unique Identifier (OUI) which identifies the manufacturer. The following MAC OUIs were registered by MikroTik with the Institute of Electrical and Electronics Engineers (IEEE) in late 2017[1]:

- 4C:5E:0C
- 64:D1:54
- 6C:3B:6B
- D4:CA:6D
- E4:8D:8C

[1]http://standards-oui.ieee.org/oui.txt

RouterOS can auto-generate random MAC addresses for virtual interfaces as they come online. ARP is used to resolve network layer protocol addresses to link layer addresses, most commonly in IPv4 networks. With IPv6 the mechanism is a bit different, and network layer to link layer resolution is done via Neighbor Discovery Protocol (NDP). Network clients, switches, and routers maintain a table of these IPv4-to-MAC relationships, most often known as the "ARP Table".

8.4.1 ARP Table

The ARP table contains IP and MAC addresses that the router has learned. These can be local interfaces on the router or remote clients on networks that the router is attached to. The entire ARP table can be printed, or the output filtered by interface using the following commands:

```
/ip arp
print
print where interface=bridge
```

An example of the first command output is shown in Figure 8.8. It can be especially useful to filter the ARP output by interface when your network has hundreds or thousands of hosts. Depending on the model and resources assigned to a RouterOS device the maximum amount of addresses in the ARP table can differ. However, RouterOS documentation [11] states the following:

"Note: Maximal number of ARP entries is 8192."

8.4.2 ARP for Inventory

Printing the ARP table can be helpful when doing device inventory. Use the "*/ip arp print*" command to print the ARP table as shown in Figure 8.8 (output trimmed for brevity):

```
[admin@MikroTik] > /ip arp print
1 DC 192.168.88.147    E4:CE:8F:08:29:5E bridge
2 DC 192.168.88.148    E8:4E:06:43:FD:6B bridge
...
7 DC 192.168.1.1       80:2A:A8:1D:43:D8 ether5
8 DC 1.2.3.1           E0:2F:6D:6D:6E:D9 ether1
[admin@MikroTik] > _
```

Figure 8.8: ARP Table

It's also possible to export the ARP table to a text file for inventory purposes:

```
/ip arp
print detail file=arp_inventory.txt
```

Download the *arp_inventory.txt* file that's generated and open it in a robust text editor like Notepad++ or Microsoft Visual Studio Code. Use that MAC information in the text file to support your inventory program.

8.4.3 Finding MACs by OUI

One of the OUIs registered to VMware® is "00:50:56", so any MAC starting with that OUI could be a virtual machine running on a VMware hypervisor. That device could also be a virtual network switch as well. It's possible to search the MAC address table by OUI using a Regular Expression (Regex) string as shown in the following command:

```
/ip arp
print where mac-address~"^00:50:56"
```

Using the same command with MAC OUI *6C:3B:6B* will identify RouterBoard interfaces. It's important to remember that multiple MACs could belong to the same physical RouterBoard; Just because three addresses are in the ARP table there aren't necessarily three separate units attached to the network.

> **NOTE**: The tilde character indicates this is a Regex-type search, and the carat character is the symbol for "starts with ...".

8.4.4 ARP Modes

ARP requests are limited to the broadcast domain in which they originate. ARP requests aren't forwarded outside a broadcast domain and the router only answers ARP queries if it has the entry in its ARP table. When configuring ARP in RouterOS there are other modes you should be aware of as well:

- Disabled
- Proxy ARP
- Local Proxy ARP
- Reply Only

8.4.5 Disabled

In *Disabled* mode the router will not respond to any ARP request received on an interface with this setting. This can be useful on interfaces that are attached to a network segment and used to "sniff" traffic transparently.

```
/interface ethernet
set arp=proxy-arp ether2
set arp=proxy-arp ether3
```

8.4.6 Proxy ARP

Proxy ARP is useful when clients on separate networks need to be able to ARP for a MAC address in another subnet. When the router sees an ARP request in one network for a MAC it knows about in another the router answers with its own MAC address. The router then forwards traffic destined for the MAC on the other network. This process is transparent to the client that originally sent the ARP request.

> **NOTE**: Be aware that implementing Proxy ARP can increase ARP traffic on the network and may have unintended consequences. Other devices on the network with smaller ARP caches may not be able to handle the larger amount of address entries.

For an example of Proxy ARP consider the topology in Figure 8.9 where *192.168.1.2* needs to ARP for *192.168.2.2*:

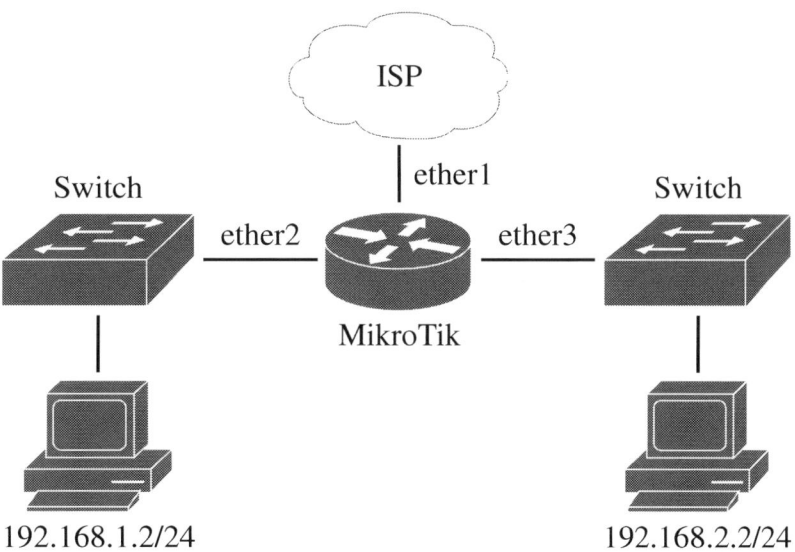

Figure 8.9: Proxy ARP

To enable Proxy ARP on interfaces *ether2* and *ether3* use the following commands: When *192.168.1.2* sends an ARP request to the broadcast MAC address *FF:FF:FF:FF:FF:FF* querying "Who has *192.168.2.2*?" the router will answer *with its own MAC address*. As traffic flows from *192.168.1.2* to *192.168.2.2* the router acts as the "middle-man" forwarding traffic across networks it's attached to. There are a few scenarios where using this type of "work-around" is necessary:

- When devices in different networks need Layer 2 reachability because of legacy software limitations

- If versions of hypervisors in use require Layer 2 communications between physical hosts for VM replication

8.4.7 Reply Only

In *Reply Only* mode the router will reply to an ARP broadcast if it has an answer in its ARP table. If the router doesn't have a good answer it simply won't reply. To operate in this mode technicians may have to configure static ARP entries for local devices on the router as shown below:

```
/ip arp
add mac-address=00:11:22:aa:bb:cc address=192.168.88.2 interface=ether3
```

8.5 Wake on LAN

Being familiar with MAC addresses and methods of extending ARP allows for interesting uses of WOL. The WOL tool sends a "magic packet"[2] to a MAC address and wakes up the host if that feature is enabled on the host's network interface. The following command wakes up a host with the MAC address *0A:1B:2C:3D:4E:5F* via *ether2*:

```
/tool wol interface=ether2 mac=0A:1B:2C:3D:4E:5F
```

This tool is not listed under any Winbox or Webfig menus as of mid-2017, though it is available from the terminal. Using WOL to remotely boot up hosts can help computers stay updated with the latest patches and antivirus updates, even if the host's primary user is away for days or weeks. Once the hosts are updated an administrator can power them down again remotely via SSH, PowerShell, or other third party management tools.

8.6 DNS and Name Records

RouterOS can run both DNS servers and clients. On RouterBOARD units or virtual CHRs with a DHCP client running on the default WAN interface much of the DNS configuration is already done. The router will automatically use the upstream DNS servers dynamically assigned for name resolution. Router-initiated lookups for domain names could happen while doing the following:

- Locating MikroTik update servers
- Pinging well-known domain names for troubleshooting
- Resolving IP addresses for domain names used in address lists

---

[2] https://wiki.wireshark.org/WakeOnLAN

If a RouterOS device is not configured to receive dynamic addresses it takes very little effort to manually configure DNS servers. The following commands set the router to use Google's public[3] DNS servers [4] for name resolution:

```
/ip dns set servers=8.8.8.8,8.8.4.4
```

Upstream DNS servers provided by an ISP or other provider can also be used. It's always a good idea to specify multiple upstream DNS servers if possible to prevent a loss of name resolution if one server goes down.

8.6.1 RouterOS DNS Server

To allow the router itself to be used as a DNS server the *"allow-remote-requests=yes"* option must be set. Figure 8.10 shows a RouterOS instance with both static and dynamic DNS servers configured and remote requests enabled:

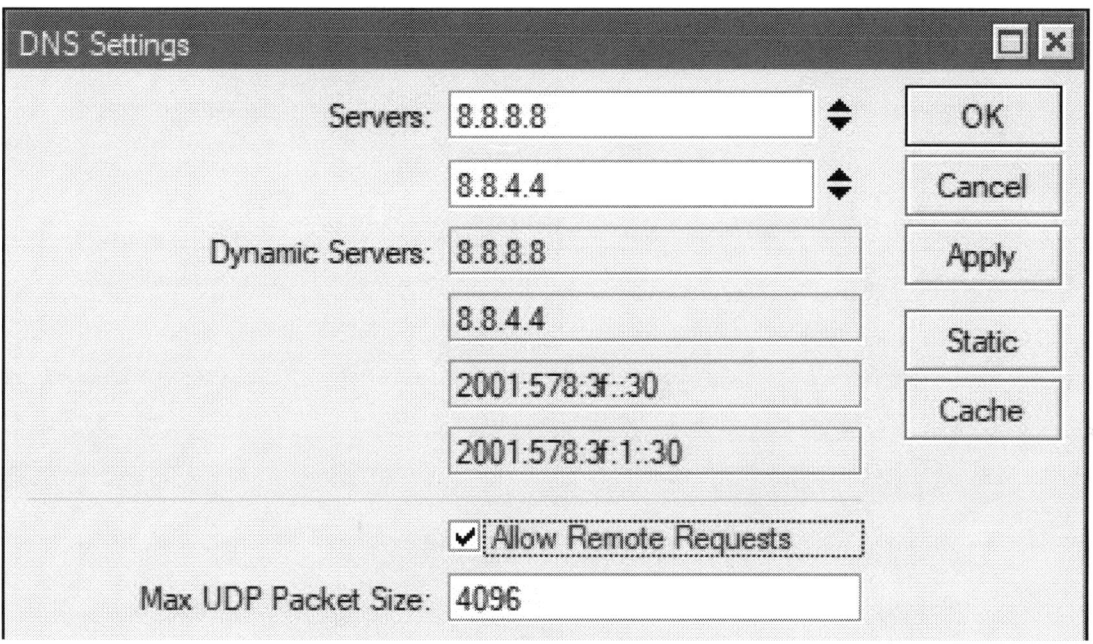

Figure 8.10: DNS Allow Remote Requests

Once this setting is in place the router will answer name resolution queries on its own if it has a valid cached record. If a cached record isn't available for a given domain it will forward the request to an upstream server already configured in the previous steps. The following command allows a RouterOS device to operate as a DNS server:

```
/ip dns
set servers=8.8.8.8,8.8.4.4 allow-remote-requests=yes
```

---

[3]https://developers.google.com/speed/public-dns/

> **WARNING**: Unsecured DNS servers that allow remote queries from the internet can be co-opted into DNS Amplification DDoS attacks. Double-check firewall rules on public-facing network interfaces before enabling this feature.

If the "*allow-remote-requests=yes*" option is set it's important to specify the upstream name resolver servers and periodically audit them. If someone is able to change the configured DNS servers they could hijack network traffic and steal login credentials. The Infrastructure Router STIG [1, Vul. ID V-3020] states the following about configuring DNS servers:

> "*Review the device configuration to ensure DNS servers have been defined if it has been configured as a client resolver (name lookup). If the device is configured as a client resolver and DNS servers are not defined, this is a finding.*"

As users inside the network perform name lookups via the RouterOS device those records will be cached locally until their Time To Live (TTL) expires. In Winbox click the *Cache* button under *IP > DNS* to see cached name records. This local caching can result in faster name resolution for local users. Cached entries for some example websites are shown in Figure 8.11:

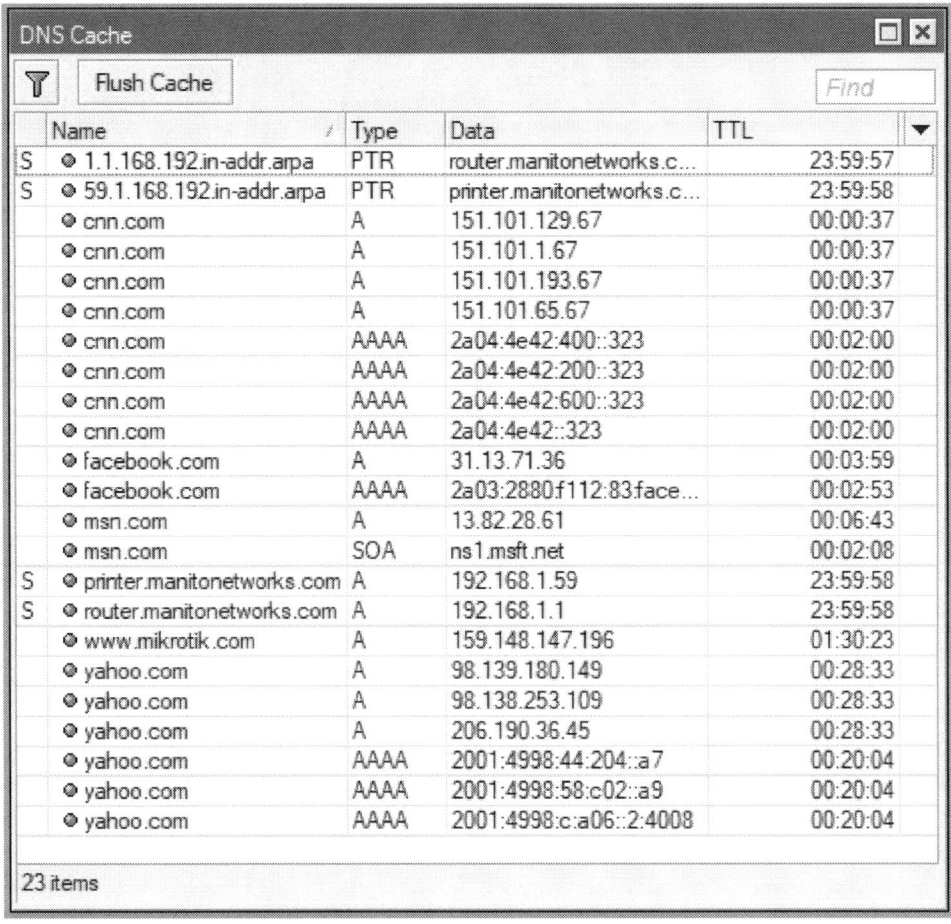

Figure 8.11: Local DNS Cache

To view cached entries via the terminal use the "*ip dns cache print*" command. For a list of all records, including Pointers (PTRs) for reverse lookups, use the "/ip dns cache all print" command. To flush entries in the cache use the following command:

```
/ip dns cache flush
```

Unfortunately as of this writing it's not possible to flush individual entries, either via the console or another interface like Winbox. The example in Figure 8.11 on the previous page includes two entries that were created statically for *printer.manitonetworks.com* and *router.manitonetworks.com*. To create a static entry use a command like the following:

```
/ip dns
static add name=web.manitonetworks.com address=192.168.1.66
```

8.7 Review Questions

1. Multiple IP addresses can be added to the same Ethernet interface.

    (a) True

    (b) False

2. Which CIDR masks can be used for point-to-point IPv4 connections?

    (a) /30

    (b) /31

    (c) /32

    (d) /33

3. MAC addresses use which type of numbering?

    (a) Binary

    (b) Base-10

    (c) Dotted Decimal

    (d) Hexadecimal

4. In each /30 network there are two "wasted" IP addresses.

    (a) True

    (b) False

5. What is the third step in the DHCP request process?

    (a) Acknowledge

    (b) Request

    (c) Offer

    (d) Discover

6. How can administrators force dynamic addresses to always be assigned to the same client?

    (a) Create a reservation

    (b) Extend the lease duration

    (c) Configure additional DHCP servers

    (d) Set a static address on the client

7. How many sets of numbers make up a MAC address OUI?

    (a) Two

    (b) Three

    (c) Four

    (d) Five

8. Creating a DHCP _____ ensures a client receives the same address all the time.

    (a) Relay

    (b) Adjacency

    (c) Reservation

    (d) Advertisement

9. Which table contains MAC addresses and their associated IPs?

    (a) Routing table

    (b) ARP table

    (c) RIB

    (d) NAT table

10. Which DHCP option specifies the router address?

    (a) 3

    (b) 2

    (c) 1

    (d) 15

8.8 Review Answers

1. Multiple IP addresses can be added to the same Ethernet interface.

   A – True (p. 115)

2. Which CIDR masks can be used for point-to-point IPv4 connections?

   A and C – /30 and /32 (p. 124)

3. MAC addresses use which type of numbering?

   D – Hexadecimal (p. 126)

4. In each /30 network there are two "wasted" IP addresses.

   A – True (p. 124)

5. What is the third step in the DHCP request process?

   B – Request (p. 116)

6. How can administrators force dynamic addresses to always be assigned to the same client?

   A – Create a reservation (p. 122)

7. How many sets of numbers make up a MAC address OUI?

   B – Three (p. 126)

8. Creating a DHCP _____ ensures a client receives the same address all the time.

   C – Reservation (p. 119)

9. Which table contains MAC addresses and their associated IPs?

   B – ARP table (p. 127)

10. Which DHCP option specifies the router address?

    A – 3 (p. 121)

Chapter 9

Routing

Routing is the science (and art) of moving packets and data from one network to another. Routers join networks together and enable the exchange of information inside organizations and around the world. Remember that routers sit at the edge of networks and connect them to one another, forming an inter-network routed path. When large routed networks like those of universities, governments, and ISPs come together they form the largest network ever created - the Internet.

Static routes are put in place manually be administrators. Dynamic routes are put in the routing table by routing protocols like OSPF, Enhanced Interior Gateway Routing Protocol (EIGRP), and BGP.

9.1 Routes

A route is simply a path from one network to another. Routes can point the way to a specific host, or to an entire network range. When traffic arrives destined for another network the router consults its routing table. Based on what's in the table the router makes a decision about what to do with the traffic. The routing decision can also take into account routing policies as well as the Administrative Distance (AD) (p. 138). Different types of routes exist in a RouterOS routing table:

- Static
- Dynamic
- Default
- Blackhole
- Prohibit
- Unreachable

To view routes in a device's routing table run the "*/ip route print*" command shown in Figure 9.1 on the next page:

```
[admin@MikroTik] > /ip route print
Flags: X - disabled, A - active, D - dynamic, C - connect, S - static, r - rip
    , b - bgp, o - ospf, m - mme, B - blackhole, U - unreachable, P - prohibit
 #      DST-ADDRESS        PREF-SRC         GATEWAY         DISTANCE
 0 ADS  0.0.0.0/0                           192.168.1.1     1
 1 ADC  192.168.1.0/24     192.168.1.38     bridge          0
 2 A S  192.168.10.1/32                     bridge          1
 3 ADC  192.168.10.2/32    192.168.10.2     bridge          0
[admin@MikroTik] > _
```

Figure 9.1: Listing Routes

9.2 Administrative Distance

The AD of each type of route is the measure of its reliability. Routes to the same destination will have their ADs compared and the route with the lowest AD will be selected. If multiple routes exist for the same destination with the same ADs the router will make an arbitrary choice of which to use[1]. If the first route drops off for whatever reason the second identical route will be moved to an *active* state.

Table 9.1 shows the default ADs for mainstream routing protocols. Protocols not supported by MikroTik like EIGRP and Intermediate System to Intermediate System (IS-IS) are included solely for comparison.

Route Type	Administrative Distance
Connected	0
Static	1
EIGRP Summary	5
External BGP	20
Internal EIGRP	90
IGRP	100
OSPF (All versions)	110
IS-IS	115
RIP (All versions)	120
EGP	140
ODR	160
External EIGRP	170
Internal BGP	200
Unknown & Blackhole	255

Table 9.1: Default Administrative Distances

---

[1] https://wiki.mikrotik.com/wiki/Manual:IP/Route#Route_selection

9.3 Static Routes

Routes that have been entered manually by a network administrator are *static*. These could be routes pointing to a default gateway using ISP-provided information, or a route to the other side of a VPN tunnel. Since these routes were entered manually they have one of the lowest ADs, second only to directly connected routes. The following command creates a static route, telling the router to send any traffic destined for 192.168.10.0/24 via 10.1.20.1:

```
/ip route
add dst-address=192.168.10.0/24 gateway=10.1.20.1
```

View all static routes with the following command:

```
/ip route print where static
```

Unless the *"distance=..."* option is specified all static routes will have a default distance of one. Adding a route with *"distance=255"* automatically blackholes traffic matching the route (see *Blackhole Routes* on p. 143). Creating the same route with different distances can be useful for failover. To achieve this use different AD values with the lowest being the most desirable and used first. Figure 9.2 shows static routes in place on both routers, pointing to networks across a site-to-site tunnel:

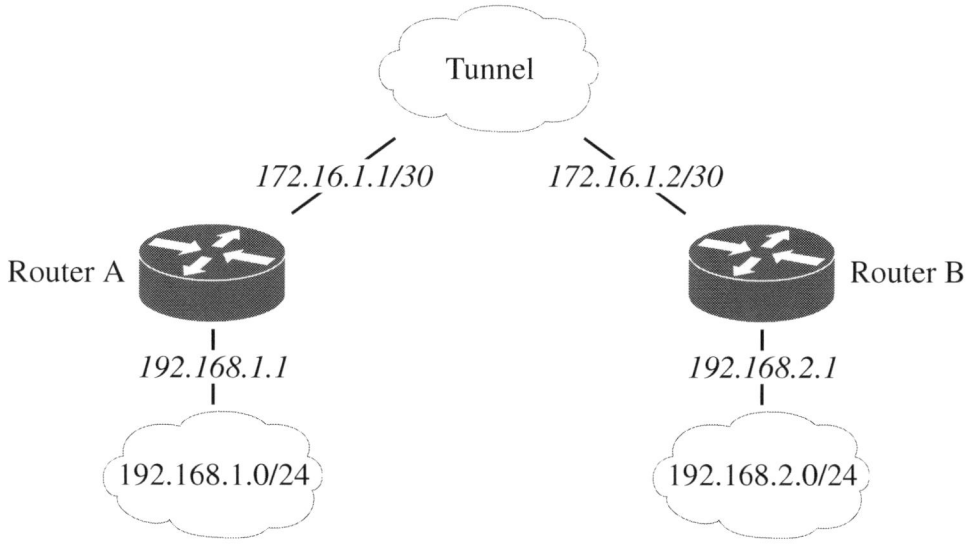

Figure 9.2: Static Route Topology

The following command on Router A points all traffic for *192.168.2.0/24* to the *172.16.1.2* gateway:

```
/ip route add dst-address=192.168.2.0/24 gateway=172.16.1.2
```

The following command on Router B points all traffic for *192.168.1.0/24* to the *172.16.1.1* gateway:

```
/ip route add dst-address=192.168.1.0/24 gateway=172.16.1.1
```

Static routes work very well for networks that don't change much and don't contain more than a handful of networks. As the number of networks grow or the topology becomes more dynamic it's necessary to implement dynamic routing.

9.4 Dynamic Routes

Dynamic routes are entered into the routing table via a routing protocol like RIP, BGP, or OSPF. These protocols allow routers and switches that run routing processes to exchange routes and build a table of which devices are connected to what networks. MikroTik supports a number of dynamic routing protocols, including the following:

- OSPF
- OSPF v3
- RIP
- RIPng
- BGP
- Mesh Made Easy (MME)

These protocols are covered as part of other certification tracks and aren't part of the MTCNA. Be aware that you'll most likely encounter both static and dynamic routing protocols in typical enterprise networks. OSPF is covered in the MikroTik Certified Routing Engineer (MTCRE), and BGP is included in the MikroTik Certified Inter-Networking Engineer (MTCINE). As a quick OSPF primer, however, I'm including the following configuration using the same topology in Figure 9.2 on the previous page.

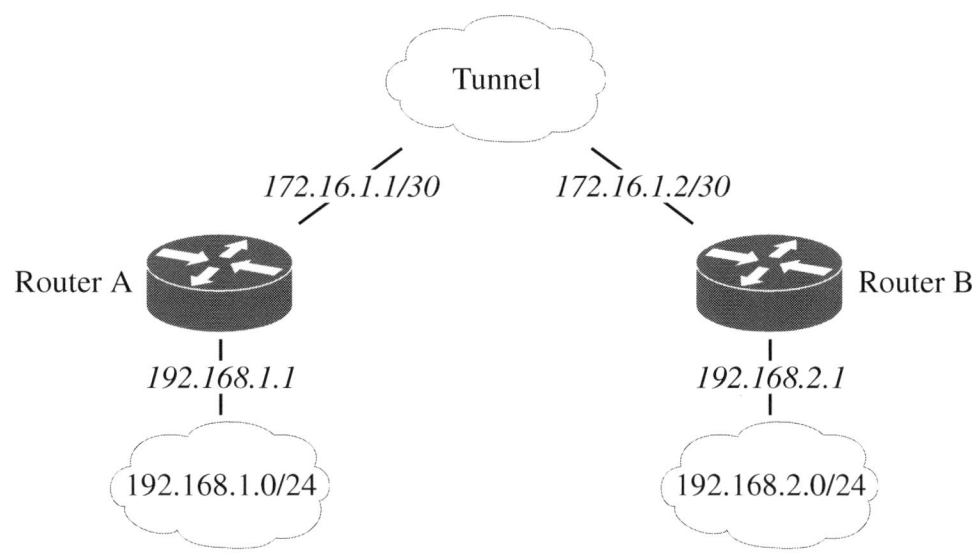

Figure 9.3: Dynamic Route Topology

This is a very simple OSPF configuration that puts all networks in the same OSPF Area[2]. The following commands on Router A advertise its connection to the LAN and tunnel subnets:

```
/routing ospf
network add area=backbone network=172.16.1.0/30 comment=Tunnel
network add area=backbone network=192.168.1.0/24 comment=LAN
```

The following commands on Router B advertise its connection to the LAN and tunnel subnets:

```
/routing ospf
network add area=backbone network=172.16.1.0/30 comment=Tunnel
network add area=backbone network=192.168.2.0/24 comment=LAN
```

Both routers A and B advertise the same network for the tunnel because they are both connected to it. This allows the routers to become OSPF Neighbors. Once they establish this relationship then they can exchange information about the other networks they are connected to. This is a very bare-bones OSPF configuration, but hopefully it's enough to interest you in OSPF routing and the MTCRE.

9.5 Default Routes

A default route is a static route that's designed as a "catch-all" for traffic that doesn't match anything in the routing table. Often a default route points upstream to an ISP's gateway, or to a router running OSPF or BGP with more learned routes in its table. That upstream router or other device *hopefully* knows where traffic should be going and passes it along. Routers hand-off traffic upstream until the destination is reached or the packet's TTL is exceeded[3].

---

[2] Area 0 is always the backbone Area number.
[3] ICMP Type 11 - Time Exceeded[2]

9.5. DEFAULT ROUTES

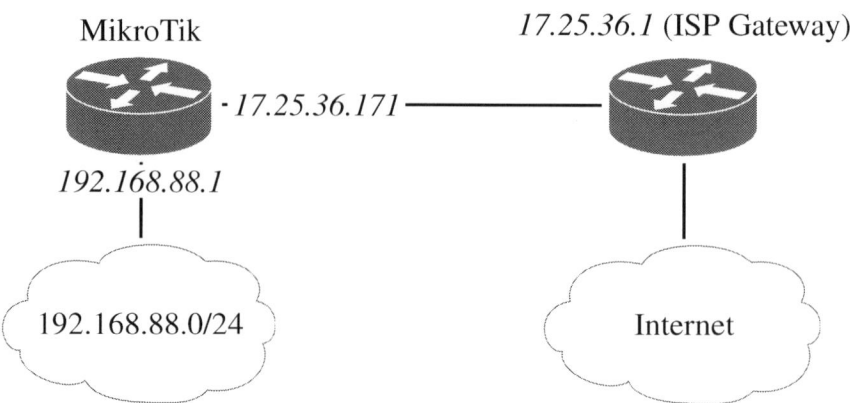

Figure 9.4: Default Route

The following command creates a default route for the network shown in Figure 9.4, telling the router to send any traffic that doesn't match a route to *17.25.36.1*:

```
/ip route add dst-address=0.0.0.0/0 gateway=17.25.36.1
```

The special *"dst-address=0.0.0.0/0"* option matches all traffic for all hosts or networks. Traffic that doesn't have a more specific match in the routing table will always match this criteria. Clients in the *192.168.88.0/24* network have their default gateway set to the MikroTik router at *192.168.88.1*. When *192.168.88.1* receives packets from local computers destined for networks it doesn't have in its routing table it uses the default gateway to send traffic upstream. Each upstream router that receives this traffic will route it directly to its destination or send it via a default route again. This happens until the traffic reaches its destination or the TTL is exceeded.

Without a default route configured, packets destined for a network not in the routing table would simply be dropped. The sending host would then receive a "No route to host" ICMP reply. Multiple gateways can be entered if you have more than one upstream ISP for redundancy. Simply enter the gateway addresses in a comma-separated list as follows:

```
/ip route
add dst-address=0.0.0.0/0 gateway=17.25.36.1,132.45.76.1
```

If you want to prefer one gateway over another modify the route distance for each. Routes with the lowest ADs will be used first. If those routes go offline the next-lowest will be used, and so on:

```
/ip route
add dst-address=0.0.0.0/0 gateway=a.b.c.d distance=1
add dst-address=0.0.0.0/0 gateway=w.x.y.z distance=2
```

Once all default gateways have been configured they can be viewed in more detail with the command in Figure 9.5 on the following page:

```
[admin@MikroTik] > /ip route nexthop print
0 address=192.168.1.1 gw-state=reachable forwarding-nexthop="" interface=""
  scope=10 check-gateway=none
[admin@MikroTik] > _
```

Figure 9.5: Print Route Nexthops

The RouterBOARD used in this example is behind another router whose address is *192.168.1.1*, so that's the current gateway. Configuration of route scopes is beyond the MTCNA outline, but be aware that the default scope value for typical routes is ten.

9.6 Blackhole Routes

Undesirable traffic can be filtered by the firewall but in some cases that's not the most efficient use of resources. "Blackholing" traffic with the use of a special route is less resource-intensive and easy to implement. A blackhole route is basically a "route to nowhere", and any traffic matching the route is discarded (or "shunted") by the router. This can be very useful when dealing with traffic floods or DDoS attacks that would otherwise overwhelm a router's firewall. Large ISPs regularly deploy automated blackhole routes to their networks to shunt DDoS attacks before they can hit the subscriber and affect network stability for everyone else. Inside organizations, blackhole routes can also be used to shunt outbound traffic from infected hosts that have been looped into a botnet or spamming campaign. The following command would cause all traffic with the destination address *1.2.3.4* to be discarded while containing a virus infection:

```
/ip route add type=blackhole dst-address=1.2.3.4
```

Figure 9.6 shows the result of a ping to the IP *1.2.3.4* with a blackhole route in place:

```
PS C:\Users\Tyler> ping 1.2.3.4

Pinging 1.2.3.4 with 32 bytes of data:
Reply from 192.168.1.1: Destination net unreachable.
Reply from 192.168.1.1: Destination net unreachable.
Reply from 192.168.1.1: Destination net unreachable.
Reply from 192.168.1.1: Destination net unreachable.

Ping statistics for 1.2.3.4:
Packets: Sent = 4, Received = 4, Lost = 0 (0% loss)
```

Figure 9.6: Blackhole Route Ping Result

The router at *192.168.1.1* responds directly to the host sending the ping that the network is unreachable. The packet statistics show zero percentage loss because each ping got a reply, but it was an ICMP reply from the router instead of *1.2.3.4*. A traceroute to the *1.2.3.4* address stops at the router and eventually dies at 30 hops. Some organizations that block certain websites on their network will use DNS records on internal name resolvers pointing to a blackholed address. This isn't a fool-proof way to block websites but it typically does a good enough job for zero cost. The following commands implement this type of filtering for "*badspamsite.com*":

```
/ip dns static
add name=badspamsite.com address=172.16.0.254 comment="Blackhole address"

/ip route
add type=blackhole dst-address=172.16.0.254 comment="Blackhole route"
```

The static DNS record associates that domain name with an IP address set aside in the organization as a blackhole destination. The blackhole route then uses that IP address to shunt all traffic to that destination. Multiple domain names can have records added with that same IP address.

9.7 Prohibit Routes

A route of this type behaves like a blackhole route, but the ICMP responses to the sender will state the destination is "administratively prohibited"[4]. This type of route isn't commonly used, as most administrators prefer to not give attackers information about the operations of their networks or traffic filtering mechanisms.

9.8 Route States

Routes can be in one or more states, depending on whether they are configured correctly, are duplicates or redundant, or have a higher or lower cost than another. A number of route states exist in RouterOS:

- Active
- Connected
- Disabled
- Unreachable

---
[4]ICMP Type 3, Code 13, "Communication Administratively Prohibited"

9.8.1 Active

An active route in the routing table can be used to forward traffic. Its gateway is reachable and no other route supersedes it. To view all active routes use the command in Figure 9.7 on the following page:

```
[admin@MikroTik] > /ip route print where active
Flags: X - disabled, A - active, D - dynamic, C - connect, S - static, r - rip
    , b - bgp, o - ospf, m - mme, B - blackhole, U - unreachable, P - prohibit
 #      DST-ADDRESS         PREF-SRC         GATEWAY            DISTANCE
 0 ADS  0.0.0.0/0                            192.168.1.1               1
 1 ADC  192.168.1.0/24      192.168.1.38     bridge                    0
 2 A S  192.168.10.1/32                      bridge                    1
[admin@MikroTik] > _
```

Figure 9.7: Printing Active Routes

9.8.2 Connected

A connected route is a route for a network that the router has a direct connection to. This could be a physical network attached to an Ethernet or SFP port, or a virtual network created by a GRE or EoIP tunnel interface. The command in Figure 9.8 prints routes that have a direct connection to the router itself:

```
[admin@MikroTik] > /ip route print where connect
Flags: X - disabled, A - active, D - dynamic, C - connect, S - static, r - rip
    , b - bgp, o - ospf, m - mme, B - blackhole, U - unreachable, P - prohibit
 #      DST-ADDRESS         PREF-SRC         GATEWAY            DISTANCE
 0 ADC  192.168.1.0/24      192.168.1.38     bridge                    0
[admin@MikroTik] > _
```

Figure 9.8: Printing Connected Routes

The example uses the same router as in Figure 9.7, but in that example only one network is directly connected. That's why only one out of the three appears in Figure 9.8.

9.8.3 Disabled

A disabled route is in the routing table but not available for lookups. Other states like *unreachable* do not apply to disabled routes, though they may when the route becomes *active*. View all disabled routes with the following command:

```
/ip route print where disabled
```

9.8.4 Unreachable

An unreachable route could be configured perfectly but the router can't reach specified gateway. A default route pointing to an ISP's gateway would become unreachable if the ISP's link was powered off on their side, or if a cable was disconnected or cut. This isolates the router from any upstream gateways, making the route unreachable. RouterOS will not prevent you from creating this kind of route if you enter the wrong gateway address. However, until it's corrected no traffic will use the route. Sending hosts using the incorrect route will receive an ICMP reply[5] stating that the destination is unreachable.

9.9 Check Gateway

The *check-gateway* option for a route configures the router to regularly test if a gateway is still reachable. This function can use two different protocols to check the gateway's reachability:

1. ICMP
2. ARP

Some service providers filter ICMP traffic addressed directly for their gateway interfaces. For this reason it may be necessary to choose the ARP protocol option. The check is done every ten seconds regardless of the protocol selected. Once the check fails twice the route will be flagged as unreachable [13].

9.10 Source Routing

A long-time feature of the Internet Protocol is Source Routing. This feature allows the sending host to specify the route that traffic will take to its destination. The source routing functionality is great for troubleshooting and traffic shaping, but it can also be used in network attacks to get around firewalls and proxies. For this reason almost all compliance standards require that source routing requests be disregarded by network routers. The Infrastructure Router STIG [1, Vul. ID V-3081] states the following about how to handle source routing:

> "Review the configuration to determine if source routing is disabled. If IP source routing is enabled, this is a finding."

Use the following command to disable source routing in RouterOS:

```
/ip settings set accept-source-route=no
```

While the topic of source routing is not part of the official MTCNA outline, it's a common audit hit for many organizations. Fortunately, the one-line command fix is very simple, and it's easy to avoid this compliance trip-up.

---

[5]ICMP Type 3, Code 1, "Host Unreachable"

9.11 Review Questions

1. Which type of route is typically put into the routing table by a software process?

    (a) Dynamic

    (b) Static

    (c) Active

    (d) Blackhole

2. What will a route become when the connection to its gateway is lost?

    (a) Invalid

    (b) Blackhole

    (c) Prohibit

    (d) Unreachable

3. Two static routes for *10.10.10.0/24* are configured by an administrator:

    ```
    /ip route
    add dst-address=10.10.10.0/24 gateway=172.16.1.2/30 distance=1
    add dst-address=10.10.10.0/24 gateway=172.16.1.6/30 distance=2
    ```

    Which gateway will be used first if both gateways are reachable?

    (a) 172.16.1.2

    (b) 172.16.1.6

    (c) 172.16.1.1

    (d) 172.16.1.5

4. Static routes have a lower AD than Connected routes.

    (a) True

    (b) False

5. Which type of route will force a router to silently discard traffic to a destination address?

    (a) Prohibit

    (b) Unreachable

    (c) Blackhole

    (d) Dynamic

6. Which route option makes a router regularly verify a gateway is still online?

    (a) *ping-gateway*

    (b) *check-gateway*

    (c) *arp-gateway*

    (d) *verify-gateway*

7. A route entered into the table by RouterOS for a dynamic tunnel that's being used to route traffic will have which flags set?

    (a) AC

    (b) AS

    (c) AD

    (d) SD

8. Which type of route will force a router to discard traffic to a destination address and return an ICMP message to the sender?

    (a) Prohibit

    (b) Unreachable

    (c) Blackhole

    (d) Dynamic

9. The following commands are entered:
```
/ip route
add dst-address=0.0.0.0/0 gateway=17.25.36.1,132.45.76.1
```

    What distance value will be automatically assigned to the route?

    (a) 0

    (b) 1

    (c) 5

    (d) 10

10. An OSPF route will be chosen before a RIP route for the same given source and destination addresses.

    (a) True

    (b) False

9.12 Review Answers

1. Which type of route is typically put into the routing table by a software process?

    A – Dynamic (p. 140)

2. What will a route become when the connection to its gateway is lost?

    D – Unreachable (p. 146)

3. Which gateway will be used first if both gateways are reachable?

    A – 172.16.1.2 (p. 142)

4. Static routes have a lower AD than Connected routes.

    B – False (p. 138)

5. Which type of route will force a router to silently discard traffic to a destination address?

    C – Blackhole (p. 143)

6. Which route option makes a router regularly verify a gateway is still online?

    B – *check-gateway* (p. 146)

7. A route entered into the table by RouterOS for a dynamic tunnel that's being used to route traffic will have which flags set?

    C – AD (p. 144 and p. 140)

8. Which type of route will force a router to discard traffic to a destination address and return an ICMP message to the sender?

    A – Prohibit (p. 144)

9. What distance value will be automatically assigned to the route?

    B – 1 (p. 138)

10. An OSPF route will be chosen before a RIP route for the same given source and destination addresses.

    A – True (p. 138)

Chapter 10

VPNs and Tunnels

Having local networks that work well is great, but being able to combine networks allows technology to be leveraged even more. RouterOS is unique in the number of VPN and tunnel types it supports, and is a big reason why I think MikroTik is the most cost-effective platform available. The MTCNA outline doesn't cover all the possible ways of connecting networks but it's a great introduction. The critical different between a VPN and a tunnel is that VPNs use encryption to provide *confidentiality*. Tunnels like GRE and EoIP don't provide *confidentiality* by default.

10.1 PPP

The PPP is a protocol used by itself and as the foundation of different protocols. It connects remote hosts and networks both in service provider and enterprise environments. MikroTik supports mainstream PPP implementations, as well as PPPoE and PPTP. PPP can work over a variety of transport mediums including Ethernet (Section 10.3), phone lines, Synchronous Optical Networking (SONET), Asynchronous Transfer Mode (ATM), Serial connections, and more. With the proliferation of broadband connections, MPLS circuits, and high-speed wireless PPP is used less but it's still an important technology for some service providers.

10.1.1 PPP Profiles

PPP Profiles are configured to set the behavior of PPP clients that dial-in. Profiles contain a number of options for addressing PPP clients and enforcing security policy:

- Local IP Address
- Remote IP Address / Pool
- Compression
- Encryption

- Session Timeout
- Idle Timeout
- TX / RX Speed
- Session Count Limit
- DNS Server
- Universal Plug and Play (UPnP) Usage

Two PPP profiles exist be default in typical RouterOS installations:

- *default*
- *default-encryption*

The *default-encryption* profile should be used whenever possible unless you create custom profiles with secure options. Since PPPoE and PPTP uses PPP for authentication it's important to secure PPP as much as possible. The following command changes encryption settings in the *default-encryption* profile to *require* that encryption be used:

```
/ppp profile set default-encryption use-encryption=required
```

Additional options secure the profile even more, protecting all traffic for PPP connections utilizing that profile. The *only-one=yes* option allows only one active connection per PPP secret. The *use-encryption=required* forces encryption to be used, because not all clients will use by default. The following commands create a custom PPP profile with important security settings in place:

```
/ppp profile
add name=VPN comment="VPN Users"
set VPN local-address=192.168.1.1 remote-address=Customers dns-server
   =8.8.8.8,8.8.4.4
set VPN only-one=yes use-encryption=required idle-timeout=5m
```

> **NOTE**: The PPP profile can be created in one command but was not does so here to prevent difficult-to-read text wrapping.

The *only-one=yes* option limits each PPP credential to a single concurrent login. *idle-timeout=5m* limits an inactive connection to five minutes, so an unattended computer connected to the network remotely can't be exploited by an attacker who sits down at the computer. The *local-address=192.168.1.1* option combines with the *'remote-address="PPP Pool"'* option to put PPP clients in the IP Pool with a connection to 192.168.1.1. The *"use-encryption=required"* option forces PPP clients to use whatever encryption they are capable of, and almost all clients can do encryption. Setting *"use-encryption=required"* also helps enforce data security policies on remote users.

10.1.2 IP Pools for PPP

The same type of IP Pool configured on page 117 can be used for PPP profiles as well. The following command creates an IP Pool just for PPP users that's used in the custom PPP profile above:

```
/ip pool
add name=Customers ranges=192.168.1.2-192.168.1.10
```

10.1.3 PPP Encryption

While PPP connections are not encrypted by default a MikroTik PPP server can force encryption. However, the most robust encryption possible with this protocol is MS-CHAP v2 (MS-CHAPv2) which is considered weak and easily cracked with modern hardware. Microsoft Challenge-Handshake Authentication Protocol (MS-CHAP) and Challenge-Handshake Authentication Protocol (CHAP) are both trivial to compromise and should not be used in any case.

10.1.4 PPP Secrets

Individual PPP Secrets leverage the Profiles built on page 151. Each remote user should have a Secret of their own so it's possible to monitor who logged in remotely and when. Create a Secret for a PPP user with the following command:

```
/ppp secret
add name=tyler password=abc123! service=any profile="Remote Users"
```

PPP users can be restricted to a particular service by modifying the *service* option. Some options for *service* include "PPTP" and "PPPoE". The PPP Secrets created in this section will be used in the following sections, including PPTP and PPPoE, so it's important to understand how to create and manage them.

10.1.5 RADIUS Users

In service provider and larger enterprise networks PPP typically uses RADIUS for AAA, allowing for robust user management and accounting. MikroTik routers can function both as RADIUS servers and clients for PPP credentials. PPP, PPPoE, wireless clients, and other protocols can use RADIUS for centralized AAA. Enable RADIUS for AAA using the following command:

```
/ppp aaa set use-radius=yes
```

> **NOTE**: A RADIUS server must be configured under */radius* for this functionality to work. Configuring RADIUS and RADIUS clients is beyond the scope of the MTCNA.

10.1.6 Monitoring PPP Users

It's important to monitor what users are actively dialed into your networks, and if multiple failed login attempts have occurred. Use the following command to view active PPP users:

```
/ppp active print
```

Monitoring router logs for PPP events is easy when using a search string:

```
/log print where message~"ppp"
```

In the logs it's important to look for failed login attempts or any PPP secrets being created or removed that you can't account for. Sending PPP log entries to a centralized Syslog server for archiving and monitoring is a good step to take as well.

10.2 PPTP

PPTP is a VPN technology that encapsulates PPP packets using TCP and GRE[1]. Like PPP, PPTP can be encrypted natively but only up to MS-CHAPv2 which isn't robust. However, PPTP is still widely supported and used in organizations that need basic VPN capabilities.

10.2.1 PPTP Server

The PPTP server running on a MikroTik router listens for inbound connections and authenticates VPN users. The PPTP service runs using a combination of TCP for 1723 and the GRE protocol. Enable the PPTP server process with the following command:

```
/interface pptp-server
server set authentication=mschap2 enabled=yes
```

MS-CHAP version two[2] is specified for authentication, but it should be noted that any version of CHAP is no longer considered secure.

10.2.2 PPTP Users

Each PPTP user is created as a PPP secret which was already described on page 153. Secrets for PPTP required a little more information, including the IP addresses they will be assigned. The following command creates a PPP user who will be assigned the IP address *10.0.0.2* and have a direct connection to *10.0.0.1*:

---

[1] IANA protocol number 47
[2] https://technet.microsoft.com/en-us/library/cc957983.aspx

```
/ppp secret
add local-address=10.0.0.1 remote-address=10.0.0.2 name=manitonetworks
   password=abc123! service=pptp
```

The *service=pptp* option ensures that this credential can only be used for PPTP connections.

10.2.3 PPTP Client

The PPTP client connects to a PPTP server and establishes a PPP connection. Clients are included in Microsoft Windows and Apple macOS® and iOS® operating systems, as well as Linux. RouterOS has a built-in PPTP client that can connect to another MikroTik router, establishing a routed point-to-point VPN connection. A PPTP Client on a RouterOS device can connect to the PPTP Server configured on page 154. The PPP Secret defined on page 154 is used to authenticate the Client in the following commands:

```
/interface pptp-client
add connect-to=vpn.manitonetworks.com user=manitonetworks password=abc123!
   disabled=no
```

Once the Client connects a virtual PPTP interface will be created and assigned the *10.0.0.2* address based on the PPP Secret.

10.3 PPPoE

With many customers connecting to service providers via Metro Ethernet or DSL lines, PPPoE remains an ISP mainstay in some markets. It allows service providers with high-speed connections to continue using PPP connections and AAA but over modern infrastructure. MikroTik routers can function as both PPPoE servers and clients.

10.3.1 PPPoE Server

A PPPoE server must be running on an interface reachable by PPPoE clients. There are a few options for encryption and sessions per host that are important. An example is shown in Figure 10.1 on the next page, with the new service running on interface *ether1*:

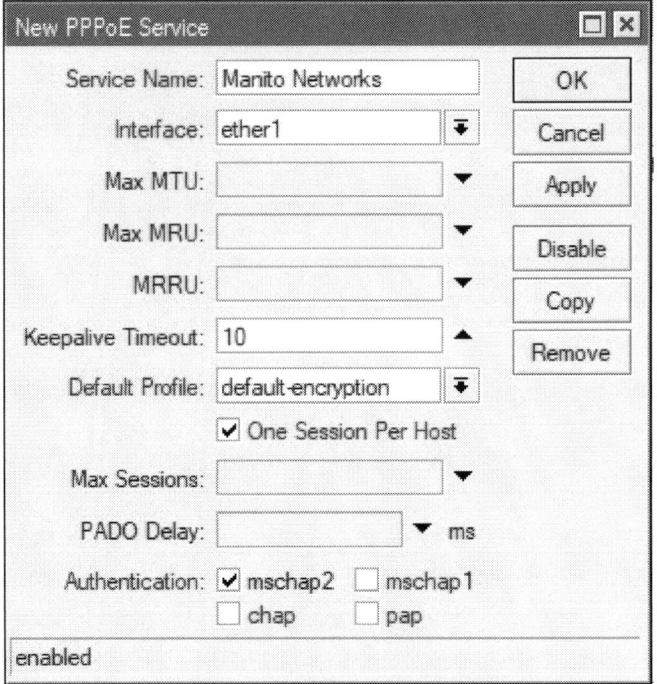

Figure 10.1: New PPPoE Service

The most robust authentication is the only option allowed, and the "*One Session Per Host*" box is checked as well. This option prevents the same user from authenticating via more than one host at a time. The credentials used to authenticate to the new PPPoE service were defined in PPP Secrets on page 153. PPP Secrets configured on the router can be used, or centralized credentials on a RADIUS server for more robust authentication.

10.3.2 PPPoE Client

The PPPoE Client scans for available Servers and attempts to connect using the specified credentials. The scanning mechanism is done via broadcasts to the *FF:FF:FF:FF:FF:FF* MAC address. Since the client relies on L2 broadcasts, both the server and client must be part of the same broadcast domain. Request for Comments (RFC) 2516[3] describes the inner-workings of PPPoE and the different types of packets it uses to discovery and provision services.

A new PPPoE Client that connects to the upstream PPPoE Server via *ether1* is added using the following commands:

```
/interface pppoe-client
add name=ISP user=tylerh password=abc123! interface=ether1
```

---

[3]https://tools.ietf.org/html/rfc2516

10.4 SSTP

Secure Socket Tunneling Protocol (SSTP) leverages SSL and Transport Layer Security (TLS) to secure PPP communications. Virtually all mainstream operating systems have SSTP clients available. With PPTP falling out of favor due to security concerns SSTP is seeing increasing popularity. Another benefit of using SSTP is that it can traverse most firewalls easily, since it only uses the typical TCP port 443. This also makes firewalling inbound connections from clients easy as well.

10.4.1 SSTP Server

The SSTP server listens for inbound connections from SSTP clients and authenticates remote users. PPP secrets (p. 153), either local or on a RADIUS server, are used to authenticate tunnel users. By default the SSTP server isn't running and must be enabled just like PPTP or PPPoE servers. Enable the SSTP server with the following command:

```
/interface sstp-server server set enabled=yes
```

Verify the server is running using the *"interface sstp-server server print"* command as shown in Figure 10.2:

```
[admin@MikroTik] > /interface sstp-server server print
                 enabled: yes
                    port: 443
                 max-mtu: 1500
                 max-mru: 1500
                    mrru: disabled
       keepalive-timeout: 60
         default-profile: default
          authentication: pap,chap,mschap1,mschap2
             certificate: none
 verify-client-certificate: no
               force-aes: no
                     pfs: no
             tls-version: any
[admin@MikroTik] > _
```

Figure 10.2: SSTP Server Enabled

10.4.2 Securing SSTP Access

By default both Password Authentication Protocol (PAP), CHAP, and MS-CHAP are used for authentication. Unfortunately, none of those have been reliably secure for a long time. Even MS-CHAP and MS-CHAPv2 aren't the most secure, but MS-CHAPv2 isn't bad when combined with other types of security. Remove *PAP*, *CHAP*, and *MS-CHAP* from the authentication settings using the following commands:

```
/interface sstp-server server
set authentication=mschap2
```

This ensures the strongest possible authentication will be used each time a user connects. Additional settings like "*force-aes=yes*" and "*pfs=yes*" add additional layers of security. Depending on your organization's security needs it may be necessary to specify the TLS version using the "*tls-version*" option due to recent encryption security disclosures.

> **NOTE**: Not all SSTP clients support the Advanced Encryption Standard (AES) and Perfect Forward Secrecy (PFS) functionality, so test authentication with all different clients before rolling out SSTP VPNs to your users.

10.4.3 Creating an SSTP User

The following commands create an SSTP user as a PPP secret that can only be used for SSTP:

```
/ppp secret
add name="tyler" service=sstp password=abc123! profile=default local-address
    =192.168.90.1 remote-address=192.168.90.10
```

The "*tyler*" user will be given the IP address 192.168.90.10/32 when he connects, and can use 192.168.90.1 as the remote gateway via the SSTP tunnel. The PPP profile (in this command "*profile=default*") is the same type of profile already outlined on page 151.

10.4.4 SSTP Client

Much like the PPTP client, the SSTP client connects to an SSTP server and establishes a VPN link. Once the SSTP server has been enabled and users created it's ready to accept inbound connections. Assuming the VPN in this example is a site-to-site from one MikroTik to another, the first step is to create the SSTP client:

```
/interface sstp-client
add connect-to=172.16.0.1 user=tyler password=abc123!
```

Verify the status of the SSTP connection by using the "*/interface sstp-client print*" command. Use the *ping* tool to verify connectivity with the other side of the tunnel.

10.5 Review Questions

1. Which protocol is used by both PPTP and PPPoE?

    (a) PPP

    (b) GRE

    (c) L2TP

    (d) EoIP

2. Where are the IPs available for client use configured?

    (a) DHCP Servers

    (b) IP Filters

    (c) IP Pools

    (d) Access Lists

3. PPP connections are encrypted by default.

    (a) True

    (b) False

4. Which protocol and port does SSTP use?

    (a) User Datagram Protocol (UDP)/4343

    (b) UDP/443

    (c) TCP/4343

    (d) TCP/443

5. The PPTP server listens for connections on TCP/1723.

    (a) True

    (b) False

6. Which protocol can be used to authenticate remote PPP users on RouterOS?

    (a) TACACS

    (b) RADIUS

    (c) TACACS+

    (d) LDAP

7. What protocol beside TCP is used to establish PPTP tunnels?

    (a) TCP

    (b) UDP

    (c) GRE

    (d) ICMP

8. ISPs use which protocol to run PPP over commodity connections like broadband?

    (a) EoIP

    (b) GRE

    (c) PPTP

    (d) PPPoE

9. 1600 is the default MTU for SSTP connections.

    (a) True

    (b) False

10. Which option allows each PPP user to only have one connection established at a time?

    (a) *only-one*

    (b) *default-authenticate*

    (c) *default-forward*

    (d) *pfs*

10.6 Review Answers

1. Which protocol is used by both PPTP and PPPoE?

   A – PPP (p. 151)

2. Where are the IPs available for client use configured?

   C – IP Pools (p. 153)

3. PPP connections are encrypted by default.

   B – False (p. 153)

4. Which protocol and port does SSTP use?

   D – TCP/443 (p. 157)

5. The PPTP server listens for connections on TCP/1723.

   A – True (p. 154)

6. Which protocol can be used to authenticate remote PPP users on RouterOS?

   B – RADIUS (p. 153)

7. What protocol beside TCP is used to establish PPTP tunnels?

   C – GRE (p. 154)

8. ISPs use which protocol to run PPP over commodity connections like broadband?

   D – PPPoE (p. 155)

9. 1600 is the default MTU for SSTP connections.

   B – False (p. 157)

10. Which option allows each PPP user to only have one connection established at a time?

    A – *only-one* (p. 152)

Chapter 11

Queues

RouterOS queues can make for a complex topic. Using queues allows you to shape, balance, and limit network traffic based on your needs and policies. To do this correctly requires a good understanding of how your network is built, what traffic profiles you're dealing with, and how to best distribute network resources. Two kinds of queues exist in RouterOS:

- Simple Queue
- Queue Tree

11.1 Scheduling Algorithms

RouterOS supports many different kinds of algorithms that determine when packets will be sent out an interface or dropped because of traffic thresholds or congestion. The following algorithms are supported:

- First In, First Out (FIFO)
    - Packet FIFO (PFIFO)
    - Byte FIFO (BFIFO)
    - Multiple Queue PFIFO (MQ-PFIFO)
- Random Early Detection (RED)
- Stochastic Fair Queuing (SFQ)
- Per-Connection Queuing (PCQ)
- None

11.1.1 FIFO

This is one of the simplest types of algorithms and does what the name implies. The first packet in will be the first out, regardless of other packets in the queue. BFIFO measures queue size in *bytes*, and PFIFO uses *packets*. As of this writing the following algorithms are used in these default queues:

- PFIFO:
    - *default*
    - *default-small*
    - *ethernet-default*
- BFIFO: None
- mq PFIFO:
    - *multi-queue-ethernet-default*

11.1.2 RED

The RED scheduler compares the current queue size against minimum and maximum thresholds. If the size of the queue is below the minimum threshold packets aren't dropped. If the queue size increases to between the minimum and maximum threshold then random packets will be dropped. The probability that packets will be dropped increases as the queue fills up. When the queue fills completely all new packets will be dropped. The RED algorithm is used by the *synchronous-default* queue.

11.1.3 SFQ

SFQ uses hashing to identify network flows. Once flows have been identified a Round-Robin methodology is used to distribute bandwidth between the flows. It's not possible with SFQ to choose which kind of network flows get more bandwidth than others. The SFQ algorithm is used by the *hotspot-default* queue.

11.1.4 PCQ

This type of algorithm works like SFQ but you can choose flows to prioritize based on network addresses and port numbers. Different types of flows can have their speeds limited as well. PCQ is commonly used to throttle upload and download speeds for individual hosts or networks using address lists. As of this writing the following queues use PCQ by default:

- *pcq-download-default*

- *pcq-upload-default*

11.1.5 None

Queues don't always have to use a scheduling algorithm. The following default queues don't use an algorithm in RouterOS:

- *only-hardware-queue*
- *wireless-default*

11.2 Priority Levels

There are a total of eight priority levels that can be assigned to each queue, numbered 1 – 8 [17]. The highest priority is one, and the lowest is eight. Queues with a higher priority will get the first "shot" at available network bandwidth. All queues are configured with a default priority value of eight. Once queues have been successfully configured and your network performance needs are understood it's possible to effectively priority traffic further by changing this value.

11.3 Simple Queues

Simple queues are designed to put boilerplate network policies in place quickly with limited management overhead. There is a limit to what can be done with these but for many organizations this is all that's needed. Many of my customers get started with queues because they need to manage download bandwidth. This is especially true in rural areas where faster connections aren't always available or easily affordable. Bear in mind that Simple queues running on a specified interface only police traffic headed *outbound*.

The following Simple queue example limits the *total download bandwidth* for the *192.168.10.0/24 network* to *5 Megabit per Second (Mbit/s)*.

```
/queue simple
add name="192.168.10.0 Download" target=192.168.10.0/24 max-limit=0M/5M
    comment="192.168.10.0/24 Download Limit"
```

NOTE: When "*0*" is specified for an upload or download value that means "*unlimited*".

The equivalent configuration in Winbox is shown in Figure 11.1 on the next page:

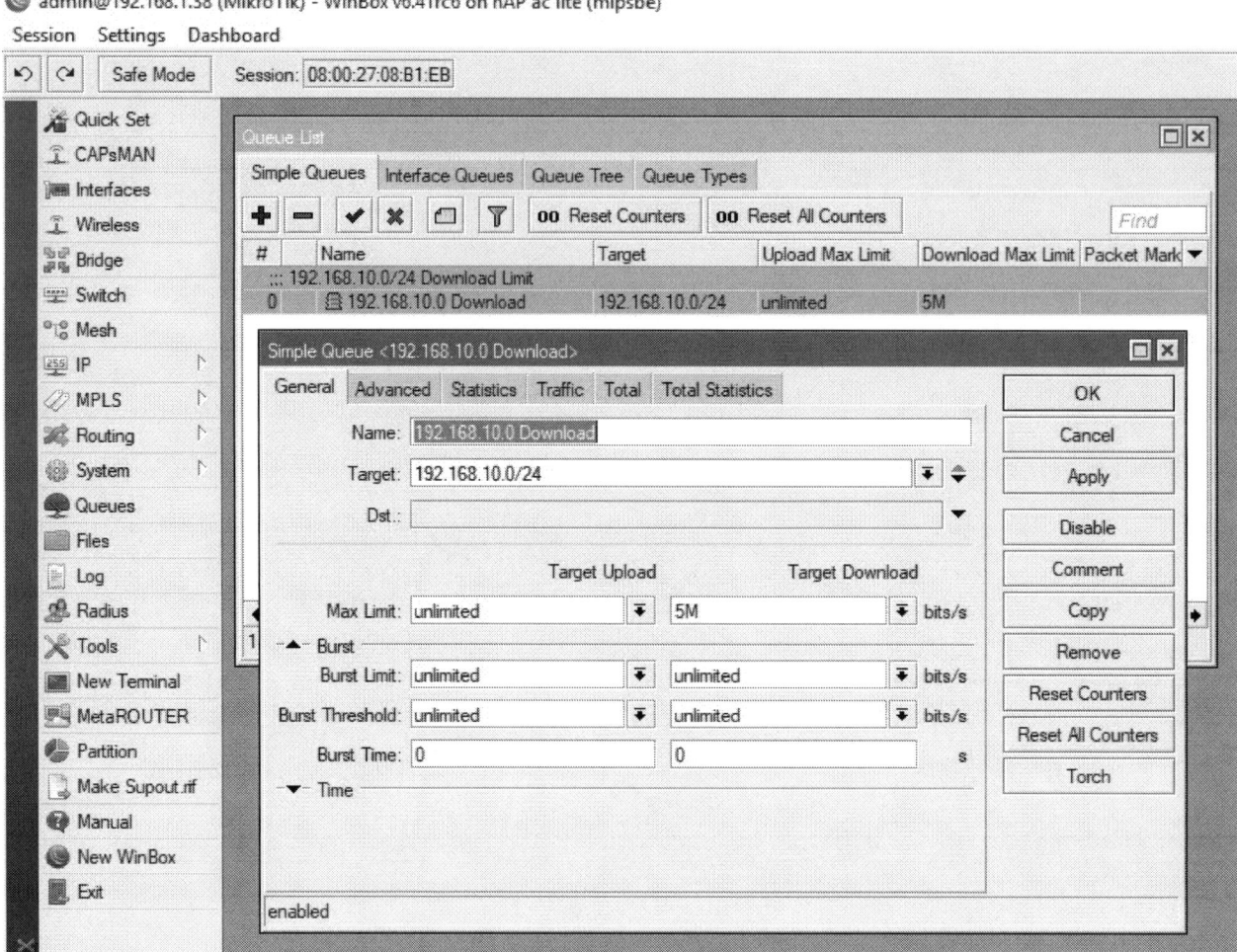

Figure 11.1: Simple Queue Download Limit

11.4 Bursting

The Bursting feature allows network users to exceed the maximum allotted bandwidth in a queue for short periods of time. This allows short downloads and bursts of media-heavy content to download quicker while still policing longer bandwidth-heavy sessions. The average traffic rate allowed is calculated every one-sixteenth of the *Burst Time* duration. Each time the traffic rate is calculated an adjustment is made if necessary. The *Burst Limit*, *Burst Threshold*, and *Burst Time* fields all work together to determine how fast and for how long traffic can run at burst speed. The longest burst duration possible is calculated with the following formula[1]

$$LongestBurstTime = BurstThreshold * BurstTime/BurstLimit$$

Bursting should be tuned over time to provide a good network performance experience based on your organization's available bandwidth, usage patterns, and needs.

---

[1] https://wiki.mikrotik.com/wiki/Manual:Queues_-_Burst#Example

11.5 Interface Queues

Interface queues allow traffic to be policed as it heads *inbound* to an interface. This is different than Simple queues because those use Source (SRC) and Destination (DST) addresses instead to identify traffic to be policed. Either the built-in queues can be applied to an interface or you can create your own and apply it. Only one type of queue can be active on an interface at a time. The *"queue interface print"* command lists which queues are active on each interface as shown in Figure 11.2:

```
[admin@MikroTik] > /queue interface print
# INTERFACE        QUEUE                    ACTIVE-QUEUE
0 ether1           only-hardware-queue      only-hardware-queue
1 ether2           only-hardware-queue      only-hardware-queue
2 ether3           only-hardware-queue      only-hardware-queue
3 ether4           only-hardware-queue      only-hardware-queue
4 ether5           only-hardware-queue      only-hardware-queue
5 wlan1            wireless-default         wireless-default
6 wlan2            wireless-default         wireless-default
7 ;;; defconf
  bridge           no-queue                 no-queue
[admin@MikroTik] > _
```

Figure 11.2: Interface Queue Print

Each of these queues uses one of the queue algorithms already covered on page 163. On most networks the default interface queues already in-place are perfectly fine. Before creating your own and assigning them to an interface in production be sure to bench-test and ensure that regular traffic won't be negatively impacted.

11.6 Queue Trees

Queue trees allow for more complex nested queues that serve robust traffic policing needs. Unlike interface queues that handle traffic *inbound* to an interface, queue Trees only police traffic heading *outbound* from an interface. Figure 11.3 on the next page shows download traffic inbound on *ether1* and outbound to the LAN on *ether2*.

11.6. QUEUE TREES

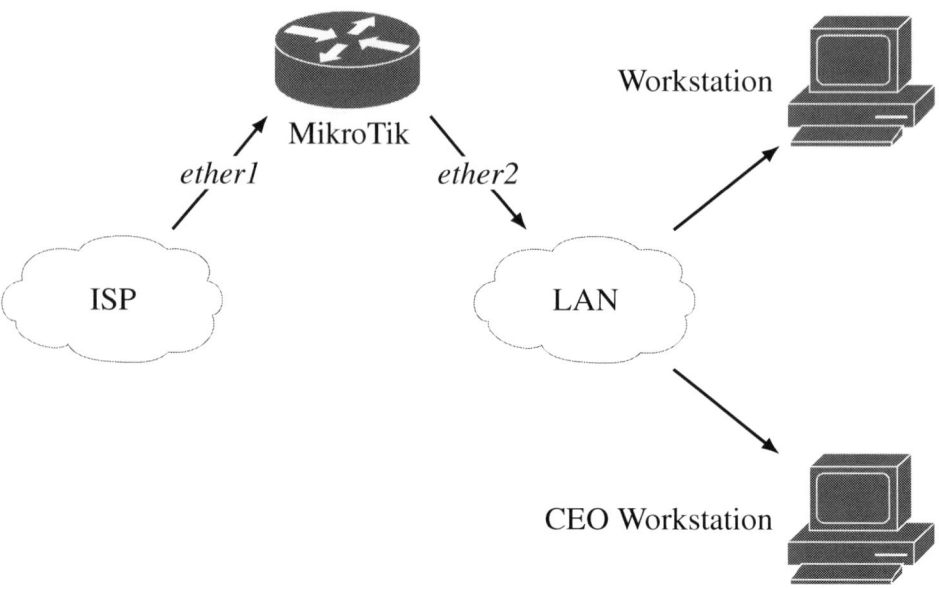

Figure 11.3: Queue Tree Download Topology

For limiting downloads to the LAN the queue tree's *parent* would be *ether2*, because that's the first interface where that traffic is headed *outbound*. The second command shown below limits downloads out *ether2* to 50Mb/sec maximum. It also guarantees each host at least a 1Mb/sec download connection using PCQ:

```
/ip firewall mangle
add chain=forward dst-address=192.168.1.199 action=mark-packet new-packet-mark
   =CEO

/queue tree
add name="LAN Download" parent=ether2 limit-at=1M max-limit=50M queue=pcq-
   download-default

add name="CEO Download" parent="LAN Download" packet-mark=CEO limit-at=5M max-
   limit=50M queue=pcq-download-default
```

Additional Queues can be placed further down the tree below the original Queue ("*parent=LAN Download*"). A common configuration in business networks is to allow additional bandwidth for an organization's conference rooms or VIPs. A new firewall Mangle rule (the first command above) marks each packet addressed for the CEO's workstation at *192.168.1.199*. The child queue tree rule uses the packet mark to modify traffic further down the Queue tree.

11.7 Review Questions

1. BFIFO uses packets to measure the queue size.
   - (a) True
   - (b) False

2. What does FIFO stand for?
   - (a) First In, First Out
   - (b) First In, Final Out
   - (c) Filter In, Filter Out
   - (d) Forward In, Filter Out

3. Which type of algorithm is good for managing traffic on a per-connection basis?
   - (a) None
   - (b) RED
   - (c) PCQ
   - (d) PFIFO

4. Simple queues manage traffic inbound to the router.
   - (a) True
   - (b) False

5. Interface queues allow traffic to be policed as it heads inbound to an interface.
   - (a) True
   - (b) False

6. What is the default interface queue type assigned to bridged?
   - (a) *only-hardware-queue*
   - (b) *wireless-default*
   - (c) *ethernet-small*
   - (d) *no-queue*

7. What value for upload and download means "unlimited"?
   (a) "100"
   (b) "100%"
   (c) "0"
   (d) "None"

8. How many priority levels can be assigned to a queue?
   (a) Five
   (b) Six
   (c) Seven
   (d) Eight

9. One is the highest priority level that can be assigned to a queue.
   (a) True
   (b) False

10. The default priority assigned to a queue is seven.
    (a) True
    (b) False

11.8 Review Answers

1. BFIFO uses packets to measure the queue size.

    B – False (p. 164)

2. What does FIFO stand for?

    A – First In, First Out (p. 164)

3. Which type of algorithm is good for managing traffic on a per-connection basis?

    C – PCQ (p. 164)

4. Simple queues manage traffic inbound to the router.

    B – False (p. 165)

5. Interface queues allow traffic to be policed as it heads inbound to an interface.

    A – True (p. 167)

6. What is the default interface queue type assigned to new bridges?

    D – *no-queue* (p. 167)

7. What value for upload and download means "unlimited"?

    C – "0" (p. 165)

8. How many priority levels can be assigned to a queue?

    D – Eight (p. 165)

9. One is the highest priority level that can be assigned to a queue.

    A – True (p. 165)

10. The default priority assigned to a queue is seven.

    B – False (p. 165)

Chapter 12

Firewalls

Firewalls filter traffic that is undesirable and allow authorized traffic into and across your networks. With the right rules you can block port scanners and reconnaissance attempts, stop devices being co-opted into DDoS attacks, troubleshoot network performance, and gather traffic statistics. The RouterOS firewall implementation is very closely related to the Linux *iptables* firewall. Both use much of the same technology and terminology, but RouterOS brings additional features and management functionality.

The RouterOS firewall is a stateful, meaning that it tracks connections from source to destination. This stateful inspection of traffic means that each type of allowed traffic doesn't need a rule allowing it in one direction, then in the other.

A good example of this behavior is Webfig traffic over HTTP from an IT workstation at *192.168.88.185* to the router at *192.168.88.1*. There could easily be a rule allowing HTTP inbound only from the *192.168.88.185* address. However, there does not need to be a rule allowing HTTP traffic back out to the IT workstation. With stateful firewall logic the router expects there will be return traffic. If inbound HTTP was already permitted, then it stands to reason that the router should be allowed to respond. It's possible to break this behavior by adding a *drop* rule in the output chain for HTTP, but it'd be easier to simply not allow HTTP inbound in the first place (best practice # 1).

12.1 Best Practices

To keep your networks secure and firewall rules from becoming too complicated there are some guidelines to follow. Consider your network operations in the context of these best practices:

1. Allow traffic you need, block everything else
2. Consolidate rules if possible for simplicity
3. Sort rules for efficiency
4. Block all traffic at the end of each chains with final "catch-all" rules

5. Periodically audit firewall configurations for consistency and security

Remember these best practices while learning more about the mechanics of firewalls in MikroTik devices.

12.2 Firewall Components

The RouterOS firewall uses three components to police traffic:

- Chains
- Rules
- Actions

Chains are mechanisms that process network traffic at different stages during routing and bridging. Each chain has groups of rules that filter traffic based on source, destination, protocol, and other matching criteria. All rules have actions assigned that affect traffic matching the rule. These actions include *drop*, *log*, *accept*, *reject*, and more. The packet flow documentation provided by MikroTik, shown in Figure 12.1, details the flow of packets through different interfaces and chains:

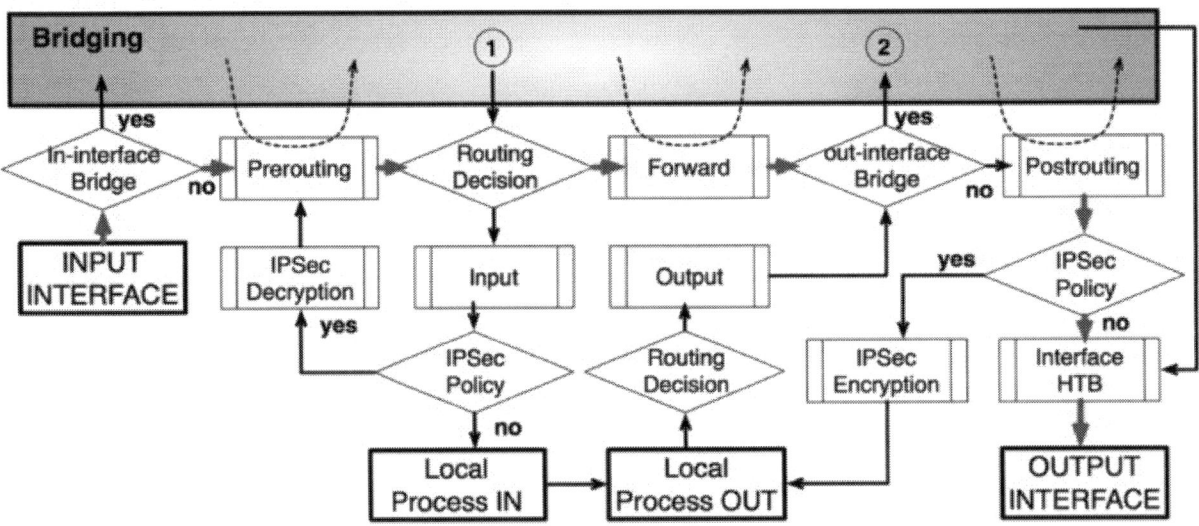

Image Credit: *MikroTik*

Figure 12.1: Routing Packet Flow

12.3 Firewall Chains

Three chains exist by default and cannot be removed:

- Input
- Forward
- Output

You can also create your own chains for more advanced firewalling and traffic monitoring. Each chain is a group of rules that processes a certain kind of traffic.

12.3.1 Input Chain

The input chain processes packets inbound to the router itself. An example of input traffic would be an administrator pinging a router's interface. Another example would be a Winbox session to a router. A diagram of output traffic is shown in Figure 12.2:

Figure 12.2: Input Chain Traffic

List all firewall Input chain rules with the command shown in Figure 12.3:

```
[admin@MikroTik] > /ip firewall filter print where chain=input
Flags: X - disabled, I - invalid, D - dynamic
 0    ;;; defconf: accept established,related,untracked
      chain=input action=accept connection-state=established,related,untracked

 1    ;;; defconf: drop invalid
      chain=input action=drop connection-state=invalid

 2    ;;; defconf: accept ICMP
      chain=input action=accept protocol=icmp

 3    ;;; defconf: drop all not coming from LAN
      chain=input action=drop in-interface-list=!LAN

[admin@MikroTik] > _
```

Figure 12.3: Listing Default Input Rules

Input traffic should be blocked on outside connections like ISP uplinks because port scanners are constantly looking for open ports and running services[1]. Router access via services like SSH and Winbox should also be allowed only from known subnets, so network administrators have the opportunity to access device configurations and no one else.

12.3.2 Forward Chain

The Forward chain processes packets being forwarded through a router. A diagram of forward traffic is shown in Figure 12.4:

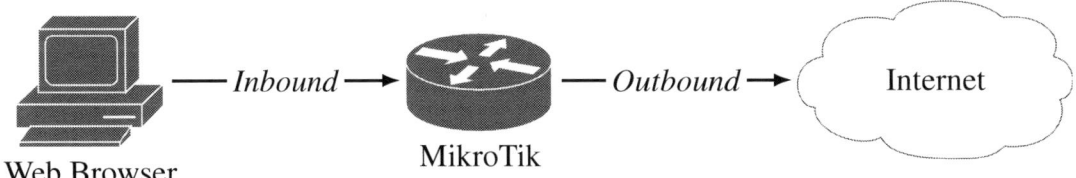

Figure 12.4: Forward Chain Traffic

This is routed traffic that the device is handing off from one network to another. While the router is handling this traffic it isn't destined specifically for the router itself, which means the input chain does not apply. On most routers the majority of the traffic being processed matches for forward chain. List all firewall Forward chain rules with the command shown in Figure 12.5 on the following page:

---

[1] Both HIPAA and PCI-DSS compliance standards require that direct connections to the router be filtered.

```
[admin@MikroTik] > /ip firewall filter print where chain=forward
Flags: X - disabled, I - invalid, D - dynamic
 0  D ;;; special dummy rule to show fasttrack counters
chain=forward action=passthrough

 1    ;;; defconf: accept in ipsec policy
chain=forward action=accept ipsec-policy=in,ipsec

 2    ;;; defconf: accept out ipsec policy
chain=forward action=accept ipsec-policy=out,ipsec

 3    ;;; defconf: fasttrack
chain=forward action=fasttrack-connection connection-state=established,related

 4    ;;; defconf: accept established,related, untracked
chain=forward action=accept connection-state=established,related,untracked

 5    ;;; defconf: drop invalid
chain=forward action=drop connection-state=invalid

 6    ;;; defconf:  drop all from WAN not DSTNATed
chain=forward action=drop connection-state=new connection-nat-state=!dstnat in
   -interface-list=WAN

[admin@MikroTik] > _
```

Figure 12.5: Listing Default Forward Rules

12.3.3 Output Chain

The Output chain processes traffic sent from the router. An example of traffic that matches the Output chain is a ping sent directly from the router's console. An OSPF *hello* packet sent to another router or a Syslog message would also match the Output chain because it was sent from the router. A diagram of output traffic is shown in Figure 12.6:

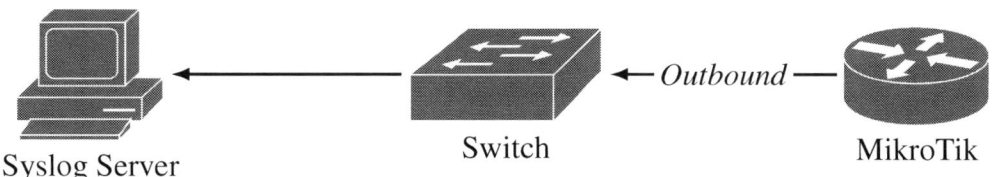

Figure 12.6: Output Chain Traffic

List all firewall Output chain rules with the command shown in Figure 12.7 on the next page:

```
[admin@MikroTik] > /ip firewall filter print where chain=output
Flags: X - disabled, I - invalid, D - dynamic

[admin@MikroTik] > _
```

Figure 12.7: Listing Default Output Rules

NOTE: Many administrators don't apply much filtering to the Output chain because traffic originating from a router (like OSPF advertisements) is considered trusted.

12.3.4 Custom Chains

Custom chains are easily created to serve more specialized firewall needs. The following command creates a custom chain called *ospf*:

```
/ip firewall filter
add chain=ospf comment="OSPF Chain"
```

We can put any rules built for OSPF into this chain to keep things organized and easier to understand. On page 186 we put this chain to work processing OSPF traffic with separate rules.

12.4 Firewall Rules

Each rule entry in the firewall tells RouterOS what to do with matching packets. These rules are applied to chains and contain the criteria for matching packets. If a packet matches the criteria in a rule then the rule's action is applied. RouterOS allows for very flexible rules driven by many available criteria. The following are selections of typical criteria used for rules:

- Protocol
- Source Address
- Destination Address
- Source Port
- Destination Port
- Interface In
- Interface Out
- ICMP Options
- TCP Flags
- Connection State
- NAT State

There are dozens of other criteria and any number of combinations for matching traffic that you're targeting with a rule. The final *drop* rule in a chain that catches all traffic not already allowed has no criteria set at all so it can match all remaining traffic.

12.4.1 Rule Evaluation

Firewall rules are evaluated in a top-down fashion. This means the firewall evaluates packets against rules starting at the top of a chain and moves down until a rule is matched or there are no more rules. If no rule matches traffic in the chain then the traffic is automatically allowed. For this reason it's critical to have a final "catch-all" drop rule at the end of each chain.

12.4.2 Rule Sorting

In many networks there are a small handful of rules that match the majority of traffic through a chain. Once identified those rules can be moved higher up the chain to eliminate wasteful processing of rules that don't get many matching packets. It's easy to see which rules these are by using the following commands:

```
/ip firewall filter
print stats
print stats chain=input
print stats chain=forward
print stats chain=output
```

Once they are at the top they will match the majority of traffic first, stopping the router from having to process other rules needlessly. For high-traffic networks this kind of sorting can result in huge processing overhead reductions.

12.5 Default Firewall Rules

The default firewall filter rules do a good job of protecting typical networks from outside attackers. While these rules can't protect against DDoS attacks they will deter in-depth port scans, remote authentication attempts, and more. Local connections from inside the router are generally allowed, while connections to external interfaces that don't belong to an internal host are dropped.

12.5.1 Default Input Rules

The default input rules allow traffic addressed to the router from LAN networks while dropping most from outside the LAN. List all input chain rules with the command shown in Figure 12.8:

```
[admin@MikroTik] > /ip firewall filter print where chain=input
Flags: X - disabled, I - invalid, D - dynamic
 0   ;;; defconf: accept established,related,untracked
chain=input action=accept connection-state=established,related,untracked

 1   ;;; defconf: drop invalid
chain=input action=drop connection-state=invalid

 2   ;;; defconf: accept ICMP
chain=input action=accept protocol=icmp

 3   ;;; defconf: drop all not coming from LAN
chain=input action=drop in-interface-list=!LAN

[admin@MikroTik] > _
```

Figure 12.8: Default Input Rules

1. Rule 0: Allows packets that are part of an *established*, *related*, or *untracked* connection. This is the first static rule at the top so most of the traffic that's *established* doesn't have to pass through a bunch of different rules.

2. Rule 1: *Invalid* connections headed inbound to the router are dropped in this rule. This can be spoofed or port scan traffic.

3. Rule 2: ICMP traffic inbound to the router is allowed by this rule. Many technicians leave this rule in place for remote troubleshooting purposes. In organizations beholden to HIPAA or PCI-DSS this kind of unfiltered ICMP connection from any network or host isn't allowed.

4. Rule 3: All remaining input traffic not originating from the LAN is dropped.

12.5.2 Default Forward Rules

These rules allow traffic outbound from local networks and block most traffic inbound from the WAN headed to local networks. List all forward chain rules with the command shown in Figure 12.9:

```
[admin@MikroTik] > /ip firewall filter print where chain=forward
Flags: X - disabled, I - invalid, D - dynamic
 0  D ;;; special dummy rule to show fasttrack counters
       chain=forward action=passthrough

 1     ;;; defconf: accept in ipsec policy
       chain=forward action=accept ipsec-policy=in,ipsec

 2     ;;; defconf: accept out ipsec policy
       chain=forward action=accept ipsec-policy=out,ipsec

 3     ;;; defconf: fasttrack
       chain=forward action=fasttrack-connection connection-state=established,related

 4     ;;; defconf: accept established, related, untracked
       chain=forward action=accept connection-state=established,related,untracked

 5     ;;; defconf: drop invalid
       chain=forward action=drop connection-state=invalid

 6     ;;; defconf:  drop all from WAN not DSTNATed
       chain=forward action=drop connection-state=new connection-nat-state=!dstnat in
          -interface-list=WAN

[admin@MikroTik] > _
```

Figure 12.9: Default Forward Rules

1. Rule 0: This is a built-in dynamic rule that can't be removed. It shows how many packets have taken advantage of the FastTrack feature.

2. Rules 1 & 2: Accept IPSEC traffic heading both directions. These rules aren't required if you're not using IPSEC VPNs.

3. Rule 3: All traffic that is *established* or *related* has the *fasttrack-connection* applied. This action is covered on page 185.

4. Rule 4: This rule allows all traffic that is *established* or *related*. It works with Rule number 3 to lower the resource utilization in the firewall for packets already allowed.

5. Rule 5: Any *invalid* traffic being forwarded into or out of networks attached to the router is dropped. Ideally very little or no traffic at all should be matching this rule. PCI-DSS requirement number 1.3.5 [3, p. 3] is partially satisfied by this rule:

   "Permit only 'established' connections into the network."

6. Rule 6: The final rule drops all traffic being forwarded into or out of WAN interfaces that has not been through the NAT process. This is typically a good rule in most organizations that NAT traffic through a single public IP assigned by their ISP.

12.5.3 Default Output Rules

List all firewall output chain rules with the command shown in Figure 12.10:

```
[admin@MikroTik] > /ip firewall filter print where chain=output
Flags: X - disabled, I - invalid, D - dynamic

[admin@MikroTik] > _
```

Figure 12.10: Default Output Rules

No default rules are configured to filter outbound traffic from the router.

12.6 Connection Tracking

RouterOS firewalls are *stateful*, meaning they track packets as part of an overall stream or connection. Packets in a connection that match a firewall rule allowing traffic will be permitted. Packets that aren't part of an active connection but have spoofed sequence numbers are dropped or rejected. This connection tracking capability is critical to robust firewalling and device security. Tracking connections also gives us the ability to filter and analyze traffic depending on its connection state.

12.6.1 Connection States

Every packet is part of a connection, whether that connection has only a few packets or millions. All connections exist in one of four possible states:

1. New
2. Established
3. Related
4. Invalid

Firewall rules can be built around these connection states to filter traffic efficiently and log suspicious traffic.

New Connections

The first packet observed by the firewall in a stream of packets will be marked as *New*. This packet will be evaluated by firewall rules, and if it is allowed then the next packet going the other direction in that stream will create an *Established* connection.

Established Connections

A stream of network traffic that successfully passes packets both directions through the firewall is considered *Established*. Further packets in that connection will not be evaluated by the firewall because the first packets through were already allowed. Additional checking of the packets by the firewall would simply be a waste of resources since traffic going both directions in the connection was already checked against firewall rules.

Related Connections

Packets that are marked *Related* aren't part of a connection itself but they are related to one. An example mentioned in MikroTik's documentation[2] is an ICMP packet notifying the sender of an error in a connection. Protocols like FTP that use multiple ports can generate *Related* traffic. PPTP is another good example, with the connection using both TCP port 1723 and the GRE protocol. Having a firewall entry that allows *Related* traffic cuts down on unnecessary rules.

Invalid Connections

Network traffic that creates *Invalid* connections should almost always be dropped in the firewall. These types of packets could arrive at the router out-of-order or with an invalid sequence number. In production networks attached to the internet I often find *Invalid* connections are created by port scanners looking for open services. A router under extreme utilization that's dropping packets could also see traffic as *Invalid* because connections aren't able to properly initiate.

---

[2]https://wiki.mikrotik.com/wiki/Manual:IP/Firewall/Filter#Properties

12.7 Firewall Actions

Firewall actions determine what the router actually does with packets that match a firewall rule. The main actions are discussed here, though there are others than enable more advanced traffic policing.

12.7.1 Accept

The *accept* action allows a packet through the firewall. The packet will not be processed by any further rules, and continues on to its destination. When accepting firewall traffic be sure to only accept traffic that is necessary - everything else should be dropped. The following command accepts ICMP traffic from a trusted network monitoring host at *a.b.c.d*:

```
/ip firewall filter
add chain=input protocol=icmp src-address=a.b.c.d action=accept comment="
   Network Monitoring"
```

12.7.2 Add to Address List

This is actually two separate actions, but they both add an IP address to an address list. The two individual actions are as follows:

- *add-src-to-address-list*
- *add-dst-to-address-list*

One adds the SRC IP to a list, the other adds the DST IP.

The example command below adds the *source IP* of any telnet traffic (*TCP, port 23*) inbound to the WAN (*ether1*) to the "*Port Scanners*" address list. No production network should have Telnet open on the WAN interface, so any source IP of traffic matching this rule is probably a port scanner looking for soft targets. Create the rule with the following command:

```
/ip firewall filter
add chain=input protocol=tcp dst-port=23 in-interface=ether1 action=add-src-to
   -address-list address-list="Port Scanners"
```

The following firewall rule references that address list and blocks traffic inbound on *ether1*:

```
/ip firewall filter
chain=input action=drop in-interface=ether1 src-address-list="Port Scanners"
   comment="Drop port scanners"
```

> **NOTE**: The *Drop* rule should be moved ABOVE the *add-src-to-address-list* rule so that IPs already on the list are blocked immediately, instead of being constantly re-added to the list.

12.7.3 Drop

The *drop* action forces the router to stop processing a packet. No further action is taken, and the traffic matching the rule is silently dropped. This is the preferred method for discarding unwanted traffic. It is considered a best practice to *accept* necessary traffic and *drop* everything else with a final rule at the end of each chain. The following rule drops all traffic that hasn't already been allowed and should be sorted to the end of the chain:

```
/ip firewall filter
add chain=input action=drop comment="DROP ALL"
```

> **NOTE**: This rule is effective as a "catch-all" because it has no criteria - it matches all protocols, all ports, all types of traffic.

12.7.4 FastTrack Connection

The *FastTrack* firewall action is special, and using it can have a tangible impact on your routers. Once a connection is FastTracked all future packets in the connection won't be checked against the firewall. If the first packet in a connection matches an *allow* rule there isn't any value in checking the packets that follow. For high-throughput devices or firewalls with a lot of rules not checking every single packet can save significant processing resources.

The default configuration for RouterOS firewalls is to FastTrack all connections that have a state of *established* or *related*. If a connection has already been established it's passed through the firewall successfully, so FastTracking the rest of the connection makes sense. The following two firewall rules work together to FastTrack connections:

```
/ip firewall filter
add chain=forward action=fasttrack-connection connection-state=established,
    related
add chain=forward action=accept connection-state=established,related
```

For this example the first packet in a connection passes through the firewall successfully. This creates an *established* session on the firewall. The second packet of that established session to hit the firewall will match the first rule that has *action=fasttrack-connection* set. From that point onward the rest of the packets in the connection will bypass the firewall.

> **NOTE**: For best performance these rules should be placed at the top of the forward chain.

12.7.5 Jump

The *jump* action takes a packet being evaluated and moves it over to a different chain. Often this is used when custom chains have been built with special firewall rules. For example, the following rule takes any *input* chain traffic matching the *ospf protocol* and jumps it over to the *ospf chain* we already created on page 178.

```
/ip firewall filter
add protocol=ospf chain=input action=jump jump-target=ospf
```

The traffic will now be evaluated against rules in the custom *ospf* chain.

12.7.6 Log

The *log* action adds source and destination information for matching packets to the router's log. Traffic is passed on to the next firewall rule in the chain. As with the *passthrough* rules, it's recommended you disable or delete *log* rules when you're finished with them. Be aware that the log action could create a significant amount of log entries that fill up a device's storage and cause instability. The following command uses the *log* action to record inbound SSH traffic:

```
/ip firewall filter
add chain=input protocol=tcp dst-port=22 action=log
```

Figure 12.11 shows the result of the firewall rule's *log* action. Notice the log data that matches the firewall rule criteria (TCP protocol, port 22).

```
[admin@MikroTik] > /log print
16:23:55 firewall, info input: in:bridge out:(none), src-mac e8:4e:06:43:fd:6b, proto TCP (SYN),
    192.168.1.40:9477->192.168.1.38:22, len 52
16:23:55 firewall, info input: in:bridge out:(none), src-mac e8:4e:06:43:fd:6b, proto TCP (ACK),
    192.168.1.40:9477->192.168.1.38:22, len 40
16:23:55 firewall, info input: in:bridge out:(none), src-mac e8:4e:06:43:fd:6b, proto TCP (ACK,PSH),
    192.168.1.40:9477->192.168.1.38:22, len 68
16:23:55 firewall, info input: in:bridge out:(none), src-mac e8:4e:06:43:fd:6b, proto TCP (ACK,PSH),
    192.168.1.40:9477->192.168.1.38:22, len 712
16:23:55 firewall, info input: in:bridge out:(none), src-mac e8:4e:06:43:fd:6b, proto TCP (ACK,PSH),
    192.168.1.40:9477->192.168.1.38:22, len 64
16:23:55 firewall, info input: in:bridge out:(none), src-mac e8:4e:06:43:fd:6b, proto TCP (ACK,PSH),
    192.168.1.40:9477->192.168.1.38:22, len 312
...
16:24:17 system,error,critical login failure for user admin from 192.168.1.40 via ssh
16:24:17 system,info,account user admin logged in via local

[admin@MikroTik] > _
```

Figure 12.11: SSH Firewall Log

For troubleshooting you can also specify a *log-prefix* that adds custom text to the log message. This is useful for troubleshooting and easy to implement with the following command:

```
/ip firewall filter
add chain=input protocol=icmp action=log log-prefix="ICMP Traffic!"
```

> **NOTE**: Move this filter rule above the final *drop* rule or it'll never log any traffic.

An example of log entries created by the rule are shown in Figure 12.12:

```
17:17:19 firewall,info ICMP Traffic! input: in:bridge out:(none), src-mac 74:
   c6:3b:64:05:89, proto ICMP (type 3, code 3), 192.168.88.253->192.168.88.1,
   len 145
```

Figure 12.12: Logged ICMP Traffic

In higher-security environments is often necessary to enable logging on the final drop rule in each chain so possible attacks can be investigated. The Infrastructure Router STIG [1, Vul. ID V-3000] states the following about logging dropped traffic:

> "Review the network device interface ACLs to verify all deny statements are logged. If deny statements are not logged, this is a finding."

12.7.7 Passthrough

The *passthrough* action adds byte and packet counts to the rule's statistics then allows the traffic to continue being processed. This is helpful when determining if a certain kind of traffic is hitting your firewall. Disable or remove passthrough rules when you're done with them so as not to add processing overhead. The following command uses passthrough to get counter information for SSH traffic:

```
/ip firewall filter
add chain=input protocol=tcp dst-port=22 action=passthrough
```

View the statistics for all rules with the *passthrough* action:

```
/ip firewall filter print stats where action=passthrough
```

12.7.8 Reject

The *reject* action forces the router to discard matching packets but doesn't do it silently like the drop action does. Instead an ICMP message is sent to notify the sender that traffic was dropped. This could allow an attacker running port scans to fingerprint your device and continue reconnaissance efforts. For this reason the reject action is not the preferred method for discarding unwanted traffic. Some compliance standards like PCI-DSS and HIPAA specifically require that unwanted traffic be silently dropped, not discarded.

For testing purposes a firewall rule blocking all ICMP from *192.168.88.253* to the router was created and moved to the top of the input chain:

```
/ip firewall filter
chain=input action=reject protocol=icmp src-address=192.168.88.253
```

Figure 12.13 shows the result of an ICMP echo (*ping*) that matches the rule just created.

```
[admin@MikroTik] > ping 192.168.88.1
Pinging 192.168.88.1 with 32 bytes of data:

Reply from 192.168.88.1: Destination net unreachable.
[admin@MikroTik] > _
```

Figure 12.13: ICMP Reject Results

Note the "*Reply from 192.168.88.1 ...*" portion of the text response. The ICMP type three[3] message informs an attacker doing reconnaissance that a device is online with some kind of filtering. That attacker can now further tailor reconnaissance attempts to unmask the device. Figure 12.14 shows the result of that same rule and test *ping* but with the *drop* action instead of *reject*.

```
[admin@MikroTik] > ping 192.168.88.1
Pinging 192.168.88.1 with 32 bytes of data:

Request timed out.
[admin@MikroTik] > _
```

Figure 12.14: ICMP Drop Results

This is what an attacker doing reconnaissance should see - nothing at all. The difference in results is why it's so important to understand the consequences of using *reject*.

---

[3]https://www.iana.org/assignments/icmp-parameters/icmp-parameters.xhtml#icmp-parameters-types

12.7.9 Return

The *return* action sends traffic back to the chain that it was originally *jumped* from (p. 186). If you have a special chain set up for traffic analysis or troubleshooting you can *return* traffic to the original chain so it gets processed by the rest of its rules.

12.7.10 Tarpit

The *tarpit* action keeps TCP connections open and deliberately slows responses to traffic sources that match a firewall rule. These traffic sources could be port scanners, spammers, or other unsavory types. Some DDoS mitigation providers and large enterprises who deal with DDoS attacks use tarpitting to slow them down. However with botnets numbering in the thousands or tens-of-thousands this can have a limited effectiveness. Be aware that using tarpit keeps connections open so applying this action on a lot of traffic places significant load on a device.

12.8 Address Lists

Address lists help you consolidate and simplify firewall rules. They can also help with the network documentation process. Address lists are objects that firewall rules can reference made up of individual hosts or entire subnets. An example of a network topology that can use an address list is shown in Figure 12.15:

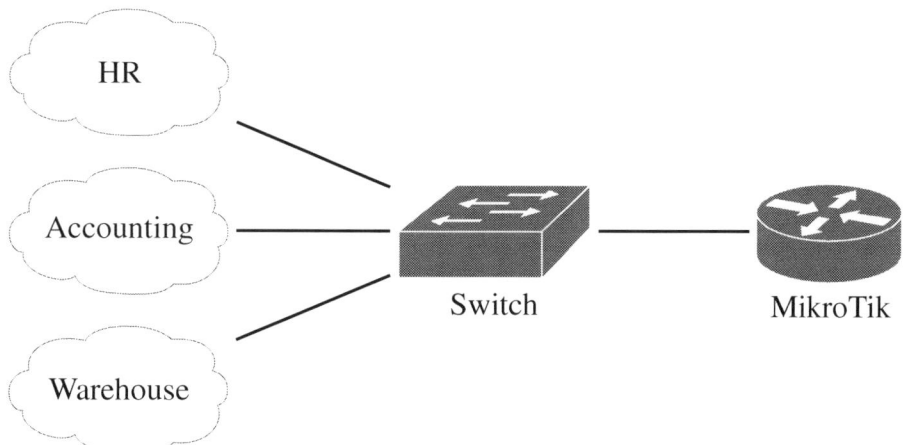

Figure 12.15: Address Group Topology

To create an address list just add an entry. If the list didn't exist before it will be created automatically. Deleting the final entry in an address list removes the list as well. The following command creates an address list containing three subnets, each one a local network behind a router:

```
/ip firewall address-list
add address=192.168.1.0/24 list="LANs" comment=HR
add address=192.168.2.0/24 list="LANs" comment=Accounting
add address=192.168.3.0/24 list="LANs" comment=Warehouse
```

Each network gets its own entry and comment, but they are all part of the "Local Nets" list. Entries can be added or removed from Address Lists without changing the firewall rules that reference them. If a new network *192.168.4.0/24* was brought online a simple */ip firewall address-list add ...* command adds the network to the list and all firewall rules will automatically apply. The following command uses the address list to allow traffic out *ether1* from all those networks:

```
/ip firewall filter
add chain=forward src-address-list="LANs" out-interface=ether1 action=accept
   comment="LANs to WAN"
```

What would have taken three total rules (one for each network) now is done in one rule. This solution scales really well as your networks grow and firewalling becomes more complex. Sorting rules becomes easier as well, because just one rule needs to be moved up or down the firewall chain instead of three. This kind of simplicity also helps prevent human error (and downtime).

12.9 Comments

Adding comments to firewall rules as they are built is an important step that can save time in the future with minimal effort in the present. Having comments in place for rules also helps onboard new network administrators faster since they don't have to puzzle out what each rule is for. Most examples in this part of the book feature comments, even if they are just one word like on page 189. Comments should be descriptive - assume someone other than yourself is reading them as you're creating comments. They don't need to be overly complicated, but they should point a person who doesn't know the network intimately in the right direction.

> **WARNING**: Avoid comments that require additional documentation to identify such as "Network 1", "Network 2", "Network 35", etc.

12.10 Review Questions

1. Which firewall chain filters traffic inbound to the router itself?

    (a) Input

    (b) Forward

    (c) Output

    (d) NAT

2. What protocol is allowed for monitoring via the Input chain in the default firewall rules?

    (a) TCP

    (b) UDP

    (c) IP

    (d) ICMP

3. An ICMP packet notifying a sender that a host cannot be found will be a *related* packet.

    (a) True

    (b) False

4. What firewall action blocks a packet without sending a reply to the sender?

    (a) Reject

    (b) Drop

    (c) Jump

    (d) Accept

5. Which firewall action speeds packets through the filtering process once they've been allowed?

    (a) Passthrough

    (b) Jump

    (c) FastPath

    (d) FastTrack

6. Rules are evaluated in alphabetical order by name in their respective chains.

    (a) True

    (b) False

7. Sending a ping from the router to another device creates traffic in which firewall chain?

    (a) Input

    (b) Forward

    (c) Output

    (d) Jump Chain

8. Once traffic has passed in both directions between a source and destination, what type of connection is created?

    (a) New

    (b) Related

    (c) Established

    (d) Invalid

9. Port scan traffic, like from a TCP SYN scan, inbound to the router can typically create what type of connection?

    (a) New

    (b) Established

    (c) Related

    (d) Invalid

10. Which rule should be placed at the end of each firewall chain?

    (a) Drop Invalid

    (b) Drop All

    (c) Drop Connections

    (d) Drop Source Routing

12.11 Review Answers

1. Which firewall chain filters traffic inbound to the router itself?

    A – Input (p. 175)

2. What protocol is allowed for monitoring via the Input chain in the default firewall rules?

    D – ICMP (p. 179)

3. An ICMP packet notifying a sender that a host cannot be found will be a *related* packet.

    A – True (p. 183)

4. What firewall action blocks a packet without sending a reply to the sender?

    B – Drop (p. 185)

5. Which firewall action speeds packets through the filtering process once they've been allowed?

    D – FastTrack (p. 185)

6. Rules are evaluated in alphabetical order by name in their respective chains.

    B – False (p. 179)

7. Sending a ping from the router to another device creates traffic in which firewall chain?

    C – Output (p. 177)

8. Once traffic has passed in both directions between a source and destination, what type of connection is created?

    C – Established (p. 183)

9. Port scan traffic, like from a TCP SYN scan, inbound to the router can typically create what type of connection?

    D – Invalid (p. 183)

10. Which rule should be placed at the end of each firewall chain?

    B – Drop All (p. 173)

Chapter 13

NAT

Network Address Translation (NAT) translates connections from one IP address to another. The router keeps track of connections between the inside and the outside, moving traffic in a way that's mostly transparent to the client. It's important to note that NAT is not routing. The function of NAT is to simply track and translate connections.

The most common use for NAT is translating connections from private internal IPs to a single outside public IP. Using NAT in this way satisfies the PCI-DSS requirement to not disclose private IP addresses [3, p. 4]:

> "Do not disclose private IP addresses and routing information to unauthorized parties. Note: Methods to obscure IP addressing may include, but are not limited to...Network Address Translation (NAT)"

Hundreds of internal clients can connect to the internet via a single publicly routed address. This prevented the complete exhaustion of public IPv4 addresses for quite a while, though most regions of the world are at the point where there are very few IPv4 addresses left to allocate. Another use for NAT is translating connections from the outside to inside resources like HTTPS or SMTP servers. This is known as "port forwarding".

13.1 NAT Overview

Two types of NAT are available in RouterOS:

- Source NAT (SRC-NAT)
- Destination NAT (DST-NAT)

Bot NAT types have their uses in enterprise and service provider networks. It's important to understand what traffic directions each handles, and which NAT actions translate connections the way you want.

13.1.1 Source NAT

SRC-NAT handles traffic originating from inside (or behind) the router destined for an external resource. This is most often private IPs being NAT'd out a single public IP to the internet. An example of where SRC-NATing would occur is shown in dashed lines between the router and ISP in Figure 13.1:

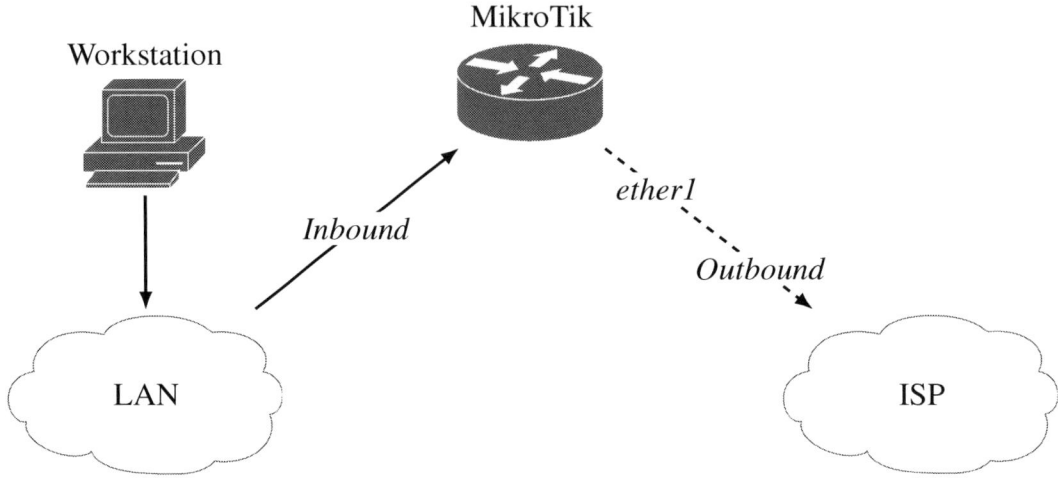

Figure 13.1: Source NAT Topology

The following command configures NAT for translating outbound connections through *ether1* using the *masquerade* action:

```
/ip firewall nat
add chain=srcnat action=masquerade out-interface=ether1
```

Most traffic that uses this rule will probably be routed by the default gateway route (p. 141).

13.1.2 Destination NAT

DST-NAT handles traffic inbound to the router destined for an internal resource. This could be a connection from a client outside the network that will be translated to an internal web or email server. An example of this is shown in Figure 13.2 with the DST-NAT translated connection in dashed lines:

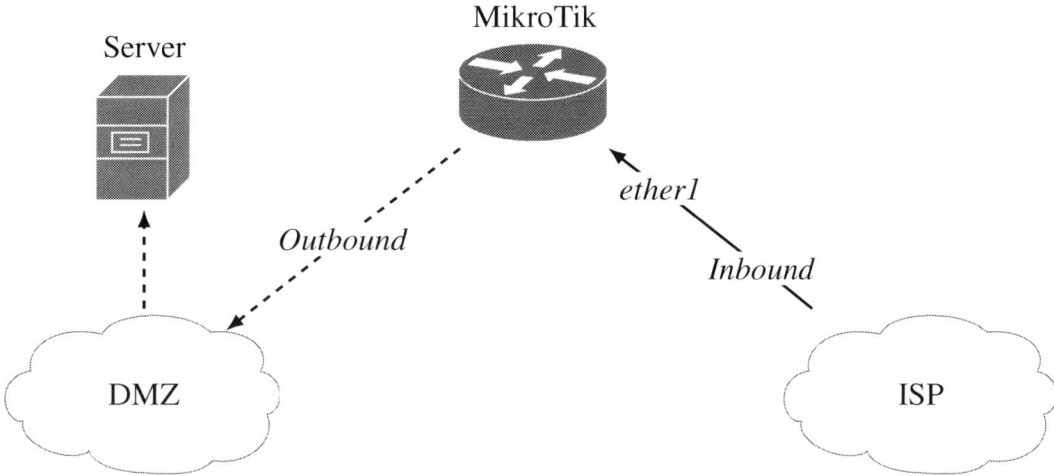

Figure 13.2: Destination NAT Topology

The following command would NAT inbound connections on *ether1* using *TCP port 80* to *192.168.10.100*, a web server:

```
/ip firewall nat
add chain=dstnat action=dst-nat in-interface=ether1 protocol=tcp dst-port=80
    to-addresses=192.168.10.100 to-ports=80
```

It is considered a best practice to only NAT specific ports and protocols inbound that are absolutely required. This is why the rule above specifies both the port and the protocol, so only HTTP traffic will match the rule.

13.2 RFC-1918 Addresses

The addresses whose connections are translated through NAT are most often in the private ranges defined by RFC-1918. The following networks are set aside for private internal use [21]:

- 10.0.0.0/8: 10.0.0.0 – 10.255.255.255
- 172.16.0.0/12: 172.16.0.0 – 172.31.255.255
- 192.168.0.0/16: 192.168.0.0 – 192.168.255.255

Most SOHO MikroTik routers SRC-NAT connections from the private 192.168.88.0/24 default subnet outbound through *ether1* to an upstream provider. For both general professional purposes and the MTCNA it's important to know the RFC-1918 ranges and which addresses are usable for network hosts.

13.2.1 NAT and IPv6

IPv4 networks often rely heavily on NAT due to IPv4 address exhaustion. However, there is no such NAT function available natively in IPv6. Due to the number of possible IPv6 addresses NAT is not needed. IPv6 addresses are fully routable, achieving the end-to-end reachability without NAT for all devices that IPv4 originally had.

While organizations transition from IPv4 to IPv6 over the very long-term there are some stop-gap measures that can be put in place. If you have IPv6 addresses assigned internally but your upstream ISP still doesn't offer IPv6 connectivity you can use a "6to4" virtual interface. Some vendors also support the "NAT64" feature that translates outside IPv6 addresses to internal IPv4 addresses. This feature is not supported by RouterOS as of this writing, however.

13.3 NAT Chains

Two default NAT chains process traffic depending on its direction. Figure 13.3 shows the two available chains in the Winbox interface:

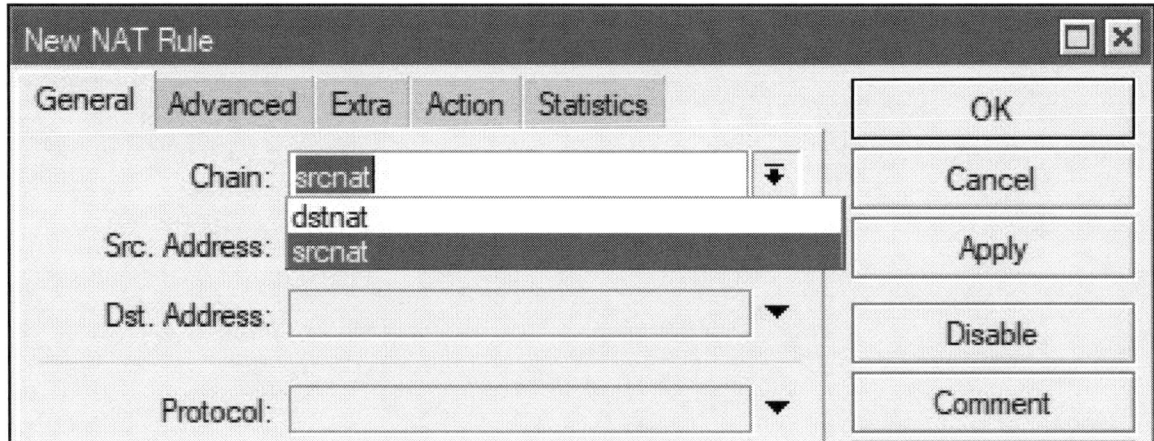

Figure 13.3: NAT Chains, Winbox

Like in the RouterOS firewall it's possible to create your own NAT chains if your NAT configuration is complex. Custom chains, however, are beyond the scope of the MTCNA.

13.4 NAT Actions

There are a number of things NAT can do to a packet when it matches a NAT rule, though some are only used rarely. Understanding each action allows you to handle translated connections properly as they ingress or egress the network.

13.4.1 Accept

The *Accept* action is used in rules referred to as "NAT-Bypass" rules. Some protocols can't function across NAT connections including IPSEC for VPNs and SIP for Voice over IP (VoIP). For traffic that uses these protocols it's best to put an *Accept* rule in so that NAT won't "grab" that traffic and break it. Packets matching a rule with this action do not get processed by NAT and don't passthrough to the next rule.

13.4.2 Add to Address List

This functions the same as the Firewall action on page 184 bearing the same name. Matching traffic is added to an Address List for monitoring purposes, or whatever else can be done with an Address List. A timeout can be specified as well so entries don't stay on the address list forever (unless they should).

13.4.3 Destination NAT

The *DST-NAT* action translate traffic inbound to a specified IP address and port number. The following command uses the *DST-NAT* action to translate *HTTP* (TCP port 80) connections inbound to *1.1.1.1* to an internal server at *192.168.1.10*:

```
/ip firewall nat
add chain=dstnat action=dst-nat to-addresses=192.168.1.10 to-ports=80 protocol
   =tcp dst-address=1.1.1.1 dst-port=80 comment="HTTP Server"
```

13.4.4 Jump

Just like the firewall *Jump* action (p. 186) the NAT version "jumps" traffic matching a rule to another specified chain. Once in the new chain the traffic will be evaluated in the typical top-down fashion. The *Return* action sends traffic back to the original chain where the *Jump* occurred.

13.4.5 Log

The *Log* action adds an entry to the device log about traffic that matches the rule, then passes that traffic to the next rule. This action is very helpful when troubleshooting if traffic is matching a rule being implemented.

13.4.6 Masquerade

MikroTik's RouterOS documentation describes this action as a "unique subversion" of the Source NAT action [12]. The *Masquerade* action translates connections from an internal network out an interface where a dynamic address is assigned. Unlike the SRC-NAT action, you aren't able to choose a specific address to use for translating connections. For most SOHO networks this is a good solution because the local service provider typically only assigns a single public dynamic address. The following commands configure a NAT rule that Masquerades outbound traffic through *ether1*:

```
/ip firewall nat
add chain=srcnat action=masquerade out-interface=ether1
```

This rule works together with a default route (p. 141) that points outbound traffic through *ether1* to a service provider gateway. Even though the router's dynamic address might change as leases come and go, the gateway's address never will, so traffic will continue going out *ether1*. It is also the same default NAT rule referenced on page 42.

13.4.7 Netmap

One-to-one NAT is implemented with the *Netmap* action. This action maps external addresses to internal addresses, translating all connections on all ports. This is commonly used to map a group of publicly routable addresses to corresponding servers in a DMZ.

The following rule maps all inbound traffic to the public address *1.1.1.1* to a DMZ host *10.1.0.1*:

```
/ip firewall nat
add chain=dstnat action=netmap dst-address=1.1.1.1 to-addresses=10.1.0.1
```

13.4.8 Passthrough

This action allows traffic that matches the rule to pass through to the next. In the process of passing the connection to the next rule the system will increment packet and byte counters. Using this action is a good way to troubleshoot what traffic profiles are matching a NAT rule without breaking production network flow.

13.4.9 Redirect

The *Redirect* action rewrites port numbers to whatever port the administrator specifies in the "to-ports" option. For example, this action could be used to redirect external traffic to TCP port 80 to 8080 on an internal server.

13.4.10 Return

The *Return* action sends traffic back to the chain where the *Jump* action was originally used.

13.4.11 Source NAT

This action translates connections outbound from a local network using a specific external address. If an organization has multiple static public IPs it's possible to be very specific about which networks or hosts NAT via what public address. This action is not appropriate when dynamic external addresses are assigned to the router.

13.5 Review Questions

1. What NAT chain processes traffic inbound to the router on its way to an internal resource?

    (a) SRC-NAT

    (b) DST-NAT

    (c) Pre-Routing

    (d) Masquerade

2. In the default RouterOS configuration, which NAT action translates connections outbound on *ether1*?

    (a) Masquerade

    (b) Passthrough

    (c) Drop

    (d) Accept

3. What NAT action should be used for traffic between subnets that is passed over an IPSEC tunnel?

    (a) Masquerade

    (b) Passthrough

    (c) Drop

    (d) Accept

4. NAT is used on IPv6 networks.

    (a) True

    (b) False

5. Which address will *masquerade* NAT traffic appear to originate, from the perspective of a web server on the internet?

    (a) LAN private address

    (b) LAN public address

    (c) WAN public address

    (d) WAN private address

6. What NAT action maps an external port to a different port for a public resource hosted in a DMZ?

    (a) Masquerade

    (b) SRC-NAT

    (c) Redirect

    (d) OSPF

7. Which NAT action maps an external public IP address to an internal private IP address?

    (a) Netmap

    (b) Redirect

    (c) Masquerade

    (d) Translate

8. Which RFC set aside private internal IPv4 ranges?

    (a) RFC-1917

    (b) RFC-1918

    (c) RFC-1919

    (d) RFC-1920

9. Which subnet is configured as the internal network that is translated outbound via NAT in the default RouterOS configuration?

    (a) 192.168.0.0/24

    (b) 192.168.1.0/24

    (c) 192.168.88.0/24

    (d) 192.168.81.0/24

10. IPSEC uses NAT to hide IP addresses for security.

    (a) True

    (b) False

13.6 Review Answers

1. What NAT chain processes traffic inbound to the router on its way to an internal resource?

   B – DST-NAT (p. 197)

2. In the default RouterOS configuration, which NAT action translates connections outbound on *ether1*?

   A – Masquerade (p. 200)

3. What NAT action should be used for traffic between subnets that is passed over an IPSEC tunnel?

   D – Accept (p. 199)

4. NAT is used on IPv6 networks.

   B – False (p. 195)

5. Which address will NAT traffic appear to originate, from the perspective of a web server on the internet?

   C – WAN public address (p. 195)

6. What NAT action maps an external port to a different port for a public resource hosted in a DMZ?

   C – Redirect (p. 201)

7. Which NAT action maps an external public IP address to an internal private IP address?

   A – Netmap (p. 200)

8. Which RFC set aside private internal IPv4 ranges?

   B – RFC-1918 (p. 197)

9. Which subnet is configured as the internal network that is translated outbound via NAT in the default RouterOS configuration?

   C – 192.168.88.0/24 (p. 42)

10. IPSEC uses NAT to hide IP addresses for security.

    B – False (p. 199)

Chapter 14

Wireless

With many companies moving steadily in a "mobile-first" direction, and with the continued drop in desktop sales, it's clear mobility is necessary in modern networks. Many organizations no longer purchase desktop computers for their employees, instead relying on robust laptops or tablets with external displays. The BYOD movement means that tablets, mobile phones, laptops, and convertible devices will come and go and customers expect those devices to "just work". Wireless communications covered in the MTCNA are defined in the IEEE 802.11 standard. Other licensed and unlicensed technologies are covered in more advanced certifications.

14.1 Wireless Protocols

MikroTik provides a unique mix of wireless protocols that's made it very popular in the wireless industry. Each protocol has its own purpose and benefits, and choosing the right protocol is important for building resilient, high-performance wireless networks. Figure 14.1 shows the available wireless protocols in Winbox:

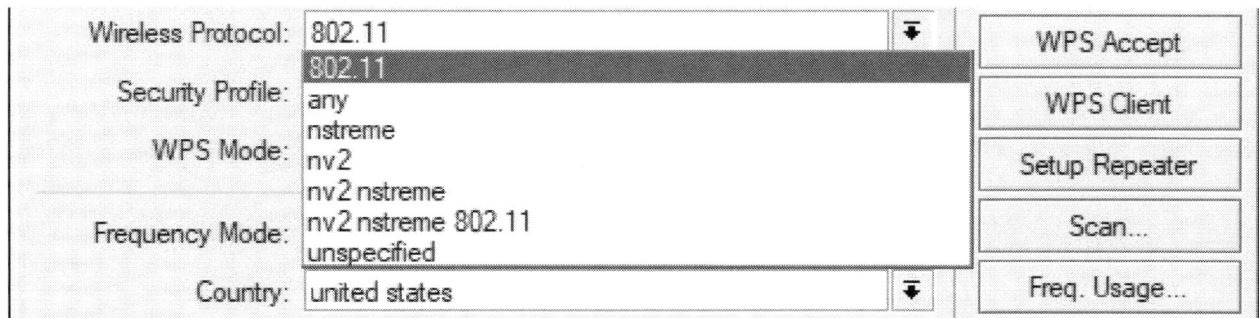

Figure 14.1: Wireless Protocols

The main focus is the 802.11 protocol for the purposes of the MTCNA. This is the protocol most users and network administrators associate with wireless networks outside the WISP market.

The *Nstreme* protocol is proprietary to MikroTik and is designed for high-performance point-to-point links. It combines the Carrier-Sense Multiple Access with Collision Avoidance (CSMA-CA) used in 802.11 with additional polling. This polling adds some overhead to the wireless network but can allow for decreased collisions and improved throughput [15]. Bear in mind that 802.11 hosts cannot join a *Nstreme* network.

The *Nv2* protocol is the successor to *Nstreme*. This newer protocol uses Time-Division Multiple Access (TDMA) multiplexing instead of CSMA-CA used in 802.11 and *Nstreme* networks. It also does away with the polling because it's no longer necessary. Each AP gets its own dedicated time slots for transmitting with *Nsteme*, so connections can be quite robust. However, this protocol can only be used between two MikroTik units and it only works on Atheros-brand wireless chipsets [15]. Just like with *Nstreme*, 802.11 hosts cannot join an *Nv2* network.

14.2 802.11 Wireless Standards

The IEEE 802.11 standard governs physical and data-link wireless network communications. Wireless network technologies are often known as WLAN (Wireless LAN) or Wi-Fi. "Wi-Fi" is a trademark of the non-profit Wi-Fi Alliance[1] that certifies devices as compliant with existing and draft standards.

Standard	Frequency Band	Speeds	Multiplexing
802.11a	5 GHz	6-54 Mbit/s	OFDM
802.11b	2.4 GHz	1-11 Mbit/s	DSSS
802.11g	2.4 GHz	6-54 Mbit/s	OFDM
802.11n	2.4 and 5 GHz	Up to 150 Mbit/s	MIMO-OFDM
802.11ac	5 GHz	Up to 7 Gbit/s	MIMO-OFDM

Table 14.1: 802.11 Wireless Standards

14.3 Frequency Bands

Wireless network equipment often runs in unlicensed frequency bands that are set aside in many countries for industry use. This means that WLAN equipment is subject to interference on those bands, and they must not utilized reserved frequencies unless specifically licensed. Some high-speed microwave backhaul connections utilize higher power or other frequencies that require a license but those fall outside the scope of this book.

Frequency ranges have been set aside in the United States and around the world for WLAN and other industry use. This includes the Industrial, Scientific, and Medical (ISM) band in the United States and Unlicensed National Information Infrastructure (U-NII) globally. Wireless transmit power is limited to one Watt without additional licenses to operate in most countries. Table 14.2 on the following page shows the frequency bands for both ISM and U-NII:

---
[1] https://www.wi-fi.org

Frequency Band	Frequency Range
ISM	2.4 - 2.5 GHz
U-NII	5.150 - 5.925 GHz

Table 14.2: Wireless Frequency Ranges

Other wireless bands are often used by WISPs for point-to-point backhauls between buildings or towers. These networks operate at various frequencies that don't require a license like 900MHz, 24GHz, or 60GHz. For the purposes of the MTCNA only the ISM and U-NII bands are important.

14.4 ISM

The ISM frequency band was set aside globally in the 1940's to accommodate devices we now take for granted [22]. This includes the 2.4-2.5 Gigahertz (GHz) band used for wireless networking, though there are other bands set aside in ISM. Versions of the 802.11 wireless standard that utilize the ISM band include 802.11b, 802.11g, and 802.11n.

Omni-directional devices operating in this band are free to utilize the spectrum at one Watt of transmit power or less, and fixed directional devices may use up to four Watts in the United States. Regardless of antenna type they must accept interference from other devices in the ISM band. This means that non-networking products like microwave ovens, baby monitors, and Bluetooth headsets can interfere with network traffic. Over the years the ISM band has become increasingly crowded as more mobile devices come online. Many modern devices utilize more than just the ISM band for wireless networking to cope with the crowded frequency space.

14.5 U-NII

The U-NII band occupies the 5.150-5.925 GHz spectrum. Wireless standards 802.11a and 802.11n occupy this space, as well as the newer 802.11ac standard. While the higher frequency allows for more data throughput than in the ISM band it is more susceptible to attenuation from obstructions. Most modern wireless devices can use both the ISM and U-NII bands to optimize connectivity.

14.6 DFS

The Dynamic Frequency Selection (DFS) feature implements government-mandated avoidance of frequencies used by military, aviation, and weather radar systems in the 5GHz band. If radar signals are detected on a channel that the MikroTik device is operating in DFS functionality takes over. The wireless device will disassociate connected clients, pick a new frequency, and shift wireless operation. Ideally this process is seamless, though in practice not all clients handle the transition well. In the United States as of 2016 DFS functionality is no longer optional, and wireless device makers who participate in the U.S. market have had to accommodate this requirement.

On MikroTik devices compliance with DFS can be accomplished by setting the *Frequency Mode* to *Regulatory Domain* and then selecting your country in the *Country* field. An example of this configuration in Winbox is shown in Figure 14.2:

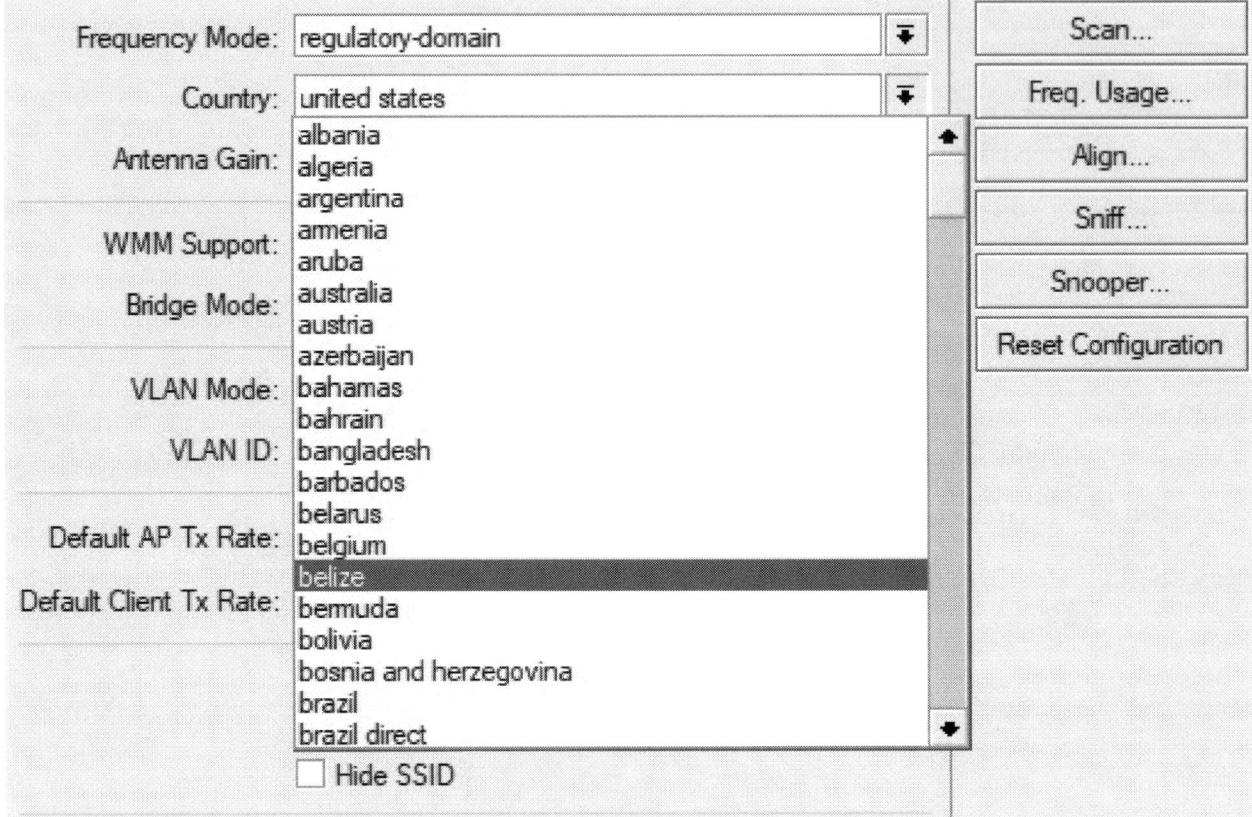

Figure 14.2: Frequency Mode, Country Selection

Updates to the country profiles are included in regular RouterOS upgrades when applicable.

> **WARNING**: Making changes to the *Frequency Mode* and *Country* will briefly disassociate wireless clients as the frequency changes.

14.7 Channels

The ISM band has a total of 14 wireless network channels, with some differences in the channels used depending on the country and local regulations. The U-NII band has 60 channels available for networking but they vary by country and authorized indoor or outdoor usage. By staggering the frequency between access points close to one another it's possible to have clients and access points "playing nice" and not interfering with each other. Non-overlapping channels for the United States are shown in Table 14.3 on the following page.

Standard	Non-Overlapping Channels
802.11a	36, 40, 44, 48, 149, 153, 157, 161 (Non-DFS only)
802.11b	1, 6, 11, 14
802.11g	1, 6, 11
802.11n	None
802.11ac	Depends on channel size

Table 14.3: 802.11 Non-Overlapping Channels (U.S.)

It's difficult to list non-overlapping channels for 802.11ac because available channel widths vary significantly. The 802.11ac standard allows for 20, 40, 80, and 160 Megahertz (MHz) channel widths. Larger channel widths allow for higher speeds but leave little or no room for other APs in close proximity to use non-overlapping channels. For this reason channel width and available speed must be balanced with AP density and physical spacing.

For all 802.11 standards overlapping channels can be used in close proximity but it should be avoided if possible. Modern wireless networks include APs in the ISM and U-NII bands to balance spectrum usage. Many hardware manufacturers like Atheros also include proprietary features like *Adaptive Noise Immunity* to compensate for interference and crowded frequencies. Even with extra features built into hardware it's a good idea to plan for non-overlapping channels first and space APs appropriately. Once you've figured out which channels to use and installed the APs then implement those extra features.

> **NOTE**: To see which channels are in use around your location use the Wireless Snooper tool on page 220.

14.8 Wireless Scanner

RouterOS includes a tool for wireless scanning that can show what access points and clients are in the area and which frequencies are in-use. Knowing which parts of the available spectrum are congested can help you maximize wireless performance. Recently a new feature was introduced in RouterOS that allows for wireless scanning while clients remain connected to an AP. On-the-fly wireless scanning for troubleshooting and optimization is much easier now. Figure 14.3 on the next page shows the wireless scanner running with the *"background=yes"* option:

```
[admin@MikroTik] > /interface wireless scan wlan1 background=yes
Flags: A - active, P - privacy, R - routeros-network, N - nstreme, T - tdma, W
       - wds, B - bridge
         ADDRESS            SSID              CHANNEL               SIG
 AP      50:6A:03:8A:F0:B6  8AF0B6            2412/20/gn(30dBm)     -90
 AP      E4:F4:C6:19:71:DC  NETGEAR92         2427/20/gn(30dBm)     -84
 A       00:80:E1:B8:34:5C  WiFi_B8345C       2437/20/g(30dBm)      -49
 P       A0:63:91:E1:3F:A3  dogewireless      2437/20/gn(30dBm)     -84
 AP      9C:AD:97:E2:AF:CE  E2AFCE-2.4G       2412/20/gn(30dBm)     -90
 AP      10:78:5B:46:2B:31  NETGEAR87         2412/20/gn(30dBm)     -88
 P       78:23:AE:86:1F:29  861F29            2437/20/gn(30dBm)     -89
 AP      C0:C5:22:05:81:4A  05814A            2412/20/gn(30dBm)     -92
 P       A4:2B:8C:9C:43:F4  NETGEAR85         2442/20/gn(30dBm)     -88
 P       6A:54:FD:D3:A5:35                    2427/20/gn(30dBm)     -78
 AP      C0:C5:22:D5:0D:55  D50D55            2462/20/gn(30dBm)     -89
 AP      10:0D:7F:DC:E0:20  DCE020            2462/20/gn(30dBm)     -84
 AP      5C:8F:E0:2B:5C:24  2B5C24            2437/20/gn(30dBm)     -89
 --     [Q quit|D dump|C-z pause]
```

Figure 14.3: Wireless Scanner Running

The same tool is available in Winbox with the ability to sort values in the different columns. Click *"Wireless > WLAN Interface > Scan"* to access the graphical tool. Figure 14.4 on the following page shows the scanner tool running in Winbox:

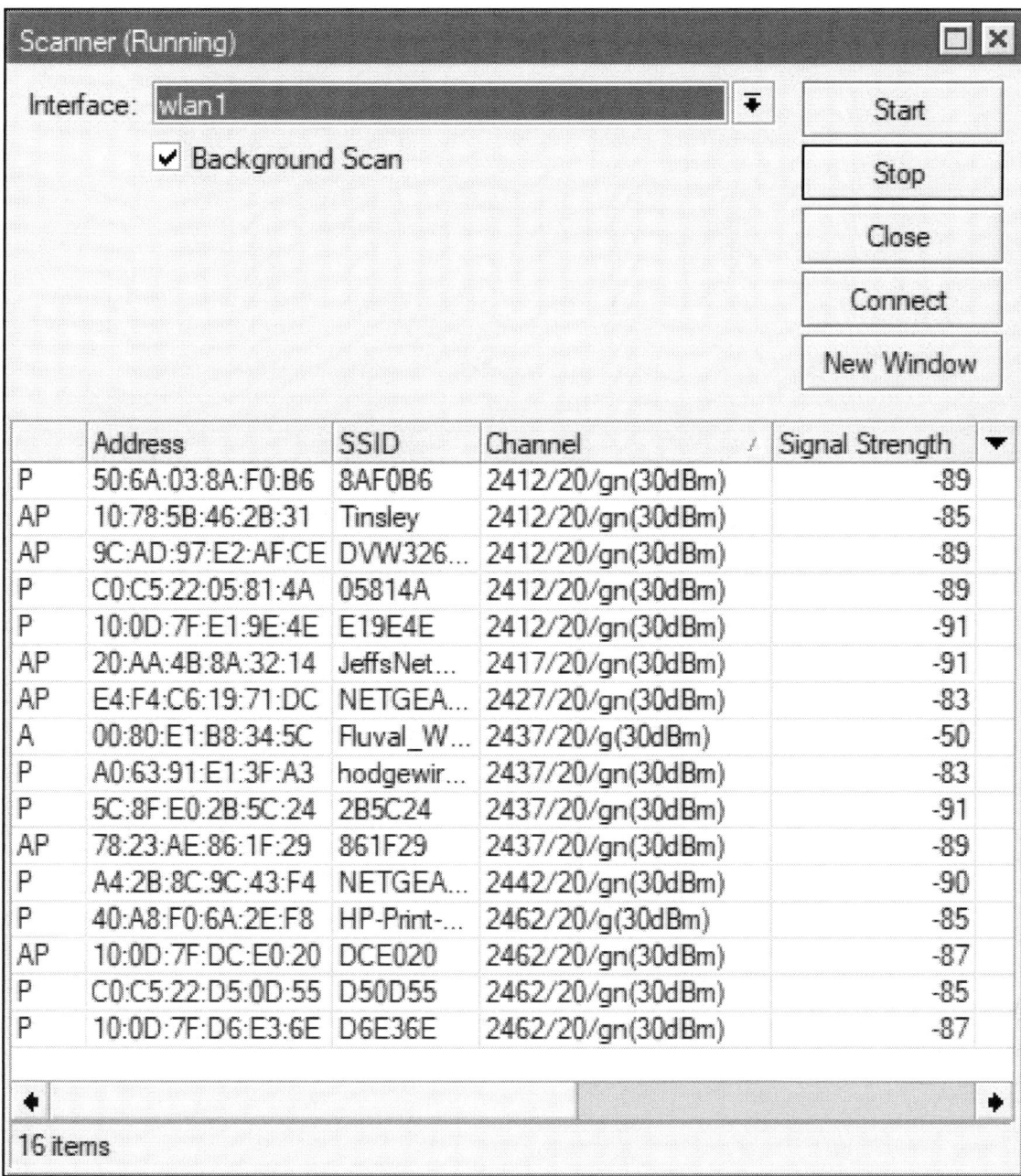

Figure 14.4: Wireless Scanner Running - Winbox

From the results of the scan it looks like most clients are using channels one (2412), six (2437), and eleven (2462). None of these channels overlap with the other, however each channel on its own is fairly congested. At this location it would be worthwhile to test throughput on channels between those in heavy use. This tool can also be used to satisfy the PCI-DSS requirement to scan for rogue access points [3, p. 18]:

> "Implement processes to test for the presence of wireless access points (802.11), and detect and identify all authorized and unauthorized wireless access points..."

14.9 Data Rates

The 802.11 wireless standards are fairly tolerant of interference produced by other devices, walls, furniture, and the natural environment. With that said, it's sometimes necessary to reduce data speeds in order to maintain connectivity in a "noisy" environment. Most wireless devices will "fall back" to slower speeds to maintain connectivity until there are no more slower speeds left. In RouterOS the *Supported Rates* are speeds that wireless clients will use if possible. The *Basic Rates* are speeds that devices associate to the AP and send multicast with. They are also the lowest speeds that a device can use before it has to drop off the wireless network. A default example of configurable data rates is shown in Figure 14.5:

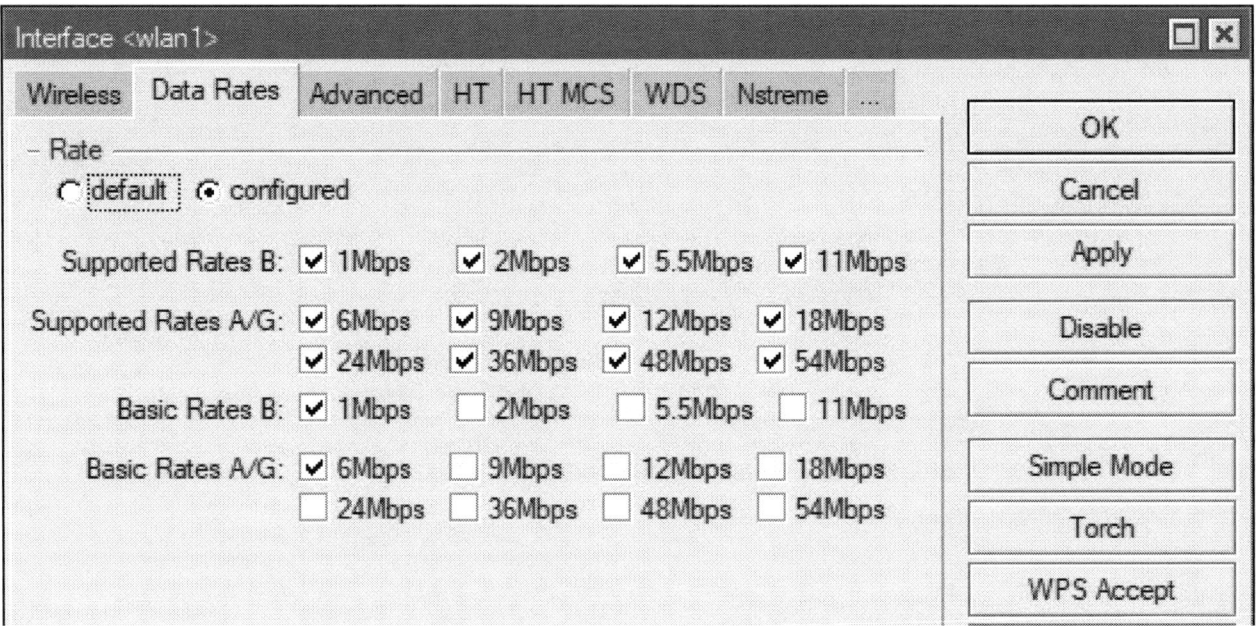

Figure 14.5: Wireless Data Rates

14.10 Multiplexing

Multiplexing is how multiple devices communicate simultaneously over a shared medium like Radio Frequency (RF). Many different types of multiplexing exist but only a few are used in networking. For the MTCNA you don't need to know about multiplexing in-depth, but you should be aware that 802.11 relies on frequency-division and time-division multiplexing. This is where multiple clients use different parts of a frequency or different time slots to broadcast their RF signal. Newer wireless standards like 802.11n and 802.11ac also feature Multiple Input, Multiple Output (MIMO). This allows devices compliant with the new standards to utilize multiple antennas for transmitting and receiving.

Standard	Multiplexing Type
802.11a	Orthogonal Frequency Division Multiplexing (OFDM)
802.11b	Direct Sequence Spread Spectrum (DSSS)
802.11g	OFDM
802.11n	MIMO-OFDM
802.11ac	MIMO-OFDM

Table 14.4: 802.11 Multiplexing

14.11 Chains

A wireless chain (transceiver) can be used to transmit and receive wireless data. Older wireless interfaces typically had only one chain. Some MikroTik WLAN interfaces still feature one chain, though many built-in WLAN chips and add-on MPCI cards have two or three. Using multiple chains allows for increased throughput in a configuration known as MIMO. A MIMO access point can transmit multiple streams at once, which can be received simultaneously by a MIMO station. Generally speaking the more chains and antennas in use, the higher wireless performance can be scaled if MIMO clients can support it. Each chain has its own transmit power and receive sensitivity levels based on the interface's chipset and antenna.

14.11.1 Transmit Power

Depending on the wireless interface and chipset each chain has its own transmit power limit. Figure 14.6 shows the available options for a wireless interface in Winbox:

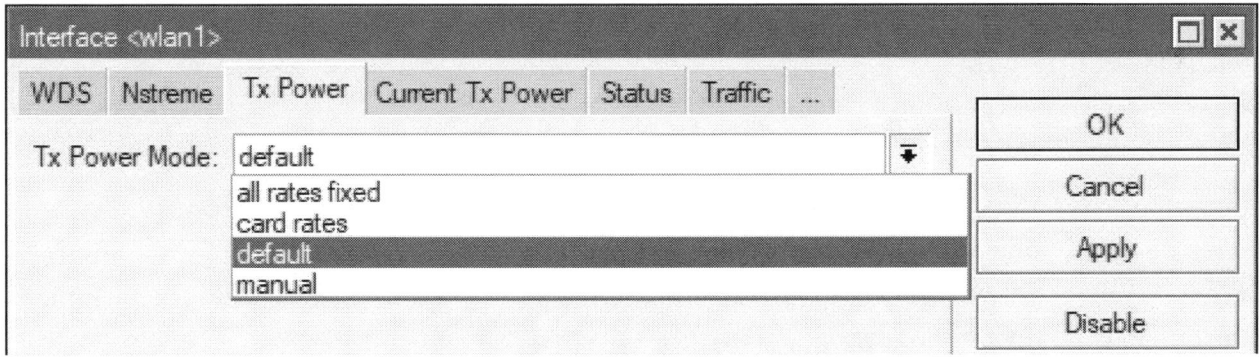

Figure 14.6: Transmit Power Modes

MikroTik recommends using the *card-rates* mode for newer Atheros chipsets [18]. This mode scales power output as client speed changes using values programmed into the WLAN chipset. It's also possible to manually set the transmit power for each speed, though this isn't recommended by the vendor. Figure 14.7 on the next page shows the current power levels per speed set automatically with the built-in values on the WLAN card:

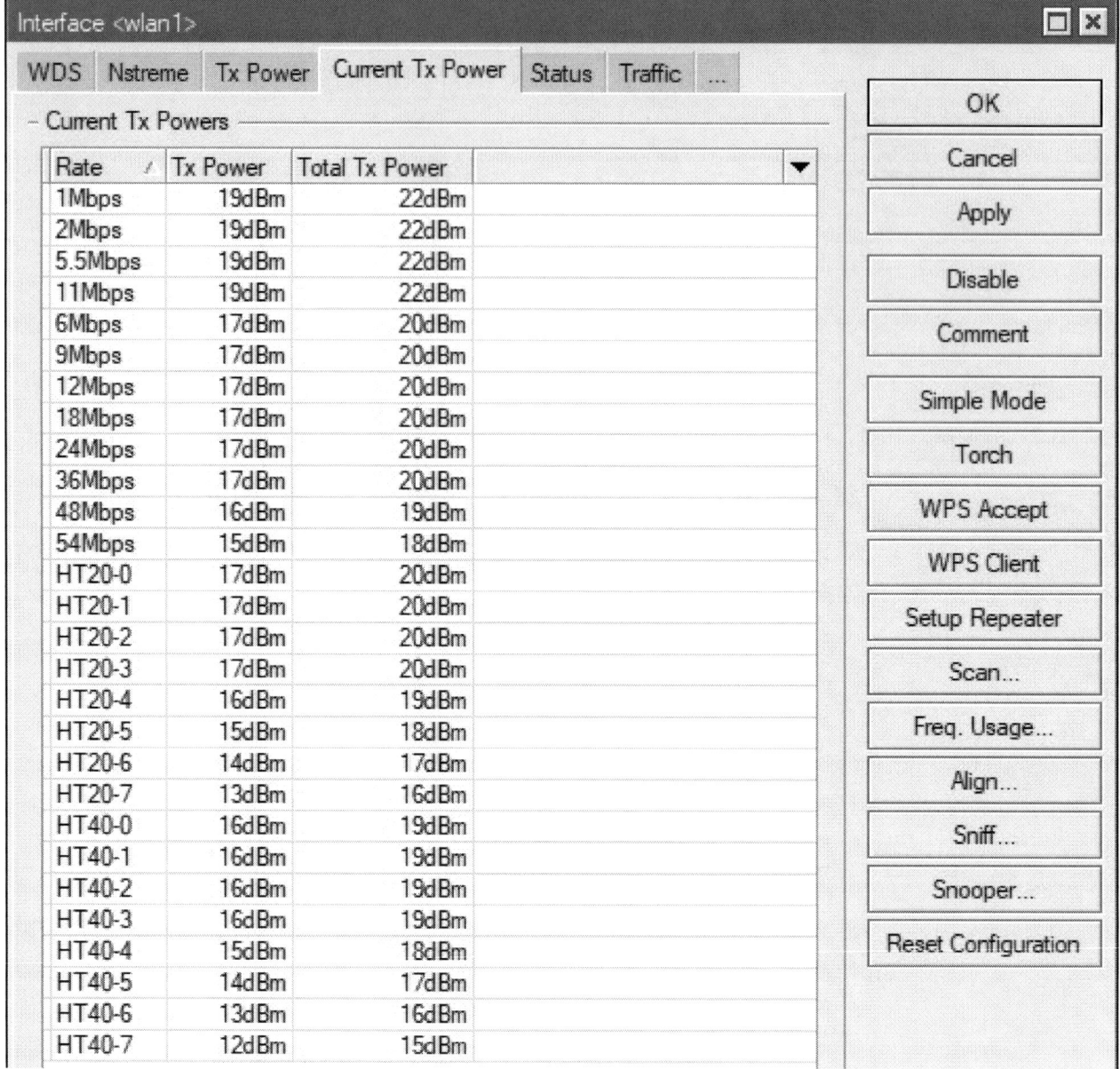

Figure 14.7: Current Wireless TX Power

Some organizations that operate high-security networks will limit the TX power of their APs to make remote connectivity impossible. They need to know that only users within a certain distance or inside the confines of their building can access the wireless network. This is one of the few times that manually setting the TX power levels is needed. Wireless units close together in a point-to-point configuration using high-gain directional antennas can also benefit from reduced power levels. Though it may seem illogical, using too much TX power can sometimes cause problems.

14.11.2 Antenna Gain

Many RouterBOARD models like the RB900-series have built-in WLAN chips and antennas that don't require further configuration or an external antenna. Other models targeted to outdoor environments and the WISP industry like the Groove require an external antenna to function. Antennas can be directional or omnidirectional, and some are more efficient than others. The efficiency of an antenna's conversion of electrical signal and RF energy is its gain. This value is typically expressed in *dBi*, and it must be configured on each wireless interface using an external antenna to get the best possible performance. Higher-end antennas are typically more expensive, but with the price comes higher gain and better directionality.

When attaching an external antenna to a MikroTik unit, first consult the antenna's datasheet for the gain value. Then update the gain configuration for the wireless interface as shown in Figure 14.8 with a 4 dBi gain antenna:

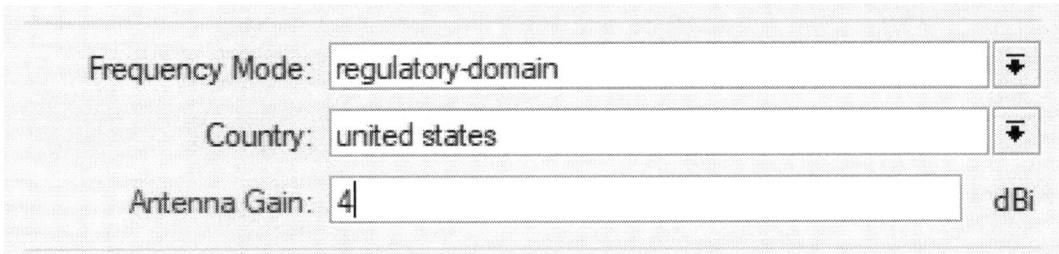

Figure 14.8: Configuring Antenna Gain

14.11.3 Noise Floor

The noise floor value for a particular frequency band is the level of background noise. Ideally this number would be very low, and the strength of the received signal from an AP or station would be very high. The ratio of background noise to received signal strength is the Signal-to-Noise Ratio (SNR). The current noise floor value for a wireless interface can be found on the Status tab in Winbox for each WLAN interface. An example value of -115 dBm is shown at the bottom of Figure 14.9 on the next page:

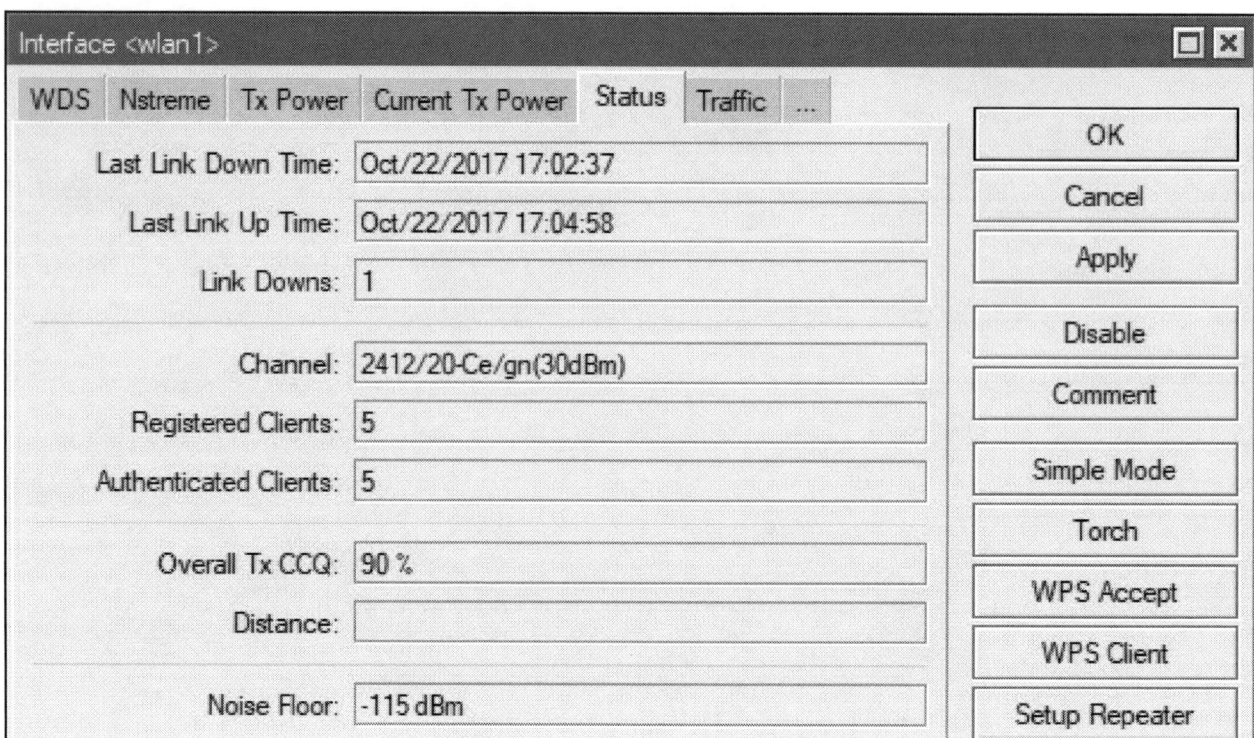

Figure 14.9: Wireless Noise Floor

The noise floor value of -115 dBm is quite good, indicating that the environment isn't very noisy. Many locations aren't so lucky though, and switching channels or even entire frequency bands (e.g. 802.11b/g to 802.11n/ac) might be necessary. If a location is very noisy it's best to switch channels, observe the noise floor value. Keep switching and observing until you find the least-noisy part of the wireless spectrum and use that.

14.12 Wireless Link Configurations

Wireless MikroTik devices can operate in a number of modes. The MTCNA covers Access Point and Station modes, and MikroTik Certified Wireless Engineer (MTCWE) topics cover the remaining modes. Figure 14.10 shows the modes that a wireless interface can operate in.

```
[admin@MikroTik] > /interface wireless set wlan1 mode=[Tab]
 alignment-only  bridge    station    station-pseudobridge    station-wds    ap
-bridge    nstreme-dual-slave    station-bridge    station-pseudobridge-clone
   wds-slave

[admin@MikroTik] > _
```

Figure 14.10: Wireless Modes

These same modes are available in a drop-down menu for each wireless interface inside Winbox and Webfig. Figure 14.11 shows the available modes in Winbox:

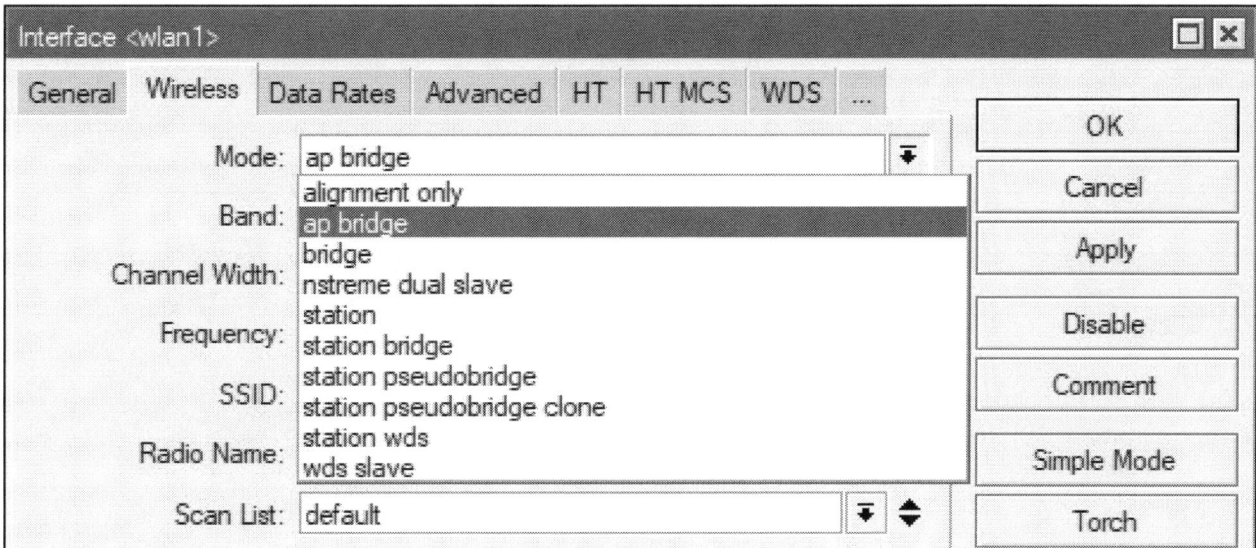

Figure 14.11: Winbox Wireless Modes

Wireless Distribution System (WDS) modes create links between two APs. Often this is used to bridge two networks together transparently. The WDS standard is used across the industry, so you can bridge a MikroTik unit with an AP from another manufacturer like Ubiquiti.

14.12.1 Access Point - Bridge Mode

AP units running in *Access Point - Bridge (AP-BR)* mode allow multiple stations to join their wireless networks. These AP units could either be dedicated APs or combination wired and wireless routers. The latter is the most common model for SOHO and branch offices. AP-BR is also the default mode for RouterBOARD-integrated wireless interfaces. Figure 14.12 shows an AP-BR topology with different types of connected stations:

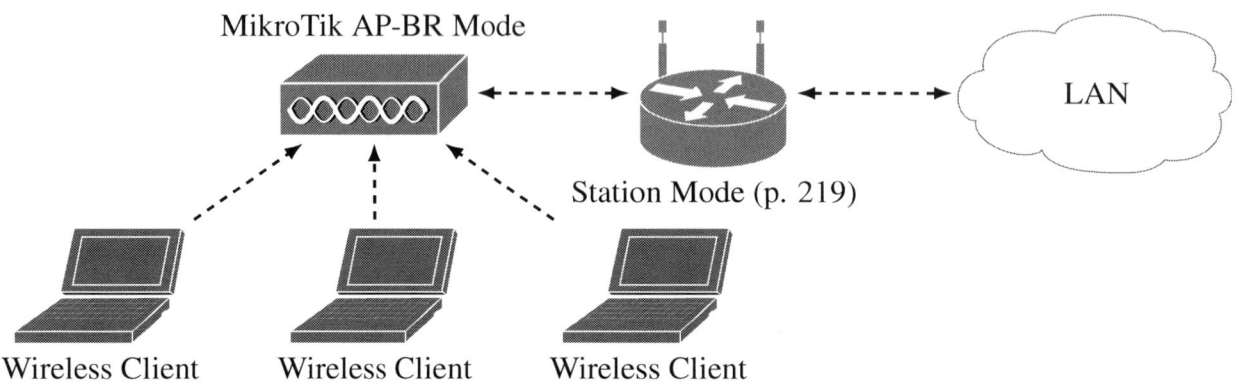

Figure 14.12: AP-BR Mode Topology

Wireless laptop clients become part of the same broadcast domain once they join the network. That broadcast domain can be extended to wired networks by using the default bridged configuration (p. 103). Even without the defaults, connecting wireless and wired networks only requires a few steps:

1. Create a bridge interface
2. Add wired and wireless ports to the bridge
3. Verify connectivity

In the following example we'll bridge ethernet interface *ether2* and wireless interfaces *wlan1* and *wlan2*:

```
/interface bridge
add name=wlan_br comment="Wireless bridge" fast-forward=yes

/interface bridge port
set bridge=wlan_br interface=ether2
set bridge=wlan_br interface=wlan1
set bridge=wlan_br interface=wlan2
```

The other station in Figure 14.12 to the right of the AP-BR device can use its wireless connection to route traffic for the networks attached to it. That type of configuration is covered more on page 219.

14.12.2 Station Mode

Station mode turns a wireless interface into a client that associates with a wireless AP. Station Mode is used on routed wireless networks, including topologies designed for end-to-end routing and MPLS. This mode uses industry-standard 802.11 wireless protocols, so a MikroTik-brand CPE unit can use this mode to connect with a non-MikroTik AP. The interface running in Station Mode will have an IP address assigned and participate in L3 routing. MikroTik recommends using this mode if possible [19]:

> "... this mode can be considered the most efficient and therefore should be used if L2 bridging on station is not necessary..."

Figure 14.13 shows a typical example of a routed wireless topology:

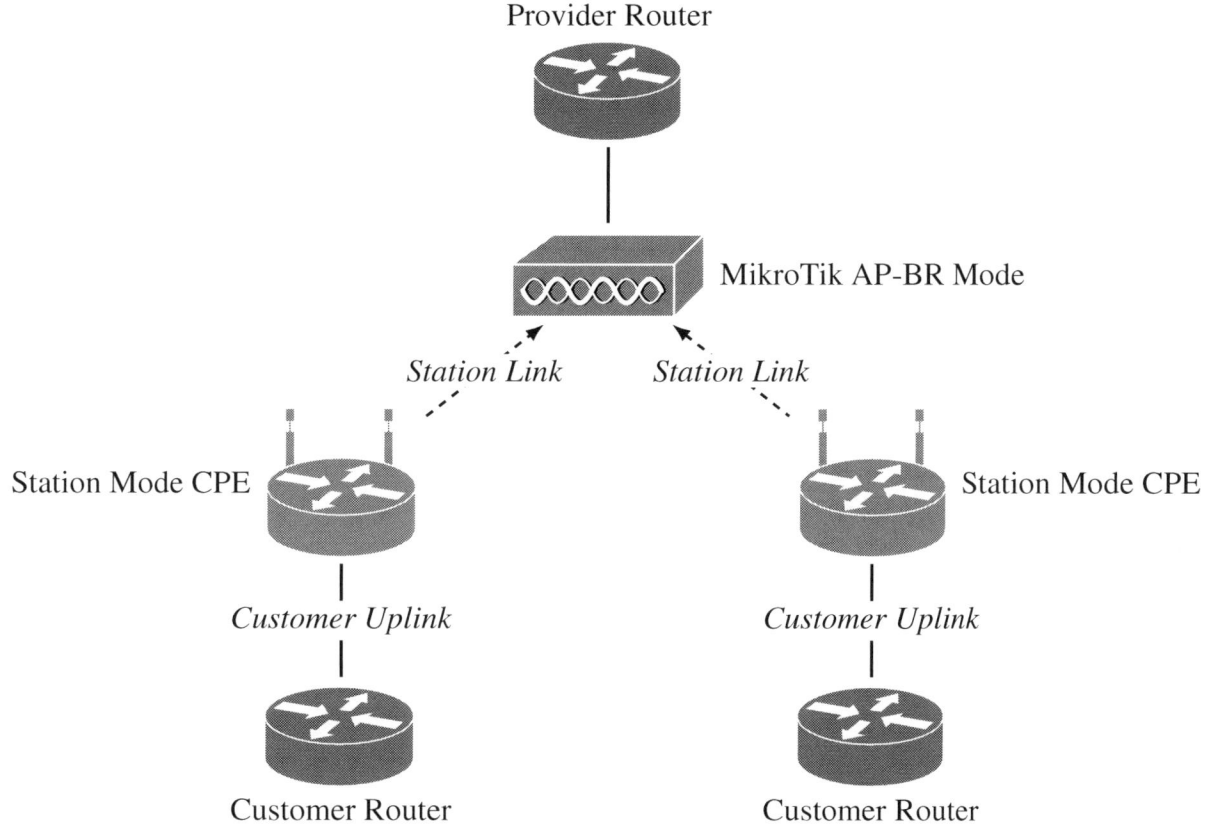

Figure 14.13: Station Mode Topology

Each station link from CPEs to the central AP is its own routed network segment. This kind of segmentation can improve network performance and help ensure customer privacy when implemented correctly.

14.13 Wireless Monitoring

Monitoring wireless devices and connectivity statistics helps tune and optimize the network experience for your users. As new wireless devices come on the market and users move devices between locations the wireless environment around them changes. For these reasons it's important to periodically survey the spectrum usage in the immediate area to ensure you're using channels and bands that have minimal interference if possible.

14.13.1 Registration Table

The registration table shows what wireless clients and access points are connected to a device. For each of those devices the registration table will show the MAC address, speed, signal level, and more. To quickly view the list of connected devices use the following command:

```
/interface wireless registration-table print brief
```

If you're troubleshooting wireless connectivity for a device (e.g. 60:45:BD:51:85:08) and wanted all the information about its wireless connection alone you can use the command shown in Figure 14.14 to see detailed statistics:

```
[admin@MikroTik] > /interface wireless registration-table print stats where
    mac-address=60:45:BD:51:85:08

0 interface=wlan1 mac-address=60:45:BD:51:85:08 ap=no wds=no bridge=no rx-rate
    ="54Mbps" tx-rate="54Mbps" packets=387,0 bytes=3904,0 frames=387,6 frame-
    bytes=6984,662 hw-frames=387,6 hw-frame-bytes=16272,870 tx-frames-timed-
    out=0 uptime=2h8m41s last-activity=19s630ms signal-strength=-36dBm@1Mbps
    signal-to-noise=79dB signal-strength-ch0=-46dBm signal-strength-ch1=-36dBm
     strength-at-rates=-36dBm@1Mbps 2h8m41s120ms,-42dBm@54Mbps 8m41s570ms tx-
    ccq=100% ...
[admin@MikroTik] > _
```

Figure 14.14: Wireless Registration Table Statistics

This outputs information about that wireless client's performance including signal strength, frame count, TX and RX Client Connection Quality (CCQ) (covered later), signal-to-noise ratio, last wireless activity, and more.

14.13.2 Snooper

The Snooper tool allows you to monitor a particular wireless band. It shows activity and devices on a given channel, and shows the overall utilization of the wireless spectrum. When planning wireless networks using the Snooper tool can help you find channels that aren't over-utilized. It can also help identify wireless APs in the vicinity that are being "noisy" on the spectrum, and rogue APs that shouldn't be online.

The Winbox version of Snooper also shows devices and access points transmitting on an interface's band as shown in Figure 14.15:

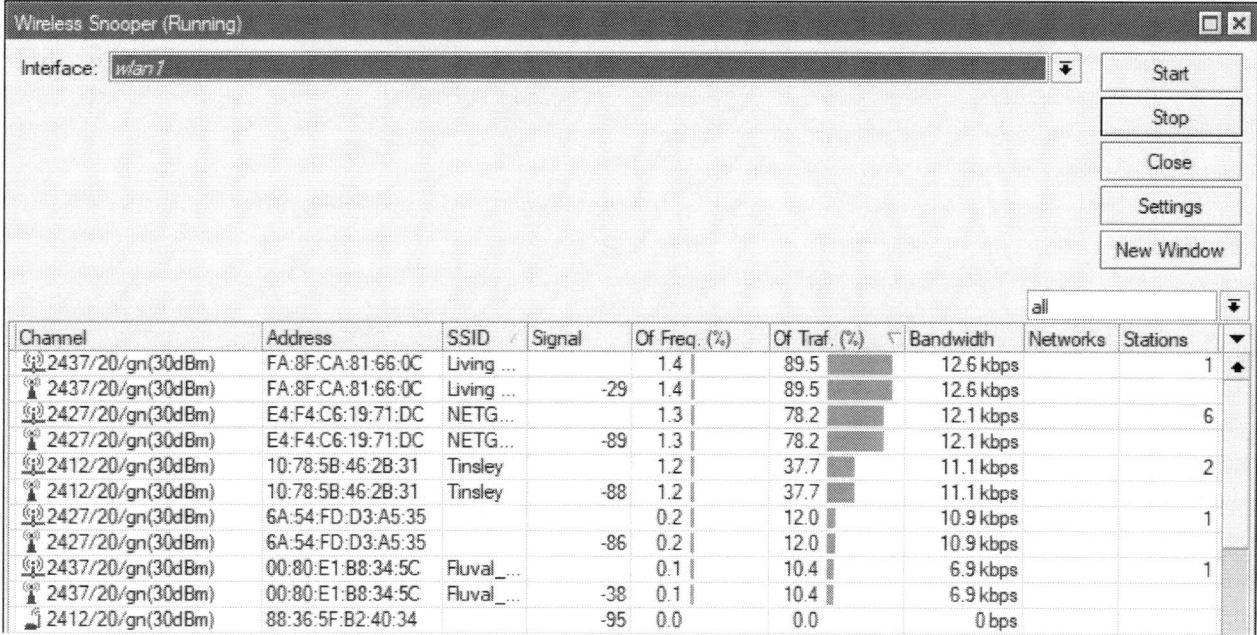

Figure 14.15: Winbox Wireless Snooper

Access the graphical version of this tool in Winbox by clicking "*Wireless > WLAN Interface > Snooper*". The CLI version of Snooper can be run using the following command (for interface *wlan2*):

```
/interface wireless snooper snoop wlan2 interval=5s
```

The "*interval=1s*" option refreshes the output every five seconds. The command line output of the wireless snooper is shown in Figure 14.16:

```
[admin@MikroTik] > /interface wireless snooper snoop wlan1 interval=1s
CHANNEL            USE      BW          NET-COUNT    NOISE-FLOOR  STA-COUNT
2412/20/gn(30dBm)  14.6%    75.3kbps    4            -116         5
2417/20/gn(30dBm)  16.2%    12.8kbps    1            -118         2
2422/20/gn(30dBm)  4.3%     25.9kbps    1            -118         2
2427/20/gn(30dBm)  8%       42.9kbps    2            -118         2
2432/20/gn(30dBm)  3.7%     11.3kbps    0            -117         0
2437/20/gn(30dBm)  6.1%     40.2kbps    3            -116         5
2442/20/gn(30dBm)  2.9%     24.5kbps    0            -116         1
2447/20/gn(30dBm)  2.9%     22.4kbps    0            -115         1
2452/20/gn(30dBm)  6%       45.6kbps    0            -116         0
2457/20/gn(30dBm)  7.6%     55.0kbps    0            -117         0
2462/20/gn(30dBm)  11.7%    88.3kbps    3            -118         5
-- [Q quit|D dump|C-z pause|n networks|s stations]
```

Figure 14.16: Console Wireless Snooper

One of my favorite things about running the Snooper from the command line is you can interact with the console output. As shown in the bottom of Figure 14.16 on the previous page you can press the [N] key to see a list of wireless networks in range, and the [D] key to see a list of broadcasting stations. Toggle back to the main screen with the list of channels by pressing the [F] key.

14.13.3 CCQ

CCQ is an aggregate score of client connection quality for a wireless interface. Higher scores mean clients are experiencing a better connection. This objective score allows you to monitor wireless quality as you change channels, tune power levels, etc. To view the current CCQ in Winbox for interface *wlan1* open *Wireless*, double-click *wlan1*, and select the *Status* tab. An example in Winbox is shown in Figure 14.17, second from the bottom:

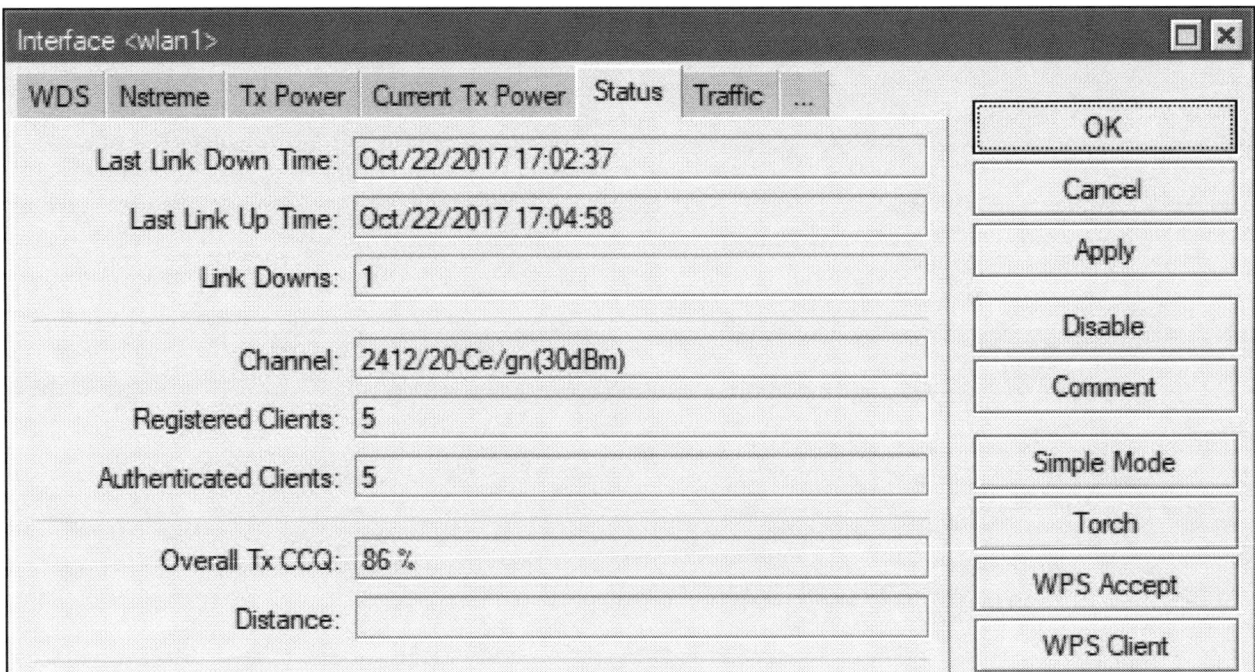

Figure 14.17: Wireless Interface CCQ

To access the same information from the CLI use the "*/interface wireless monitor wlan1*" command shown in Figure 14.18 on the following page:

```
[admin@MikroTik] > /interface wireless monitor wlan1
              status: running-ap
             channel: 2412/20-Ce/gn(30dBm)
   wireless-protocol: 802.11
         noise-floor: -116dBm
      overall-tx-ccq: 90%
   registered-clients: 5
 authenticated-clients: 5
         wmm-enabled: yes
   current-tx-powers: 1Mbps:19(19/22), 2Mbps:19(19/22), ...
  notify-external-fdb: no
-- [Q quit|D dump|C-z pause]
```

Figure 14.18: CLI Wireless Interface CCQ

14.14 Review Questions

1. Which two frequencies do commodity wireless devices use?

    (a) 60 MHz

    (b) 2.4 GHz

    (c) 2.7 GHz

    (d) 5 GHz

2. Which 802.11 wireless standards use 5 GHz frequencies?

    (a) 802.11a

    (b) 802.11b

    (c) 802.11g

    (d) 802.11n

    (e) 802.11ac

3. Which wireless band is typically used for APs and clients in the United States?

    (a) U-NII

    (b) LTE

    (c) ISM

    (d) GSM

4. What wireless features helps APs avoid military and weather radar frequencies in use for a given area?

    (a) DFS

    (b) WDS

    (c) DFS-R

    (d) RFD

5. Which tool identifies nearby wireless networks?

    (a) Wireless Scan

    (b) Wireless Sniffer

    (c) Frequency Usage

    (d) Torch

6. Which wireless standards use MIMO multiplexing?

    (a) 802.11a

    (b) 802.11g

    (c) 802.11n

    (d) 802.11ac

7. CCQ is an objective metric for gauging client connection quality.

    (a) True

    (b) False

8. Which AP mode is most common for SOHO-oriented devices?

    (a) Bridge

    (b) Station

    (c) AP-Bridge

    (d) Station-Bridge

9. The *station* mode allows an AP to join a wireless network.

    (a) True

    (b) False

10. What information about connected clients is contained in the registration table?

    (a) TX-Rate

    (b) RX-Rate

    (c) MAC Address

    (d) Signal-to-Noise Ratio

    (e) All of the above

14.15 Review Answers

1. Which two frequencies do commodity wireless devices use?

   B & D – 2.4 GHz and 5 GHz (p. 206)

2. Which 802.11 wireless standards use 5 GHz frequencies?

   A, D, and E – 802.11a, 802.11n, 802.11ac (p. 206)

3. Which wireless band is typically used for APs and clients in the United States?

   C – ISM (p. 207)

4. What wireless features helps APs avoid military and weather radar frequencies in use for a given area?

   A – DFS (p. 207)

5. Which tool identifies nearby wireless networks?

   A – Wireless Scan (p. 209)

6. Which wireless standards use MIMO multiplexing?

   C & D – 802.11n and 802.11ac (p. 212)

7. CCQ is an objective metric for gauging client connection quality.

   A – True (p. 222)

8. Which AP mode is most common for SOHO-oriented devices?

   C – AP-Bridge (p. 218)

9. The *station* mode allows an AP to join a wireless network.

   A – True (p. 219)

10. What information about connected clients is contained in the registration table?

    E – All of the above (p. 220)

Chapter 15

Wireless Security

Wireless networks are essential in a mobile-first world, but convenience needs to be balanced with security. Access lists, encryption, and forwarding controls can all be combined to create a secure wireless network.

15.1 Wireless Interface Security Options

Three checkboxes are available for security options on each wireless interface. Two of the three being very important security options. The three options include the following:

1. *Default Authenticate*

2. *Default Forward*

3. *Hide SSID*

These options are located in the same window for each wireless interface near the bottom. By default, the first two options are enabled in RouterOS. For most organizations not beholden to compliance requirements like PCI-DSS they can simply be left enabled and the third option unused.

15.1.1 Default Authenticate

The default authenticate option allows clients not on an interface's access list (p. 228) to authenticate to the access point. If the option is disabled then only clients with access list entries will be able to authenticate and join a wireless network. Regardless of the option's setting, devices must still authenticate with a pre-shared key or some other credential on secured networks.

15.1.2 Default Forward

The default forward option allows connected clients and stations to connect with each other via the same AP. With this option disabled clients connected to the same AP won't be able to directly communicate. Disabling this option and breaking communication between clients is also known as "client isolation". On many wireless networks, such as in hotels and restaurants, there is no reason for wireless devices to be reachable by each other. In that case it's a good idea to disable this option.

However, some devices can't function properly with client isolation configured on the network. Streaming devices like Google Chromecast® and Apple TV® must be able to communicate with other hosts on the same access point. Printers with wireless print capabilities must be reachable when a physical network connection isn't available. Disabling the default forward option would stop those devices from serving their purpose.

15.1.3 Hide SSID

This option will stop an interface running in AP mode from broadcasting an Service Set Identifier (SSID). This is a very simple method for hiding a wireless network from non-technical users in the area. Freely-available software or the built-in Wireless Snooper tool will show hidden SSIDs, allowing anyone in the local area to attempt a connection. While using this option could become part of your overall wireless security plan, it certainly shouldn't be relied upon to provide robust protection.

15.2 Access List

Access lists allow you to define which devices are allowed to join a wireless network and set some custom security options for each client. Device entries include a MAC address, pre-shared key, and forwarding options. It's also possible to limit access by time, as shown at the bottom of the "New AP Access Rule" sub-window. For this to be effective long-term it's important that the AP have a good time source (e.g. NTP). An example entry for a fictional wireless device with a MAC address of *00:11:22:33:44:55* is shown in Figure 15.1 on the following page:

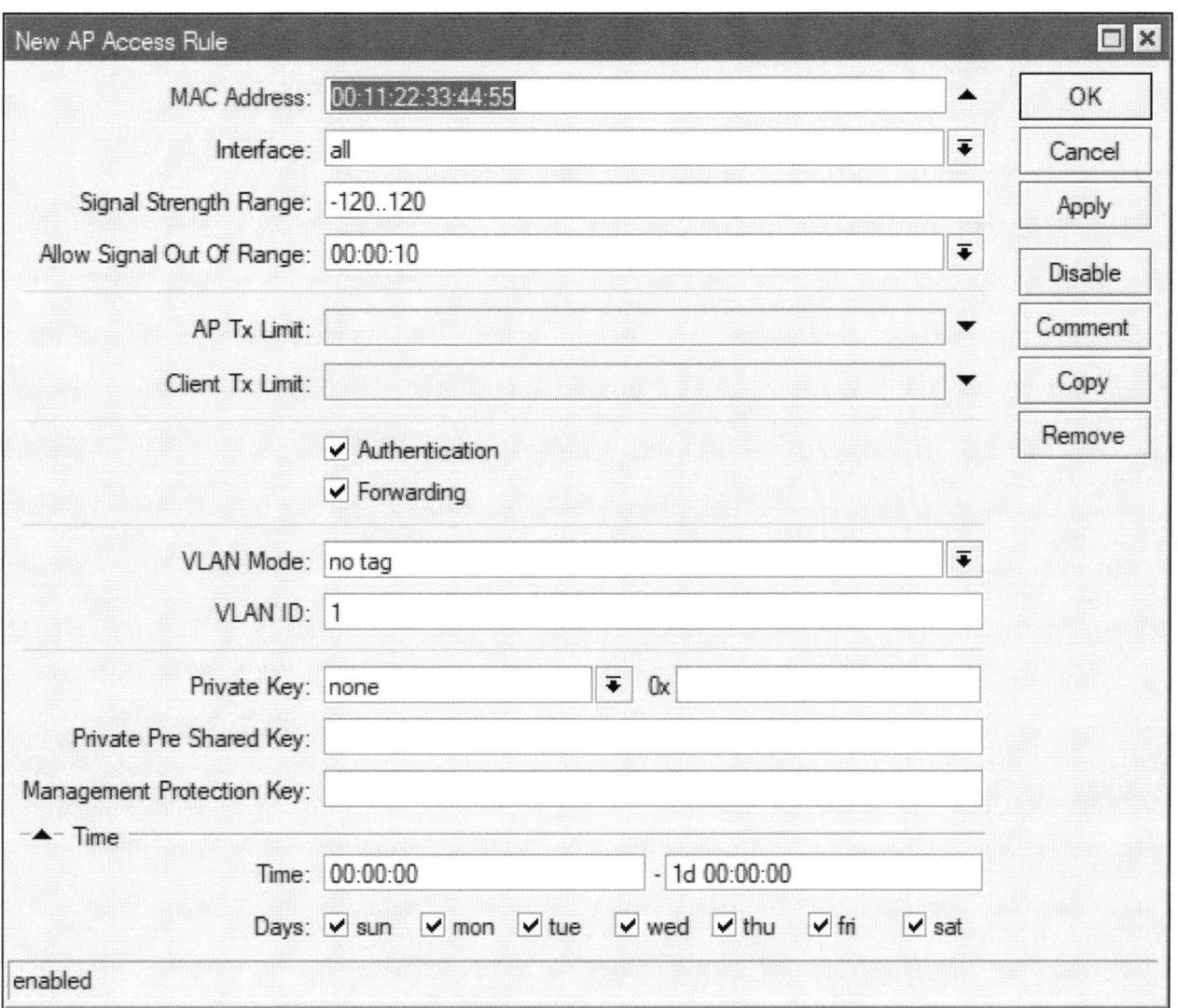

Figure 15.1: Wireless Access List

A limitation of this feature is that an access lists on one AP do not apply to others. For centralized authentication of wireless devices across many APs a more robust solution like Controlled Access Point system Manager (CAPsMAN) is needed. If multiple access list rules exist for a device only the first rule that's matched will be processed [10].

15.3 Connect List

The Connect List controls connections from remote stations to a local AP. Adding an entry on an AP's Connect List for another AP running in one of the *"station"* modes will allow it to establish a point-to-point connection. This can be used for many different wireless scenarios, like bridging local networks across an 802.11 point-to-point link between two buildings. If the remote AP appears in the local wireless Registration Table adding it to the Connect List is easy in Winbox. Figure 15.2 shows how to dynamically add a connected AP to the Connect List with pre-populated address information.

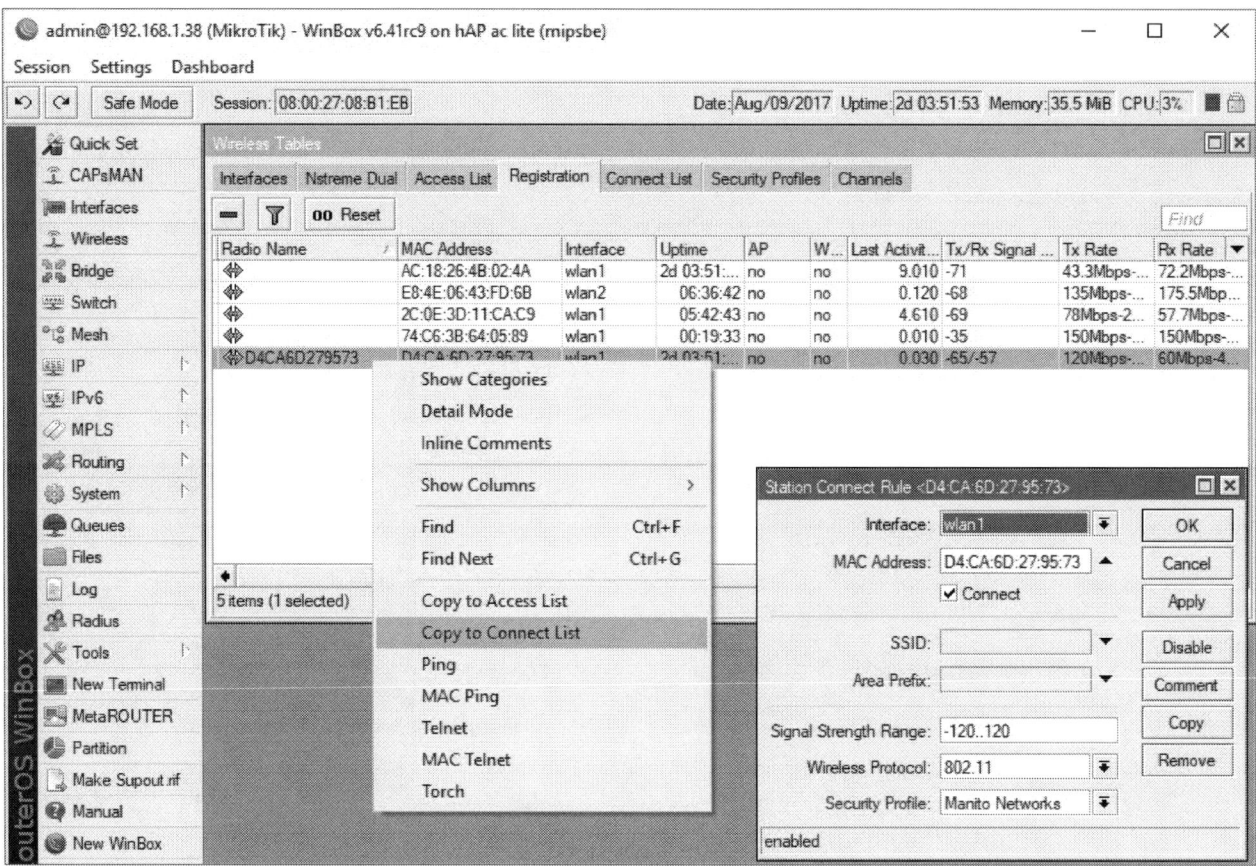

Figure 15.2: Add to Wireless Connect List

The dynamically created Connect List rule is also shown in Figure 15.2, showing the result of clicking the selected menu option. If wireless encryption is used on the network being joined by the remote AP then the wireless security profile must also be selected.

15.4 Encryption

All wireless networks should be encrypted to ensure the confidentiality of data in-flight and the privacy of network users. A number of encryption standards and best practices are available to keep your networks secure.

15.4.1 Encryption Algorithms

RouterOS supports two encryption algorithms for securing wireless networks:

- AES
- Temporal Key Integrity Protocol (TKIP)

AES is a modern standard that still provides robust security for wireless networks. TKIP on the other hand has been deprecated and is no longer considered secure. Another advantage of using AES is hardware processing offload. A dedicated hardware chip on models that feature it can handle AES encryption and decryption itself, not burdening the central processor.

15.4.2 WEP

Wired Equivalent Privacy (WEP) encryption is not officially part of the MTCNA outline but it is worth a brief mention. WEP encryption has been broken for a number of years and should not be used to secure wireless networks. A number of freely-available tools[1] exist for cracking WEP encryption keys, and with modern computers it is almost trivial to break into a WEP-encrypted network. If you absolutely must use WEP with legacy systems or networks I recommend putting the following safeguards in place:

1. Use a very robust encryption key
2. Change the encryption key on a regular basis
3. Restrict AP signal strength so only on-premise devices and users can connect to the network
4. Hide the SSID to shield it from casual observers

---
[1] e.g. Aircrack-ng

15.4.3 WPA & WPA2 Encryption

Wi-Fi Protected Access (WPA) and WPA2 encryption is used in modern networks to secure wireless access. WPA2 should be used in-lieu of WPA, and both should be used in place of WEP. WPA does have documented weaknesses but they are harder to take advantage of than those in WEP. The Wi-Fi Alliance and most major vendors recommend implementing WPA2 when possible. Fortunately WPA2 support is a standard feature in modern wireless networks and wireless clients. For the purposes of this guide encryption will be discussed in the context of using the recommended WPA2. Two types of encryption and authentication methods are available with WPA2:

1. Pre-Shared Key (PSK)
2. Enterprise

WPA2-PSK

WPA2-PSK uses a PSK to secure communications between clients and APs. Using a PSK is convenient and doesn't require any enterprise infrastructure on the back-end to process authentication. Unfortunately a change to the PSK requires that the new key be sent to all clients. If the PSK is leaked to an untrusted party a network may be compromised. An employee that leaves an organization with the PSK unchanged could access a company network from the parking lot if the signal is good enough. The robustness of protection provided by WPA2-PSK is also directly tied to the strength of the PSK. If the PSK is easily guessable (e.g. Password, P@ssw0rd, 123456789, qwerty, etc) or written somewhere in plain sight it will be ineffective.

WPA2-Enterprise

WPA2-Enterprise uses Extensible Authentication Protocol (EAP) or Protected EAP (PEAP) to authenticate clients over the network before allowing them to fully connect. The 802.1X standard enables authentication via an infrastructure server running FreeRADIUS, Microsoft Active Directory with NPS, and others. This configuration allows for the following:

1. Easier, centralized credential updates
2. Quick disabling of individual network credentials
3. Enforcement of password policies:
   - Length
   - Complexity
   - Minimum and Maximum Age
   - History
4. Central accounting of failed and successful login attempts

Unfortunately, this kind of control also requires additional infrastructure to handle AAA. For large networks with many roaming wireless clients this kind of configuration is the only way to have clients moving across networks seamlessly while using robust, regularly-updated credentials. WPA-Enterprise is covered in-depth as part of the MTCWE outline.

15.5 Security Profiles

Security profiles brings together encryption settings, PSKs, and RADIUS and EAP settings, and more. This reusable profile is then assigned to physical or virtual wireless interfaces to control network access. Each security profile is local to a RouterOS device, so changes to settings on one AP won't affect another. An example of a new wireless security profile being created with robust security settings is shown in Figure 15.3:

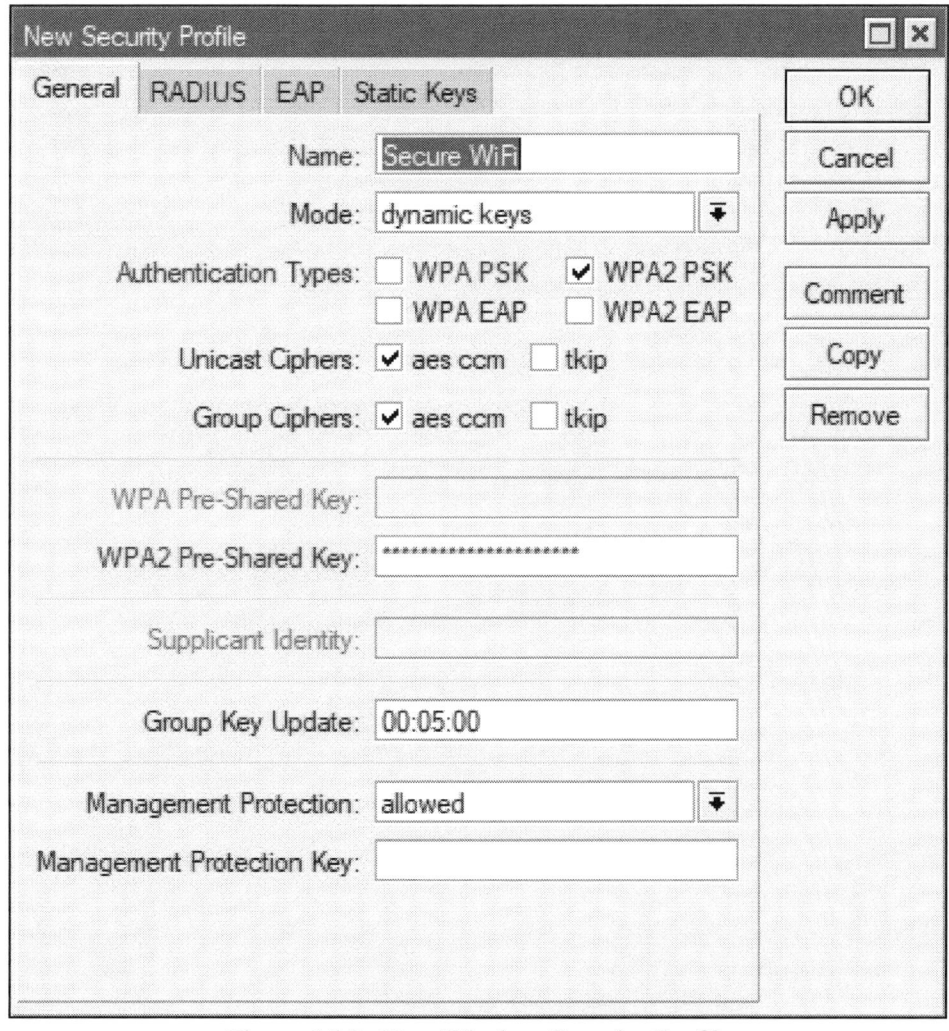

Figure 15.3: New Wireless Security Profile

The new profile is then assigned to an interface as shown in Figure 15.4 on the next page:

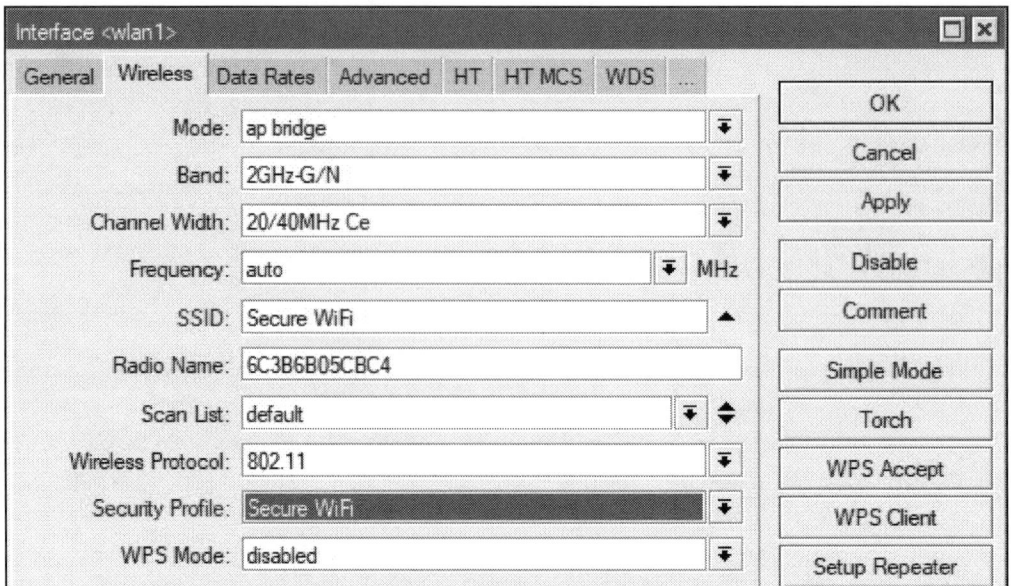

Figure 15.4: Select Wireless Security Profile

For more centralized authentication control network owners should implement Master Configuration Profiles with CAPsMAN, or use EAP and PEAP with RADIUS.

15.6 WPS

Wi-Fi Protected Setup (WPS) makes wireless configuration easy for home users. This feature simplifies the process of adding additional devices to an existing network, but a secure network must already be available to join. While WPS does offer convenience it's also easily exploited by attackers when not implemented correctly. For this reason many network administrators leave the feature turned off or only use it when other solutions aren't available.

15.6.1 WPS Mode

The following modes of adding devices to a network are available in RouterOS or typical of other platforms:

- Push Button
- Virtual Push Button
- PIN (not supported in RouterOS)

The WPS PIN method isn't available in RouterOS for security reasons. Some vendors place a sticker on their wireless units with the PIN which creates a security issue. Other router platforms have been found with hard-coded WPS PINs which provide little or no security. Not all wireless RouterBOARD models have a physical WPS button, but all RouterOS versions support the virtual button.

By default WPS is disabled but it's simple to enable the physical button (if available) for an interface with the following command:

```
/interface wireless
set wlan1 wps-mode=push-button
```

To only use the *WPS Accept* button in Winbox instead, set the "*wps-mode=push-button-virtual-only*" option for the wireless interface. For RouterBOARD models without a physical button this is the only option for enabling WPS. Having a virtual button in Winbox allows network administrators some amount of control along with the convenience of WPS.

15.6.2 WPS Client

Clicking the WPS Client button in Winbox begins the process of authenticating the wireless station to an AP configured for WPS. This is equivalent to Apple macOS® or Microsoft Windows devices joining a WPS-enabled network. On the client wireless station the WPS Client button is clicked, then the WPS Accept button must be pressed within two minutes on the wireless AP.

15.6.3 WPS Accept

The *WPS Accept* button allows devices that have initiated the WPS process to join the network. The button must be pushed in Winbox, and is shown in Figure 15.5:

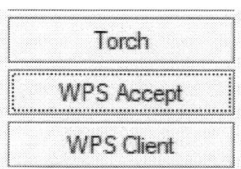

Figure 15.5: Virtual WPS Accept Button

The following command can also be run from the console for a particular WLAN interface e.g. *wlan1* within two minutes:

```
/interface wireless wps-push-button wlan1
```

15.7 Review Questions

1. Which is the preferred encryption technology for securing wireless networks?

    (a) TKIP

    (b) WPA

    (c) WPA2

    (d) WEP

2. Which list controls access to an AP from other remote access points?

    (a) Connect List

    (b) Access List

    (c) Channel List

    (d) Address List

3. Which technology allows wireless clients to connect when an administrator presses a physical or virtual button?

    (a) WDS

    (b) WPS

    (c) WPA

    (d) WEP

4. What object contains encryption settings, pre-shared keys, and available ciphers?

    (a) Dynamic Keys List

    (b) Profile Tool

    (c) Device Profile

    (d) Security Profile

5. TKIP is the most robust cipher available for WPA security.

    (a) True

    (b) False

6. Which option allows clients connected to the same AP to communicate with one another by default?

    (a) Default Security Profile

    (b) Default Authenticate

    (c) Default Forward

    (d) Default SSID

7. Which type of address does an Access List use to allow clients onto a wireless network?

    (a) MAC address

    (b) IP address

    (c) Link-local address

    (d) DNS address

8. The Default Authenticate option allows clients to connect to an AP even if they aren't on an Access List.

    (a) True

    (b) False

9. Which table shows a list of connected wireless clients and their signal strength?

    (a) FIB / RIB

    (b) ARP table

    (c) Route table

    (d) Registration table

10. Which option hides a wireless network from non-technical wireless users?

    (a) Security Profile

    (b) Hide SSID

    (c) Access List

    (d) Connect List

15.8 Review Answers

1. Which is the preferred encryption technology for securing wireless networks?

    C – WPA2 (p. 232)

2. Which list controls access to an AP from other remote access points (radios)?

    A – Connect List (p. 230)

3. Which technology allows wireless clients to connect when an administrator presses a physical or virtual button?

    B – WPS (p. 234)

4. What object contains encryption settings, pre-shared keys, and available ciphers?

    D – Security Profile (p. 233)

5. TKIP is the most robust cipher available for WPA security.

    B – False (p. 231)

6. Which option allows clients connected to the same AP to communicate with one another by default?

    C – Default Forward (p. 227)

7. Which type of address does a Access List use to allow clients into a wireless network?

    A – MAC address (p. 228)

8. The Default Authenticate option allows clients to connect to an AP even if they aren't on an Access List.

    A – True (p. 228)

9. Which table shows a list of connected wireless clients?

    D – Registration table (p. 220)

10. Which option hides a wireless network from typical wireless users?

    B – Hide SSID (p. 227)

Chapter 16

Troubleshooting Tools

Several tools are built into RouterOS to help administrators troubleshoot network connectivity and performance problems. It's also possible to augment network inventory and discovery processes with these tools. In some networks I've seen administrators deploy old RouterBoard units running updated software as "jump boxes" just for the use of these tools.

16.1 IP Scan

The *IP Scan* tool allows you to scan for hosts on a particular subnet and interface as shown in Figure 16.1. This is helpful during network discovery or while performing device inventory. If possible the tool will perform reverse lookups for DNS and NetBIOS to assist you in identifying clients that are discovered. CLI usage of the *ip-scan* tool is shown in Figure 16.1 with some output omitted for formatting purposes. The Winbox version of a running scan is shown in Figure 16.2 on the next page.

Both figures below illustrate different types of scans that are possible. The console example of a running scan is done with a specified IP address range. The Winbox example doesn't have a specified IP range but instead uses an interface. Both types of scans are useful in their own way.

```
[admin@MikroTik] > /tool ip-scan address-range=192.168.56.0/24
Flags: D - dhcp
ADDRESS           MAC-ADDRESS         TIME      DNS
192.168.56.1      0A:00:27:00:00:05   0ms       router
192.168.56.102    08:00:27:08:B1:EB   0ms       desktop
192.168.56.101    08:00:27:F8:E4:87   0ms
192.168.56.100    08:00:27:DF:D3:7B
-- [Q quit|D dump|C-z pause]
```

Figure 16.1: CLI IP Scan Tool

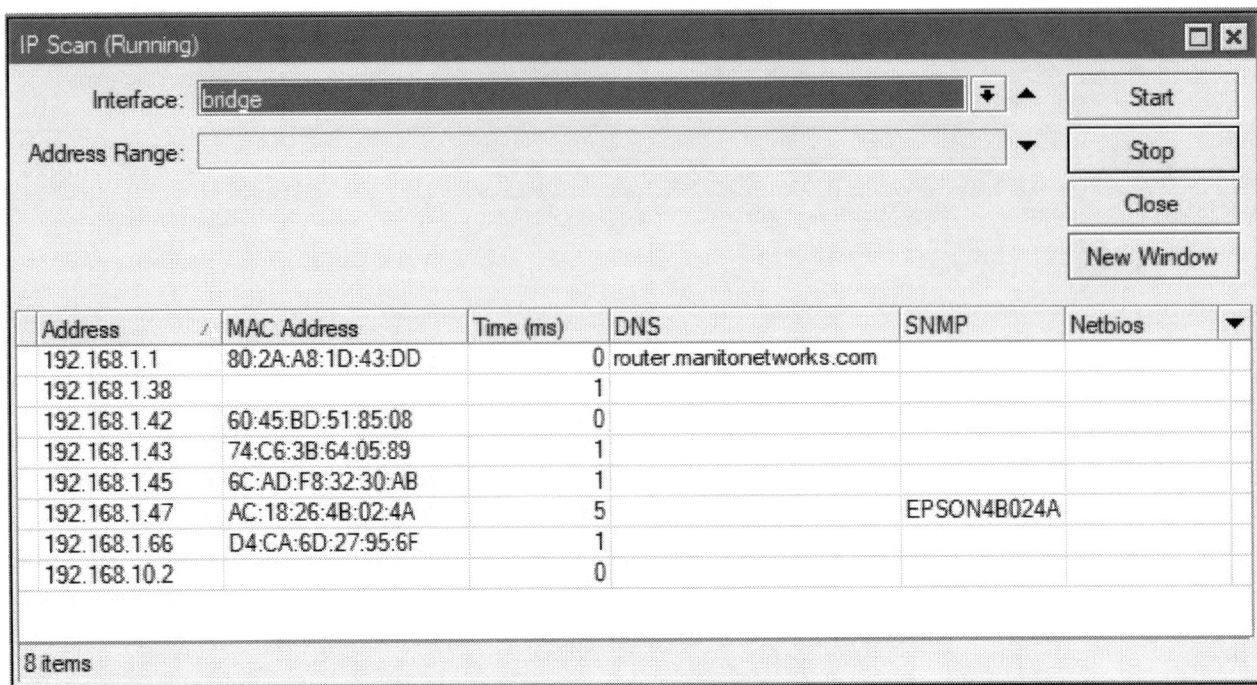

Figure 16.2: Winbox IP Scan Tool

This functions like port scanners like Nmap[1] that can do ICMP sweeps, but it lacks much of the options of a full-blown port scanner.

16.2 MAC Scan

The MAC Scan tool allows you to discover the L2 addresses of hosts in networks attached to the router. This tool will only find MAC addresses in the router's broadcast domains but it's great for finding devices that don't run a neighbor discovery protocol. Figure 16.3 show the result of a "/tool mac-scan all" command, which discovers MAC addresses attached to all interfaces.

```
[admin@MikroTik] > /tool mac-scan all
MAC-ADDRESS         ADDRESS              AGE
08:00:27:08:B1:EB   192.168.56.1          1
08:00:27:F8:E4:87   192.168.56.101        6
0A:00:27:00:00:05   192.168.56.1          1
-- [Q quit|D dump|C-z pause]
```

Figure 16.3: MAC-Scan Tool

---

[1] https://nmap.org/download.html

16.3 Additional Scanning Tools

For more in-depth network scanning check out the Nmap project. It's a staple of network auditors and administrators, is freely available, and has a lot of configurable scanning options. Browse to `https://nmap.org/` for more information on scanning with Nmap. After downloading the Nmap software the following scan commands are useful for discovering MikroTik devices:

- Winbox service scan: *nmap -sT -p 8291 -open 192.168.88.0/24*
- API service scan: *nmap -sT -p 8728,8729 -open 192.168.88.0/24*

If computers on your networks are running host-based Intrusion Prevention System (IPS) software as part of an antivirus or security suite be sure to whitelist the address of the computer running Nmap scans. Since this tool is used both by security professionals and hackers many vendors will flag an Nmap scan as a possible intrusion.

> **WARNING**: Due to its popularity with network administrators and hackers, sometimes attackers try to distribute malware via bogus Nmap downloads. Only download Nmap from the Nmap project's website.

16.4 Email

The Email tool configures mail account settings so RouterOS can email network administrators when triggered by an event. Some use cases for the email tool include the following:

- Notify administrators when *warning* or *critical*-level events occur
- Send an email "blast" to a distribution group so multiple administrators can monitor for events remotely
- Regularly send backup configuration files to administrators via a script for archiving
- Send device statistics and information via regularly scripted email for devices where there isn't a persistent connection for monitoring

Despite its usefulness the email tool can have security and operational implications that should be considered. If the email account being used is ever hacked any sensitive information in archived backup configurations like usernames or wireless keys could be compromised. The configured email address and password are also available in plaintext if configured in the *Tools* menu under *Email* as shown in Figure 16.4 on the next page:

```
[admin@MikroTik] > /tool e-mail print
address: mail.example.com
port: 25
start-tls: no
from: mikrotiks@example.com
user: mikrotiks@example.com
password: abc123!
[admin@MikroTik] > _
```

Figure 16.4: Email Tool Security Warning

Even a relatively unskilled attacker will know to try that username and password combination on other services, hoping administrators haven't been careful about password recycling. Some administrators store email usernames and passwords in script files instead, but those are also available in plaintext.

If a device doesn't have multiple WAN links all emails will fail to send if the link goes down. If that same WAN link is bouncing and creating warnings that would trigger an email it may not be send depending on how unstable the link is. As of this writing the email tool does not support Two-Factor Authentication (2FA), which many organizations now require for security. Bear these limitations in mind as you plan for how to use this particular tool.

16.4.1 Email Usage

Network administrators can send emails in the following ways:

- Manually
- Via a built-in action
- Using a script

Manually sending emails is often done from the router itself with a backup configuration file attachment. This prevents administrators from having to manually copy the file off a device, attach it, send the email, then remember to delete the file for security. Figure 16.5 on the following page shows the email tool being used manually to send a backup copy of the configuration via Google Mail:

Figure 16.5: Manually Sending Email

To use this tool automatically some credentials for an email account must be configured first. Figure 16.6 on the next page shows the credential configuration for an email account:

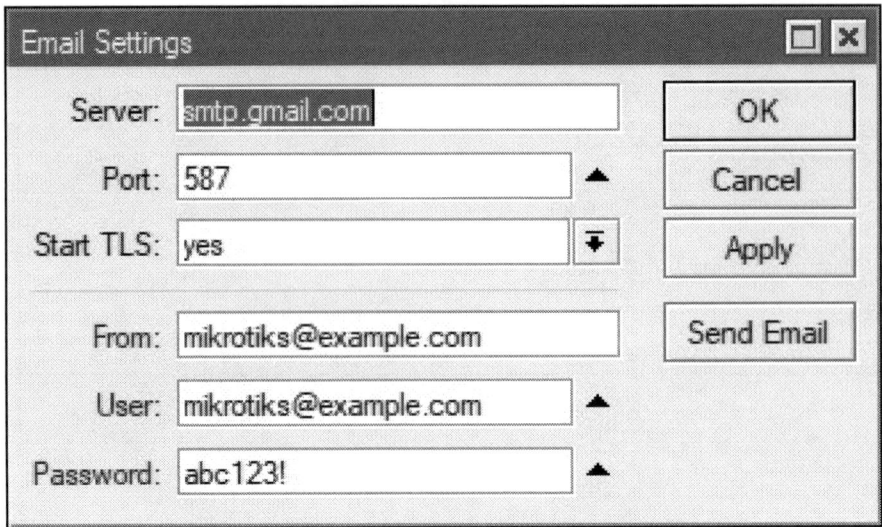

Figure 16.6: Email Account Configuration

Setting up an email action allows the logging system and others to use it without manual administrator intervention. Figure 16.7 shows a logging action being configured to send email to an administrator:

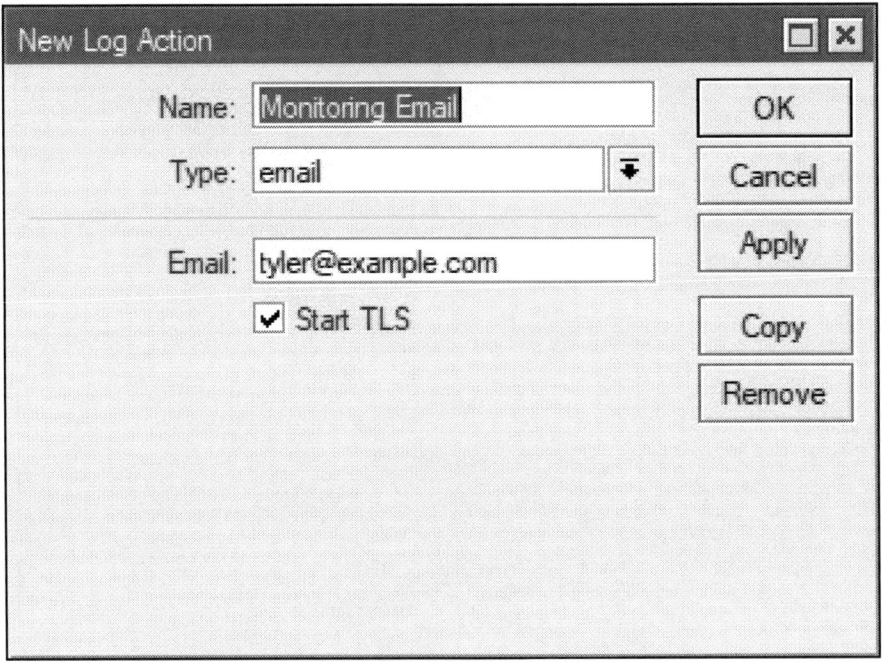

Figure 16.7: Configuring Email Log Action

16.5 MAC Server

The MAC Server allows connections to RouterOS devices without L3 addresses assigned. This can be very helpful during device provisioning, or if a misconfiguration causes loss of a routed connection.

16.5.1 MAC Server Settings

MAC Server settings control if the device can receive Winbox, Telnet, and Ping connections over L2. The MAC server is running and will accept L2 connections on all interfaces as shown in Figure 16.8:

```
[admin@MikroTik] > /tool mac-server print
Flags: X - disabled, * - default
#    INTERFACE
0  * all
[admin@MikroTik] > _
```

Figure 16.8: MAC Server Enabled

The default configuration for accepting Winbox connections over L2 is also shown in Figure 16.9. An earlier example of MAC Winbox connecting over an L2 link is shown on page 54. Again it is configured to accept connections on all interfaces.

```
[admin@MikroTik] > /tool mac-server mac-winbox print
Flags: X - disabled, * - default
#    INTERFACE
0  * all
[admin@MikroTik] > _
```

Figure 16.9: MAC Winbox Server Enabled

> **NOTE**: It's recommended that the MAC Telnet, Winbox, and Ping services be limited to trusted internal networks or be disabled entirely for security.

16.5.2 MAC Ping

With MAC Ping enabled it's possible for one host to *ping* the MAC address of another. This can be very useful when IP connectivity has been lost and administrators need to test if devices are still connected and powered on. Commands shown in Figure 16.10 on the next page enable this feature on a device and confirm it's turned on:

```
[admin@MikroTik] > /tool mac-server ping
[admin@MikroTik] /tool mac-server ping> set enabled=yes
[admin@MikroTik] /tool mac-server ping> print
enabled: yes
[admin@MikroTik] /tool mac-server ping> _
```

Figure 16.10: Enabling MAC-Server Ping

16.5.3 MAC Telnet

The MAC Telnet tool allows for Telnet sessions to be established using only L2 addresses. Unlike the */system ssh* client no IP addresses need to be assigned for this to work. In Winbox the client can be accessed via the *Tools* menu under *Telnet*, then select the *MAC Telnet* radio button.

> **NOTE**: It's easier to copy-paste MAC addresses from the Neighbor Discovery window or *"/ip neighbor print"* output than it is to type them by hand.

16.6 Netwatch

The *netwatch* tool monitors host reachability and leverages RouterOS scripting to react to an event. The router checks if a host is up by sending an ICMP echo (ping) to its address. Netwatch can trigger scripts when hosts go down and aren't reachable, or come back online and reply to pings. This could include scripts to log a network event, send an emails and text messages, or trigger route updates. Scripting and programming concepts are beyond the scope of the MTCNA but some simple monitoring can be set up easily. For example, to check every 30 seconds and log when the 192.168.10.100 host goes down use the following commands:

```
/system script
add name=monitor_down source="/log info \"192.168.10.100 down!\";"

/tool netwatch
add host=192.168.10.100 down-script=monitor_down interval=30s
```

> **NOTE**: Backslashes ("\") are used to *escape* the double-quotes. This is done so they don't break up the command text in the wrong places.

To log connectivity loss with *192.168.10.100* to a centralized server an SNMP trap could also be sent.

16.7 Packet Sniffer

The *packet sniffer* tool captures network traffic off an interface. The capture format is the typical *.pcap* and can be read by Wireshark[2], tcpdump[3], and other tools. Set the capture options, start the capture, and stop it after the file is full or you're satisfied with the amount of traffic.

Use the commands in Figure 16.11 to capture traffic on interface *ether1* in a PCAP file from the console:

```
[admin@MikroTik] > /tool sniffer
[admin@MikroTik] /tool sniffer> set file-name=traffic.pcap filter-interface=
    ether1
[admin@MikroTik] /tool sniffer> start
[admin@MikroTik] /tool sniffer> stop
[admin@MikroTik] /tool sniffer> /file print where type~"pcap"
 # NAME              TYPE         SIZE          CREATION-TIME
 0 traffic.pcap     .pcap file    6.0KiB        oct/29/2017 16:32:33
[admin@MikroTik] /tool sniffer> _
```

Figure 16.11: Packet Sniffer

Starting and stopping the command with the same *"file-name=..."* option will overwrite the named file automatically if it exists. The tool is also available with additional display options in Winbox as shown in Figure 16.12 on the next page:

---
[2]https://www.wireshark.org/
[3]http://www.tcpdump.org/

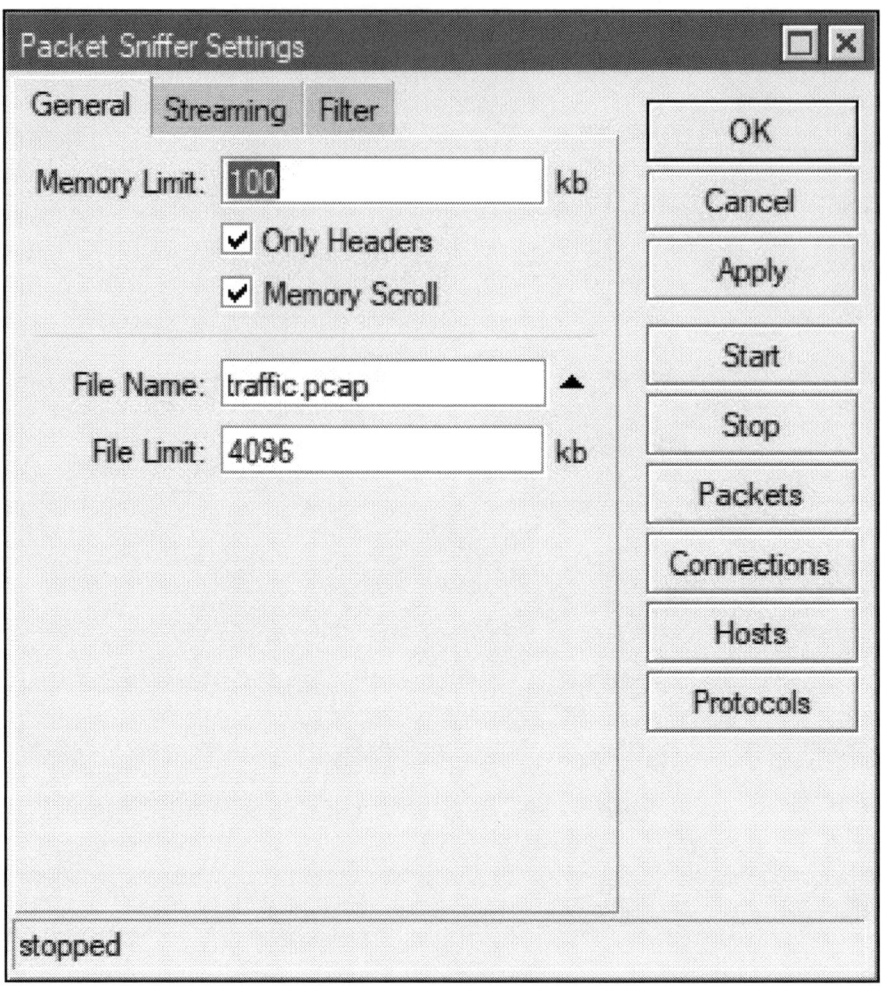

Figure 16.12: Winbox Packet Sniffer

The buttons for packets, connections, hosts, and protocols provide basic analysis of the captured traffic during on-the-fly troubleshooting. Packet capture streaming using the TaZmen Sniffer Protocol (TZSP)[4] can also be done with Wireshark or other packet capture utilities. This streams packets to a central capture host for advanced analysis and archiving. Figure 16.13 on the following page shows the configuration for a centralized host at *192.168.88.33*:

---

[4]https://wiki.mikrotik.com/wiki/Ethereal/Wireshark

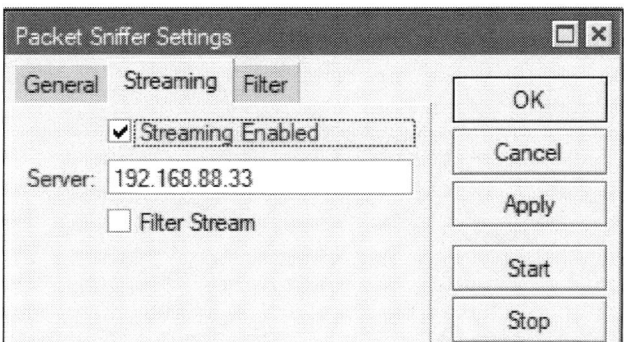

Figure 16.13: Packet Sniffer Streaming

Figure 16.14 shows the contents of an offline PCAP file captured via the sniffer tool and opened in Wireshark:

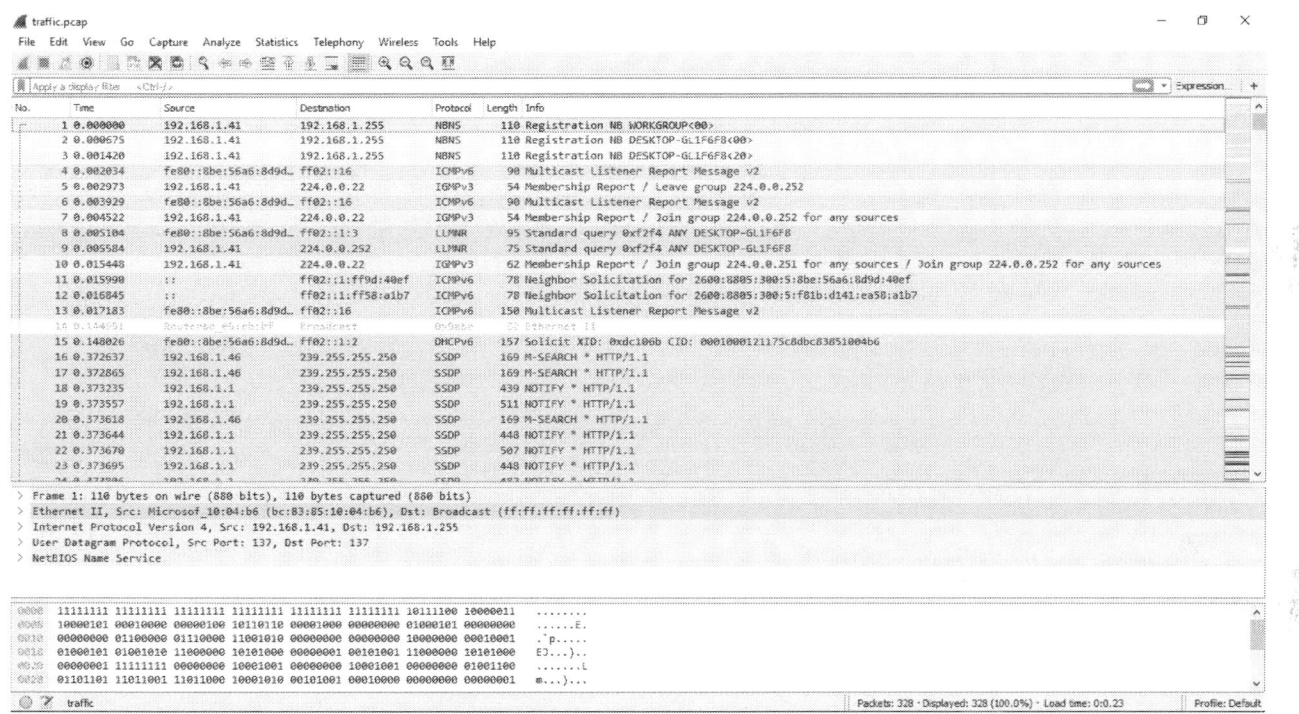

Figure 16.14: PCAP File In Wireshark

Maximum file size is specified in Kilobytes with the *file-limit=...* option. It's also possible to capture only the headers of the packets and not their payloads if you only need traffic sources and destinations. Use *only-headers* like in the following commands to get just header information:

```
/tool sniffer
set file-name=traffic.pcap filter-interface=ether1 only-headers
start
stop
```

It's also possible to dump captured traffic directly to the console for quick monitoring. This is useful when doing remote troubleshooting, or if you only need to verify that traffic is being received on an interface. Use the following command to quickly see traffic on an interface:

```
/tool sniffer quick interface=ether1
```

An example of the sniffer tool in action is shown in Figure 16.15, with both IPv4 and IPv6 traffic in-flight.

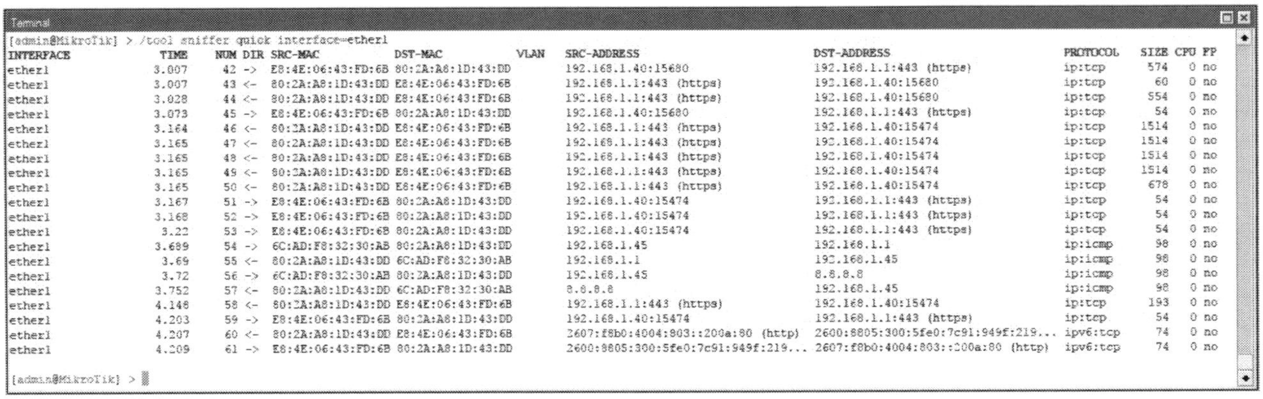

Figure 16.15: Sniffer Tool

Use the [CTRL+C] keystroke or the [Q] key to stop the capture. The [CTRL+Z] keystroke pauses the scrolling if you see something interesting and want to investigate further. If you only need to verify traffic is being received on an interface use the *direction* option:

```
/tool sniffer quick interface=ether1 direction=rx
```

16.8 Ping

The Ping tool allows for easy, customized sending of ICMP echoes[5]. You can also specify an *ARP Ping*, as well as the source interface, source IP address, and more. This makes the ping tool essential when troubleshooting connectivity issues across networks when routing policies or NAT rules are in place. The typical output of the ping tool is shown in Figure 16.16 on the following page.

---

[5]ICMP Type 8

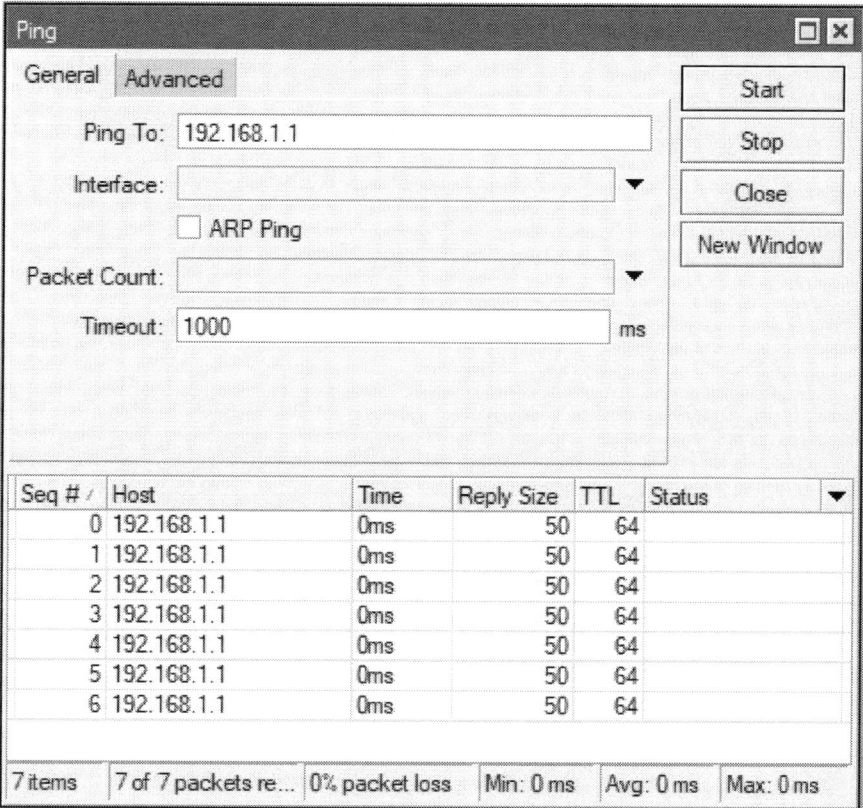

Figure 16.16: Ping Tool

The "*ping*" command can be referenced directly from the command root so, "*/tool...*" and "*/...*" aren't necessary each time it's used. Figure 16.17 shows the tool running at the console from the command root:

```
[admin@MikroTik] > ping example.com
SEQ HOST              SIZE    TTL TIME     STATUS
  0 93.184.216.34      56      47 22ms
  1 93.184.216.34      56      47 22ms
  2 93.184.216.34      56      47 22ms
  3 93.184.216.34      56      47 23ms
sent=4 received=4 packet-loss=0% min-rtt=22ms avg-rtt=22ms max-rtt=23ms

[admin@MikroTik] > _
```

Figure 16.17: Console Ping Tool

16.9 Ping Speed

The Ping Speed tool sends a flood of pings to a client to gauge network speed performance. This is analogous to other tools like iperf[6], though without a lot of protocol tuning options. Since this tool can generate an enormous amount of ICMP echoes it's important to heed the following:

- A flood of traffic could negatively impact the *Availability* of a production network
- The use of such tools against publicly-routable addresses, especially over the internet, may violate ISP terms of service

An example of Ping Speed tool output in Winbox is shown in Figure 16.18.

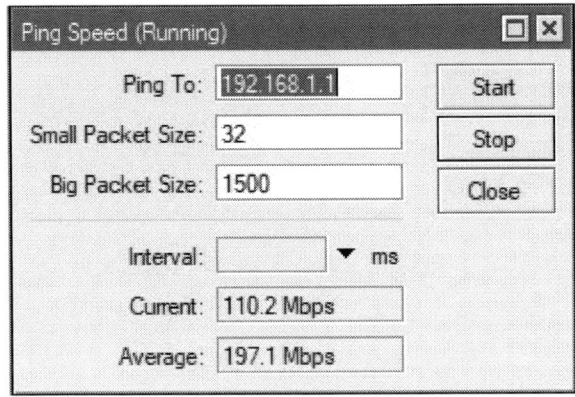

Figure 16.18: Ping Speed

Figure 16.19 shows the Ping Speed tool working from the command line.

```
[admin@MikroTik] > /tool ping-speed 192.168.88.148
    current: 45.4Mbps
    average: 146.1Mbps
-- [Q quit|D dump|C-z pause]
```

Figure 16.19: CLI Ping Speed

16.10 RoMON

The Router Management Overlay Network (RoMON) capability is a unique value-add tool in the RouterOS platform. It creates a separate network apart from the typical L2 and L3 connections, and can be used when no IP addresses are in place. Routers discover one another on directly connected network segments and create an overlay network. Via that overlay network you can Ping, SSH, and even Winbox into a device. This is a great tool to have at your disposal, especially as you're remotely provisioning devices.

---

[6]https://iperf.fr

16.10.1 Enable RoMON

RoMON must first be enabled on a device to participate in the overlay network. Use the following command to enable RoMON in RouterOS:

```
/tool romon set enabled=yes
```

16.10.2 RoMON Secrets

RoMON runs and creates an overlay network with no authentication under the default settings. This is very convenient for bootstrapping a network and getting everything configured, but it's detrimental to your long-term security posture. RoMON can be secured by using *secrets* that ensure the *confidentiality* and *integrity* of your RoMON connections. Multiple secrets can be configured using comma-separated strings in the following command:

```
/tool romon
set secrets=secret1,secret2,secret3
```

These secrets are viewable in plaintext by using a "*print*" command, so don't use a sensitive password as a RoMON secret. Using multiple secrets can be helpful when integrating two MikroTik networks together.

16.10.3 RoMON Interfaces

RoMON is allowed to run on all interfaces with an unmodified configuration. This is set in a rule that cannot be deleted or disabled, though it can be changed. RoMON should not be allowed to run on interfaces that connect to service providers or clients like desktops or mobile devices. The default rule will be updated to forbid all interfaces, then we'll selectively allow some interfaces like *ether2* to run RoMON with the following commands:

```
/tool romon
port 0 forbid=yes
port add interface=ether2 forbid=no
```

Run the final command above for any interface that should be part of the overlay network. Allow RoMON to run on point-to-point links between MikroTik devices, and on management ports for network administrators.

16.10.4 Discovery

Routers participating in RoMON can be told to discover their RoMON neighbors. The command to initiate discovery is "*/tool romon discover*", and it will continue running until [Q] is pressed. The results of the discovery are shown for the CLI in Figure 16.20 on the next page, and for Winbox in Figure 16.21 on the next page.

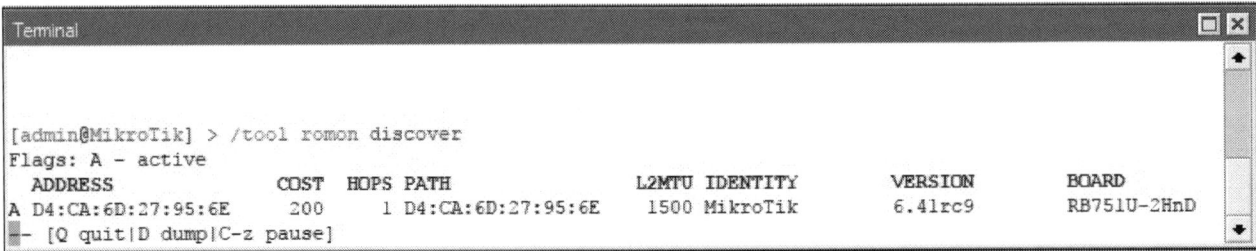

Figure 16.20: RoMON Discover CLI

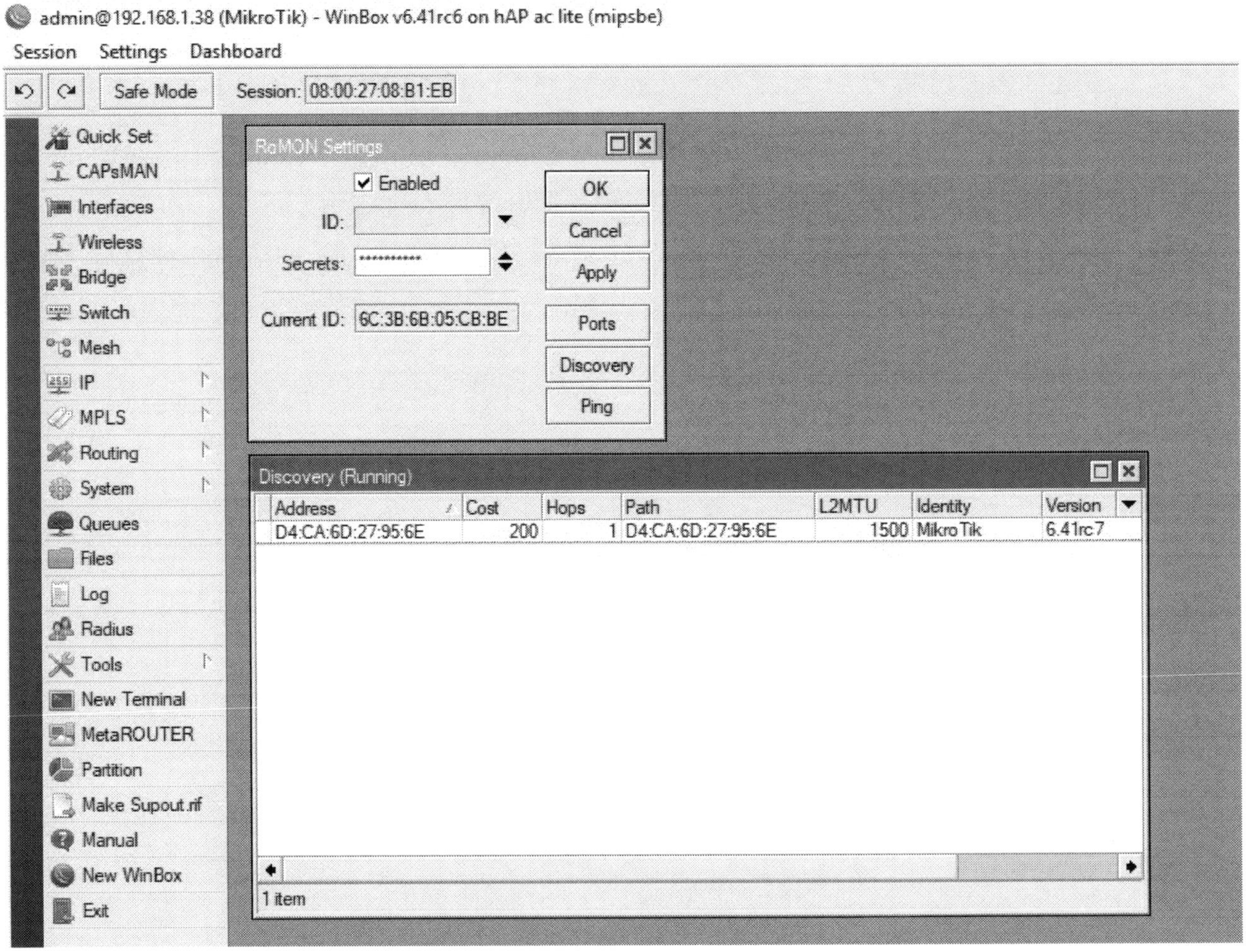

Figure 16.21: RoMON Discover

16.10.5 Connecting via RoMON

RoMON allows you to utilize the overlay network for Ping, SSH, and Winbox.

RoMON Ping

To ping a discovered host (*west.manitonetworks.com*) via RoMON use the following command:

```
/tool romon
ping id=08:00:27:3B:BC:A8
```

RoMON SSH

To SSH to a RoMON host (*west.manitonetworks.com* use the following command:

```
/tool romon
ssh user=admin address=08:00:27:3B:BC:A8
```

16.11 Telnet

The name of the Telnet tool is a bit of a misnomer in Winbox because you can choose Telnet, SSH, or MAC Telnet. Figure 16.22 shows the Telnet tool open, attempting to initiate a Telnet connection to *192.168.1.1* in Winbox.

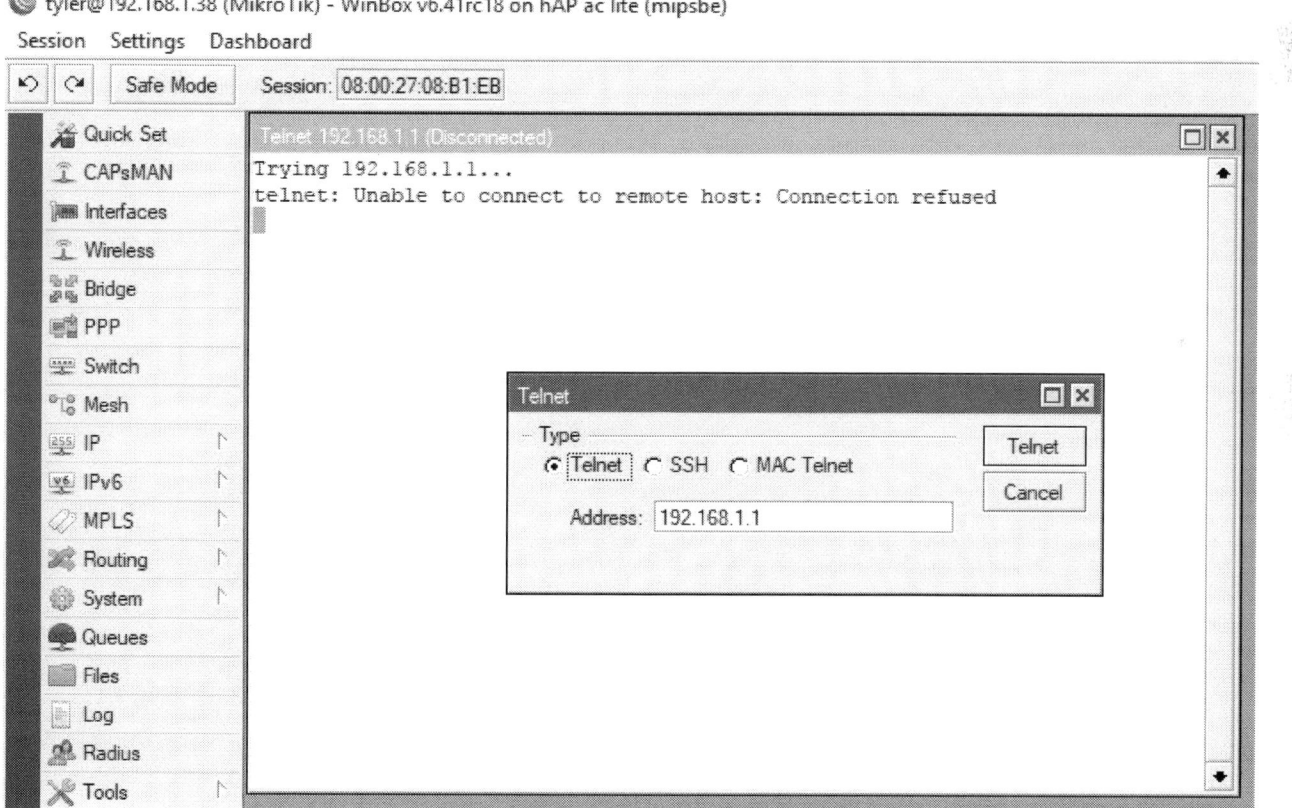

Figure 16.22: Telnet Tool

The connection was refused because Telnet has been disabled on that device per best practices in favor of SSH [?]. To access the same Telnet and SSH client tools (respectively) from the command line use the following commands:

```
/system telnet 192.168.56.101
/system ssh user=admin 192.168.56.101
```

16.12 Traceroute

Traceroute works by sending ICMP echoes to a destination address with progressively longer TTL values. Each echo makes it further down the routed path before exceeding the TTL and triggering an ICMP "Time Exceeded" response[7]. In this way the router is able to parse out the ICMP responses and infer the path that the traffic is taking. Traffic may take different paths if the network changes or is load-balanced, so the output of identical *traceroute* commands may not be the same over time. Results of a successful *traceroute* to *example.com* are shown in Figure 16.23.

```
[admin@MikroTik] > /tool traceroute example.com
# ADDRESS           LOSS   SENT   LAST    AVG    BEST   WORST   STD-DEV STATUS
1 10.4.128.1         10%    14    7.4ms   7.8    6.8    9.6     0.9
2 100.127.40.240     0%     14    9ms     9      7.6    10.7    0.8
3 172.22.51.104      0%     14    9.4ms   10.4   9.1    14.5    1.4
4 68.1.4.139         0%     14    19.6ms  17.5   15.2   20.5    2.1
5 184.187.207.206    0%     14    17.9ms  18.6   17.3   23.5    1.5
6 152.195.65.135     0%     14    15.9ms  16.5   15.1   20.4    1.4
7 93.184.216.34      0%     14    16.2ms  16.3   15.1   19.6    1.1
-- [Q quit|D dump|C-z pause]
```

Figure 16.23: CLI Traceroute Usage

16.12.1 Traceroute Usage

The traceroute tool can be used with the following commands and tweaked with command options:

```
/tool
traceroute example.com
traceroute 192.168.1.1
traceroute max-hops=10 example.com
traceroute max-hops=30 timeout=10s 192.168.1.1
```

Other options exist to specify a different protocol, source address, routing table, and more. This makes *traceroute* a very versatile troubleshooting tool but there are limitations.

---

[7]ICMP Type 11, Code 0

16.12.2 Traceroute Limitations

Traceroute does a great job parsing out the path of typical routed traffic but once a packet traverses certain tunnels or connections it becomes less useful. IPSEC tunnels and MPLS connections don't typically appear in *traceroute* output because the networks beneath those connections are transparent. IPSEC uses policies (not routing) to make decisions about traffic. MPLS is a different technology entirely, using labels and a separate forwarding table to determine the best path for traffic to take. Traceroute doesn't get the expected ICMP replies from these kinds of paths so multiple hops may be missing from output.

Network operators who filter ICMP can also interfere with the operation of *traceroute*. While ICMP is an essential part of any working network it can also be leveraged for DDoS attacks. For that reason some operators filter outbound ICMP, meaning that while a hop is successfully traversed *traceroute* never gets an ICMP message back and you don't get to see that hop. An example of missing hops is shown in Figure 16.24. A traceroute to an IP address seems to fail on hop five though the *traceroute* is actually successful.

```
[admin@MikroTik] > /tool traceroute 4.2.2.2
# ADDRESS         LOSS  SENT  LAST     AVG   BEST  WORST  STD-DEV STATUS
1 10.4.128.1      0%    4     8.3ms    7.9   7.3   8.3    0.4
2 100.127.40.240  0%    4     8.2ms    8.7   8.2   9.2    0.4
3 172.22.51.104   0%    4     14.6ms   11.1  9.6   14.6   2.1
4 4.26.66.25      0%    4     15.7ms   16.2  14.7  18.3   1.3
5                 100%  4     timeout
6 4.2.2.2         0%    3     19.6ms   22.7  19.6  27.1   3.2

[admin@MikroTik] > _
```

Figure 16.24: Traceroute Missing Hops

This kind of limitation doesn't mean traceroute is useless in modern networks but it does mean that the output should be scrutinized.

16.13 Bandwidth Test Server

The bandwidth test server is the server-side component of the bandwidth testing tool. When a bandwidth test client connects to a server and begins a bandwidth test it saturates the network link(s) between the two. This tells you the available bandwidth and robustness of the network between the client and server. By default this feature is enabled, though it should be disabled on production networks when not in use. Figure 16.25 on the next page shows the available options.

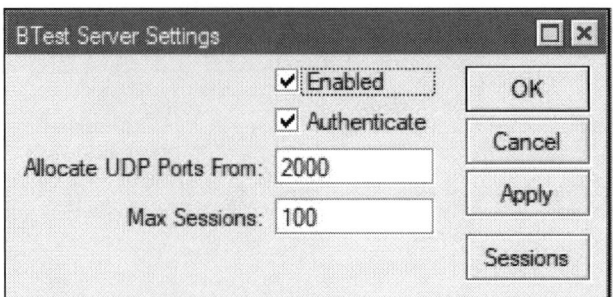

Figure 16.25: Bandwidth Test Server Settings

> **WARNING**: This tool can saturate network links and device processors, possibly causing an outage if run on production networks. Run this tool in a lab environment or during a scheduled network outage to prevent loss of service. If the feature is not disabled and the *admin* password isn't changed this feature could be leveraged by an attacker to make your network unavailable.

The *Enabled* option turns the server on and off, and the *Authenticate* option determines if the client will be forced to log in to the server using router credentials.

16.14 Bandwidth Test Client

The bandwidth test client authenticates to the server on page 257 and begins to push as much data as possible across the network. The client works via the console, Winbox, and a downloadable Windows client[8].

```
[admin@MikroTik] > /tool bandwidth-test 192.168.1.72 user=admin password=
   abc123! direction=both
              status: running
            duration: 21s
          tx-current: 8.0Mbps
tx-10-second-average: 1086.3Mbps
    tx-total-average: 571.9Mbps
          rx-current: 6.5Gbps
rx-10-second-average: 4.2Gbps
    rx-total-average: 2.0Gbps
         lost-packets: 15194
         random-data: no
           direction: both
             tx-size: 1500
             rx-size: 1500
-- [Q quit|D dump|C-z pause]
```

Figure 16.26: Bandwidth Test Client, Console

---

[8]https://mikrotik.com/download/btest.exe

An example of a test to with a local address in Winbox is shown in Figure 16.27.

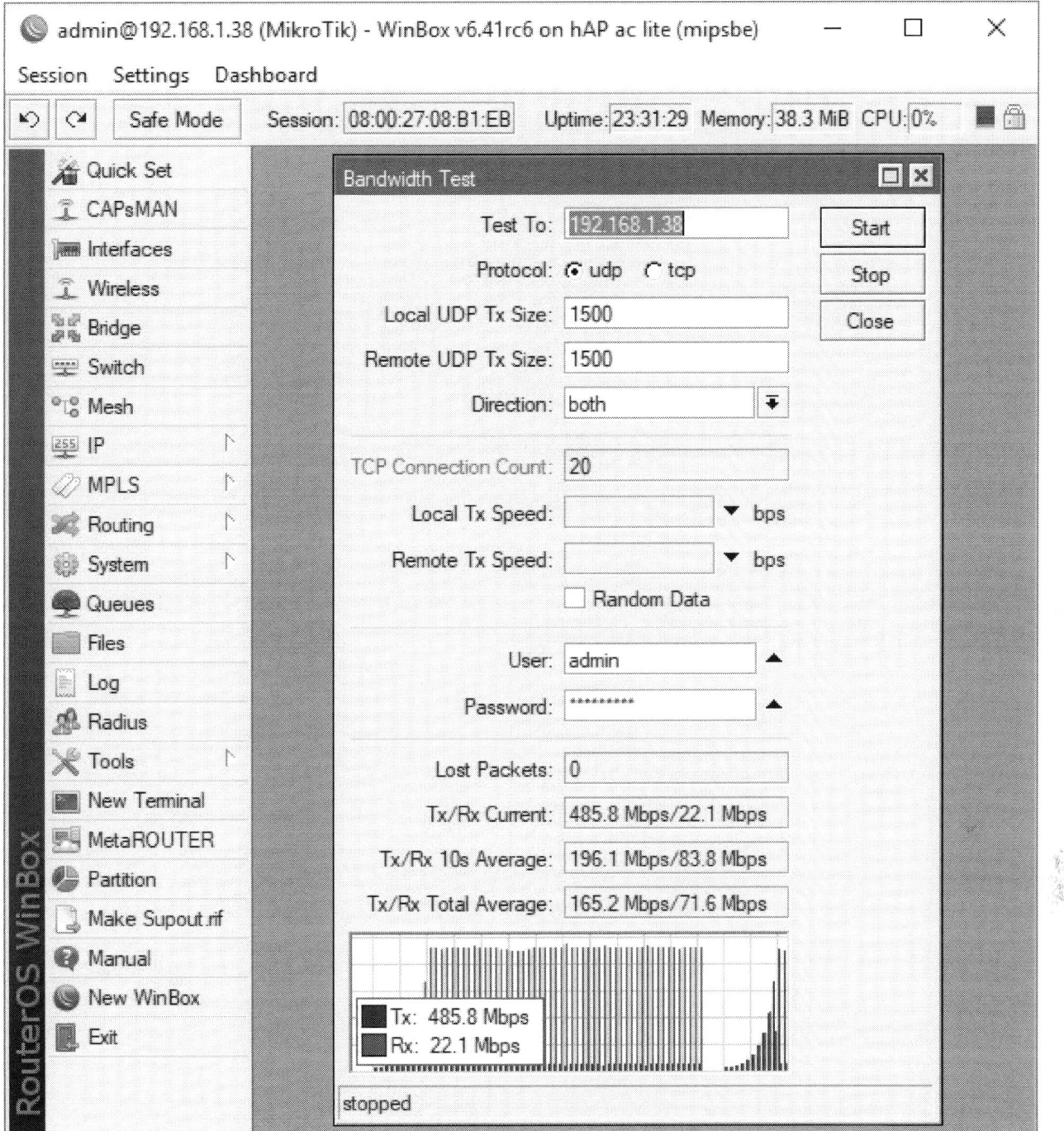

Figure 16.27: Bandwidth Test Client

The Windows client in Figure 16.28 on the next page looks and performs much like the Winbox client. The dedicated Windows client also makes it possible to save specific profiles for repeated tests:

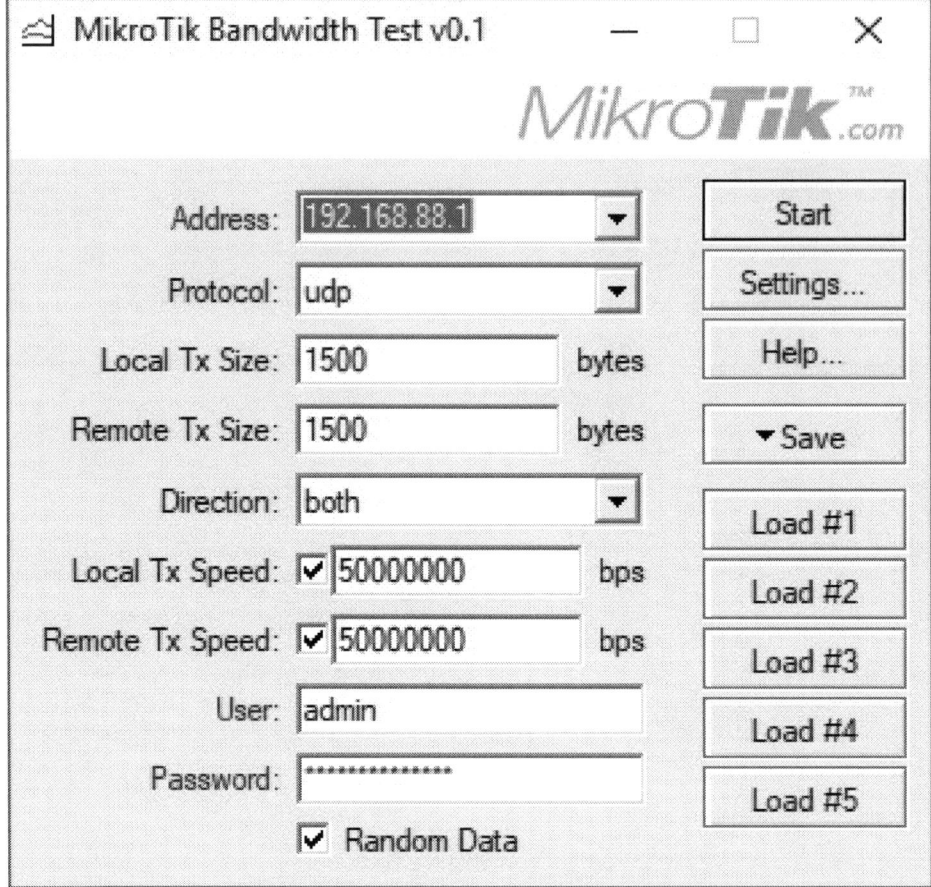

Figure 16.28: Windows Bandwidth Test Tool

The warning about impacting network links and devices by using this tool in the previous section should be taken seriously. Figure 16.29 shows a RouterBOARD unit's processor completely pegged at 100% while a bandwidth test runs:

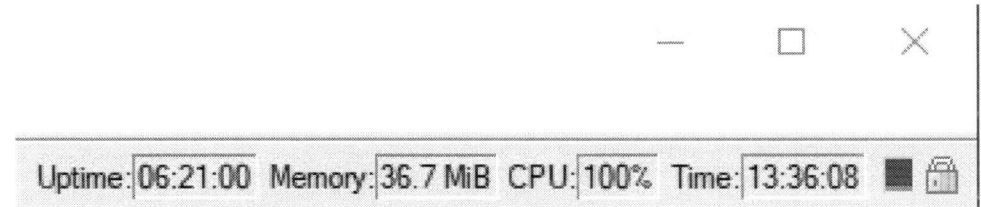

Figure 16.29: Bandwidth Test 100% CPU

16.15 Flood Ping

The ping flood tool sends a barrage of ICMP echoes to the destination specified, and gives you information about the minimum, maximum, and average Round Trip Time (RTT). This is a rudimentary tool for testing connectivity, but it can be helpful for quick troubleshooting. An example of a flood ping to a local device is shown in Figure 16.30 on the following page.

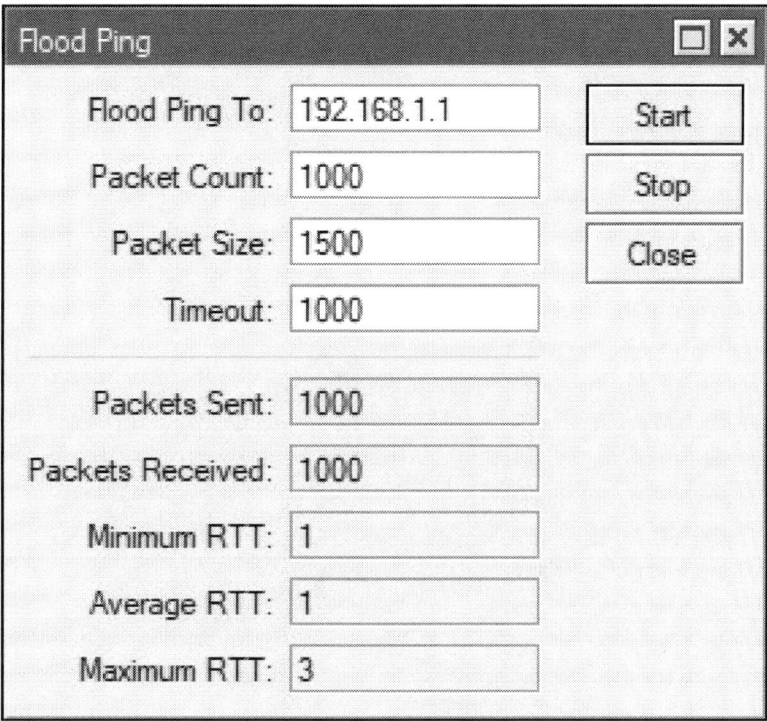

Figure 16.30: Flood Ping

The same tool is available at the console but it sends 500 packets by default instead of the 1000 sent in Winbox. Figure 16.31 shows the different amount of packets but basically the same network statistics:

```
[admin@MikroTik] > /tool flood-ping 192.168.1.1
    sent: 500
received: 500
 min-rtt: 1
 avg-rtt: 1
 max-rtt: 3

[admin@MikroTik] > _
```

Figure 16.31: Console Flood Ping

WARNING: Using this tool on production networks during business hours may have an adverse effect on network *availability*.

16.16 Review Questions

1. The Flood Ping tool tests packet loss, not speed.

    (a) True

    (b) False

2. How can RoMON connections between devices be secured?

    (a) Using EoIP

    (b) Using GRE

    (c) Using secrets

    (d) Using DH groups

3. The MAC Scan tool works within which network boundary?

    (a) Collision Domain

    (b) Broadcast Domain

    (c) Local Domain

    (d) Backbone Area

4. Which RouterOS feature creates an overlay network for device access and management?

    (a) RoMON

    (b) BoGON

    (c) ROMMON

    (d) EMCON

5. What type of network link can make *traceroute* appear to lose a hop?

    (a) EoIP

    (b) IP-IP

    (c) IPSEC

    (d) Ethernet

6. Which tool sends an ICMP echo to a destination and waits for a reply?
   (a) Bandwidth Tester
   (b) UDP
   (c) SSH
   (d) Ping

7. Which tool can fire a script or action when a network link crosses a pre-configured threshold?
   (a) Netman
   (b) Netwatch
   (c) Netboot
   (d) Netfig

8. Which tool can identify L2 device addresses present on a network?
   (a) IP Sweep
   (b) IP Scan
   (c) MAC Scan
   (d) RoMON

9. Which tool sends a barrage of ICMP echoes to a destination for network testing?
   (a) Flood Ping
   (b) Ping Sweep
   (c) Ping Surge
   (d) Ping Speed

10. Which tool tests the relative throughput of a network link with ICMP echoes?
    (a) Flood Ping
    (b) Ping Sweep
    (c) MAC Ping
    (d) Ping Speed

16.17 Review Answers

1. The Flood Ping tool tests packet loss, not speed.

    A – True (p. 260)

2. How can RoMON connections between devices be secured?

    C – Using secrets (p. 253)

3. Which RouterOS feature creates an overlay network for device access and management?

    B – Broadcast Domain (p. 240)

4. Which RouterOS feature creates an overlay network for device access and management?

    A – RoMON (p. 252)

5. What type of network link can make traceroute appear to lose a hop?

    C – IPSEC (p. 257)

6. Which tool sends an ICMP echo to a destination and waits for a reply?

    D – Ping (p. 250)

7. Which tool can fire a script or action when a network link crosses a pre-configured threshold?

    B – Netwatch (p. 246)

8. Which tool can identify L2 addresses present on a network?

    C – MAC Scan (p. 240)

9. Which tool sends a barrage of ICMP echoes to a destination for network testing?

    A – Ping Flood (p. 260)

10. Which tool tests the relative throughput of a network link with ICMP echoes?

    D – Ping Speed (p. 252)

Chapter 17

RouterOS Monitoring

Long-term operation and maintenance of high-performing networks requires monitoring of devices and network traffic. Once network monitoring is configured it's possible to determine what a network's baseline performance and behavior is. With a good baseline in mind it's possible to determine if a network is operating outside typical norms and troubleshoot proactively. Monitoring supports a network's *availability*, and keeping an eye on log events and resource utilization could reveal risks to a network *confidentiality*.

17.1 Graphs

While not a replacement for a network monitoring suites like Cacti, Nagios®, OpenNMS®, or others the *graphing* tool can produce some interesting data. Graphs can be configured for interface statistics, as well as resources usage like Central Processing Unit (CPU), RAM, and Storage. Access to these graphs is possible via the RouterOS web interface and inside Winbox.

17.1.1 Accessing Graphs

Browse to the device's web interface at *http://router-ip*, then click on the *Graphs* icon in the lower-middle of the screen as shown in Figure 17.1 on the next page:

Figure 17.1: Accessing RouterOS Graphs

The next page that loads presents links to each graph that you have access to. Clicking an interface graph link loads a page with daily, weekly, monthly, and yearly interface statistics like those shown in Figure 17.2 on the following page:

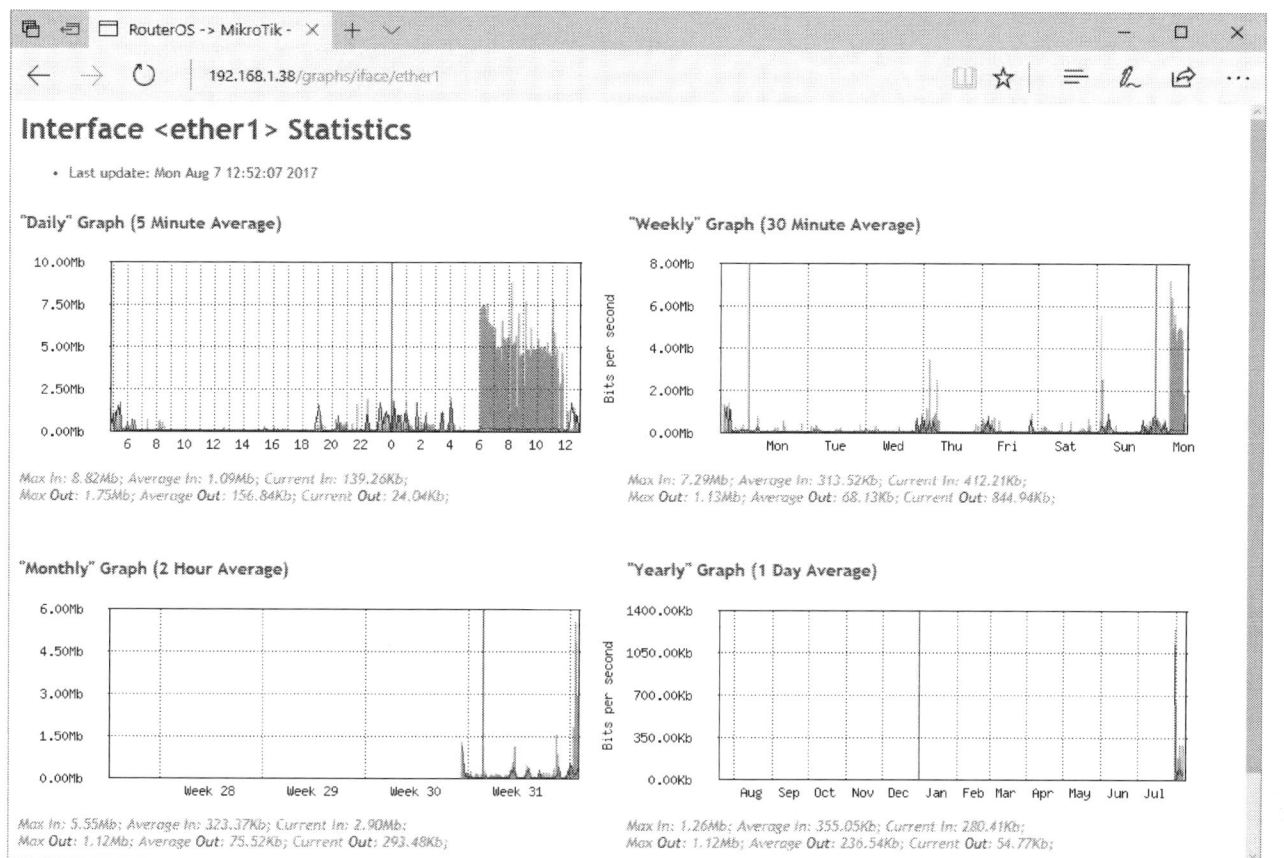

Figure 17.2: Web Console Interface Graph

17.1.2 Configuring Graphs

The first step in using graphs is to configure them on your RouterOS device. Two kinds of graphs exist:

- Interface graphs
- Resource graphs

To create Interface graphs for monitoring bandwidth on *ether1* and *ether2* use the following commands:

```
/tool graphing interface
add interface=ether1 allow-address=192.168.88.100/32
add interface=ether2 allow-address=192.168.88.100/32
```

Specifying the "*allow-address=...*" option restricts graph access to only that specific host. Figure 17.3 on the next page shows the same type of configuration in Winbox:

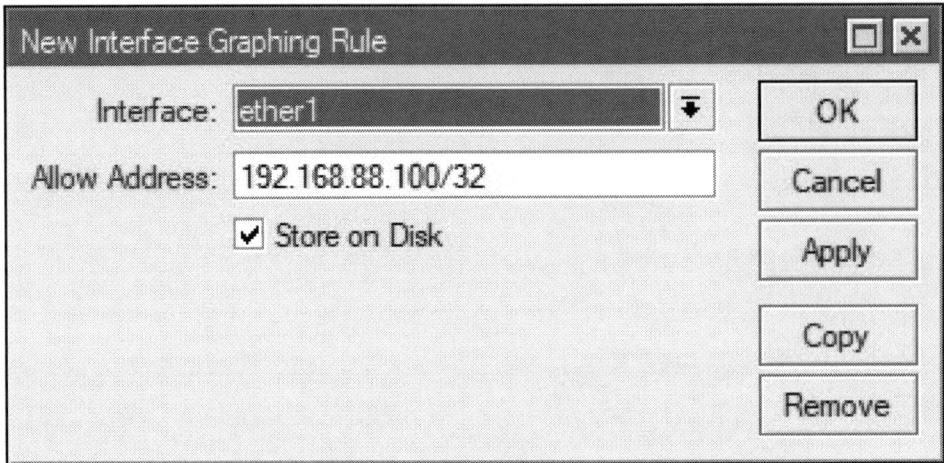

Figure 17.3: New Interface Graph, Winbox

WARNING: Access to graphs is NOT restricted by username or any authentication. The "*allow-address=a.b.c.d/x*" option restricts graph access to only authorized hosts or networks.

Opening an interface graph will show you four separate graphics:

- "Daily" Graph (5 Minute Average)
- "Weekly" Graph (30 Minute Average)
- "Monthly" Graph (2 Hour Average)
- "Yearly" Graph (1 Day Average)

An example of bandwidth graphing is shown in Figure 17.4 on the following page. Additional information about the maximum, average, and current data in and out are also shown.

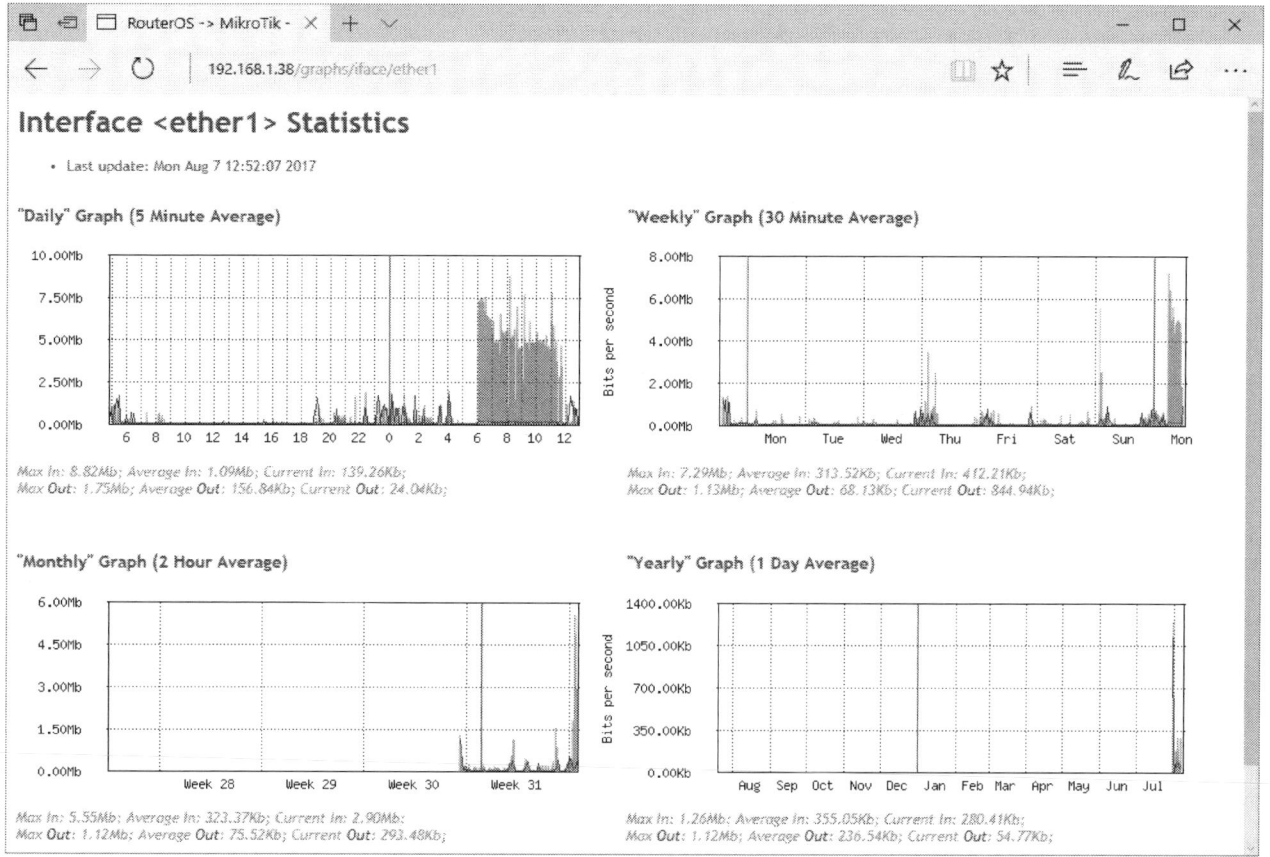

Figure 17.4: Interface Graph

To create graphs of CPU, RAM, and Storage data viewable by an administrator at "*192.168.88.100*" use the following commands:

```
/tool graphing resource add allow-address=192.168.88.100
```

An example of the Memory graphs is shown in Figure 17.5 on the next page, with Daily, Weekly, Monthly, and Yearly rolling data:

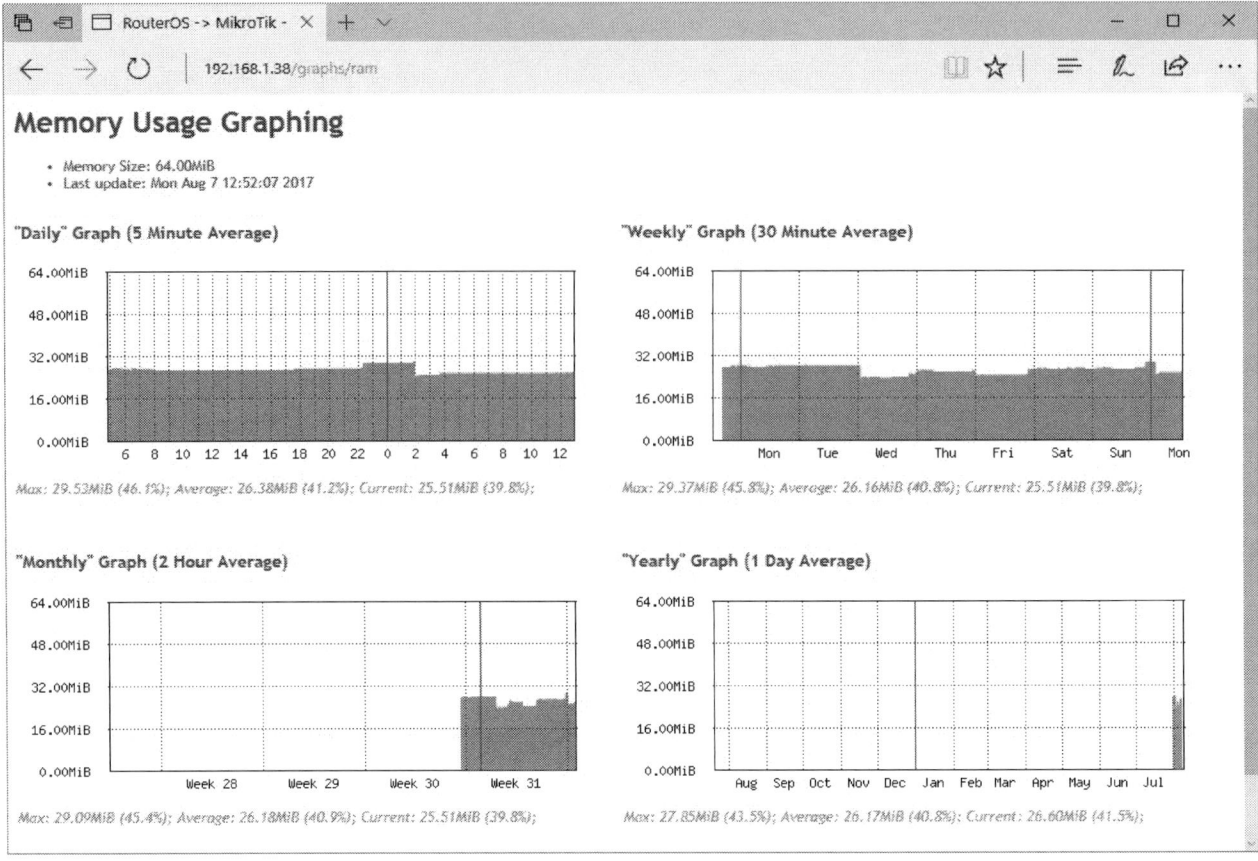

Figure 17.5: Memory Graph

17.2 Interface Monitoring

Monitoring device interfaces can provide important information about network performance and behavior. Look for the following indications when monitoring interfaces:

- RX and TX errors
- Packet drops
- Interface up and down events
- Average speed utilization over time

17.2.1 Interface Statistics

The "*/interface print stats*" and "*/interface print stats-detail*" commands show interface status and traffic. Some of the statistics information can be lengthy, and the output in Figure 17.6 on the following page is shortened.

```
[admin@MikroTik] > /interface print stats detail
Flags: D - dynamic, X - disabled, R - running, S - slave
 #     NAME           RX-BYTE          TX-BYTE      RX-PACKET    TX-PACKET RX-DROP
 0  R  ether4     153 594 557      115 250 811        961 006      822 005       0
[admin@MikroTik] > _
```

Figure 17.6: Interface Statistics

The interface *Traffic* tab in Winbox shows much of the same information, as shown in Figure 17.7:

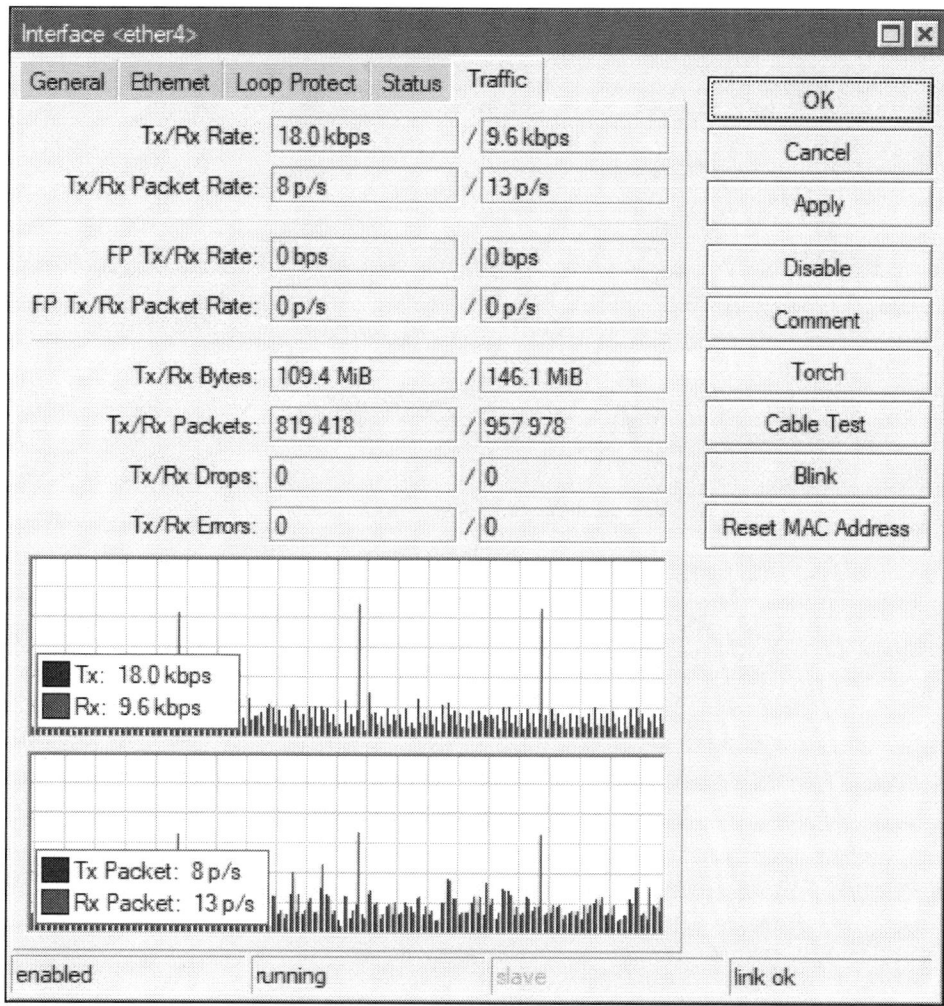

Figure 17.7: Interface Traffic Statistics

Up and down events can be seen in the output of the "*/interface print detail*" command as shown in Figure 17.8 on the next page:

```
[admin@MikroTik] > /interface print detail
Flags: D - dynamic, X - disabled, R - running, S - slave

0  R  name="ether4" default-name="ether1" type="ether" mtu=1500 actual-mtu
      =1500 mac-address=00:15:5D:7E:D8:15 fast-path=no last-link-up-time=aug
      /12/2017 07:14:43 link-downs=0
[admin@MikroTik] > _
```

Figure 17.8: Interface Up and Down Events

17.2.2 Torch Tool

The Torch tool allows you to monitor traffic on interfaces and filter by source, destination, protocol, and more. It's a very useful tool when investigating bandwidth utilization or unknown traffic. The Torch button is available in Winbox for each interface dialog shown in Figure 17.9:

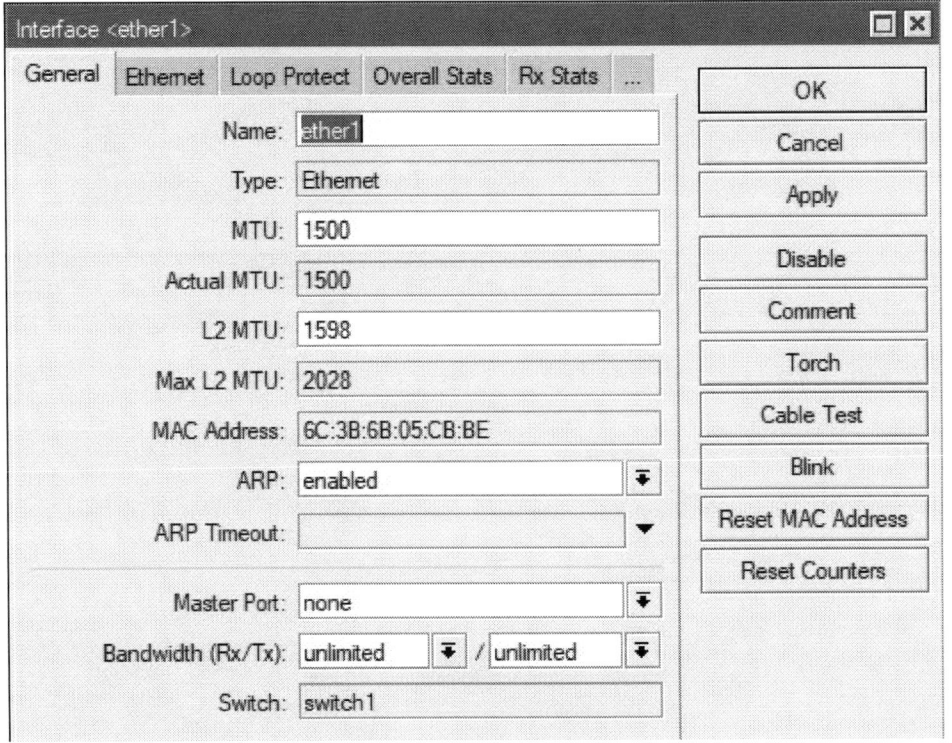

Figure 17.9: Winbox Torch Button

An example of Torch output for *ether1* on a router is shown in Figure 17.10 on the following page. In this example there is a *traceroute* running, and you can see the ICMP traffic in-flight.

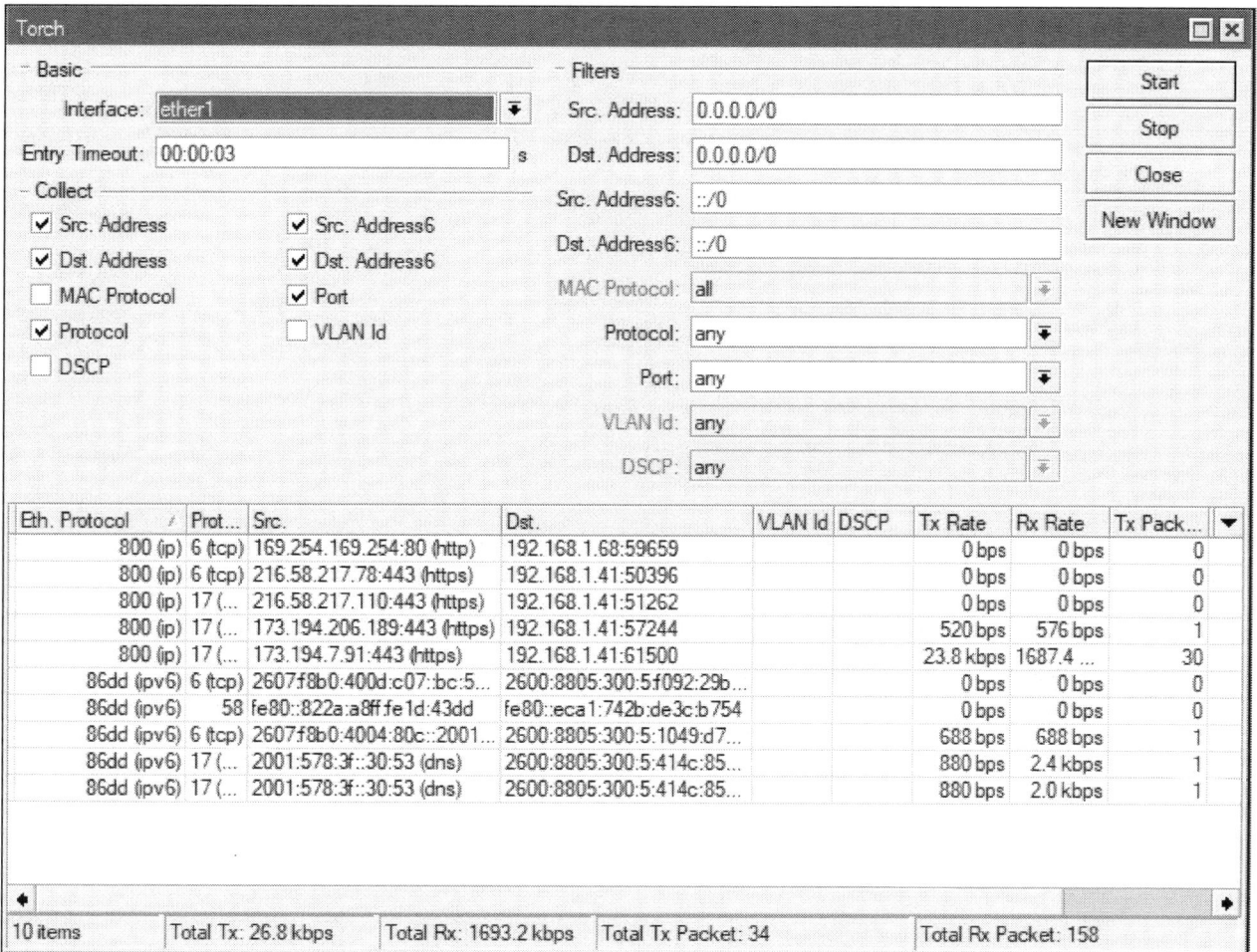

Figure 17.10: Winbox Torch Running

Torch can be run from the console with the "/tool torch ..." command as shown in Figure 17.11. The console version of the tool shows less detail about source and destination addresses but it's still useful.

```
[admin@MikroTik] > /tool torch interface=ether1 ip-protocol=any mac-protocol=any
MAC-PROTOCOL   IP-PROTOCOL    TX          RX         TX-PACKETS   RX-PACKETS
ip             icmp           0bps        4.7kbps    0            1
ip             igmp           2.6kbps     0bps       6            0
ip             tcp            5.6kbps     9.9kbps    9            8
ip             udp            83.7kbps    49.9kbps   32           27
arp            0              336bps      0bps       1            0
ipv6           udp            1520bps     0bps       2            0
ipv6           icmpv6         3.6kbps     0bps       5            0
                              97.4kbps    64.6kbps   55           36

-- [Q quit|D dump|C-z pause]
```

Figure 17.11: Console Torch Tool

17.2.3 Interface Monitor-Traffic Tool

The *"interface monitor-traffic ..."* command can be used to monitor traffic flows across an interface. It's also possible to view a real-time aggregate value of traffic with the command shown in Figure 17.12:

```
[admin@MikroTik] > /interface monitor-traffic aggregate
       rx-packets-per-second: 34
          rx-bits-per-second: 20.2kbps
    fp-rx-packets-per-second: 47
       fp-rx-bits-per-second: 25.5kbps
         rx-drops-per-second: 0
        rx-errors-per-second: 0
       tx-packets-per-second: 23
          tx-bits-per-second: 21.3kbps
    fp-tx-packets-per-second: 47
       fp-tx-bits-per-second: 25.5kbps
         tx-drops-per-second: 0
        tx-errors-per-second: 0
-- [Q quit|D dump|C-z pause]
```

Figure 17.12: Aggregate Traffic Flow Monitoring

17.2.4 Traffic Monitor Tool

If you want to be alerted when traffic hits or falls below a threshold you can use the *Traffic Monitor* tool. For a given interface it allows you to set a threshold and paste in a script that fires in response to the threshold being crossed. The command shown below logs an entry when the threshold is crossed. The following command logs an event when download traffic passes 40 Mbit/s:

```
tool traffic-monitor
add name="Ether1 Download" interface=ether1 traffic=received trigger=above
   threshold=40000000 on-event="/log info \"40 Mbits exceeded\";"
```

17.3 Performance Monitoring

Performance monitoring can provide some of the best early indications of router malfunction, network misconfiguration, or security issues. CPU utilization spikes can indicate poorly configured firewall and NAT rules, or overuse of Mangle rules. Spikes in disk utilization can indicate poorly configured logging rules, or the presence of a fault or security breach generating many alerts in the logs.

17.3.1 Console Resource Monitoring

CPU and RAM monitoring is possible from the console using command shown in Figure 17.13.

```
[admin@MikroTik] > /system resource monitor
/system resource monitor
        cpu-used: 2%
cpu-used-per-cpu: 2%
     free-memory: 24432KiBs

-- [Q quit|D dump|C-z pause]
```

Figure 17.13: Console Resource Monitoring

17.3.2 Console CPU Monitoring

The command in Figure 17.14 streams CPU utilization statistics at the console.

```
[admin@MikroTik] > /system resource cpu print follow
 #    CPU      LOAD    IRQ    DISK
 0    cpu0     3%      2%     0%

-- Ctrl-C to quit. Space prints separator. New entries will appear at bottom.
```

Figure 17.14: Console CPU Monitoring

17.3.3 Profile Tool

The Profile tool shows a list of services and how much CPU each is utilizing. Being able to see the CPU performance spread across services is very helpful when troubleshooting Queue or layer seven (L7) firewall rule impact. It can also help you gauge the impact of large routing tables or complex firewall chains. Sample output from the Profile tool is shown in Figure 17.15 on the next page.

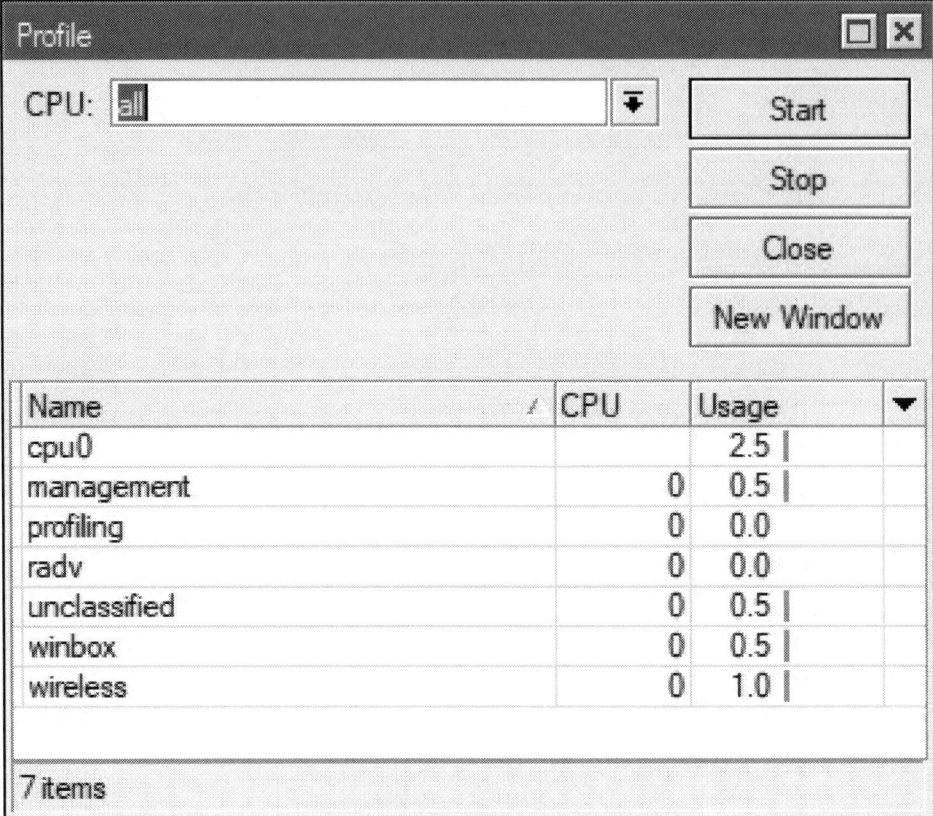

Figure 17.15: Profile Tool

While the Profile tool only shows you point-in-time information about device performance you can compare it with SNMP data gathered over time. With enough SNMP data logged you can put data from Profile against past data to see how far you've deviated from baseline. CLI usage of the Profile tool for a 10 second *duration* is shown in Figure 17.16.

```
[admin@MikroTik] > /tool profile duration=10s
NAME            CPU     USAGE
wireless                0.5%
ethernet                0%
console                 1%
dns                     0%
firewall                0%
networking              0%
winbox                  0%
management              0.5%
routing                 0%
profiling               0%
telnet                  0%
unclassified            0.5%
total                   2.5%
[admin@MikroTik] > _
```

Figure 17.16: CLI Profile Tool

17.3.4 CPU Graphs

The CPU utilization graphs created on page 267 help identify trends over time that monitoring current usage from the console can't provide. Look for the following types of trends:

- Hours of the day where CPU upswings and downswings occur
- Most resource-intensive hours of the day
- Most resource-intensive days of the week
- Unusual peaks and valleys outside typical baselines

17.4 Event Monitoring

Device event log entries are the administrator's way of seeing the rolling history of changes and events on the device. These entries also support *accountability* for who made what changes and when.

17.4.1 RouterOS Logs

Logs give you the ability to see the events taking place on your routers over time. Having good logs is critical when troubleshooting or investigating a possible security incident. An example of log entries in Winbox is shown in Figure 17.17 on the next page.

17.4. EVENT MONITORING CHAPTER 17. ROUTEROS MONITORING

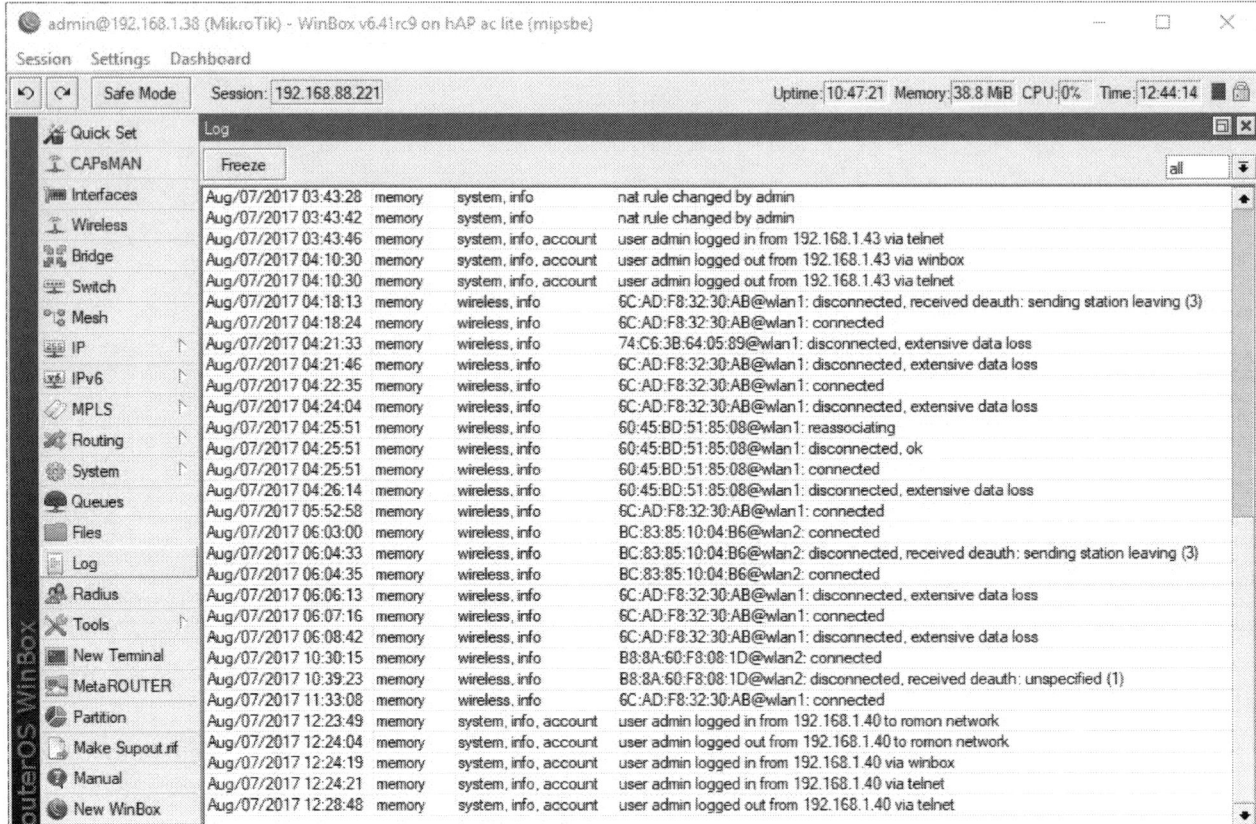

Figure 17.17: Winbox Log Entries

While examining logs in Winbox to stop them from scrolling by click the *Freeze* button in the upper-right portion of the Log window. This temporarily stops the scrolling until you either click the button again or close the Log window. Logs can be viewed from any console or terminal window including Telnet, SSH, Winbox, etc. Logs including the keyword *OSPFv2* are shown in Figure 17.18.

```
[admin@MikroTik] > /log print where message~"OSPFv2"
mar/26 21:48:03 system, info  OSPFv2 network added by admin
mar/26 21:48:32 system, info  OSPFv2 area area1 added by admin
mar/26 21:48:44 system, info  OSPFv2 network changed by admin
[admin@MikroTik] > _
```

Figure 17.18: OSPF Logs

The Tilde symbol ($\sim$) in the *"log print where..."* command below is used to indicate a Regex string search.

17.4.2 Interface Events

If you suspect an interface is malfunctioning or the device at the other end of the connection is bouncing you can view log events for interfaces. Use the *interface* topic to see all interface-related events, and use the *message* field to sort further if needed. The command in Figure 17.19 shows logs for interface *ether1*.

```
[admin@MikroTik] > /log print where topics~"interface" message~"ether1"
mar/26 20:10:03  interface , info  ether1 link up (speed 100M, full duplex)
19:45:25  interface , info  ether1 link down
19:45:33  interface , info  ether1 link up (speed 100M, full duplex)
[admin@MikroTik] > _
```

Figure 17.19: Printing *ether1* Interface Logs

17.4.3 Security Events

It's very important to regularly audit login events for infrastructure devices like routers. Password guessing attempts or login attempts outside normal working hours or by unrecognized credentials should be an immediate red-flag. Searching by the *account* topic will show most events related to router accounts. Account creation and deletion are logged under the *system* topic. Examples of both types of account events are shown in Figure 17.20 and 17.21 respectively.

```
[admin@MikroTik] > /log print where topics~"account"
mar/26 20:10:36  system,info ,account  user admin logged in  from 74:C6:3B:64:05:89 via winbox
mar/26 20:10:45  system,info ,account  user admin logged in  via local
mar/26 20:12:39  system,info ,account  user admin logged out via local
mar/26 20:13:50  system,info ,account  user admin logged out from 74:C6:3B:64:05:89 via winbox
[admin@MikroTik] > _
```

Figure 17.20: Printing Account Event Logs

The command in Figure 17.21 has some output trimmed for brevity.

```
[admin@MikroTik] > /log print where topics~"system" message~"user"
19:46:10  system,info ,account  user admin logged in from 192.168.88.253 via telnet
19:55:19  system,info  user tyler added by admin
[admin@MikroTik] > _
```

Figure 17.21: Printing Account Creation Events

17.5 SNMP

SNMP allows network administrators to monitor hardware and interface performance statistics. While the protocol can be used to be read and write data from the device, this section will focus on reading performance data. SNMP is a "pull" protocol, with a central monitoring agent polling devices for performance data. The typical polling interval for most network monitoring systems is every 30 seconds. The Dude (Chapter 18) has a native SNMP agent (p. 308) for monitoring devices, and all other Network Management System (NMS) suites can probe SNMP as well.

17.5.1 SNMP Versions

RouterOS supports all the mainstream versions of SNMP for device monitoring:

- v1
- v2c
- v3

In a mixed environment with older legacy equipment it may be necessary to continue using SNMP v1 or v2c across some networks. If your network monitoring suite includes support for multiple versions at the same time it's possible to use a mix of older and newer versions of the protocol. The Dude (p. 287) supports all versions of SNMP, so it's perfect for monitoring brand new RouterOS devices and legacy equipment from other vendors.

SNMP v1

This is the first and most basic version of SNMP. This legacy version of SNMP is still well-supported by almost all vendors but offers little security. Any SNMP client that can reach the device and has the Community String can query configuration and performance data.

SNMP v2c

Larger 64-bit counters were added in SNMP v2. The newer version also added additional security capabilities though many vendors never fully implemented them. The new security model was thought to be overly complex and convoluted, so vendors instead implemented SNMP v2c. This version uses the Community String security of v1 with no authentication or encryption built-in.

SNMP v3

The larger 64-bit counters of SNMP v2c are augmented in SNMP v3 with authentication and encryption. Message Digest 5 (MD5) and Secure Hash Algorithm 1 (SHA-1) are used for authentication. AES and Data Encryption Standard (DES) are used for encryption, though AES is much more robust than DES.

> **NOTE**: SNMP v3 should be used if possible to ensure the *confidentiality* and *integrity* of a device and its configuration data.

17.5.2 Community Strings

The SNMP Community String is a simple plaintext string that clients use to probe SNMP data sources. Almost all vendors (including MikroTik) implement a "*public*" Community String by default. Figure 17.22 shows the default community string configured on the router.

```
[admin@MikroTik] > /snmp community print
Flags: * - default
 #   NAME       ADDRESSES    SECURITY       READ-ACCESS
 0 * public     0.0.0.0/0    none           yes
[admin@MikroTik] > _
```

Figure 17.22: Default SNMP Community String

Using the "*public*" string is a violation of both best practices and established security requirements in PCI-DSS, HIPAA, etc. This well-known default configuration should be changed or removed. Unfortunately RouterOS does not allow for removal of the default string as of mid-2017, but it can be renamed. Security Technical Implementation Guide (STIG) Finding V-3210 states that:

> "The network device must not use the default or well-known SNMP Community strings public and private."
>
> –Infrastructure Router STIG Finding V-3210

One quick command will change the default string so it can't be used by hackers performing system footprinting and reconnaissance:

```
/snmp community set [find name=public] name=not-public
```

Once the default string has been changed new strings must be created on each device to be monitored. Then new strings are configured on the NMS system that will be polling for performance data. Create a read-only community string with no write access using the following command:

```
/snmp community add name=exampleorg read-access=yes write-access=no
```

17.6 Syslog

The Syslog protocol pushes event alerts from a device to a central collector. This centralized collector typically indexes, displays, and archives log events for day-to-day monitoring and possible forensic examination in the event of a breach. The Dude can function as a Syslog collector, as can many NMS and open source network monitoring suites. Syslog collectors typically listen on UDP port 514, and it's common to restrict Syslog traffic to a Management network or VLAN.

17.6.1 Logging Actions

Before event logs can be shipped to another server a logging action must be created. This new entry will specify that the logging target is *"remote"* and what the *"remote"* address is. The following command adds an action pointing to a remote Syslog server at 192.168.1.200:

```
/system logging action
add name=Syslog target=remote remote=192.168.1.200
```

17.6.2 Logging Rules

Now that a Syslog action is available we can reference it in a new logging rule. The following command creates a logging rule for any critical event, using the action created on page 282:

```
/system logging
add topics=critical action=Syslog disabled=no
```

The router will ship log events that match the *"critical"* topic to the Syslog server. Once all devices are configured to use this type of logging an organization can begin to analyze all device logs from a single locations.

17.6.3 Syslog Security

A good practice to follow in any organization is restricting network administrators from modifying or deleting logs sent to the Syslog server. While network administrators and systems analysts should be able to read logs for troubleshooting, being able to change or wipe entries creates a Conflict of Interest (COI). Creating this barrier protects against insider threats who may be trying to cover their tracks when creating the following:

- Backdoor accounts
- Firewall pinholes for remote access
- Unauthorized VPN tunnels
- DNS hijacking-related settings changes

The challenge that comes with this kind of restriction is having a senior-level person who has the authority to hold networking folks accountable while also knowing enough about security to spot suspicious behavior. Someone outside the IT department should have admin-level rights to the Syslog server, so any effort to cover tracks or purge logs would require collusion between people in two groups.

17.7 Review Questions

1. How often do most network monitoring systems poll SNMP devices for monitoring data?

   (a) 15 seconds

   (b) 30 seconds

   (c) 45 seconds

   (d) 60 seconds

2. What version of SNMP first implemented support for larger counters?

   (a) v1

   (b) v2c

   (c) v3

   (d) v4

3. What symbol is used to search logs with a Regex string?

   (a) %

   (b) &

   (c) \

   (d) ~

4. Which logging topic should be searched for user logged in / logged out events?

   (a) *account*

   (b) *authentication*

   (c) *authorization*

   (d) *accounting*

5. The Profile tool shows which system processes are utilizing the CPU.

   (a) True

   (b) False

6. Which flag in the "/system resource cpu print..." command continues to stream real-time processor performance metrics?

    (a) *monitor*

    (b) *follow*

    (c) *show*

    (d) *list*

7. Which command shows aggregated RX and TX statistics for all interfaces in real-time?

    (a) */interface snooper aggregate*

    (b) */interface monitor-traffic aggregate*

    (c) */interface scan aggregate*

    (d) */interface print-traffic aggregate*

8. The Torch tool shows protocol and port traffic statistics in real-time.

    (a) True

    (b) False

9. Which command keyword displays extended interface statistics?

    (a) *detail*

    (b) *more*

    (c) *follow*

    (d) *print-detail*

10. The two types of graphs integrated with the RouterOS web interface are "Interface" and "Resource".

    (a) True

    (b) False

17.8 Review Answers

1. How often do most network monitoring systems poll SNMP devices for monitoring data?

    B – 30 seconds (p. 280)

2. What version of SNMP first implemented support for larger counters?

    B – v2c (p. 280)

3. What symbol is used to search logs with a Regex string?

    D – "~" (p. 279)

4. Which logging topic should be searched for user logged in / logged out events?

    A – *account* (p. 279)

5. The Profile tool shows which system processes are utilizing the CPU.

    A – True (p. 275)

6. Which flag in the "*/system resource cpu print...*" command continues to stream real-time processor performance metrics?

    B – *follow* (p. 275)

7. Which command shows aggregated RX and TX statistics for all interfaces in real-time?

    B – */interface monitor-traffic aggregate* (p. 274)

8. The Torch tool shows protocol and port traffic statistics in real-time.

    A – True (p. 272)

9. Which command keyword displays extended interface statistics?

    A – *detail* (p. 271)

10. The two types of graphs integrated with the RouterOS web interface are "Interface" and "Resource".

    A – True (p. 267)

Chapter 18

The Dude

The Dude is an NMS by MikroTik that operates in a server-client architecture. A centralized server monitors devices, while remote clients display alerts and allow administrators to interact with graphs and maps. Remote Agents make it possible to monitor distant devices and networks while conserving bandwidth across the network.

18.1 Dude Server

The Dude Server is the central component of the monitoring solution. It handles device polling, data storage, and monitoring tasks. If configured it can also alert administrators when specified thresholds are exceeded. In past versions The Dude could be installed as an application on Microsoft Windows computers, however that is no longer the case. In newer releases of The Dude the only supported platform is a RouterOS instance. It doesn't matter which platform as long as there are sufficient resources to run The Dude. This chapter will guide you through the following steps to create a Dude instance running on a Microsoft Hyper-V:

1. Create a CHR VM for Dude
2. Attach a virtual storage drive for monitoring data and event logs
3. Boot the VM
4. Enable Dude services
5. Discover devices on the network
6. Configure SNMP and Syslog monitoring
7. Create resource graphs for CPU, RAM, and bandwidth usages

Once Dude is installed, configured, and running your view of the network can change dramatically.

18.2 Dude as a VM

Dude can be run on larger RouterBOARD models, x86 server installations, or CHR instances on a hypervisor. This book uses the pre-built CHR image provided by MikroTik because it's made specifically for virtualization. Running the Dude instance on a virtual CHR gives us access to the following:

- VM Snapshots or Checkpoints
- Replication and High Availability (HA) if licensed and enabled in the hypervisor
- Easy VM backups and exports (OVF, OVA, Hyper-V export, etc.)

This book uses Microsoft Hyper-V as the virtualization platform but you can easily use the same steps adjusted for VMware vSphere, Oracle VirtualBox, etc.

18.3 Creating a Virtual Machine

Open Hyper-V and click the menu option to create a new VM as shown in Figure 18.1. In Hyper-V you may or may not see the *Before You Begin* page - if you do just click *Next*.

18.3.1 Name and Location

Give the VM a name and choose a different storage location if necessary.

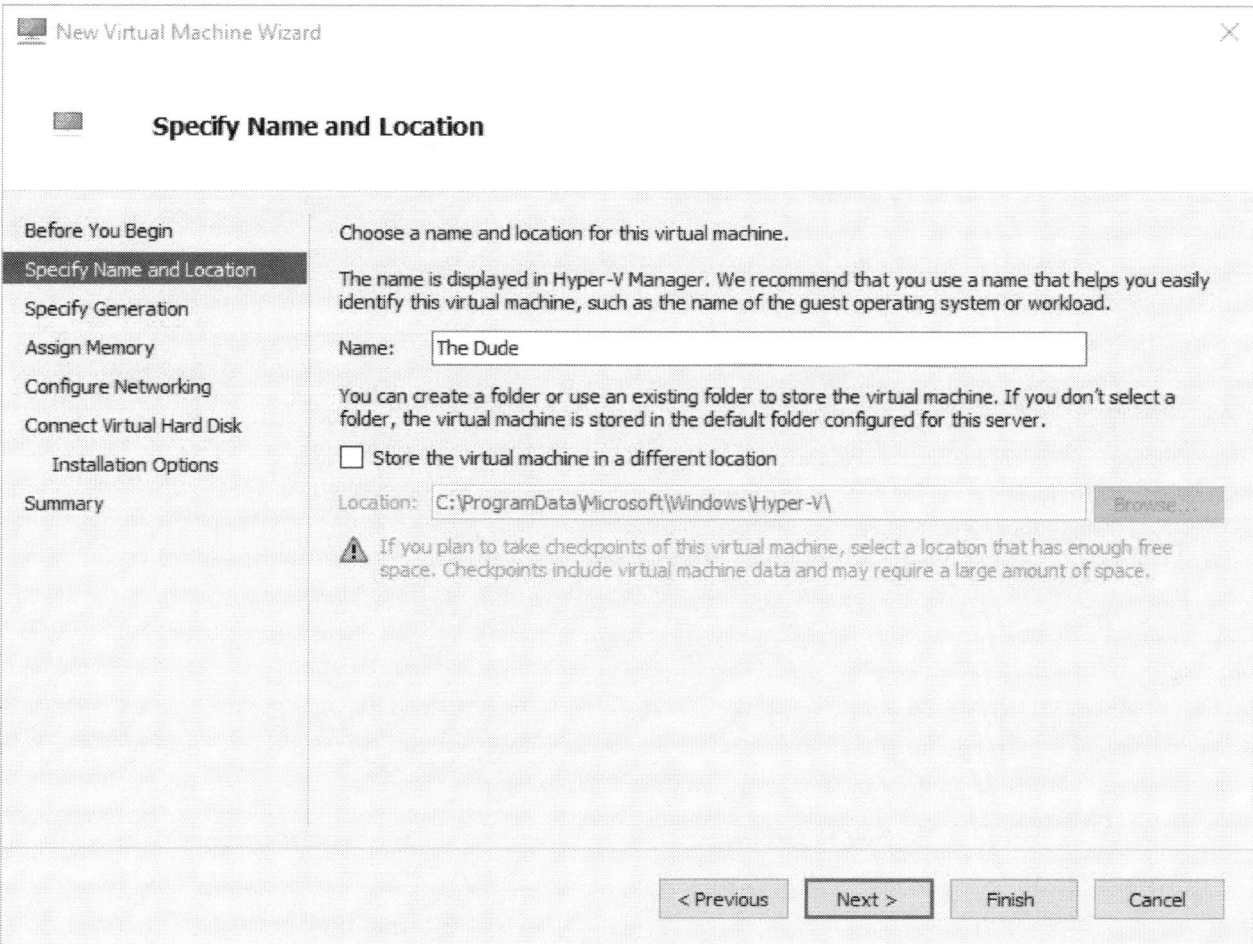

Figure 18.1: Creating a VM, First Steps

18.3.2 VM Generation

In Hyper-V the VM's generation will be "one". Generation two is reserved for more modern versions of Microsoft Windows Server and some Linux distributions that support secure booting. The MikroTik CHR also requires an IDE drive as of this writing, and IDE storage buses are no longer supported in generation two. Figure 18.2 shows generation one chosen for the Dude VM:

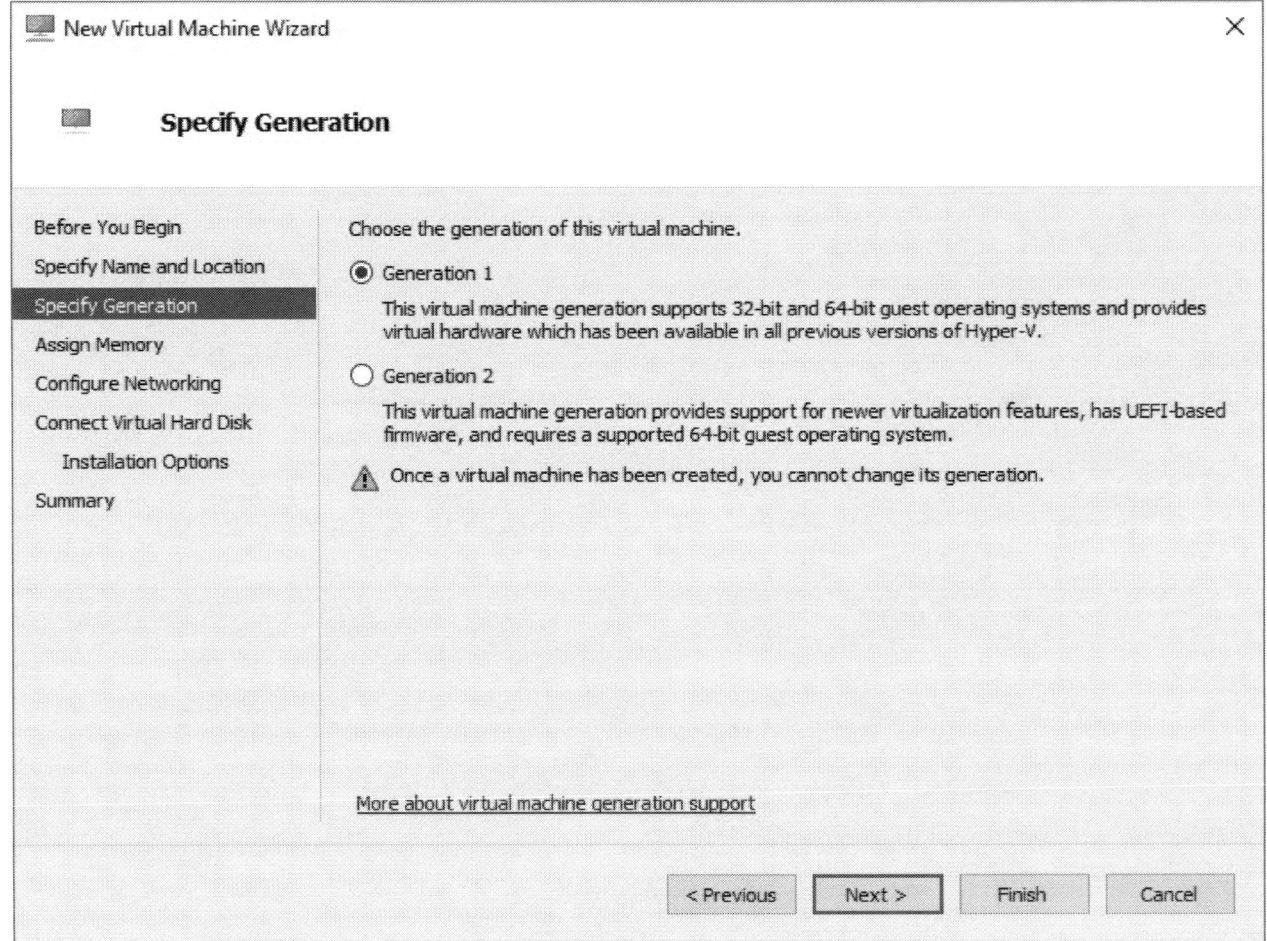

Figure 18.2: Dude VM Generation

NOTE: If you choose the wrong generation and create the VM it will have to be deleted and recreated to change the generation.

From the MikroTik documentation[1] on usable disk interfaces:

> "Note: SCSI controller Hyper-V and ESX is usable just for secondary disks, system image must be used with IDE controller"

---

[1] https://wiki.mikrotik.com/wiki/Manual:CHR#Usable_Network_and_Disk_interfaces_on_various_hypervisors:

18.3.3 Memory

I'm assigning 2 GB (2048 MB) of RAM to the Dude VM as shown in Figure 18.3. The official Dude documentation[2] doesn't list the minimum required RAM as of this writing, but 2 GB has worked well for me in the past. This can always be adjusted later depending on your organization's needs. The option to use Dynamic Memory is also turned on so the hypervisor will only allocate memory as needed to the VM. This option isn't required but it's typically good to leave on.

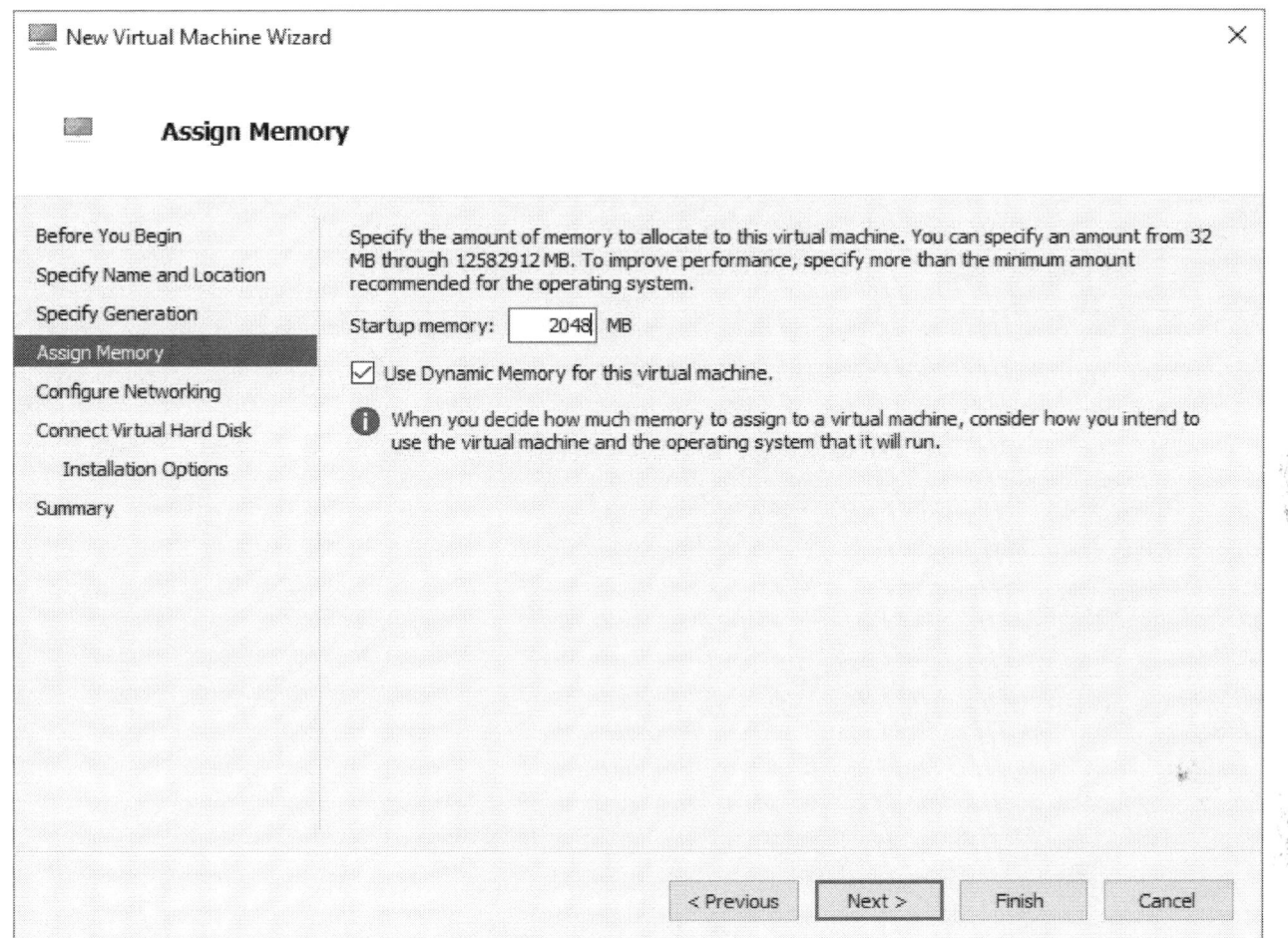

Figure 18.3: Assigning Memory

---

[2]https://wiki.mikrotik.com/wiki/Manual:The_Dude_v6/Installation#System_requirements_for_server_package

18.3.4 Virtual Network Connection

Choose the virtual network connection appropriate for your environment. Figure 18.4 shows that I've selected a virtual connection called *WAN* that has access to the rest of my network.

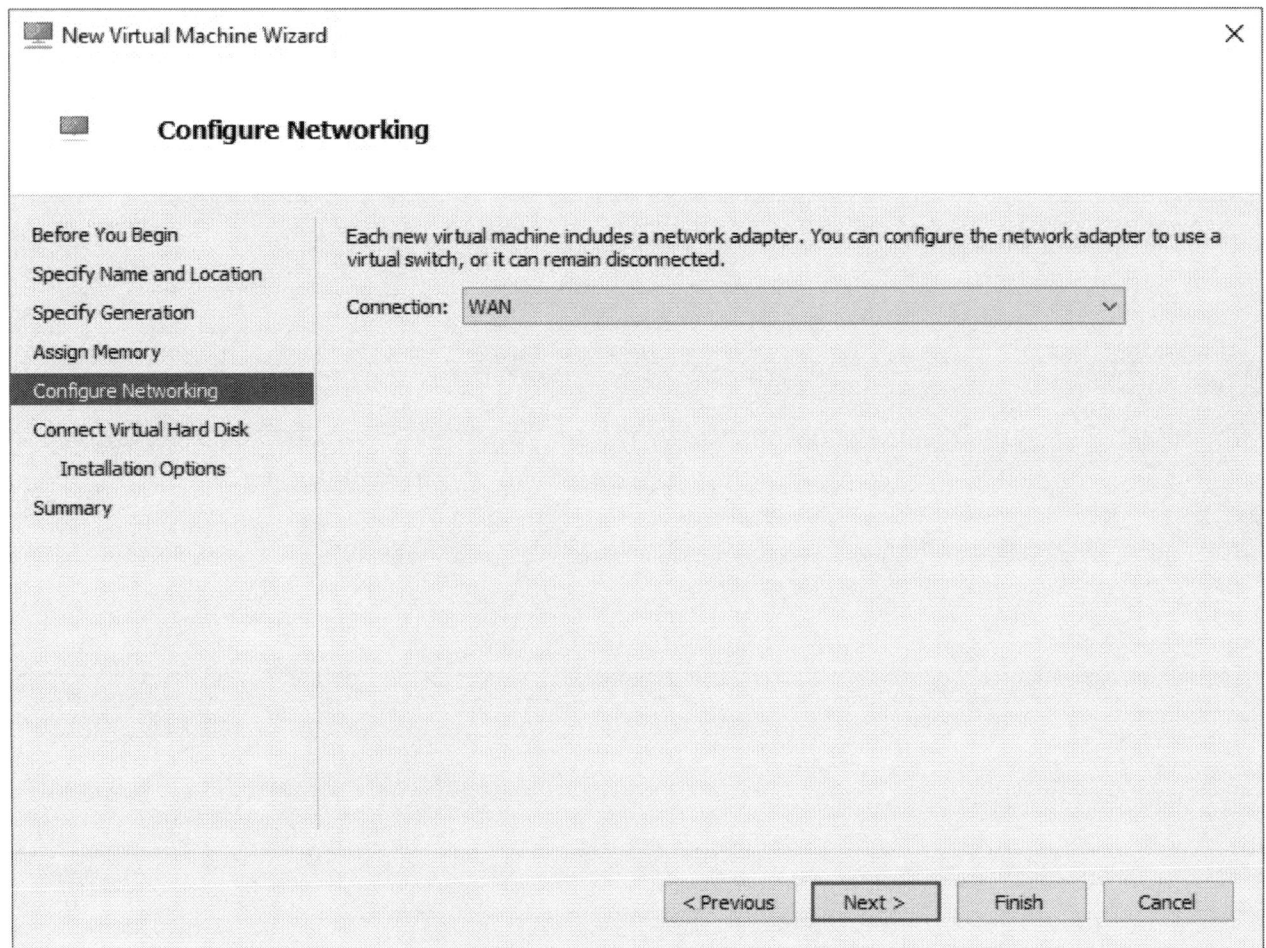

Figure 18.4: Choose Dude Network Connection

18.3.5 Install Virtual Hard Disk

Instead of creating a new virtual hard disk for the Dude installation we'll choose the downloaded VHDX file. Figure 18.5 shows the VHDX file chosen for the VM's hard drive.

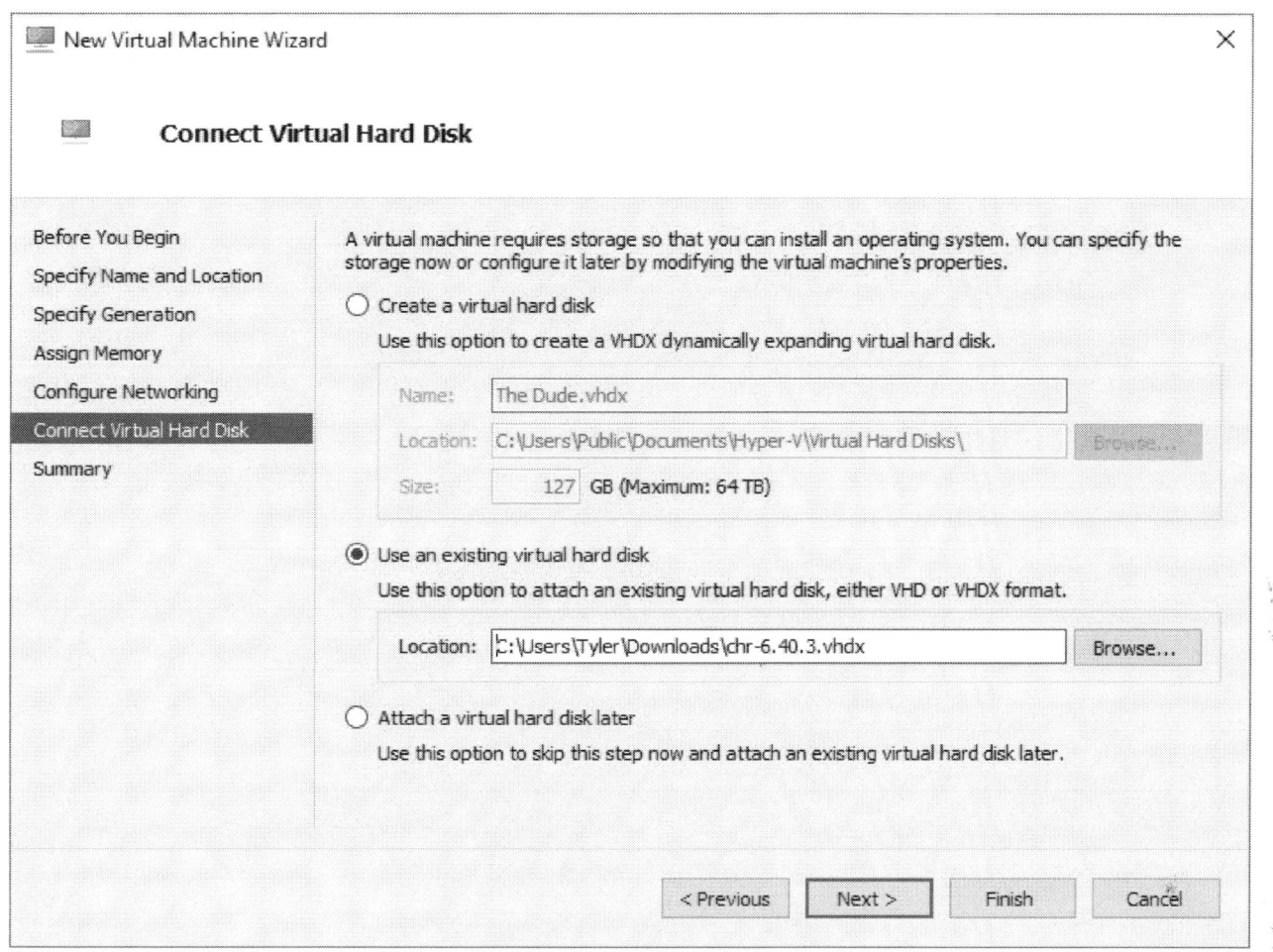

Figure 18.5: Attach Virtual Hard Disk

Click *Next* and then *Finish* on the Summary screen to create the VM on the hypervisor.

18.3.6 Attach Additional Storage

Collected network performance and log data can accumulate very quickly in even small networks depending on what's being monitored. For this reason it's a good idea to split out the Dude install drive from the data storage drive. Use the following steps in Hyper-V to create a new virtual hard disk for Dude data storage:

1. Select the VM in the left pane
2. Right-click and select *Settings*
3. Select *IDE Controller 0* or *SCSI Controller* on the left, then select *Hard Drive* on the right and click *Add*
4. On the right under *Virtual Hard Disk* click *New*
5. Choose the type, name, and size of the drive that best fits your environment. All options can be left on default values and it will work fine.

Figure 18.6 shows the additional storage drive configured on the VM:

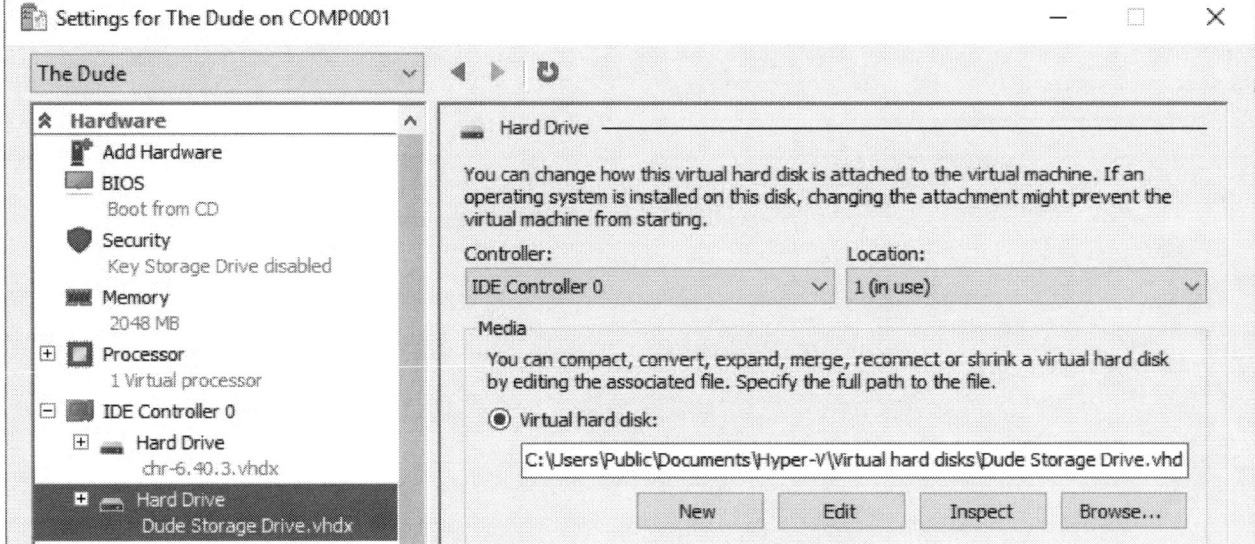

Figure 18.6: Dude Storage Drive Added

Click *OK* to return to the main Hyper-V screen. Right-click on the Dude VM and select *Start*.

18.4 VM Integration Services

Most (if not all) hypervisors offer some kind of integration services for the VMs they host, and Microsoft's Hyper-V offers quite a few[3]. Select the *Integration Options* menu item on the left. First, I recommend disabling the *Time Synchronization* option. It's generally considered good practice to not synchronize a VM's clock with the host's hardware. Instead we'll rely on NTP to update our system clock over the network. Then check the other boxes as shown in Figure 18.7:

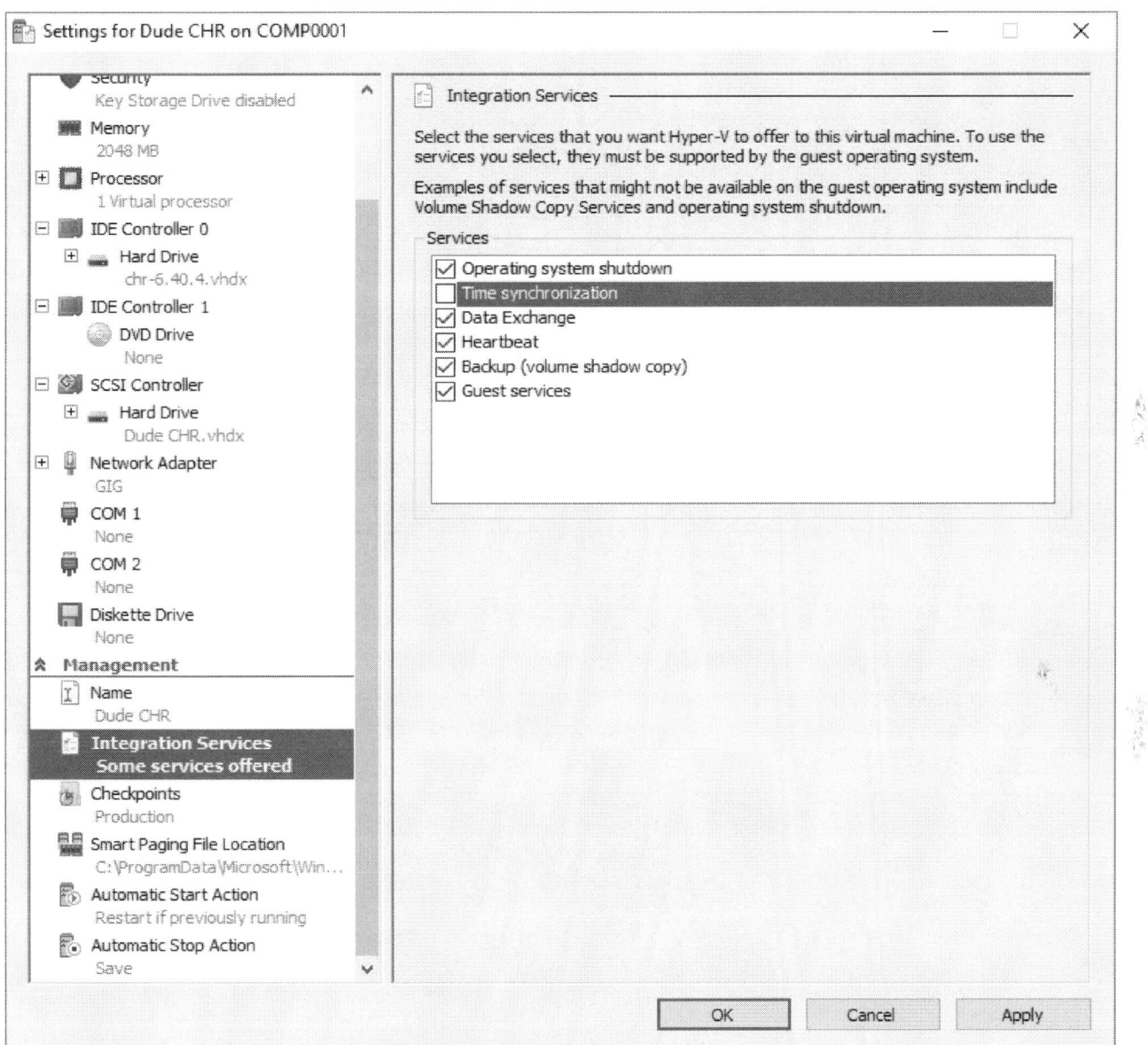

Figure 18.7: Hyper-V VM Integration Services

---

[3] https://technet.microsoft.com/en-us/library/dn798297(v=ws.11).aspx#BKMK_guest

These other options allow the hypervisor to shut down the VM autonomously in the event of a power failure. Advanced monitoring and backups (Checkpoints in Hyper-V) are also possible with via the other options.

18.5 Dude Configuration

Double-click the VM to open up a console or right-click the VM and select *Connect*. Log in with the default MikroTik credentials:

- Username: *admin*
- Password: *No password*

Set the IP addressing on *ether1* and routes so the Dude server will be available over the network. Use either static or DHCP addresses with the following commands:

- Static:
    1. Add a local IP address: */ip address add interface=ether1 address=192.168.88.199/24*
    2. Add a default route: */ip route add dst-address=0.0.0.0/0 gateway=192.168.88.1*
    3. Remove the default CHR DHCP client on *ether1*: */ip dhcp-client remove 0*
- DHCP:
    1. Verify the DHCP client has received a dynamic address on the *ether1* interface: */ip dhcp-client print*
    2. Verify the DHCP client has received a dynamic default route: */ip route print*
    3. On your local network's DHCP server mark the IP lease for the CHR instance as static or reserved so the address doesn't change.

The DHCP command above assumes that there is a router at the edge of the network handing out a typical default route along with dynamic IPs. Use the "*/ip address print*" command to show the dynamic address if applicable and make a note of it. The assigned address will be used later to access the server via the Dude Client. Connect to the router via Winbox and open a Terminal session or access the device using SSH.

18.5.1 Manage Storage

List available storage drives with the command shown in Figure 18.8:

```
[admin@MikroTik] > /disk print detail
0 name="" label="" type=unknown disk="Virtual Disk" size=127.0GiB
[admin@MikroTik] > _
```

Figure 18.8: List Storage Drives

We have an unformatted, unlabeled disk at the moment. Use the command to format and label the storage drive shown in Figure 18.9 so it's usable.

> **WARNING**: The command that formats the drive does not ask for additional confirmation. Ensure you're formatting the correct drive number!

```
[admin@MikroTik] > /disk format-drive 0 label=Dude file-system=ext3
formatted: 8%
-- [Q quit|D dump|C-z pause]
```

Figure 18.9: Disk Formatting

Having a good label ensures the disk won't be accidentally deleted. MikroTik recommends using the Ext3 file system for storing Dude monitoring data so we're in-line with their recommended practices. Figure 18.10 shows the result of a successful formatting operation:

```
[admin@MikroTik] > /disk print detail
0 name="disk1" label="Dude" type=ext3 disk="Virtual Disk" free=125.9GiB size
    =127.0GiB
[admin@MikroTik] > _
```

Figure 18.10: Properly Formatted Disk

Make note of the name "*disk1*" because it will be used in the following section.

18.5.2 Manage Services

Even with the Dude package installed it won't be running by default. The service must be enabled and pointed to the storage location for monitoring data. This is why we formatted the storage drive before enabling the Dude service. Use the following command to enable Dude services and use the newly-formatted storage drive:

```
/dude set enabled=yes data-directory=disk1
```

The command in Figure 18.11 confirms the service is running and data will be logged to the correct drive:

```
[admin@MikroTik] > /dude print
       enabled: yes
data-directory: disk1
        status: running
[admin@MikroTik] > _
```

Figure 18.11: Dude Status

At this point we're ready to transition to the Dude client and begin monitoring devices and networks.

18.6 Dude Client

Complete the following steps to begin running the Dude client on a Microsoft Windows host or in Linux with an emulator like WINE:

1. Download the Dude Client with the same version number as the Dude Server from the following URL:

    `https://mikrotik.com/download`

2. Install the downloaded executable
3. Launch the newly installed Dude client
4. Enter the IP address, username, and password for your CHR instance created previously. The username and password are for the local RouterOS credentials on the CHR.
5. Click *Connect*
6. Verify the login window displays "*Getting stuff*" while it downloads data from the server

The client should open to a blank map and an auto-discovery window that we'll use in the next section.

18.7 Auto-Discover

The Dude has robust auto-discover capabilities built-in that help you populate network maps without having to create each device manually. Figure 18.12 shows the auto-discover window with some additional options I encourage you to use.

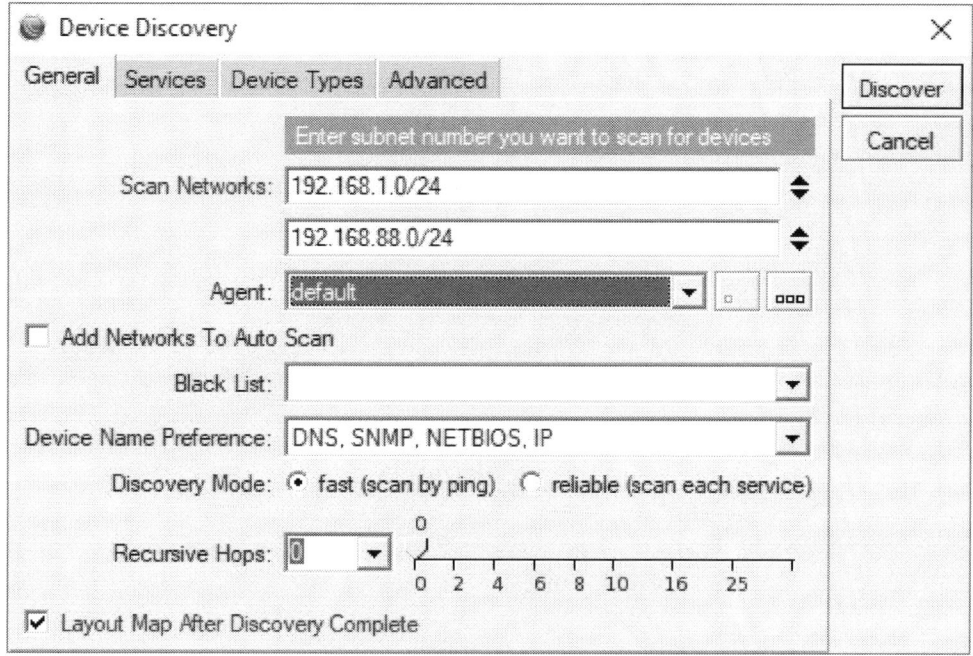

Figure 18.12: Dude Device Discovery

The *"Layout Map After Device Discovery"* option at the bottom of the window keeps the default map orderly. Otherwise all discovered devices are piled atop one another and you have to arrange them manually. In my lab environment I have both *192.168.1.0/24* and *192.168.88.0/24* networks so I've added the additional entry under *Scan Networks*.

> **WARNING**: The discovery process creates network traffic that looks like a possibly malicious port scan. It's a good idea to whitelist the Dude instance's IP address in your IDS / IPS software before running scans.

18.8 SNMP

The SNMP protocol will provide us with a wealth of device performance information once we configure a profile. On page 281 we created an SNMP community and here is where it's put to work. Figure 18.13 on the next page shows the default SNMP profiles that come pre-configured on the Dude server under the far-left *Settings* menu:

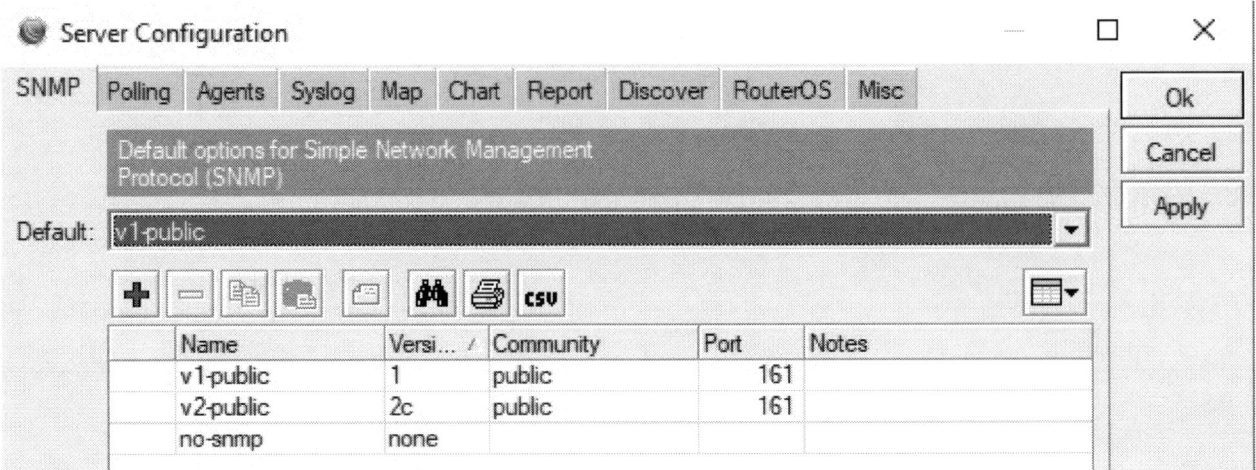

Figure 18.13: Dude Default SNMP Profiles

These would work fine for us with a device fresh out-of-the-box but we've already disabled the default *public* community. Click the button to add a new profile and fill in your SNMP community information as shown in Figure 18.14:

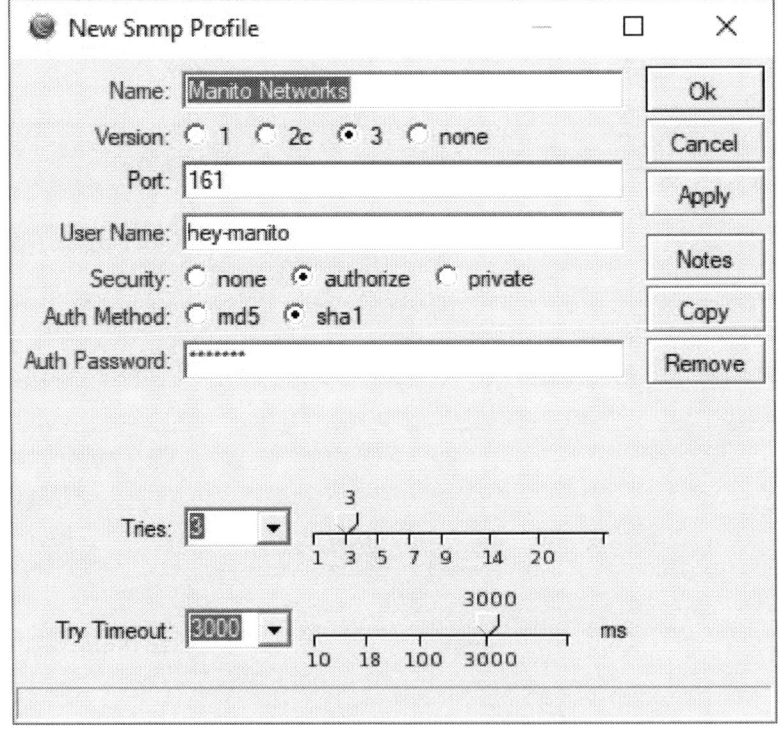

Figure 18.14: Dude New SNMP Profile

Since Dude is running on RouterOS we can also do the same configuration in Winbox as shown in Figure 18.15 on the following page:

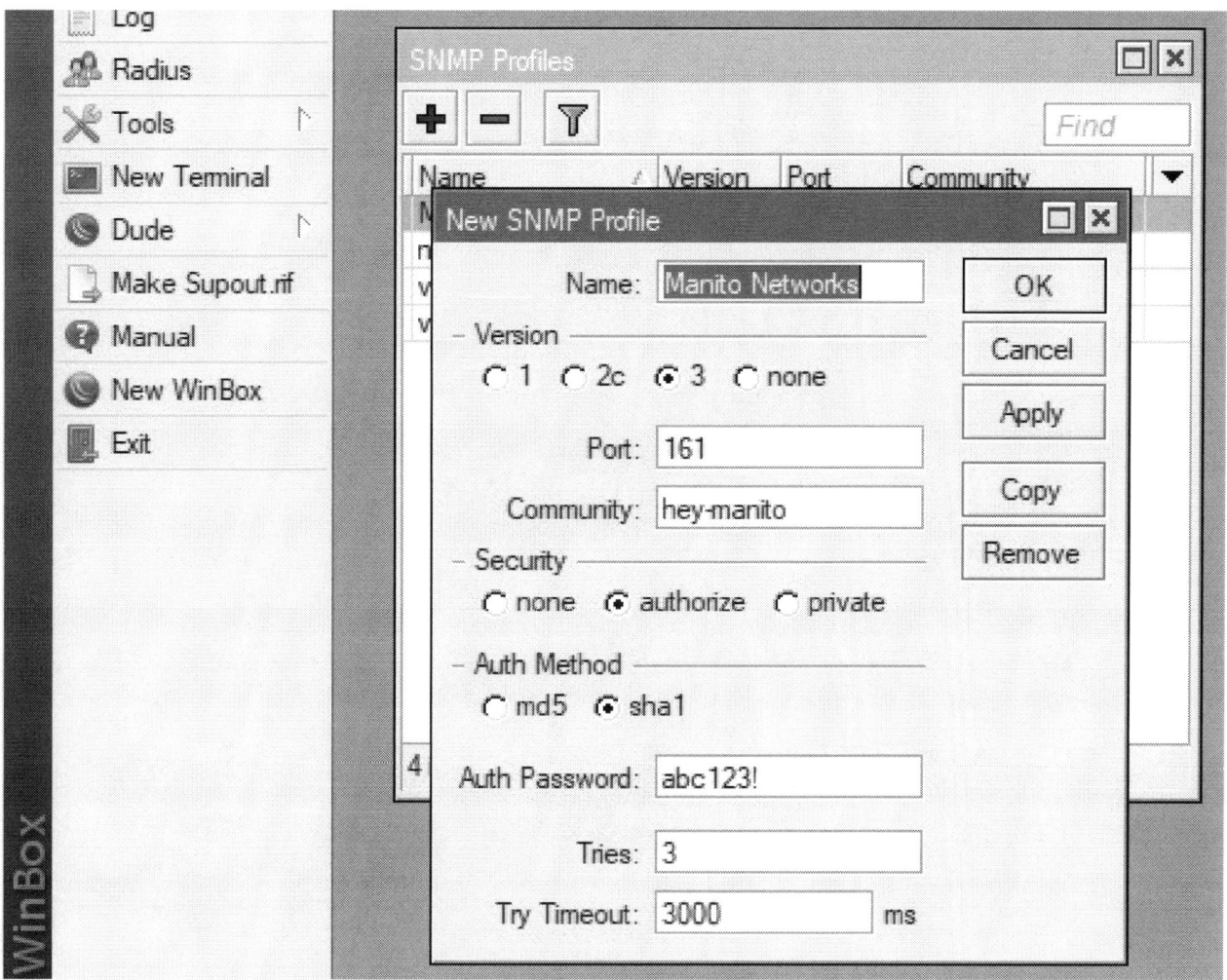

Figure 18.15: Dude SNMP Profile in Winbox

While SNMP is usually a polling protocol where nothing is exchanged unless the collector reaches out, we can configure RouterOS to send SNMP Traps. These special messages are normally sent only when something interesting happens on a device. RouterOS has limited functionality for sending traps but it can alert on interface-related events. When discussing physical security on page 281 it was mentioned that an attacker unplugging an interface should trigger an alert. These steps are where we implement that alerting and the single command on RouterOS would make a good addition to your default configuration templates.

The following RouterOS command configures SNMP traps to be sent when *ether1* through *ether3* experience a change:

```
/snmp
set trap-target=192.168.88.10 trap-community=hey-manito trap-version=3 trap-
    generators=interfaces trap-interfaces=ether1,ether2,ether3
```

Figure 18.16 on the next page shows the configuration applied in Winbox:

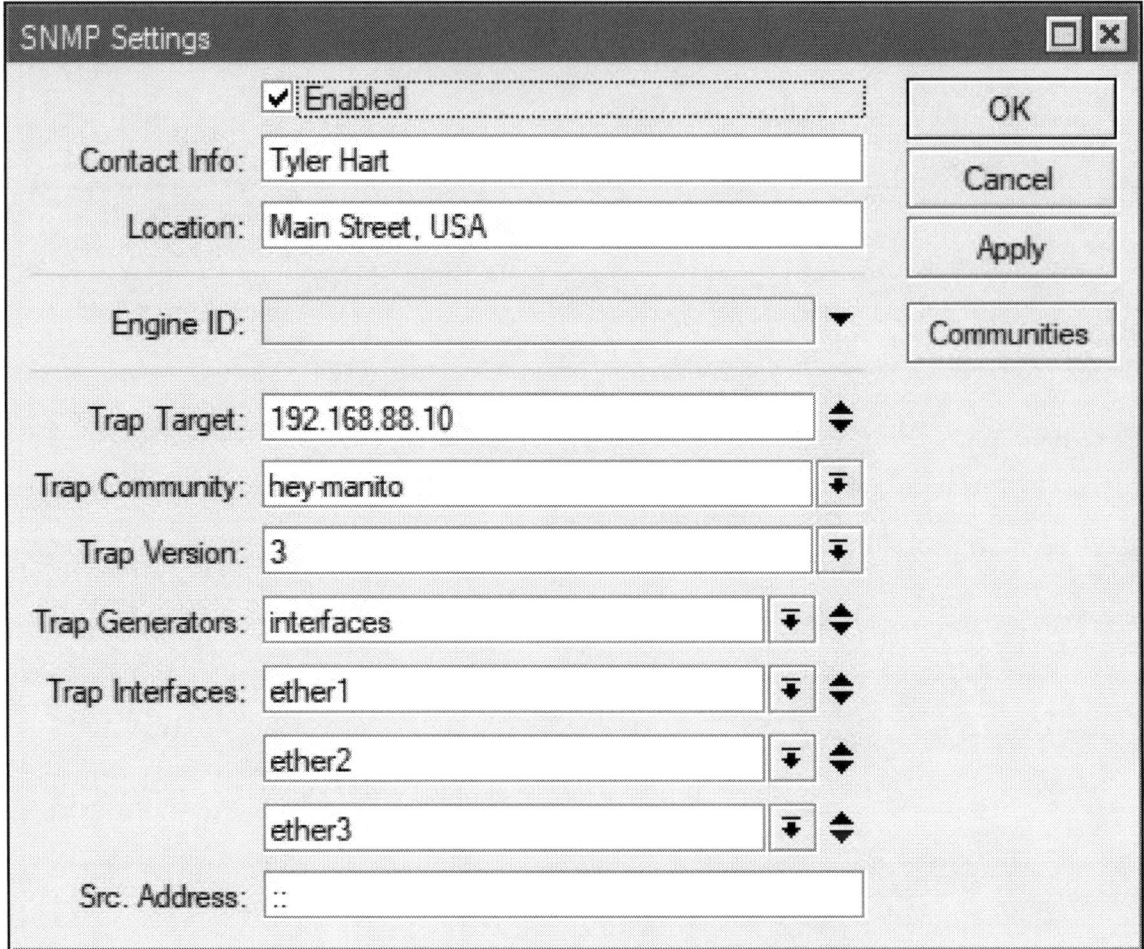

Figure 18.16: Winbox SNMP Trap Configuration

18.9 Syslog

The Dude server can act as a Syslog event collector with a quick configuration change. In Winbox under *Dude > Server Config > Syslog* select the option *Syslog Enabled*. Figure 18.17 shows the setting applied in Winbox:

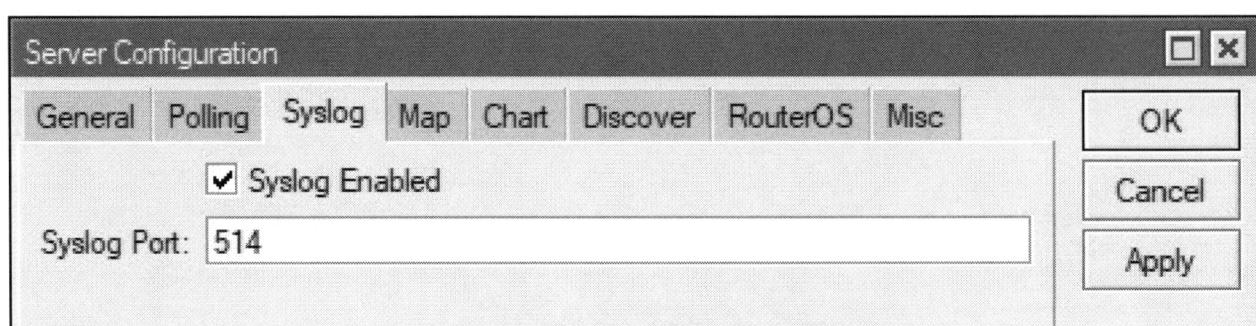

Figure 18.17: Dude Syslog Enabled in Winbox

The same setting is available in the Dude Client via the left *Settings* button as shown in Figure 18.18:

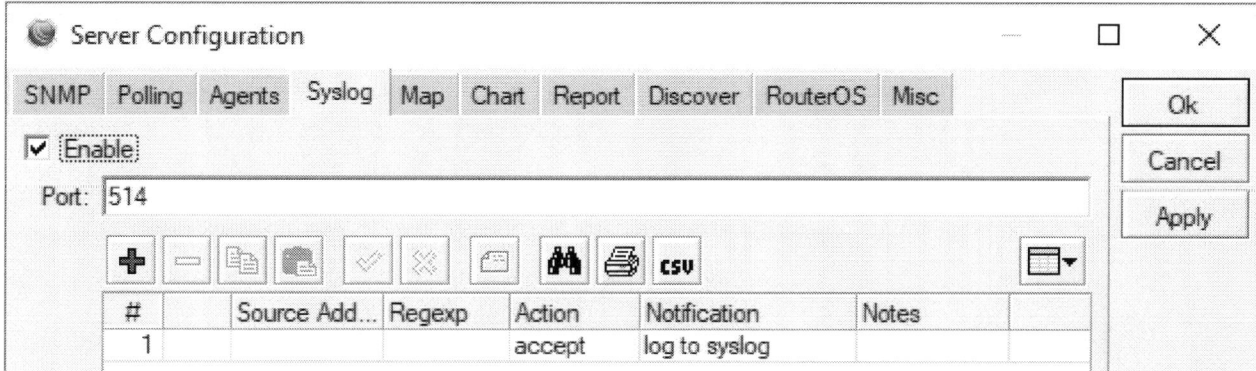

Figure 18.18: Syslog Enabled on Dude Server

18.10 Dude Client

The Dude Client is the distributed component that presents the unified monitoring picture for networking personnel. It's a Microsoft Windows executable that can also be run on Linux using the Wine emulator. Often in a Network Operations Center (NOC) an instance of the Dude Client will be running on a workstation connected to a television with multiple instances also running on NOC Analyst workstations.

Remote NOC staff working from home or other locations can use Dude Client via a VPN connection. This extends the reach of an organization's NOC support staff and allows for a more flexible workforce. The Client runs in the foreground, and when minimized runs in the Microsoft Windows system tray.

The Client is fairly easy to operate, with a function tree on the left and a large pane on the right for loading maps, graphs, etc. An empty Dude Client ready for devices to be configured is shown in Figure 18.19 on the next page:

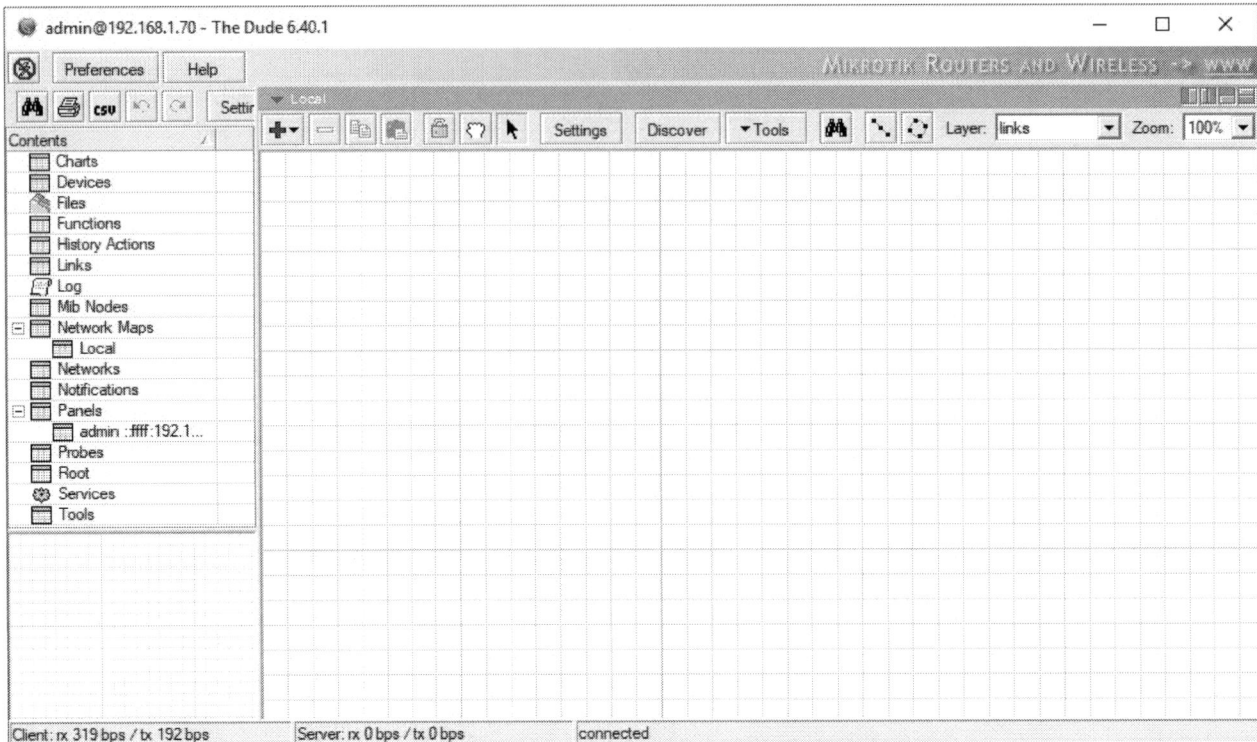

Figure 18.19: Basic Dude Client Window

18.11 Devices

All activities and graphics in The Dude revolve around devices. There are many device types and ways of connecting to those devices. The devices can be created either at the CLI or via the Dude Client, though there's not much you can do at the CLI as of this writing.

18.11.1 Device Types

Many kinds of devices are supported for monitoring as shown in Figure 18.20 on the following page. The default device types cover most of the devices used in a typical enterprise environment. If your network has devices like industrial sensors or warehouse scanners that don't fit into a pre-defined device type it's possible to create your own.

```
[admin@MikroTik] > /dude device-type print
#  NAME
0  MikroTik Device
1  Bridge
2  Router
3  Switch
4  RouterOS
5  Windows Computer
6  HP Jet Direct
7  FTP Server
8  Mail Server
9  Web Server
10 DNS Server
11 POP3 Server
12 IMAP4 Server
13 News Server
14 Time Server
15 Printer
16 Some Device
[admin@MikroTik] > _
```

Figure 18.20: Dude Device Types

Creating a new type of device can automate a lot of your monitoring requirements if a pre-defined device like those shown on page 305 don't fit your needs. An example of a new device is a "Check Printer" used in Accounting and Finance departments. Since the loss of a check printer on payroll day could be really bad some companies monitor them like servers.

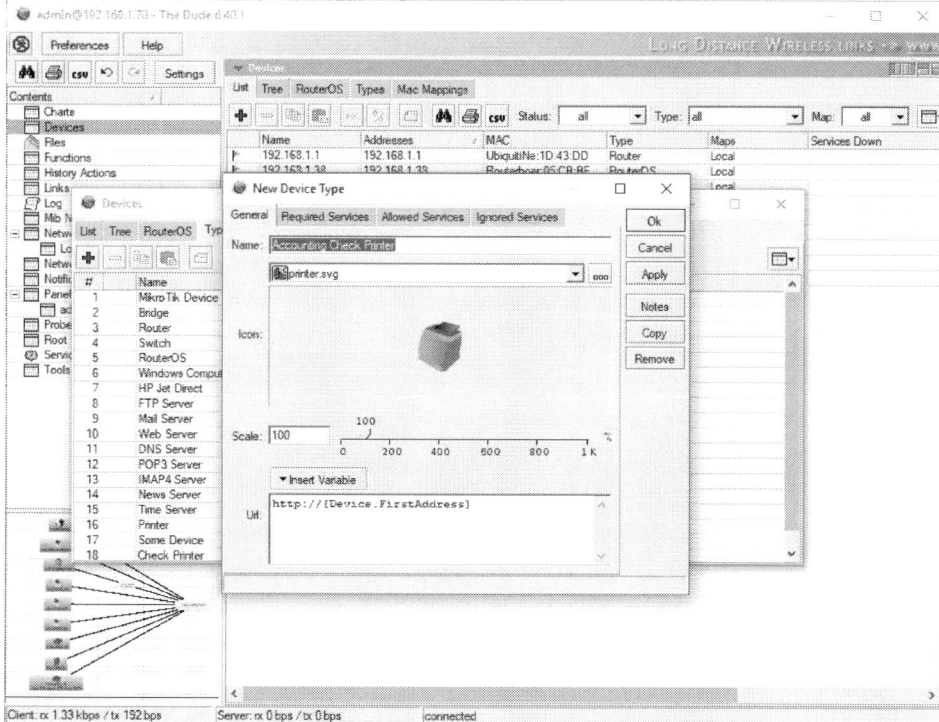

Figure 18.21: New Printer Device

It's possible to specify "*Required Services*" to automatically create those services when a Check Printer is created. Figure shows that the *Ping* and *Printer* services should be used.

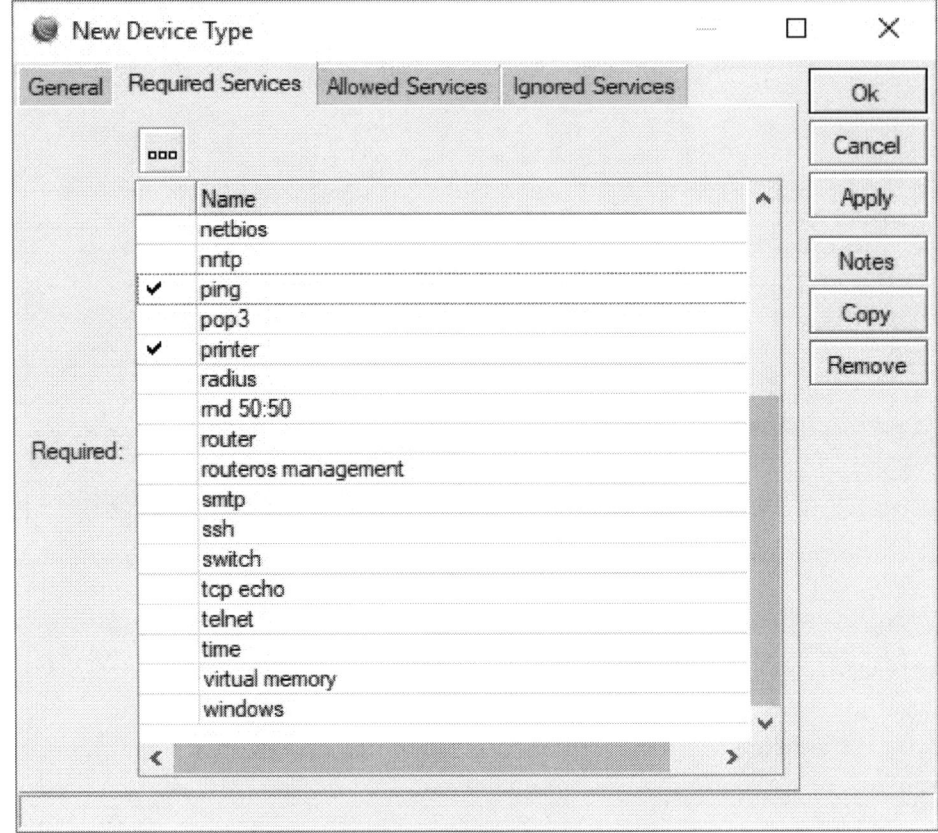

Figure 18.22: New Printer Device Services

Monitored device status can be viewed on the network map or in the list of devices located in the left panel. There are three statuses that a device can be in The Dude:

1. Up (Green)
2. Partially Down (Orange)
3. Down (Red)

18.11.2 Up

Devices that are *Up* and show in green are responding on all services that The Dude is configured to probe. A device may show as *Up* immediately after it has crashed or lost connection because the probe time interval hasn't come around again. Normally this in-between state only lasts for seconds or tens-of-seconds.

18.11.3 Partially Down

Devices that are *Partially Down* and shown in orange are responding on some services that The Dude probes for that device. A device in this category may have been *Up* but had one service fail, or it may have been *Down* and services are beginning to come back online. The auto-discovery process for devices can sometimes find open ports that don't correspond to a real running service, which can cause *Partially Down* false positives. In this case simply pruning the probed services remediates the issue.

18.11.4 Down

When a device goes *Down* and is shown in red it has stopped responding on all services being probed. This device is now completely inaccessible to The Dude for monitoring purposes.

18.11.5 Device Autodiscovery

If no devices are configured the Dude Client will prompt users who log in to auto-discover devices on the Dude instance's local network. Additional networks can be added as well, and it can be easier to auto-discover devices and prune those you don't want than it would be entering devices manually. The default auto-discover tool is shown in Figure 18.23:

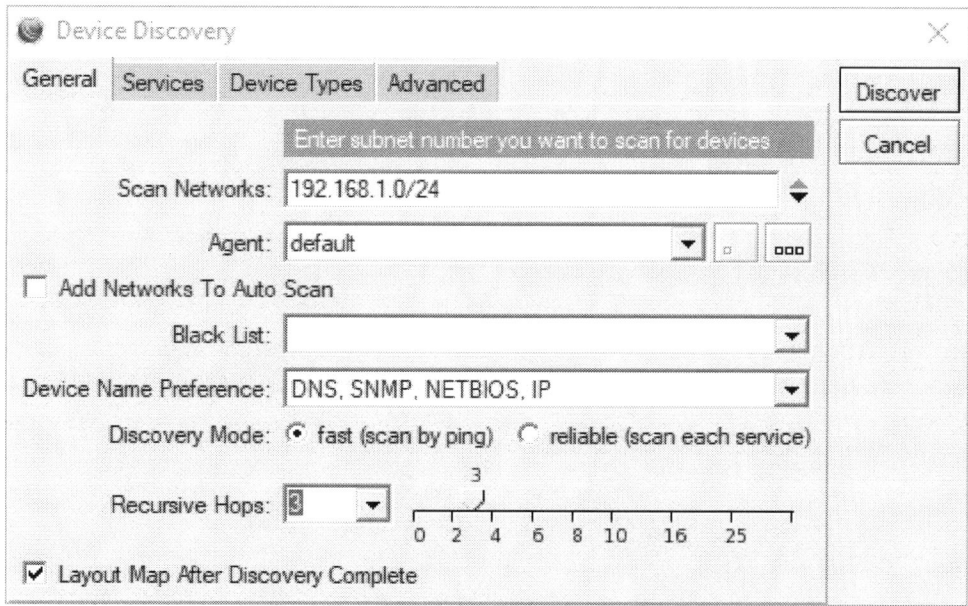

Figure 18.23: Local Network Discovery

For most networks the discovery process doesn't take long. Devices and networks that are found get added to the default "*Local*" map. Since the autodiscovery process probes DNS, SNMP, NetBIOS, and IP protocols it does a fairly good job of identifying all sorts of devices. A map with discovered devices is shown in Figure 18.24 on the next page:

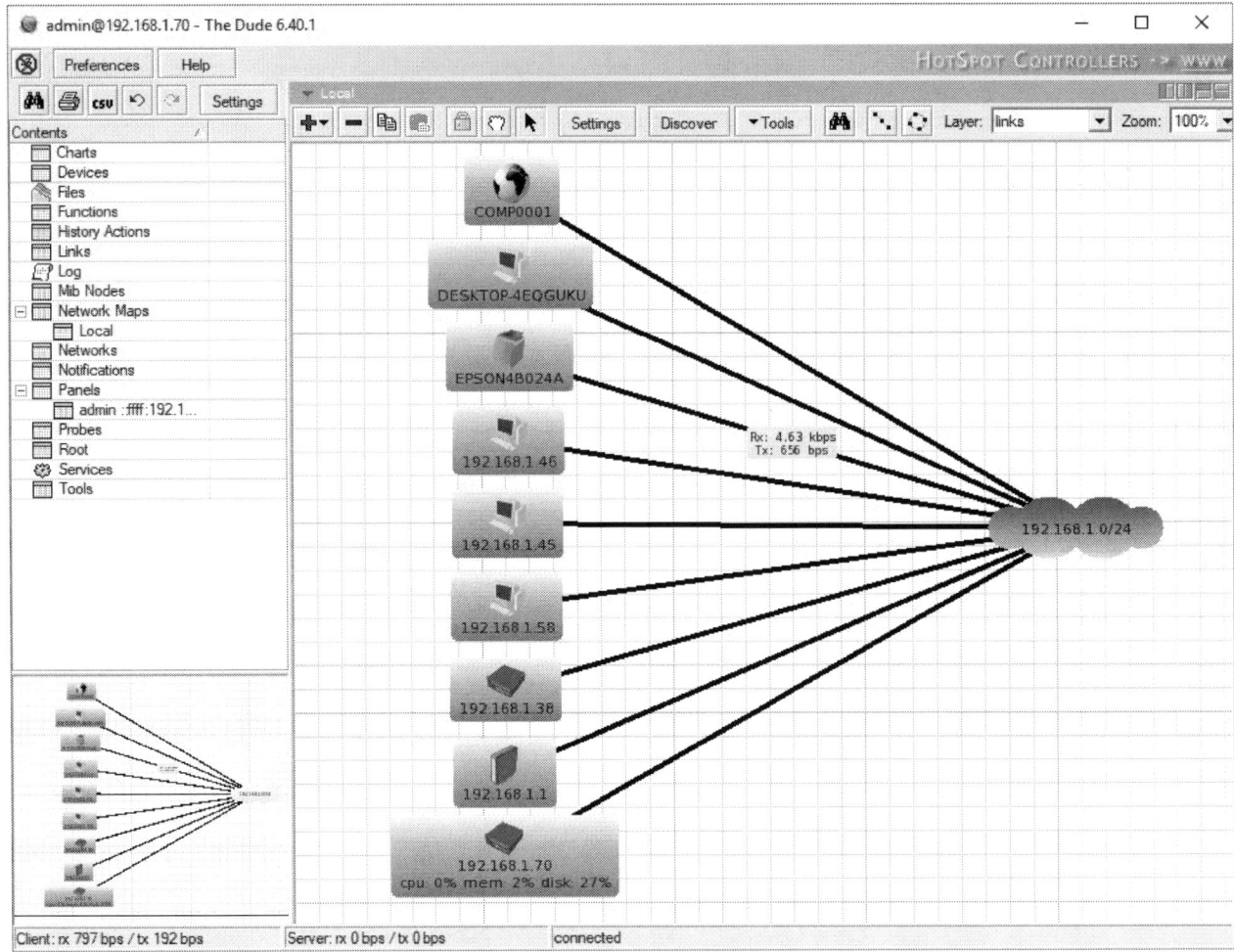

Figure 18.24: Dude Discovered Devices

The printer shown in Figure 18.24 has bandwidth utilization shown on its connecting line because the autodiscovery process tries the default "*public*" SNMP Community String.

18.12 Agents

Dude Agents are remote MikroTik Dude servers that can be used to monitor networks that you don't have a direct connection to. Using a remote Agent to monitor devices can also save bandwidth. When devices are added to the Dude server you can specify the remote Agent that should be used to connect to the device. If there aren't any remote Agents available the only option will be the local *Default* Agent. To create an Agent on a remote device simply upload the Dude *.npk* package and reboot the device.

18.13 Maps

Maps provide you with a graphical layout of devices and their status. Maps can give a high-level overview of entire networks, or be very granular and show status at the device level. Overview networks are great for NOC displays, and for use by non-technical managers and decision-makers. More specific maps showing infrastructure devices and critical links can be used by network administrators and engineers.

Each Dude server is pre-configured with a "*Local*" network map. It's possible to build out completely separate maps and to nest maps within maps (submaps). How many maps you have will depend on how your organization is structured and how you monitor your infrastructure. It's easy to start with the default map and evolve the layouts and networks as you go.

18.13.1 Network Submaps

Submaps nest one map inside another. On networks with many locations and hundreds of devices having just one map becomes unmanageable. Adding submaps is easy, as shown in Figure 18.25:

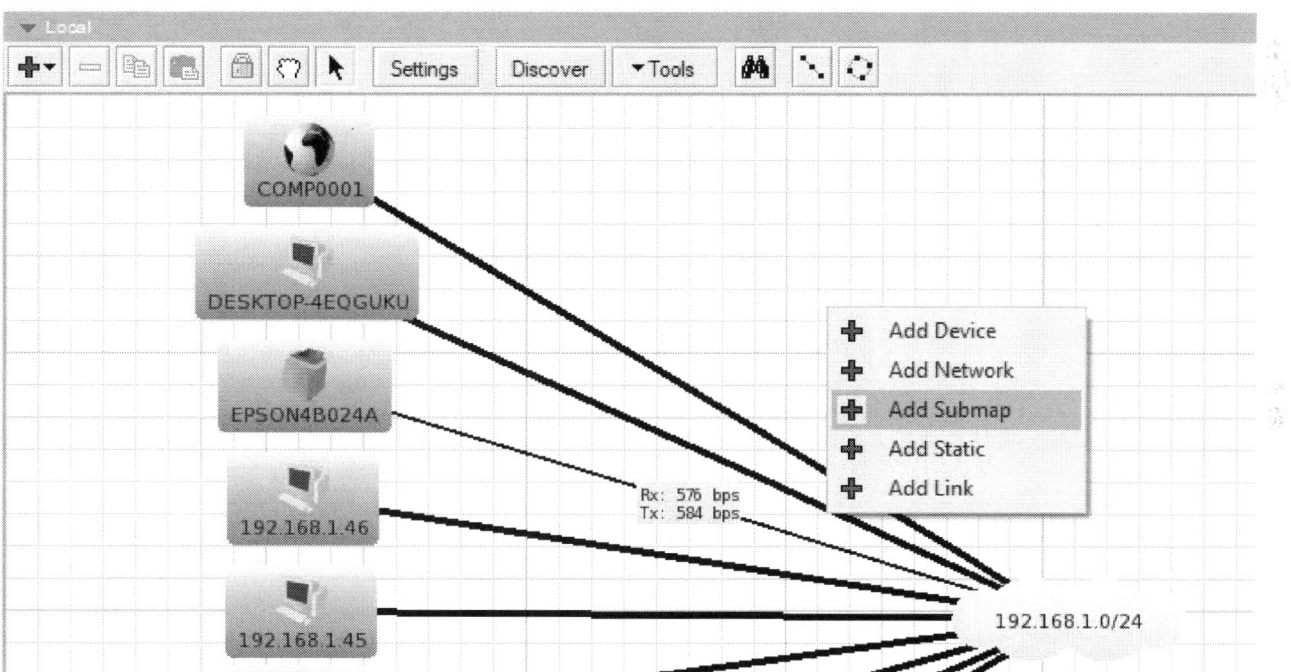

Figure 18.25: Adding Submaps

Give each submap a useful name. Once it's created you can add devices just like any other map. Submaps are displayed with their name and three numbers that show the following metrics:

1. Devices Up
2. Devices Partially Down

3. Devices Down

In figure 18.26 you can see those three metrics in the "*East Office*" submap showing *2/0/0*:

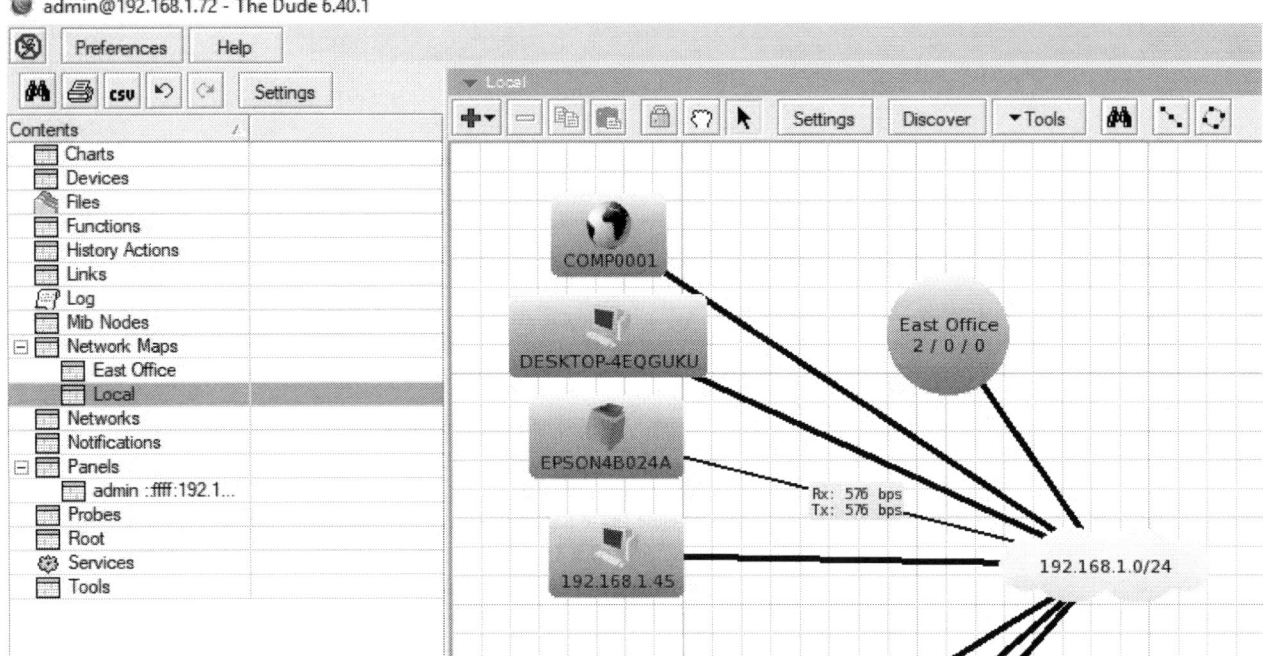

Figure 18.26: Dude Network Submap

18.13.2 Adding Devices to Maps

To begin adding a monitored device to a map or submap use the following steps:

1. Right-click in the map you want to add the device to
2. Select *Add Device*
3. Enter the IP or DNS address of the device in the *Address* field
4. If adding a RouterOS device add the following information:
    (a) User Name
    (b) Password
    (c) Select the *RouterOS* checkbox

The completed first screen will look something like Figure 18.27 on the following page:

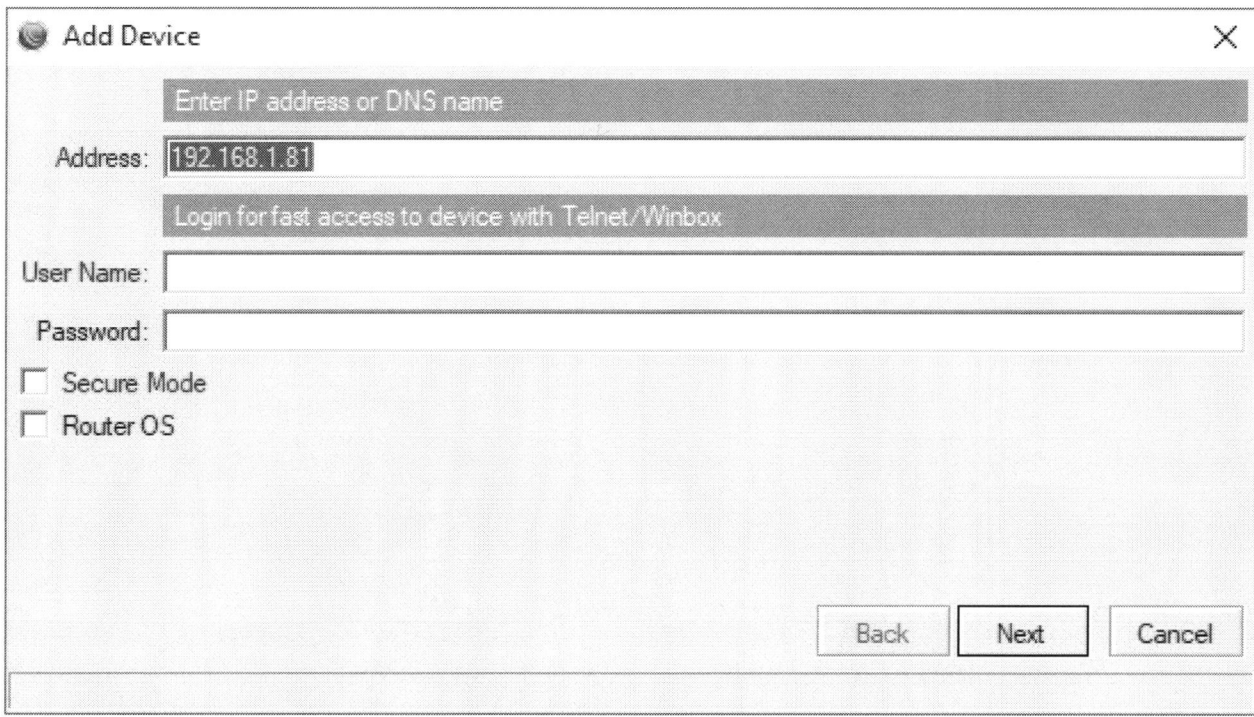

Figure 18.27: Dude Add Device

5. Click *Next*

6. To dynamically find which services are running on the new device click the *Discover* button

7. Give the system a moment to probe the services on the new device. The results will look something like that in Figure 18.28 on the next page:

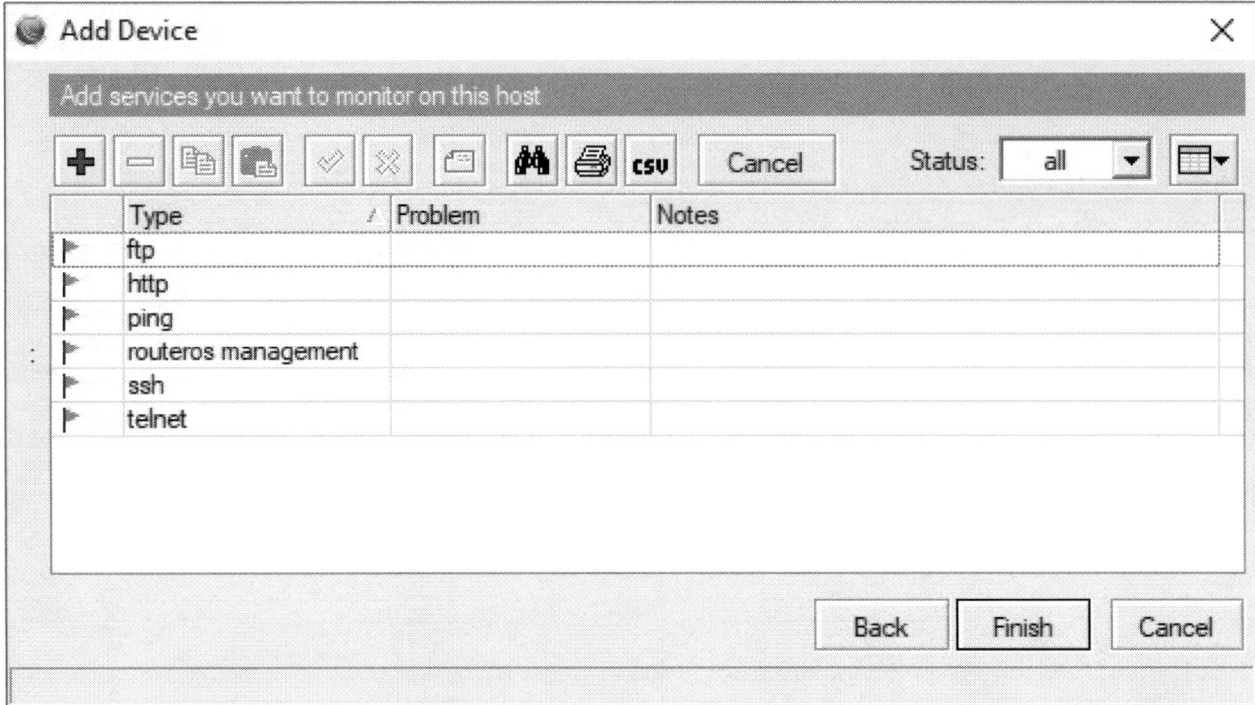

Figure 18.28: Discovered Network Services

8. Click *Finish*

18.14 Links

Links highlight the connection or relationship between two devices or networks. Depending on the type of device and how it's monitored Dude can display real-time throughput on the map for each link. It's also possible to specify thresholds for alarming as well. The following types of links, selected in the *Mastering Type* box, can be created between devices:

- Simple
- SNMP
- RouterOS

A "Simple" link is just a line between two devices that shows a connection exists. There is no monitoring of throughput or stability, it's simply there to show a connection. SNMP links are a bit more dynamic and can show throughput. RouterOS links between two MikroTik-brand devices provide the most robust monitoring of throughput and stability. Use the following steps to create a link between two devices:

1. Right-click the map with the devices to be linked
2. Click *Add Link*

3. Click the first device
4. Drag the line to the second device and release the mouse button
5. Specify the link's details in the *Add Link* window:
    (a) For a basic line link:
        i. Select *Simple* under the *Mastering Type* menu
    (b) For SNMP-only link monitoring:
        i. Select *SNMP* under the *Mastering Type* menu
        ii. Select the interface on one side of the connection under the *Interface* menu
    (c) For RouterOS link monitoring:
        i. Select *RouterOS* under the *Mastering Type* menu
        ii. Select the interface on one side of the connection under the *Interface* menu
6. Enter the maximum possible speed of the link in bits per second (optional)
7. Choose the connection type under the *Type* menu
8. Click *Finish*

Links that are created without any other options are *simple* links.

18.15 Performance Charts

While the Dude monitors whether devices are up or down, it also collects quantitative performance data for each device in the background. Performance charts display graphs over time for the following data:

1. Monitored network service latency
2. CPU usage
3. RAM usage
4. Storage usage
5. Interface throughput

Having this data graphed over time can help you create a network performance baseline and identify trends. With a good performance baseline administrators can more easily spot abnormal network conditions. Use the following steps to create a performance chart in the Dude Client:

1. Double-click the *Charts* item in the left pane
2. Click the red *Add* button

3. In the new window give the chart a useful name
4. Click the *OK* button
5. Double-click the newly created chart
6. Click the red *Add* button
7. Select a data source from the *Source* menu
8. Adjust the line style, thickness, and opacity if needed
9. Repeat the three steps above for each data source in the chart

For charts with multiple data sources it's important to group similar types of data that share the same approximate value ranges. Very small values on the same graph with very large values will render the former unreadable.

18.16 Review Questions

1. What default UDP port does Syslog run on?
   (a) 500
   (b) 507
   (c) 514
   (d) 521

2. Which version of SNMP supports authentication and encryption?
   (a) None
   (b) v1
   (c) v2c
   (d) v3

3. The storage bus of the first drive on the Dude server must be what type?
   (a) IDE
   (b) SCSI
   (c) SATA
   (d) SAS

4. In Microsoft Hyper-V, the Dude server VM must be set to Generation Two.
   (a) True
   (b) False

5. What format type does MikroTik recommend for Dude data storage?
   (a) NTFS
   (b) FAT-32
   (c) Ext2
   (d) Ext3

6. Which status will be assigned to devices that only respond on some monitored services or protocols?

    (a) Partially Down

    (b) Down

    (c) Offline

    (d) Partially Up

7. Monitored devices that are online but unreachable by the Dude server will remain in a green state on the network map.

    (a) True

    (b) False

8. Which link mastering type will still show throughput without devices at either end being RouterOS instances?

    (a) SNMP

    (b) RouterOS

    (c) Simple

    (d) Enhanced

9. Performance charts are able to display more than one data point over time on a single chart.

    (a) True

    (b) False

10. A submap showing the metrics "2/0/0" indicates what?

    (a) Two devices up, zero down, zero partially down

    (b) Two devices down, zero partially down, zero up

    (c) Two devices partially down, zero down, zero up

    (d) Two devices up, zero partially down, zero down

18.17 Review Answers

1. What default UDP port does Syslog run on?

   C – 514 (p. 302)

2. Which version of SNMP supports authentication and encryption?

   D – v3 (p. 281)

3. The storage bus of the first drive on the Dude server must be what type?

   A – IDE (p. 290)

4. In Microsoft Hyper-V, the Dude server VM must be set to Generation Two.

   B – False (p. 290)

5. What format type does MikroTik recommend for Dude data storage?

   D – Ext3 (p. 297)

6. Which status will be assigned to devices that only respond on some monitored services or protocols?

   A – Partially Down (p. 307)

7. Monitored devices that are online but unreachable by the Dude server will remain in a green state on the network map.

   B – False (p. 307)

8. Which link mastering type will still show throughput without devices at either end being RouterOS instances?

   A – SNMP (p. 312)

9. Performance charts are able to display more than one data point over time on a single chart.

   A – True (p. 314)

10. A submap showing the metrics "2/0/0" indicates what?

    D – Two devices up, zero partially down, zero down (p. 309)

Online Resources

The following online resources can help you continue your MikroTik education at no additional cost:

- Official MikroTik Resources:
    - MikroTik newsletter:

        `https://wiki.mikrotik.com/wiki/MikroTik_News`
    - Hardware and software documentation:

        `https://wiki.mikrotik.com/`
    - MikroTik forum:

        `https://forum.mikrotik.com/`
    - RouterOS Changelog:

        `https://mikrotik.com/download/changelogs/`
    - MikroTik User Meetings:

        `https://mum.mikrotik.com/`
    - MikroTik YouTube channel:

        `https://www.youtube.com/user/mikrotikrouter`
    - MTCNA outline:

        `https://www.mikrotik.com/download/pdf/MTCNA_Outline.pdf`
    - MTCNA practice exam:

        `https://www.mikrotik.com/client/trainingSessions`
- Reddit.com Subreddits:
    - `https://www.reddit.com/r/mikrotik/`
    - `https://www.reddit.com/r/networking/`
    - `https://www.reddit.com/r/netsec/`

APPENDIX . ONLINE RESOURCES

- `https://www.reddit.com/r/sysadmin/`

List of Figures

1.1	Making supout.rif	4
1.2	Supout.rif File Print	5
1.3	System Resources	7
1.4	Winbox System Resources	7
1.5	hEX POE (RB960PGS)	8
1.6	RB493AH Board	9
1.7	Daughter Board	9
1.8	MikroTik CCR Components	10
1.9	MikroTik CCR1016-12S-1S+	11
1.10	MikroTik CCR Reverse	11
1.11	MikroTik Replacement PSU	11
1.12	RB260GS Smart Switch	12
1.13	MikroTik CRS226-24G-2S+RM	13
1.14	CHR Hyper-V Console	14
1.15	VirtualBox CHR	15
1.16	CHR Speed Limitation	16
1.17	System License	17
1.18	CHR License Print	18
2.1	Showing Pre-Installed License	24
2.2	Package Selection	25
2.3	Installed Packages	27
2.4	System Packages, Winbox	27
2.5	Checking for Updates	30
2.6	New Version Available	30
2.7	Checking for Updates, Winbox	31
2.8	Winbox Package Downgrade Button	32
2.9	Winbox Downgrade Confirmation	32
2.10	Disabled Package	33
2.11	RouterBOARD Firmware Version	34
3.1	Default WAN DHCP Client	41
4.1	LCD Screen	49
4.2	Disabling Telnet Service	49

4.3	SSH Strong Crypto Enabled	50
4.4	Regenerating SSH Keys	50
4.5	Winbox Login	51
4.6	Winbox	52
4.7	Winbox Check for Updates	52
4.8	MAC Winbox	54
4.9	Webfig	55
5.1	Moving Command Location	62
5.2	Moving Up Commands	62
5.3	Using Slash	63
5.4	Default Banner Message	63
5.5	PuTTY Terminal Color Settings	64
5.6	Single Tab Results	65
5.7	Single Tab with Space	65
5.8	Double-Tab Result	66
5.9	Question Mark Results	66
5.10	Turning on HotLock	67
5.11	System History	68
5.12	Command Undo Results	68
5.13	Quick Set Configuration	69
5.14	CLI Safe Mode	70
5.15	Winbox Safe Mode	70
5.16	Winbox Safe Mode Quit	71
5.17	Setting System Hostname	71
5.18	Default Time Settings	72
5.19	Configuring Time Zones	72
5.20	Default NTP Configuration	73
5.21	Updated NTP Configuration	74
5.22	Creating Device Backup File	75
5.23	Restoring From Backup	75
5.24	Configuration Export File	76
5.25	Configuration Export Restore	77
5.26	List Disks	78
5.27	Formatting USB Storage	78
5.28	Listing Formatted USB Storage	78
5.29	Complete Device Reset	79
6.1	Listing Users	84
6.2	User Updating Password	86
6.3	Active Users	88
6.4	Winbox User Management	89
6.5	Printing Active Users	91
7.1	Default RouterBOARD Interfaces	96

7.2	Interface Count Command	96
7.3	Wireless Interface Count Command	97
7.4	Running Interface Statistics	97
7.5	Master Port	98
7.6	Ethernet Interfaces	98
7.7	Listing POE Status	99
7.8	Monitoring POE Status	99
7.9	MikroTik POE Injector	101
7.10	Copper SFP Module	102
7.11	Fiber Optic SFP Module	102
7.12	MikroTik DAC	103
7.13	Mini PCI-Express Wireless Radio	104
7.14	Interface Running, Slave Status	106
7.15	Removing Bridge Ports	106
7.16	Interface MTU	107
7.17	List Running Interfaces	108
7.18	List Offline Interfaces	108
7.19	Interface Monitor, Duplex Status	109
7.20	Spanning Tree Default Settings	110
7.21	Cable Test - Good	111
7.22	Cable Test Bad	111
8.1	Printing Static Addresses	116
8.2	DHCP Leases	119
8.3	DHCP Make Static	120
8.4	Creating DHCP Options	122
8.5	Active DHCP Client	124
8.6	/30 Point-to-Point Addressing	124
8.7	/32 Point-to-Point Addressing	125
8.8	ARP Table	127
8.9	Proxy ARP	129
8.10	DNS Allow Remote Requests	131
8.11	Local DNS Cache	132
9.1	Listing Routes	138
9.2	Static Route Topology	139
9.3	Dynamic Route Topology	141
9.4	Default Route	142
9.5	Print Route Nexthops	143
9.6	Blackhole Route Ping Result	143
9.7	Printing Active Routes	145
9.8	Printing Connected Routes	145
10.1	New PPPoE Service	156
10.2	SSTP Server Enabled	157

11.1 Simple Queue Download Limit	166
11.2 Interface Queue Print	167
11.3 Queue Tree Download Topology	168
12.1 Routing Packet Flow	174
12.2 Input Chain Traffic	175
12.3 Listing Default Input Rules	175
12.4 Forward Chain Traffic	176
12.5 Listing Default Forward Rules	177
12.6 Output Chain Traffic	177
12.7 Listing Default Output Rules	178
12.8 Default Input Rules	180
12.9 Default Forward Rules	181
12.10 Default Output Rules	182
12.11 SSH Firewall Log	186
12.12 Logged ICMP Traffic	187
12.13 ICMP Reject Results	188
12.14 ICMP Drop Results	188
12.15 Address Group Topology	189
13.1 Source NAT Topology	196
13.2 Destination NAT Topology	197
13.3 NAT Chains, Winbox	198
14.1 Wireless Protocols	205
14.2 Frequency Mode, Country Selection	208
14.3 Wireless Scanner Running	210
14.4 Wireless Scanner Running - Winbox	211
14.5 Wireless Data Rates	212
14.6 Transmit Power Modes	213
14.7 Current Wireless TX Power	214
14.8 Configuring Antenna Gain	215
14.9 Wireless Noise Floor	216
14.10 Wireless Modes	217
14.11 Winbox Wireless Modes	217
14.12 AP-BR Mode Topology	218
14.13 Station Mode Topology	219
14.14 Wireless Registration Table Statistics	220
14.15 Winbox Wireless Snooper	221
14.16 Console Wireless Snooper	221
14.17 Wireless Interface CCQ	222
14.18 CLI Wireless Interface CCQ	223
15.1 Wireless Access List	229
15.2 Add to Wireless Connect List	230
15.3 New Wireless Security Profile	233

15.4 Select Wireless Security Profile 234
15.5 Virtual WPS Accept Button 235

16.1 CLI IP Scan Tool 239
16.2 Winbox IP Scan Tool 240
16.3 MAC-Scan Tool 240
16.4 Email Tool Security Warning 242
16.5 Manually Sending Email 243
16.6 Email Account Configuration 244
16.7 Configuring Email Log Action 244
16.8 MAC Server Enabled 245
16.9 MAC Winbox Server Enabled 245
16.10 Enabling MAC-Server Ping 246
16.11 Packet Sniffer 247
16.12 Winbox Packet Sniffer 248
16.13 Packet Sniffer Streaming 249
16.14 PCAP File In Wireshark 249
16.15 Sniffer Tool 250
16.16 Ping Tool 251
16.17 Console Ping Tool 251
16.18 Ping Speed 252
16.19 CLI Ping Speed 252
16.20 RoMON Discover CLI 254
16.21 RoMON Discover 254
16.22 Telnet Tool 255
16.23 CLI Traceroute Usage 256
16.24 Traceroute Missing Hops 257
16.25 Bandwidth Test Server Settings 258
16.26 Bandwidth Test Client, Console 258
16.27 Bandwidth Test Client 259
16.28 Windows Bandwidth Test Tool 260
16.29 Bandwidth Test 100% CPU 260
16.30 Flood Ping 261
16.31 Console Flood Ping 261

17.1 Accessing RouterOS Graphs 266
17.2 Web Console Interface Graph 267
17.3 New Interface Graph, Winbox 268
17.4 Interface Graph 269
17.5 Memory Graph 270
17.6 Interface Statistics 271
17.7 Interface Traffic Statistics 271
17.8 Interface Up and Down Events 272
17.9 Winbox Torch Button 272
17.10 Winbox Torch Running 273

17.11 Console Torch Tool 273
17.12 Aggregate Traffic Flow Monitoring 274
17.13 Console Resource Monitoring 275
17.14 Console CPU Monitoring 275
17.15 Profile Tool 276
17.16 CLI Profile Tool 276
17.17 Winbox Log Entries 278
17.18 OSPF Logs 278
17.19 Printing *ether1* Interface Logs 279
17.20 Printing Account Event Logs 279
17.21 Printing Account Creation Events 279
17.22 Default SNMP Community String 281

18.1 Creating a VM, First Steps 289
18.2 Dude VM Generation 290
18.3 Assigning Memory 291
18.4 Choose Dude Network Connection 292
18.5 Attach Virtual Hard Disk 293
18.6 Dude Storage Drive Added 294
18.7 Hyper-V VM Integration Services 295
18.8 List Storage Drives 296
18.9 Disk Formatting 297
18.10 Properly Formatted Disk 297
18.11 Dude Status 297
18.12 Dude Device Discovery 299
18.13 Dude Default SNMP Profiles 300
18.14 Dude New SNMP Profile 300
18.15 Dude SNMP Profile in Winbox 301
18.16 Winbox SNMP Trap Configuration 302
18.17 Dude Syslog Enabled in Winbox 302
18.18 Syslog Enabled on Dude Server 303
18.19 Basic Dude Client Window 304
18.20 Dude Device Types 305
18.21 New Printer Device 305
18.22 New Printer Device Services 306
18.23 Local Network Discovery 307
18.24 Dude Discovered Devices 308
18.25 Adding Submaps 309
18.26 Dude Network Submap 310
18.27 Dude Add Device 311
18.28 Discovered Network Services 312

Glossary

AAA Authentication, Authorization, and Accounting. 167, 178, 181

AD Administrative Distance. 111–113

AES Advanced Encryption Standard. 165, 184, 200

AP Access Point. 11, 21, 61, 153, 154, 157, 162, 163, 166, 167, 169, 171–174

AP-BR Access Point - Bridge. xxii, 171, 172

API Application Program Interface. 41, 42, 49, 50

ARP Address Resolution Protocol. xxi, 49, 89–93, 96, 233

ATM Asynchronous Transfer Mode. 175

BFIFO Byte FIFO. 119, 120

BGP Border Gateway Protocol. 16, 111, 113, 114

BOOTP Bootstrap Protocol. 84

CAPsMAN Controlled Access Point system Manager. 162, 168

CCNA Cisco Certified Network Associate. xxviii

CCQ Client Connection Quality. xxii, 156, 158, 159

CCR Cloud Core Router. xix, 6, 13, 16, 17, 35, 43

CHAP Challenge-Handshake Authentication Protocol. 178, 180, 183

CHR Cloud Hosted Router. xix, 10, 19, 20, 22, 24, 205

CIA Confidentiality, Integrity, and Availability. 1

CIDR Classless Inter-Domain Routing. 77

CLI Command Line Interface. xx, xxii–xxiv, 41, 42, 52–54, 59, 82, 157, 159, 195, 196, 208, 226, 236, 237, 240

COI Conflict of Interest. 202

COP Common Operating Picture. 206

CPE Customer Premise Equipment. 20, 21, 173

CPU Central Processing Unit. 185, 188, 195

CRS Cloud Router Switch. 17, 18, 42, 43

DAC Direct Attach Cable. xxi, 101, 102

dB Decibel. 103

DDoS Distributed DoS. 1, 2, 68, 116, 127, 141, 241

DES Data Encryption Standard. 200

DFS Dynamic Frequency Selection. 151–153

DHCP Dynamic Host Configuration Protocol. xx, xxi, 36, 37, 57, 67, 78–87, 97

DiD Defense-in-Depth. 3, 50

DMZ Demilitarized Zone. 78, 147

DNS Domain Name Service. ii, xx, 36–38, 67–70, 80, 81, 84, 86, 87, 176, 213, 225

DoS Denial of Service. 1

DSSS Direct Sequence Spread Spectrum. 150, 155

DST Destination. 123, 135

DST-NAT Destination NAT. 144, 146

EAP Extensible Authentication Protocol. 166–168

EIGRP Enhanced Interior Gateway Routing Protocol. 111–113

EMR Electronic Medical Record. 2

EoIP Ethernet Over IP. 95, 117, 175

FIFO First In, First Out. 119

FTP File Transfer Protocol. 9, 39, 50, 66, 67, 73, 134

Gbit/s Gigabit per Second. 150

GHz Gigahertz. 150, 151

GRE Generic Route Encapsulation. 95, 117, 134, 175, 179

HIPAA Health Insurance Portability and Accountability Act. 2, 62, 129, 139, 201

HTTP Hypertext Transfer Protocol. 39, 45

HTTPS HTTP Secure. 45, 143

Glossary

IANA Internet Assigned Numbers Authority. 84

ICMP Internet Control Message Protocol. xxviii, 38, 114, 115, 117, 131, 134, 135, 139, 140, 172, 192, 223, 226, 231, 233, 235, 240, 241

IDS Intrusion Detection System. 3

IEEE Institute of Electrical and Electronics Engineers. 89, 149

IP Internet Protocol. ii, xvii, xxiii, xxviii, 7, 35–37, 39, 41, 43, 49, 50, 57, 58, 66, 67, 72, 76–81, 85–89, 91, 95, 97, 106, 135, 136, 143–147, 173, 174, 176, 177, 180, 184, 213, 225, 226, 230, 233, 236, 239, 241

IP-IP IP-IP. 95

IPS Intrusion Prevention System. 3

IPSEC Internet Protocol Security. 2, 66, 145, 241

IPv4 Internet Protocol v4. xxviii, 89, 143, 146, 233

IPv6 Internet Protocol v6. 25, 31, 89, 143, 233

IS-IS Intermediate System to Intermediate System. 112

ISM Industrial, Scientific, and Medical. 150–153

ISP Internet Service Provider. v, 37, 39, 68, 86, 87, 113–115, 117, 129, 144, 145, 181, 235

L2 Layer 2. 106, 174, 227, 229, 230

L3 Layer 3. 18, 106, 173, 174, 229

LAN Local Area Network. 37, 44, 57, 93, 96, 102, 124, 144, 149

LCD Liquid Crystal Display. 41, 43

MAC Media Access Control. xxiii, 50, 73, 81, 82, 85, 86, 89–93, 156, 161, 182, 227, 229, 230, 239

Mbit/s Megabit per Second. 121, 150, 193

MD5 Message Digest 5. 200

MHz Megahertz. 153

MIMO Multiple Input, Multiple Output. 150, 155

MIPS Microprocessor without Interlocked Pipeline Stages. 11–13

MPCI Mini PCI. 14, 15, 95, 102

MPCI-E Mini PCI-Express. xxi, 15, 95, 102, 103

MPLS Multiprotocol Label Switching. 25, 103, 173, 175, 241

MQ-PFIFO Multiple Queue PFIFO. 119

MS-CHAP Microsoft Challenge-Handshake Authentication Protocol. 178, 183

MS-CHAPv2 MS-CHAP v2. 178, 179, 183

MTCINE MikroTik Certified Inter-Networking Engineer. 114

MTCNA MikroTik Certified Network Associate. xxviii, 18, 23, 65, 95, 114, 149, 155, 165, 171, 175, 179, 222, 231

MTCRE MikroTik Certified Routing Engineer. 114

MTCWE MikroTik Certified Wireless Engineer. 167, 171

MTU Maximum Transmission Unit. 106, 107

MUM MikroTik User Meeting. 7

NAC Network Access Control. 167

NAT Network Address Translation. 10, 35, 38, 39, 57, 78, 143–147, 194, 233

NDP Neighbor Discovery Protocol. 89

NMS Network Management System. 199, 201, 205

NOC Network Operations Center. 207, 214

NTP Network Time Protocol. xx, 38, 71, 72, 80, 84–87, 162

OFDM Orthogonal Frequency Division Multiplexing. 150, 155

OSI Open Systems Interconnect. xxviii, 89, 103

OSPF Open Shortest Path First. 88, 103, 111, 113, 114, 130, 131

OUI Organizationally Unique Identifier. 89–91

OVA Open Virtualization Archive. 22

OVF Open Virtualization Format. 22

PAP Password Authentication Protocol. 183

PCI-DSS Payment Card Industry - Data Security Standard. 2, 38, 62, 129, 139, 201

PCQ Per-Connection Queuing. 119, 120

PEAP Protected EAP. 166, 168

PFIFO Packet FIFO. 119, 120

PFS Perfect Forward Secrecy. 184

PIN Personal Identification Number. 43, 169

POE Power Over Ethernet. xix, xxi, 14, 99, 100

Point-to-Point Point-to-Point. 174

PPC Power PC. 12, 13

PPP Point-to-Point Protocol. xxii, 95, 175–184

PPPoE PPP over Ethernet. xxii, 175, 176, 178, 181–183

PPTP Point-to-Point Tunnel Protocol. 134, 175, 176, 178–180, 182–184

PSK Pre-Shared Key. 166, 167

PSU Power Supply Unit. xix, 16, 17

RADIUS Remote Authentication Dial-In User Service. 166–168, 178, 179, 182

RAM Random Access Memory. 14, 185, 188

RED Random Early Detection. 119, 120

Regex Regular Expression. 90, 91

RF Radio Frequency. 155

RFC Request for Comments. 182

RIP Routing Information Protocol. 88, 113, 114

RoMON Router Management Overlay Network. 236–238

RSTP Rapid STP. 109

RTT Round Trip Time. 223

RX Receive. 107, 156, 176

SFP Small Form-Factor Pluggable. xxi, 16, 95, 100–102, 117

SFP+ SFP Plus. 16, 95, 100, 101

SFQ Stochastic Fair Queuing. 119, 120

SHA-1 Secure Hash Algorithm 1. 200

SNMP Simple Network Management Protocol. xxiii, 58, 195, 199–201, 213, 214, 216, 231

SNTP Simple NTP. 162

SOHO Small Office, Home Office. 6, 13, 14, 35–37, 97, 102, 107, 171, 172

SONET Synchronous Optical Networking. 175

SRC Source. 123, 135

SRC-NAT Source NAT. 144

SSH Secure Shell. xxi, 2, 9, 38, 41, 44, 50, 67, 73, 129, 138, 139, 197, 236, 238, 239

SSL Secure Socket Layer. 49, 182

SSTP Secure Socket Tunneling Protocol. xxii, 182–184

STIG Security Technical Implementation Guide. 201

STP Spanning Tree Protocol. 109

SwOS SwitchOS. 18

TCP Transmission Control Protocol. 45, 46, 49, 106, 131, 134, 135, 138, 141, 145, 147, 179, 182

TCP/IP TCP/IP. xxviii, 106

TKIP Temporal Key Integrity Protocol. 165

TLS Transport Layer Security. 182, 184

TTL Time To Live. 69, 114, 240

TX Transmit. 107, 156, 176

U-NII Unlicensed National Information Infrastructure. 150–153

UDP User Datagram Protocol. 201

UPnP Universal Plug and Play. 176

VAR Value-Added Reseller. 85

VHD Virtual Hard Disk. 24

VLAN Virtual LAN. 44, 81, 95, 201

VM Virtual Machine. 19, 24

VoIP Voice over IP. 145

VPLS Virtual Private LAN Service. 96

VPN Virtual Private Network. 2, 113, 145, 175, 179, 180, 184, 207

VRRP Virtual Router Redundancy Protocol. 95

WAN Wide Area Network. xx, 36–38, 57, 67, 102, 135, 236

WAP Wireless Access Point. 85

WEP Wired Equivalent Privacy. 165, 166

Wi-Fi Wi-Fi. 149, 166, 168

WISP Wireless ISP. v, xxvii, 6, 20, 21, 173, 174

WLAN Wireless LAN. 37, 149, 150, 170, 172

WOL Wake on LAN. 93

WPA Wi-Fi Protected Access. 166, 167

WPA2 WPA2. 166

WPS Wi-Fi Protected Setup. 168–170

Bibliography

[1] Defense Information Systems Agency. Network infrastructure router l3 switch. Available at "https://nvd.nist.gov/ncp/checklist/382.

[2] Internet Assigned Numbers Authority. Internet control message protocol (icmp) parameters. Available at http:/www.iana.org/assignments/icmp-parameters/icmp-parameters.xhtml.

[3] PCI Security Standards Council. Pci dss prioritized approach for pci dss 3.2. Available at https://www.pcisecuritystandards.org/documents/Prioritized-Approach-for-PCI_DSS-v3_2.pdf?agreement=true.

[4] Google. Google public dns. Available at https://developers.google.com/speed/public-dns/.

[5] Microsoft. Dhcp option parameters. Available at https://technet.microsoft.com/en-us/library/cc958929.aspx.

[6] MikroTik. About us. Available at https://mikrotik.com/aboutus.

[7] MikroTik. Manual:chr. Available at https://wiki.mikrotik.com/wiki/Manual:CHR#Minimal_requirements:.

[8] MikroTik. Manual:interface/bridge. Available at http://wiki.mikrotik.com/wiki/Manual:Interface/Bridge.

[9] MikroTik. Manual:interface/ethernet. Available at https://wiki.mikrotik.com/wiki/Manual:Interface/Ethernet.

[10] MikroTik. Manual:interface/wireless. Available at https://wiki.mikrotik.com/wiki/Manual:Interface/Wireless#Access_List.

[11] MikroTik. Manual:ip/arp. Available at https://wiki.mikrotik.com/wiki/Manual:IP/ARP.

[12] MikroTik. Manual:ip/firewall/nat. Available at https://wiki.mikrotik.com/wiki/Manual:IP/Firewall/NAT#Masquerade.

[13] MikroTik. Manual:ip/route. Available at https://wiki.mikrotik.com/wiki/Manual:IP/Route.

[14] MikroTik. Manual:license. Available at https://wiki.mikrotik.com/wiki/Manual:License#License_Levels.

[15] MikroTik. Manual:nv2. Available at https://wiki.mikrotik.com/index.php?title=Manual:Nv2&redirect=no#How_Nv2_compares_with_Nstreme_and_802.11.

[16] MikroTik. Manual:poe-out. Available at https://wiki.mikrotik.com/wiki/Manual:PoE-Out#Port_settings.

[17] MikroTik. Manual:queue. Available at https://wiki.mikrotik.com/wiki/Manual:Queue#HTB_Properties_2.

[18] MikroTik. Manual:wireless faq. Available at https://wiki.mikrotik.com/wiki/Manual:Wireless_FAQ#What_TX-power-mode_is_the_best.3F.

[19] MikroTik. Manual:wireless station modes. Available at https://wiki.mikrotik.com/wiki/Manual:Wireless_Station_Modes#Mode_station-bridge.

[20] MikroTik. Mikrotik certified network associate study guide. Available at https://www.mikrotik.com/download/pdf/MTCNA_Outline.pdf.

[21] et al Rekhter. Address allocation for private internets. Available at https://tools.ietf.org/pdf/rfc1918.pdf.

[22] International Telecommunication Union. Documents of the international radio conference (atlantic city, 1947). Available at https://www.itu.int/dms_pub/itu-s/oth/02/01/S020100002B4813PDFE.pdf.

Made in the USA
Monee, IL
24 August 2020